GEORGE W.E. NICKELSBURG IN PERSPECTIVE

SUPPLEMENTS

TO THE

JOURNAL FOR THE STUDY OF JUDAISM

Editor

JOHN J. COLLINS

The Divinity School, Yale University

Associate Editor

FLORENTINO GARCÍA MARTÍNEZ

Qumran Institute, University of Groningen

Advisory Board

J. DUHAIME — A. HILHORST— P.W. VAN DER HORST
A. KLOSTERGAARD PETERSEN — M.A. KNIBB — J.T.A.G.M. VAN RUITEN
J. SIEVERS — G. STEMBERGER — E.J.C. TIGCHELAAR — J. TROMP

VOLUME 80

GEORGE W.E. NICKELSBURG IN PERSPECTIVE

An Ongoing Dialogue of Learning

EDITED BY

JACOB NEUSNER & ALAN J. AVERY-PECK

VOLUME 1

BRILL

LEIDEN · BOSTON

2003

This book is printed on acid-free paper.

Library of Congress Cataloging-in Publication data

George W.E. Nickelsburg in perspective : an ongoing dialogue of learning / edited by Jacob Neusner & Alan J. Avery-Peck.
   p. cm. Supplements to the Journal for the study of Judaism, 1384-2161 ; v. 80
  Includes bibliographical references and index.
   ISBN 9004129871 (set)
1. Ethiopic book of Enoch. 2. Bible. N.T.—Criticism, interpretation, etc. 3. Apocryphal books (Old Testament)—Criticism, interpretation, etc. 4. Apocalyptic literature—History and criticism.   5. Judaism—History—Post-exilic period, 586 B.C.-210 A.D. I Nickelsburg, George W. E.,
1934- II Neusner, Jacob, 1932- III Avery-Peck, Alan J. (Alan Jeffery), 1953-

BS1700 .G46 2003
229/.91/0046—dc21

2003049589

ISSN 1384-2161

ISBN 90 04 12985 5 (vol. 1)
ISBN 90 04 12986 3 (vol. 2)
ISBN 90 04 12987 1 (set)

CONTENTS

Volume One

VOLUME TWO

PART THREE
REVIEWS OF BOOKS ON EARLY JUDAISM

PART FOUR
EARLY CHRISTIANITY IN ITS JEWISH CONTEXT

PART FIVE
PERSONAL RECOLLECTIONS

PART SIX
A CODA (TO WHAT SHOULD THIS LEAD US?)

PREFACE

One day there was a dispute in the school house [on the following matter]: As to a sword, knife, dagger, spear, hand-saw, and scythe—at what point in making them do they become susceptible to become unclean? It is when the process of manufacturing them has been completed [at which point they are deemed useful and therefore susceptible]. And when is the process of manufacturing them completed?

R. Yohanan said, "When one has tempered them in the crucible."

R. Simeon b. Laqish said, "When one has furbished them in water."

[R. Yohanan] said to him, "[Having been a thug before you studied Torah, you would know.] Never con a con-man" [lit.: a robber is an expert at robbery].

He said to him, "So what good did you [who drew me to Torah-study] ever do for me? When I was a robber, people called me, 'my lord' [*lit.*: rabbi], and now people call me 'my lord.'"

He said to him, "I'll tell you what good I've done for you, I brought you under the wings of the Presence of God."

R. Yohanan was offended, and R. Simeon b. Laqish fell ill. . . .

R. Simeon b. Laqish died, and R. Yohanan was much distressed afterward. Rabbis said, "Who will go and restore his spirits? Let R. Eleazar b. Pedat go, because his traditions are well-honed."

He went and took a seat before him. At every statement that R. Yohanan made, he comments, "There is a Tannaite teaching that sustains your view."

He said to him, "Are you like the son of Laqisha? When I would state something, the son of Laqisha would raise questions against my position on twenty-four grounds, and I would find twenty-four solutions, and it naturally followed that the tradition was broadened, but you say to me merely, 'There is a Tannaite teaching that sustains your view.' Don't I know that what I say is sound?"

So he went on tearing his clothes and weeping, "Where are you, son of Laqisha, where are you, son of Laqisha," and he cried until his mind turned from him.

Rabbis asked mercy for him, and he died.

(*Bavli Baba Mesia* 84A/7:1 I.12)

The great Talmudic master, Yohanan, misses his contentious colleague unto death, and dies from an excess of affirmation of his views. In our context, he perished from receiving too many honorary degrees. He had the integrity not to believe the citations—or to crave the reassurance. He did not require them.

Scholarship and politics do not mix. The great scholars are rarely adept politicians. That is no accident. The authentic scholar values criticism. The true path of greatness in learning leads to contention above all else. That is not argument for the sake of contention to be sure, but argument in a pure spirit. It is intellectual confrontation for the sake of purifying truth and extending learning, broadening its scope and deepening its grasp. In that spirit—the spirit of Talmudic learning—we assemble in these pages to contend with principal parts of the scholarly heritage of George W.E. Nickelsburg. We propose to sift through his principal ideas and initiatives and to argue with him where in our view argument is called for.

So we come to reread his more important articles and encounter afresh some of his books, to criticize them and to attend to his response to the criticism. In these pages, he sets the agenda for scholarly debate, he does not dictate the outcome. We share his view, testing it against evidence, argument, alternative readings of matters. That is because, as in the story of Yohanan and Simeon b. Laqish, scholarship finds its nourishment in contention and conflict, not in compromise and conciliation. The great Rabbinic sages declare, "Let reason pierce the mountains," and their counterparts in every academic culture in the tradition of Western philosophy and science concur.

This set of *Auseinandersetzungen*—no word in English does the job of expressing what we are about—carries forward the life of learning and debate that yields a rich harvest of scholarship. For nothing so sustains tough-minded learning, nothing so transforms information into knowledge, knowledge into truth and meaning, as do criticism and debate. These empower reason. They accord priority to logic and clear-thinking and accurate writing. In so doing, they transform scholarship from an exchange of opinion—accompanied by political negotiation as to what "our crowd" thinks worthy of affirmation—into a rigorous debate concerning reason, argument, and evidence. The particular heritage of intellectual tradition that sustains the Western academy, deriving as it does from the commitment to criticism and rationality characteristic of philosophy and Enlightenment, affords no option but to engage, debate and criticize, test and challenge, correct and revise—renew. These are the activities institutionalized in Mathematics and the Natural Sciences, but no less enduring in the living traditions of the academic Humanities and the Social Sciences.

What this book does—with few models or antecedents to guide

the editors in their work—is pay tribute to a scholar through acts of engaged, critical scholarship. These essays do not set forth mere words of praise. They form actions of authentic tribute: empowering Nickelsburg to define the program of debate, not only episodically through scattered articles and books, but cogently and systematically through collected articles, reread as a group, and reviews of some of the more important books he has written. In each case, a specialist rereads an article reproduced in these pages and responds to it, and then Nickelsburg joins issue—a protracted engagement, spanning an entire intellectual career and many of its more important moments.

Nickelsburg's heritage not only deserves the rigors of academic praise in the form of contention, it also sustains them. On any list of scholars who over the past forty years have defined and cultivated the field of Second Temple Judaism and early Christianity, Nickelsburg is included, at or near the top. But he is one among many. What makes him particular, and worth of the honor paid to him through criticism, is that he has defined a field for learned cultivation that before him had long lain fallow. Nickelsburg helped to re-found the field of Apocryphal and Pseudepigraphic studies, neglected from the years following the great work of R.H. Charles until its renewal with the discovery of the Dead Sea Scrolls. He did not do this alone; others of his age group joined in the work of renewal. Others helped to give the field a new beginning. But none doubts that Nickelsburg stands tall indeed.

Accordingly we come not to praise George W.E. Nickelsburg nor to celebrate him. Some of those in the present book—four in all—did that in the Festschrift organized by his students from the University of Iowa, entitled *For a Later Generation*.[1] Nor do we assemble to bury him. This is a landmark, not a grave stone. We wish him a full one hundred twenty years of hard and productive labor. Rather it is to accord him the respect that he has earned for his intellectual *oeuvre*: to engage with his ideas, to argue with him and once more to invite him to take up the challenges of criticism and reconstruction. In so doing, we situate him at the center of his field and seek a proportionate, balanced view of his position therein.

---

[1] Randal A. Argall, Beverly A. Bow, and Rodney A. Werline, eds., *For a Later Generation. The Transformation of Tradition in Israel, Early Judaism, and Early Christianity* (Harrisburg, 2000: Trinity Press International).

So this is no Festschrift, the personal tribute, through scholarship, of scholarly colleagues and students. It is something else, for which we have no known precedent, indeed, no name in English, only the borrowed German word used above. This we do who devote our lives to critical learning, who do our work to solve problems, ask questions, clarify, explain, rethink, analyze and synthesize learning in fresh ways. All of us, in collaboration with Nickelsburg and in engagement with his ideas, here take our place in the long line of learning that preserves and hands on the traditions that sustain culture. That is why there are not only schools and students, libraries and textbooks to record the known, but facilities for research and scholarly inquiry and lavish opportunities afforded us to test what we think we know, to renew knowledge.

Here we present the natural outcome of the academy: scholars in contention over truth.

The editors thank the contributors to this volume, who, as a group, cooperated to make the work easy. All those who originally undertook to participate in this venture kept their commitment and honored the deadline we set. We believe all of them have given us their best work, their most rigorous criticism—a wonderful tribute to George Nickelsburg. We also thank the editor of this series, a long-time friend and colleague, for including the project under his aegis. We further express appreciation to our editors at Brill for encouraging this novel enterprise and bringing it to fruition. No generation has been better served by its scholarly media than is this generation by Brill and its current editors and professional staff.

Finally, we offer this volume as a model, an alternative to the conventional Festschrift, however well intended. So we underscore: this is a new venture in scholarly debate. But we do not subject it to our copyright. Celebrating a career by critical engagement and on-going debate—that is an enterprise free for others to imitate and appropriate.

Let many colleagues now take up the experiment of *Auseindersetzungen* with noteworthy scholars and their life's work.

Jacob Neusner, Bard College

Alan J. Avery-Peck, College of the Holy Cross

PERMISSIONS

Chapter 1
"The First Century: A Time to Rejoice and a Time to Weep," in *Religion & Theology/Religie & Teologie* 1 (1994), pp. 4–17. Reprinted by permission of Unisa and *Religion & Theology*.

Chapter 2
"The Apocalyptic Construction of Reality in 1 Enoch," in John J. Collins and James H. Charlesworth, eds., *Mysteries and Revelations: Apocalyptic Studies since the Uppsala Colloquium* (JSPSup 9; 1991), pp. 51–64. Reprinted by permission of Sheffield Academic Press.

Chapter 3
"Salvation Without and With a Messiah: Developing Beliefs in Writings Ascribed to Enoch" in Jacob Neusner, William S. Green, and Ernest Frerichs, eds., *Judaism and Their Messiahs at the Turn of the Christian Era* (Cambridge: Cambridge University Press, 1987), pp. 49–68. Reprinted by permission of Cambridge University Press.

Chapter 4
"The Epistle of Enoch and the Qumran Literature," in *Journal of Jewish Studies* 33 (1982) = *Essays in Honour of Yigael Yadin*, pp. 333–348. Reprinted by permission of the *Journal of Jewish Studies*.

Chapter 5
"Religious Exclusivism: A World View Governing Some Texts Found at Qumran," in Michael Becker and Wolfgang Fenske, eds., *Das Ende der Tage und die Gegenwart des Heils; Begegnungen mit dem Neuen Testament und seiner Umwelt; Festschrift für Heinz-Wolfgang Kuhn zum 65. Geburtstag* (Leiden: E.J. Brill, 1999), pp. 45–67. Reprinted by permission of E.J. Brill Publishers.

Chapter 6
"Patriarchs Who Worry about Their Wives: A Haggadic Tendency in the Genesis Apocryphon," in Michael E. Stone and Esther G. Chazon, eds., *Biblical Perspectives: Early Use and Interpretation of the Bible in Light of the Dead Sea Scrolls. Proceedings of the First International Symposium of the Orion Center for the Study of the Dead Sea Scrolls and Associated Literature,*

12–14 May, 1996 (Studies on the Texts of the Desert of Judah 28; Leiden: E.J. Brill, 1998), pp. 137–158. Reprinted by permission of E.J. Brill Publishers.

Chapter 7
"Tobit and Enoch: Distant Cousins with a Recognizable Resemblance," in *Society of Biblical Literature Seminar Papers* 27 (Scholars Press, 1988), pp. 54–68. Reprinted by permission of the Society of Biblical Literature.

Chapter 8
"The Search for Tobit's Ancestry: A Historical and Hermeneutical Odyssey," in RevQ 17 (1996) = Milik Festschrift, pp. 339–349. Reprinted by permission of RevQ.

Chapter 9
"Wisdom and Apocalypticism in Early Judaism: Some Points for Discussion," in *Society of Biblical Literature Seminar Paper* 33 (Atlanta: Scholars Press, 1994), pp. 715–732. Reprinted by permission of the Society of Biblical Literature.

Chapter 13
"Enoch, Levi, and Peter: Recipients of Revelation in Upper Galilee," in *Journal of Biblical Literature* 100 (1981), pp. 575–600. Reprinted by permission of the Society of Biblical Literature.

Chapter 14
"The Genre and Function of the Markan Passion Narrative," in *Harvard Theological Review* 73 (1980), pp. 153–184. Reprinted by permission of the *Harvard Theological Review*.

Chapter 15
"Riches, the Rich, and God's Judgment in 1 Enoch 92–105 and the Gospel According to Luke," in *New Testament Studies* 25 (1979), pp, 324–344. Reprinted by permission of Cambridge University Press.

Chapter 16
"Revisiting the Rich and the Poor in 1 Enoch 92–105 and the Gospel according to Luke," in *Society of Biblical Literature Seminar Paper* 37 (Atlanta: Scholars Press, 1998), vol. 2, pp. 579–605. Reprinted by permission of the Society of Biblical Literature.

Chapter 17
"The Incarnation: Paul's Solution to the Universal Human Predicament," in Birger Pearson, ed., *The Future of Early Christianity* (Minneapolis:

Fortress Press, 1991), pp. 348–357. Reprinted by permission; © 1991 Augsburg Fortress.

Chapter 18
"Jews and Christians in the First Century: The Struggle over Identity," in *Neotestamentica* 27 (1993), pp. 365–390. Reprinted by permission of *Neotestamentica.*

Chapter 19
"1 and 2 Maccabees—Same Story, Different Meaning," in *Concordia Theological Monthly* 42 (1971) = *Festschrift for Martin Franzmann*, pp. 515–526. © 1971 CPH. Used with permission.

Chapter 20
"Why Study the Extra-Canonical Literature: A Historical and Theological Essay," in *Neotestamentica* 28 (1994). Special edition = *Essays in Memory of Willem Vorster*, pp. 181–204. Reprinted by permission of *Neotestamentica.*

BIBLIOGRAPHY OF GEORGE W.E. NICKELSBURG

Books

Resurrection, Immortality, and Eternal Life in Intertestamental Judaism (HTS 26; Cambridge: Harvard University and London: Oxford University, 1972).
Jewish Literature Between the Bible and the Mishnah: A Historical and Literary Introduction (Philadelphia: Fortress, 1981; paperback edition, 1987).
With Michael E. Stone, *Faith and Piety in Early Judaism: A Reader of Texts and Documents* (Philadelphia: Fortress, 1983; Paperback edition, Valley Forge: Trinity International, 1991).
1 Enoch 1: A Commentary on the Book of 1 Enoch Chapters 1–36; 81–108 (Hermeneia; Minneapolis: Fortress, 2001).
Ancient Judaism and Christian Origins: Diversity, Continuity, and Transformation (Minneapolis: Fortress, 2003).

Books Collaborated on

A Complete Concordance to Flavius Josephus 2 (ed., K.H. Rengstorf; Leiden: Brill, 1975).
A Complete Concordance to Flavius Josephus 3 (ed., K.H. Rengstorf; Leiden: Brill, 1979).

Books Edited

Studies on the Testament of Moses (SBLSCS 4; Cambridge: Society of Biblical Literature, 1973).
Studies on the Testament of Joseph (SBLSCS 5; Missoula: Scholars Press, 1975).
Studies on the Testament of Abraham (SBLSCS 6, Missoula: Scholars Press, 1976).
With John J. Collins, *Ideal Figures in Ancient Judaism: Profiles and Paradigms* (SBLSCS 12; Chico: Scholars Press, 1980).
Christians among Jews and Gentiles: Essays in Honor of Krister Stendahl on His Sixty-Fifth Birthday (Philadelphia: Fortress, 1986 = *HTR* 79:1–3).
With Robert A. Kraft, *Early Judaism and its Modern Interpreters* (Philadelphia: Fortress and Atlanta: Scholars Press, 1986).
With Birger A. Pearson (principal editor), A. Thomas Kraabel, and Norman R. Petersen, *The Future of Early Christianity: Essays in Honor of Helmut Koester* (Minneapolis: Fortress, 1991).
Associate Editor, *Dictionary of Judaism in the Biblical Period* (ed., Jacob Neusner and William Scott Green; 2 vols., New York: Macmillan, 1996).

Articles and Book Chapters

"1 and 2 Maccabees—Same Story, Different Meaning," in *CTM* 42 (1971), pp. 515–526.
"Eschatology in the Testament of Abraham: A Study of the Judgment Scenes in the Two Recensions," in Robert A. Kraft, ed., *1972 Proceedings* (SBLSCS 2; The International Organization for Septuagint and Cognate Studies and the Society of Biblical Literature Pseudepigrapha Seminar), pp. 180–227.
"Narrative Traditions in the Paralipomena of Jeremiah and 2 Baruch," in *CBQ* 35 (1973), pp. 60–68.

"An Antiochan Date for the Testament of Moses," in George W.E. Nickelsburg, ed, *Studies on the Testament of Moses* (1973), pp. 33–37.

"Miscellaneous Small Finds," in Paul W. Lapp and Nancy L. Lapp, eds., *Discoveries in the Wâdi ed-Dâliyeh* (AASOR 41; Cambridge: American Schools of Oriental Research, 1974), pp. 101–102 and eleven plates.

With Nancy L. Lapp, "The Roman Occupation and Pottery of ʿArâq en-Naʿsaneh (Cave II)," in ibid., pp. 49–54 and ten plates.

"Enoch 97–104: A Study of the Greek and Ethiopic Texts," in Michael E. Stone, ed., *Armenian and Biblical Studies* (SionSup 1; Jerusalem: St. James, 1976), pp. 90–156.

"Enoch, Book of," pp. 265–268; "Future Life in Intertestamental Literature," pp. 348–351, in Keith Crim, ed., *The Interpreter's Dictionary of the Bible*, Supplementary Volume (Nashville: Abingdon, 1976).

"Eschatology in the Testament of Abraham," in George W.E. Nickelsburg, ed., *Studies on the Testament of Abraham* (1976), pp. 23–64. Revision of the 1972 article.

"Structure and Message in the Testament of Abraham," in ibid., pp. 85–93.

"Summary and Prospects for Future Work," in ibid., pp. 289–298.

"Simon—A Priest with a Reputation for Faithfulness," in *BASOR* 223 (1976), pp. 67–68.

"The Apocalyptic Message of 1 Enoch 92–105," in *CBQ* 39 (1977), pp. 309–328.

"Apocalyptic and Myth in 1 Enoch 6–11," in *JBL* 96 (1977), pp. 383–405.

"Good News/Bad News: The Messiah and God's Fractured Community," in *CurTM* 4 (1977), pp. 324–332.

Review article, Charlotte Klein, *Anti-Judaism in Christian Theology*, in *RelSRev* 4 (1978), pp. 161–168.

"Reflections upon Reflections: A Response to John Collins,' 'Methodological Issues in the Study of 1 Enoch,'" in Paul J. Achtemeier, ed., *Society of Biblical Literature 1978 Seminar Papers* 13 (2 vols.; Missoula: Scholars, 1978), vol. 1, pp. 311–314.

"Riches, the Rich, and God's Judgment in 1 Enoch 92–105 and the Gospel according to Luke," in *NTS* 25 (1979), pp. 324–344.

"Resurrection," in *The Encyclopedia Americana* (International ed.; Danbury: Americana, 1980), vol. 23, pp. 447–448.

"Good and Bad Leaders in Pseudo-Philo's Liber Antiquitatum Biblicarum," in John J. Collins and George W.E. Nickelsburg, eds., *Ideal Figures in Early Judaism* (1980), pp. 49–65.

"The Genre and Function of the Markan Passion Narrative," in *HTR* 73 (1980), pp. 153–184.

Review article "The Books of Enoch in Recent Research," in *RelSRev* 7 (1981), pp. 210–217.

"Some Related Traditions in the Apocalypse of Adam, the Books of Adam and Eve, and 1 Enoch," in Bentley Layton, ed., *The Rediscovery of Gnosticism*, vol. 2: Sethian Gnosticism (SHR 41; Leiden: Brill, 1981), pp. 515–539.

"Enoch, Levi, and Peter: Recipients of Revelation in Upper Galilee," in *JBL* 100 (1981), pp. 575–600.

"The Epistle of Enoch and the Qumran Literature," in *JJS* 33 (1982) = Geza Vermes and Jacob Neusner, eds., *Essays in Honour of Yigael Yadin*, pp. 333–348.

"Reading the Hebrew Scriptures in the First Century: Christian Interpretations in Their Jewish Context," in *WW* 3 (1983), pp. 238–250.

"Social Aspects of Palestinian Jewish Apocalypticism," in David Hellholm, ed., *Apocalypticism in the Mediterranean World and the Near East: Proceedings of the International Colloquium on Apocalypticism, Uppsala, August 12–17, 1979* (Tübingen: Mohr/Siebeck, 1983), pp. 641–654.

"Stories of Biblical and Early Post-Biblical Times," in Michael E. Stone, ed., *Jewish Writings of the Second Temple Period*, Compendia Rerum Iudaicarum ad Novum Testamentum 2:2 (Assen: Van Gorcum/Philadelphia: Fortress, 1983), pp. 33–87.

"The Bible Rewritten and Expanded," in ibid., pp. 89–156.

"The God of the Bible in a Nuclear Age?" in *CurTM* 11 (1984), pp. 213–224.

"Aaron," in *Reallexikon für Antike und Christentum*, Supp. Vol. 1 (Stuttgart: Anton Hiersemann, 1985), cols. 1–11.

"Revealed Wisdom as a Criterion for Inclusion and Exclusion: From Jewish Sectarianism to Early Christianity," in Jacob Neusner and Ernest S. Frerichs, eds., *"To See Ourselves as Others See Us:" Christians, Jews, "Others" in Late Antiquity* (Chico: Scholars Press, 1985), pp. 73–91.

"An *Ektroma*, Though Appointed from the Womb: Paul's Apostolic Self-Description in 1 Corinthians 15 and Galatians 1," in George W.E. Nickelsburg, ed., *Christians Among Jews and Gentiles* (1986), pp. 198–205.

With Robert A. Kraft, "Introduction: The Modern Study of Early Judaism," in Robert A. Kraft and George W.E. Nickelsburg, eds., *Early Judaism and its Modern Interpreters* (1986), pp. 1–30.

"1 Enoch and Qumran Origins: The State of the Question and Some Prospects for Answers," in Kent Harold Richards, ed., *Society of Biblical Literature 1986 Seminar Papers* 25 (Atlanta: Scholars Press, 1986), pp. 341–360.

"Salvation Without and With a Messiah: Developing Beliefs in Writings Ascribed to Enoch," in Jacob Neusner, William S. Green, and Ernest Frerichs, eds., *Judaisms and Their Messiahs* (New York: Cambridge University, 1987), pp. 49–68.

"Tobit," in James L. Mays, ed., *Harpers Commentary on the Bible* (San Francisco: Harper & Row, 1988), pp. 791–803.

"Tobit and Enoch: Distant Cousins with a Recognizable Resemblance," in David J. Lull, ed., *Society of Biblical Literature 1988 Seminar Papers* 27 (Atlanta: Scholars Press, 1988), pp. 54–68.

"Introduction to the Apocrypha," in Bernhard W. Anderson, ed., *The Books of the Bible* (2 vols.; New York: Charles Scribners, 1989), vol. 2, pp. 3–11.

"Two Enochic Manuscripts: Unstudied Evidence for Egyptian Christianity," in Harold W. Attridge, John J. Collins, and Thomas H. Tobin, eds., *Of Scribes and Scrolls: Studies on the Hebrew Bible, Intertestamental Judaism, and Christian Origins* (Resources in Religion 5; Lanham: University Press of America, 1990), pp. 251–260.

"The Apocalyptic Construction of Reality in 1 Enoch," in John J. Collins and James H. Charlesworth, eds., *Mysteries and Revelations: Apocalyptic Studies since the Uppsala Colloquium* (JSPSup 9; Sheffield: Sheffield Academic Press, 1991), pp. 51–64.

"The Qumranic Radicalizing and Anthropologizing of an Eschatological Tradition (1QH 4:29–40), in Dwight R. Daniels, Uwe Glessmer, and Martin Rösel, eds., *Ernten, was man sät: Festschrift für Klaus Koch zu seinem 65. Geburtstag*, (Neukirchen-Vluyn: Neukirchener, 1991), pp. 423–435.

"The Qumran Fragments of *1 Enoch* and Other Apocryphal Works: Implications for the Understanding of Early Judaism and Christian Origins," in *Jewish Civilization in the Hellenistic-Roman Period* (ed. Shemaryahu Talmon; JSPSup 10; Sheffield: Sheffield Academic Press, 1991), pp. 181–195.

"The Incarnation: Paul's Solution to the Universal Human Predicament," in Birger A. Pearson, ed., in collaboration with A. Thomas Kraabel, George W.E. Nickelsburg, Norman R. Petersen, *The Future of Early Christianity: Essays in Honor of Helmut Koester* (Minneapolis: Fortress, 1991), pp. 348–357.

"Enoch, First Book of," vol. 2, pp. 508–516; "Eschatology, *Early Jewish Literature*," vol. 2, pp. 579–594; "Jeremiel," vol. 3, pp. 722–723; "Passion Narratives," vol. 5, pp. 172–177; "Resurrection, *Early Judaism and Christianity*," vol. 5, pp. 684–691; "Son of Man," vol. 6, pp. 137–150, in David Noel Freedman, ed., *The Anchor Bible Dictionary* (6 vols.; New York: Doubleday, 1992).

"The Qumranic Transformation of a Cosmological and Eschatological Tradition (1QH 4:29–40)," in *The Madrid Qumran Congress: Proceedings of the International Congress on the Dead Sea Scrolls, Madrid 18–21 March, 1991* (ed. Julio Trebolle Barrera and

Luis Vegas Montaner, eds.; 2 vols.; STDJ 11; Leiden: Brill, 1992), vol. 2, pp. 648–659. Revision of article in Klaus Koch Festschrift).

Annotations for "The Book of Tobit," in *The HarperCollins Study Bible: New Revised Standard Version* (New York: HarperCollins, 1993), pp. 1437–1458.

"Jews and Christians in the First Century: The Struggle over Identity," in *Neot* 27 (1993), pp. 365–390.

"The First Century: a Time to Rejoice and a Time to Weep," *R & T* 1 (1994), pp. 4–17.

"Dealing with Challenges and Limitations: A Response," in *DSD* 1 (1994), pp. 229–237.

"Wisdom and Apocalypticism in Early Judaism: Some Points for Discussion," in Eugene H. Lovering, ed., *Society of Biblical Literature 1994 Seminar Papers* 33 (Atlanta: Scholars Press, 1994), pp. 715–732.

"Why Study the Extra-Canonical Literature: A Historical and Theological Essay," in *Neot* 28 (1994) Special edition = Essays in Memory of Willem Vorster, pp. 181–204.

"Scripture in 1 Enoch and 1 Enoch as Scripture," in Tord Fornberg and David Hellholm, eds., *Texts and Contexts: Biblical Texts in their Textual and Situational Contexts, Essays in Honor of Lars Hartman*) (Oslo: Scandanavian University Press, 1995), pp. 333–354.

"The Jewish Context of the New Testament," in Leander E. Keck, ed., *The New Interpreter's Bible* (Nashville: Abingdon, 1995), vol. 8, pp. 27–42.

"Son of Man," in Karel van der Toorn, et al., eds., *Dictionary of Deities and Demons in the Bible* (Leiden: Brill, 1995), cols. 1510–1520.

Jacob Neusner and William Scott Green, eds., *Dictionary of Judaism in the Biblical Period* (2 vols.; New York: Macmillan, 1996), 252 entries.

"The Search for Tobit's Mixed Ancestry: A Historical and Hermeneutical Odyssey," in *RevQ* 17/65–68 (1996) = *Hommage à Jozef T. Milik*, ed. F. García Martínez et Émile Puech; Paris: Gabalda, 1996), pp. 339–349.

"4Q551: A Vorlage to Susanna or a Text Related to Judges 19?" *JJS* 48 (1997), pp. 349–351.

"Patriarchs Who Worry about their Wives: A Haggadic Tendency in the Genesis Apocryphon," in Michael E. Stone and Esther G. Chazon, eds., *Biblical Perspectives: Early Use and Interpretation of the Bible in Light of the Dead Sea Scrolls. Proceedings of the First International Symposium of the Orion Center for the Study of the Dead Sea Scrolls and Associated Literature, 12–14 May, 1996* (STDJ 28; Leiden: Brill, 1998), pp. 137–158.

"Enochic Wisdom: An Alternative to the Mosaic Torah?," in Jodi Magness and Seymour Gitin, eds., *Hesed ve-Emet: Studies in Honor of Ernest S. Frerichs* (BJS 320; Atlanta: Scholars Press, 1998), pp. 123–132.

"Revisiting the Rich and the Poor in 1 Enoch 92–105 and the Gospel According to Luke," in *Society of Biblical Literature 1998 Seminar Papers* 37 (Atlanta: Scholars Press, 1998), vol. 2, pp. 579–605.

"Abraham the Convert: A Jewish Tradition and its Use by the Apostle Paul," in Michael E. Stone and Theodore A. Bergren, eds., *Biblical Figures Outside the Bible* (Harrisburg, Trinity International, 1998), pp. 151–175.

"Response to Paolo Sacchi's *Jewish Apocalyptic and its History*," in *Hen* 20 (1998), pp. 89–106.

"The Nature and Function of Revelation in 1 Enoch, Jubilees, and Some Qumranic Documents," in Esther G. Chazon and Michael E. Stone, eds., *Pseudepigraphic Perspectives: The Apocrypha and Pseudepigrapha in Light of the Dead Sea Scrolls, Proceedings of the International Symposium of the Orion Center for the Study of the Dead Sea Scrolls and Associated Literature, 12–14 January, 1997* (STDJ 31; Leiden: Brill, 1999), pp. 91–119.

"The Books of Enoch at Qumran: What We Know and What We Need to Think About," in Berndt Kollmann, ed., *Antikes Judentum und Frühes Christentum: Festschrift*

für Hartmut Stegemann zum 65. Geburtstag (BZNW 97; Berlin: Walter de Gruyter, 1999), pp. 99–113.
"Religious Exclusivism: A World View Governing Some Texts Found at Qumran," in Michael Becker and Wolfgang Fenske, eds., *Das Ende der Tage und die Gegenwart des Heils: Begegnungen mit dem Neuen Testament und seiner Umwelt: Festschrift für Heinz-Wolfgang Kuhn zum 65. Geburtstag* (Leiden: Brill, 1999), pp. 45–67.
"Currents in Qumranic Research: The Interplay of Data, Agendas, and Methodology," in Robert A. Kugler and Eileen M. Schuller, eds., *The Dead Sea Scrolls at Fifty: Proceedings of the 1997 Society of Biblical Literature Qumran Section Meeting* (Atlanta: Scholars Press, 1999), pp. 79–99, 143–146.
"Seeking the Origins of the Two-Ways Tradition in Jewish and Christian Ethical Texts," in Benjamin G. Wright, ed., *A Multiform Heritage: Studies on Early Judaism and Christianity in Honor of Robert A. Kraft* (Scholars Press Homage Series 24; Atlanta: Scholars Press, 1999), pp. 95–108.
"'Enoch' as Scientist, Sage, and Prophet: Content, Function, and Authorship in 1 Enoch," in *Society of Biblical Literature 1999 Seminar Papers* 38 (Atlanta: Society of Biblical Literature, 1999), pp. 203–230.
"Judgment, Life-After-Death, and Resurrection in the Apocrypha and the Non-Apocalyptic Pseudepigrapha," in Alan J. Avery-Peck and Jacob Neusner, eds., *Death, Life-After-Death, Resurrection, and the World-to-Come in the Judaisms of Antiquity* (Judaism in Late Antiquity 4; Leiden: Brill, 2000), pp. 141–162.
"Apocalyptic Texts," pp. 29–35; "Daniel, Book of, Greek Additions," pp. 174–176; "Enoch, Books of," pp. 249–53; "Eternal Life," pp. 270–272; "Resurrection," pp. 764–767; "Revelation," pp. 770–772, in Lawrence H. Schiffman and James C. VanderKam, eds., *Encyclopedia of the Dead Sea Scrolls* (2 vols.; New York: Oxford University Press, 2000).
"Tobit," in James L. Mays, ed., *The Harper-Collins Bible Commentary* (San Francisco: Harper, 2000), pp. 719–731. Revision of commentary in *Harper's Bible Comentary* (1988).
"Tobit, Genesis, and the Odyssey: A Complex Web of Intertextuality," in Dennis R. MacDonald, ed., *Mimesis and Intertextuality in Antiquity and Christianity* (Harrisburg: Trinity Press International, 2001), pp. 41–55.
"Prayer of Manasseh," in John Barton and John Muddiman, eds., *The Oxford Bible Commentary* (Oxford: Oxford University Press, 2001), pp. 770–773.
"From Roots to Branches: 1 Enoch in Its Jewish and Early Christian Contexts," in Hermann Lichtenberger and Gerbern S. Oegema, eds., *Jüdische Schriften in ihrem antik-jüdischen und urchristlichen Kontext* (Studien zu den Jüdischen Schriften aus hellenistisch-römischer Zeit 1; Gütersloh: Gütersloher Verlagshaus 2002), pp. 335–346.

Book Reviews

Matthew Black, *An Aramaic Approach to the Gospels and Acts* (1967), in *The Pulpit* (October, 1968), p. 27.
Raymond E. Brown, et al., *The Jerome Biblical Commentary* (1968), in *ChrCent* (May 28, 1969), p. 754.
Reginald C. Fuller, *A New Catholic Commentary on Holy Scripture* (1969), in *ChrCent* (February 18, 1970), p. 214.
Wolfgang Harnisch, *Verhängnis und Verheissung der Geschichte* (1969), in *JBL* 89 (1970), p. 486.
Otto Plöger, *Aus der Spätzeit des Alten Testaments* (1971), in *CBQ* 34 (1972), pp. 102–103.
Erling Jorstad, *That New Time Religion: The Jesus Revival in America* (1972), in *ChrCent* (November 22, 1972), pp. 1197–1198.
Gerhard Maier, *Mensch und freier Wille* (1971), in *JBL* 92 (1973), pp. 293–296.
M. Didier, ed., *L'Évangile selon Matthieu* (1972), in *CBQ* 35 (1973), pp. 525–527.

Günther Stemberger, *Der Leib der Auferstehung* (1972), in *CBQ* 35 (1973), pp. 555–556.
H.C.C. Cavallin, *Life After Death* (1974), in *JSJ* 6 (1975), pp. 100–102.
John H. Hayes, *Son of God to Superstar: Twentieth Century Interpretations of Jesus* (1976), in *ChrCent* (May 19, 1976), pp. 501–502.
Ibid. in *CurTM* 3 (1975), pp. 250–251.
"Review of the Literature," in *Studies on the Testament of Abraham*, ed., George W.E. Nickelsburg (1976), pp. 9–22.
W. Stewart McCullough, *The History and Literature of the Palestinian Jews*, in *CurTM* 3 (1976), pp. 368–370.
Raymond F. Surburg, *Introduction to the Intertestamental Period* (1975), in *CBQ* 38 (1976), pp. 600–601.
John Dart, *The Laughing Savior* (1976), in *ChrCent* (March 30, 1977), pp. 306–307.
H.C.C. Cavallin, *Life After Death* (1974), in *Int* 31 (1977), pp. 331–332.
William Barclay, *Jesus of Nazareth* (1977); David L. Edwards, *Today's Story of Jesus* (1977), in *ChrCent* (July 20–27, 1977), pp. 664–666 (with Marilyn M. Nickelsburg).
David M. Rhoads, *Israel in Revolution* (1976), in *CurTM* 4 (1977), p. 313.
James M. Robinson, ed., *The Nag Hammadi Library* (1977), in *ChrCent* (May 31, 1978), pp. 595–596.
J.T. Milik, *The Books of Enoch* (1976), in *CBQ* 40 (1978), pp. 411–419.
M. de Jonge, ed. *Studies on the Testaments of the Twelve Patriarchs* (1975), in *CBQ* 40 (1978), pp. 438–440.
The Oxford Annotated Apocrypha (1977), in *PSB* N.S. 2 (1978), pp. 58–59.
E.P. Sanders, *Paul and Palestinian Judaism* (1977), in *CBQ* 41 (1979), pp. 171–175.
James C. VanderKam, *Textual and Historical Studies in the Book of Jubilees* (1977), in *JAOS* 100 (1980), pp. 83–84.
Michael A. Knibb, *The Ethiopic Book of Enoch: A New Edition in the Light of the Aramaic Dead Sea Fragments* (1978), in *CBQ* 43 (1981), pp. 133–135.
Ferdinand Dexinger, *Henochs Zehnwochenapokalypse und offene Probleme der Apokalyptikforschung* (1977), in *JBL* 100 (1981), pp. 669–670.
Lars Hartman, *Asking for a Meaning: A Study of 1 Enoch 1–5* (1979), in *CBQ* 44 (1982), pp. 327–328.
Paul J. Kobelski, *Melchizedek and Melchiresaʿ* (1981), in *CBQ* 45 (1983), pp. 492–493.
John C. Meagher, *Five Gospels: An Account of How the Good News Came to Be* (1983), in *ChrCent* (January 4–11, 1984), pp. 24–25.
G.H.R. Horsley, *New Documents Illuminating Early Christianity: A Review of the Greek Inscriptions and Papyri Published in 1976* (1981), in *CBQ* 46 (1984), pp. 348–349.
Otto Neugebauer, *The "Astronomical" Chapters of the Ethiopic Book of Enoch (72–82)* (1981), in *JBL* 103 (1984), p. 457.
Ryszard Rubinkiewicz, *Die Eschatologie von Hen 9–11 und das Neue Testament* (1984), in *JBL* 106 (1987), pp. 535–537.
James H. Charlesworth, ed., *The Old Testament Pseudepigrapha*, 2 vols. (1983–85) and H.F.D. Sparks, *The Apocryphal Old Testament* (1984), in *CBQ* 50 (1988), pp. 288–291.
Matthew Black, *The Book of Enoch or 1 Enoch: A New English Edition with Commentary and Textual Notes* (1985), in *JBL* 107 (1988), pp. 342–344.
Roger Beckwith, *The Old Testament Canon of the New Testament Church and Its Background in Early Judaism* (1985), in *CBQ* 50 (1988), pp. 706–707.
Margaret Barker, *The Older Testament: The Survival of Themes from the Ancient Royal Cult in Sectarian Judaism and Early Christianity* (1987), in *JBL* 109 (1990), pp. 335–337.
Albert-Marie Denis, *Concordance grecque des Pseudépigraphes d'Ancien Testament* (1987), in *CBQ* 53 (1991), pp. 463–465.
J. Dominic Crossan, *The Cross that Spoke: The Origins of the Passion Narrative* (1988), in *JAAR* 59 (1991), pp. 159–162.
Michael E. Stone and David Satran, eds., *Emerging Judaism: Studies on the Fourth and Third Centuries* B.C.E. (1989), in *CBQ* 54 (1992), pp. 199–200.

Michael E. Stone, *History of the Literature of Adam and Eve* (1992), in *JR* 74 (1994), p. 94.

Florentino Garcia Martinez, *Qumran and Apocalyptic: Studies on the Aramaic Texts from Qumran* (1992), in *DSD* 2 (1995), pp. 235–238.

James C. VanderKam, *The Book of Jubilees* (2 vols.; Louvain: Peeters, 1989), in *JSP* 13 (1995), pp. 110–112.

John J. Collins, *The Scepter and the Star: The Messiahs of the Dead Sea Scrolls and Other Ancient Literature* (1995), in *JR* 77 (1997), pp. 457–458.

Merten Rabenau, *Studien zum Buch Tobit* (1994), in *JBL* 116 (1997), pp. 348–350.

James C. VanderKam and William Adler, eds., *The Jewish Apocalyptic Heritage in Early Christianity*, Compendia Rerum Iudaicarum ad Novum Testamentum 3:4 (1996), in *CBQ* 60 (1998), pp. 804–806.

Magen Broshi, et al., *Qumran Cave 4, XIV, Parabiblical Texts, Part 2. Discoveries in the Judaean Desert, XIX* (1995), in *JSP* 17 (1998), pp. 120–123.

George Brooke, et al., *Qumran Cave 4, XVII, Parabiblical Texts, Part 3. Discoveries in the Judaean Desert, XXII* (1996), in *DSD* 6 (1999), pp. 194–199.

PART ONE

JEWISH AND CHRISTIAN PERSPECTIVES:
SEEKING ANOTHER VIEW

CHAPTER ONE

THE FIRST CENTURY:
A TIME TO REJOICE AND A TIME TO WEEP*

George W.E. Nickelsburg

Most of us have seen it happen many times. The final whistle is blown; the game is over, and people with opposing emotions cannot sympathize with one another. On the one side, among team and fans, there is the joy and ecstasy of victory—shouts and cheers and hopes realized, and, in my country, maybe a goal post to tear down. On the other side, the sorrow and agony of defeat—silence and sadness and *nothing* to do but lick one's wounds and think of broken expectations and scenarios that will never be played out. Good sports shake hands, but the tears shed on both sides, in joy and in sorrow, have little more in common than the salt and the water. Understanding there may be, but sympathy—hardly; for it is quickly swallowed up by one's own emotions, which leave no room for the other's.

This example may seem trivial and far removed from the serious concerns of biblical history; but its familiar human dimension illustrates the central point of my topic, and its triviality highlights the seriousness of my concern. The events of first century Jewish and Christian history were inextricably bound up with human expectations, beliefs, and emotions. But what happened was no game. When it was over, life did not go on as usual. The competitors—Jews and Christians—were, in a way, children of the same mother. And the

* This paper was first read on April 13, 1986, as the Thomas J. King Memorial Lecture at Washburn University, Topeka Kansas, U.S.A. In its present form, in which only a few sentences were revised from the original for the sake of clarity, it was given as a public lecture at the Powell Bible Centre at UNISA on April 1, 1993. That a lecture about ancient history prepared for delivery in the midwestern United States should seem to speak so pointedly to the situation in South Africa may seem uncanny. In fact, my remarks deal with a common human problem that arises when cultures undergo fundamental, divisive changes. The tragic two thousand year story of Jewish-Christian relations is a reminder that understanding, empathy, and communication are crucial if communities in conflict with one another are to move toward productive rather than destructive scenarios. I offer it for publication in this spirit and with hope.

passing of time confirmed their contradictory reactions to the same historical events and intensified their inability to sympathize with each other. At best, Judaism and Christianity went their own ways. But often they became locked in bitter dispute and violent conflict, the consequences of which are still with us. That long, unhappy history is not my topic today. Rather, I want to look at the origins of that history in the first century, when the two sides, governed by their mutually exclusive beliefs and experiences, found it impossible to sympathize and difficult to communicate with one another. The issues were the death and resurrection of Jesus of Nazareth and the destruction of the Temple in the year 70.

JESUS OF NAZARETH IN FIRST CENTURY ROMAN PALESTINE

Let us begin around the turn of the era—the Year One, if you will—before the parting of the ways. Jews in the Roman Empire lived in a kind of tension between the religious and cultural traditions of their past and the concrete realities of their present life. Their heritage included a consciousness that they were God's chosen people, a desire to live out their elect status in obedience to God's will revealed in the Torah, and the belief that God would reward their obedience and punish their disobedience. The facts of life were another matter. Health and prosperity did not always accompany the just and pious life. And what did one make of Roman rule, which sometimes could be harsh and cruel? Was God rightly punishing the nation for its sins? If so, repentance could bring divine reward and blessing. Or were the people suffering unjustly? In such a case, one anticipated that God would intervene, overthrow Rome, and usher in God's kingly reign. People expected that this might happen in a variety of ways. Some awaited a messianic king who would sit on the Davidic throne, vacant now for almost six centuries. He would drive the Romans into the sea, shepherd the people of God, and restore the glories of the ancient kingdom. Others anticipated a heavenly savior, who would condemn the oppressive rulers of the earth and the demonic powers that possessed them and would usher in a new and eternal age of blessing. There was no lack of persons and groups who claimed to know how and when this would come to pass, and there were many who claimed to be the agents or harbingers of the coming divine intervention.

One such person was a Jewish itinerant preacher called Jesus of Nazareth. We know less about him that we would like to—and, probably, less than we *think* we know. But some facts are certain. His preaching centered on the assertion that in his words and deeds the awaited kingly rule of God was breaking into the world. Through his healing of the sick, he was expelling the demonic powers that were confounding God's good intentions in creation. His gathering of the lowly and outcasts bespoke divine justice and forgiveness. As to the Torah, his conduct presumed a divinely given wisdom to distinguish between God's intention and human interpretation, and the authority to act accordingly.

Not surprisingly, Jesus of Nazareth met with mixed reactions. The down-and-outers—the sick and the social and religious outcasts—joyfully received his words and actions as the voice and the healing, reconciling presence of God. The more religious and established elements of society viewed him with skepticism, with concern for true religion and the public welfare, and probably some fearful hostility which derived from this skepticism and concern. But the ultimate threat came from Rome and its representative Pontius Pilate. For regardless of what the Jews believed or thought or said, it was Pilate who condemned Jesus as a threat to the Empire; it was he who brought the benevolent career of Jesus of Nazareth to an abrupt halt.

Things had come to an end!

For Christians—A Time to Rejoice

But the end was not the end. In fact, it was the beginning. That death—the end—should be the beginning was an idea already present in the religious beliefs of Judaism. Many Jewish scenarios for the new age included the event which we call the resurrection; God the judge would restore life to those unjustly put to death. And so, in the present instance, the end that was the crucifixion gave way to the beginning that was the resurrection. But Jesus' resurrection constituted another beginning, a beginning of the parting of the ways, a beginning of the inability of two sides to comprehend and sympathize with one another. The resurrection, which was the difference between death and life, also came to make all the difference between Jews and Christians. Was the crucifixion the end? Most Jews certainly thought so. Even if they earnestly believed in a resurrection,

it had not started in the case of Jesus of Nazareth. For other Jews
it was different. They came to believe that God had raised the
crucified Jesus from the dead. This crucial belief made these Jews
into Christians, persons for whom the resurrection attested to Jesus'
special significance. What was that significance, and how did the resurrection attest to it?

The resurrection of Jesus was not a simple, uninterpreted, physical fact—the resuscitation of a corpse. From the outset, the resurrection was an event with meaning. Indeed, in a very short time, it
acquired multiple meanings. On a very basic level, the resurrection
was significant for Jesus himself—in two different ways. In the first
place, the resurrection was God's vindication of Jesus—whose death
had been an evil act of violent injustice. God's supreme court had
overruled the earthly court. The activity for which Jesus has been
wrongly condemned was approved by God. Secondly, with a nod
to the inscrutability of God's will, the crucifixion itself was given a
positive meaning. Jesus' death was a necessary event that possessed
redeeming significance for sinful humanity, and the resurrection was
God's way to restore the life which the innocent Jesus had *had* to
surrender.

If Jesus' *death* had significance for others, so did his resurrection.
A new age was dawning for humanity. Resurrection was, by definition,
an event of the end times, and Jesus' resurrection meant that those
times had come.

In one respect, the resurrection had *already* changed things. Jesus
was now exalted in heaven as God's Messiah, God's anointed king.
In other language, Jesus was Lord of the universe—of things in
heaven and on earth and under the earth. Moreover, the quality of
human life had changed. The Spirit of the risen Christ dwelt in
those who believed in him and that spirit gave life to the church,
the community of believers, binding them together in love.

The new order of things had implications also for the future. When
the exalted Jesus brought the world into subjection, he would return
on the clouds of heaven as judge. Then the spirit of Christ given
in baptism would give life to those who had died in Christ, and the
dead and the living would be transformed into the likeness of Christ's
glorious resurrection body.

So for Christians of the first decades, the resurrection of Christ
had made all things new. In the excitement and joy of their new
status and the new order of things in the cosmos, they anxiously

awaited the final events, when God's sovereignty and will would become visible on earth, finally, fully, and forever. They lived in the joy that promises had been fulfilled, and they anxiously anticipated the final consummation of what had already begun to happen. It was a liberating, transforming experience that enabled them to endure the bitter and harsh facts of life in the Mediterranean world. It was *a time for rejoicing*, and that joy overcame the sorrow and weeping that attended suffering, imprisonment, and the death of loved ones.

For Most Jews—Nothing Special

But this joy was not shared by all. For most Jews in the first century, the crucifixion was the end. Jesus had not been raised from the dead. He was not the Messiah or the exalted Lord. Neither the world, nor the times, nor human existence had changed one bit because of Jesus of Nazareth. The joy and enthusiasm that characterized the early Christian community did not substantially affect the vast majority of the Jewish people. Here we must note an ironic turn of events. The early Christian community, which sprang from the womb of Judaism, came to be composed increasingly of non-Jews—Gentiles.

We take this transformation for granted, because we have lived with it for nineteen centuries. However, for one Christian of the first century it was the cause of considerable puzzlement and intense personal sorrow. Listen to the poignant lament of the Jewish-Christian apostle Paul:

> I have great sorrow and unceasing anguish in my heart. For I wish that I myself were accursed and cut off from Christ for the sake of my brethren, my kinsmen by race. They are Israelites, and to them belong the sonship, the glory, the covenants, the giving of the law, the worship, and the promises; to them belong the patriarchs, and of their race, humanly speaking, is the Messiah. (*Rom.* 9:2–5)

But Paul's sorrow over Jewish unbelief did not dampen his faith in the power and purpose of God. Once the gospel had been preached to all the gentiles, Israel would turn in faith to Jesus.

Paul's exuberant hope was not realized. Most Jews continued to live in their own religious world. Neither in the first century nor thereafter did they come to share the specific new mode of joyous existence that characterized life in the first century church. Indeed, exactly the opposite happened.

THE JEWISH REVOLT AGAINST ROME

Toward the end of Paul's life, a series of events began to unfold in
Palestine which resulted in disaster, sorrow, and tragedy for the Jews.
That is the second part of our story. As the Christians celebrated
the party which they hoped would soon turn into the Messiah's banquet, the remainder and the majority of the Jews mourned the
destruction of Jerusalem, the obliteration of the Temple, and the
death of their national existence as they had known it.

The tragedy that burst upon Palestine in the latter half of the first
century had its roots in the same events and circumstances that gave
birth to Christianity: the Roman presence and the social, economic,
and religious factors that coexisted with it. John the Baptist and Jesus
of Nazareth were not the only prophetic and messianic figures who
spoke to first century Palestinian Jews. As the decades of the forties
and fifties and sixties passed, the landscape became populated with
leaders, demagogues, and bandit chieftains who promised release
from Roman oppression and the domination which the powerful
upper classes exerted over the poor of the land. Eventually, a flame
was lit that had to burn itself out. Sporadic outbursts contributed to
widespread revolt against Rome. And before the armies of Vespasian
and Titus put out the fire, the land and the people had been crushed
and devastated by a massive revolt that was also, in many places, a
bitter and bloody civil war.

The events of the Jewish Revolt of 66–74 are chronicled in grue-
some detail by the Jewish historian, Flavius Josephus in *The Jewish
War*, and we need not rehearse them. The *results* can hardly be over-
estimated. Widespread death and casualties in the civilian population, destruction of property, disruption of the agricultural cycles,
dissolution of social and political institutions, the breaking up of families and the obliteration of family identity through death and slav-
ery, reprisals by the victorious occupying powers. When the smoke
and dust had settled, the countryside was desolated, cities had been
destroyed, and the population was decimated. But the single most
devastating event, because of its symbolic value, was the destruction
of Jerusalem in the year 70. The nation's capital and central religious institution had been obliterated. Jerusalem was in ruins, the
Temple was a pile of rocks, and the sacrificial cult had permanently
ceased. It was *a time to weep*, a time for doubt, and a time for despair.

For Jews—A Time to Weep

Several Jewish sources from the last decades of the first century testify to these sentiments—unambiguously, and sometimes poignantly and with eloquence. One anonymous author, whom scholars call "Pseudo-Philo," composed a rewritten version of biblical history from creation to the time of Samuel, known as *The Book of Biblical Antiquities*. His concerns are evident in the way that he embellishes the old stories. With an eye toward the demagoguery and inadequate leadership which led to the revolt, he seldom misses an opportunity to place an appropriate speech in the mouth of an ancient leader—whether a prophet, a patriarch, or a judge. These speeches resound with the same questions: Does the present crisis threaten the continued existence of God's people? Is the covenant still intact, or has our God forsaken us? The stories also suggest the answer. In the past, in spite of bad leadership, and through good leaders, God delivered the people from imminent destruction and restored them to favor. The implication is clear. In the present crisis, such leadership will emerge again and the nation will recover. For all of the questions and doubts that he verbalizes, the author maintains a sense of hope.

A similar tension between despair and hope is evident in two other writings from around the turn of the first century. Both are written pseudonymously, that is, under an assumed name. Both are ascribed to figures associated with Nebuchadnezzar's destruction of Jerusalem in 587 B.C.E.

The first of these two documents is attributed to Baruch, the scribe of Jeremiah, who lived through the destruction of Jerusalem and the first Temple. The sorrowful tone of the apocalypse known as *2 Baruch* is reminiscent Jeremiah's Book of Lamentations. The story opens on the eve of the destruction of Jerusalem. Baruch pleads that God prevent the destruction of city and Temple. After the destruction occurs, Baruch agonizes over its consequences and their implications. His questions are big ones: Why has God allowed his people and city to fall to a pagan and unjust nation? What has happened to the covenantal relationship? How can the people continue to serve God and obey God's commandments? In a manner that recalls the book of Jeremiah, the author depicts Baruch moving from private, questioning confrontations with God to public interactions with the people and their leaders. The book ends as Baruch becomes the convinced exponent of the promise that God will furnish teachers who will interpret the Torah and enable the people to obey and thus obtain the blessings of heaven and the new age. The book is remarkable for its progression from sorrow, gloom, and doubt to hope and faith.

The second text, written around the year 100, is attributed to Ezra, the scribe who came to Jerusalem after the Babylonian Exile in order to restore and establish the Torah to its rightful place as the center and foundation of Jewish society. *Fourth Ezra* is set in Babylon, where Ezra is brooding over the destruction of Jerusalem and the Temple. Like *2 Baruch*, it is composed of a series of revelatory discourses between the sage and God's angel. However, the tone of the book differs from Baruch. The skepticism is deeper, and the questions are more profound. The author is less concerned about practical matters of restoration and wrestles more with the implications that the destruction of Jerusalem has for one's faith in divine justice. The discourses are reminiscent of the dialogues in the book of Job; the author's challenge to God is more explicit than in Baruch and the implications of this challenge are far-reaching. The destruction of Jerusalem is God's punishment for sin, but has God not rigged the course of events ahead of time? Has not the propensity to sin been built into the human heart? And if that is the case, how can God punish God's people for the sins they were bound to commit and unable to avoid? Thus the historical event of the destruction of Jerusalem becomes the occasion for profound and massive questions about human nature and about God's success as a Creator and God's fairness as the Lord of history. Although the book is not permeated with the acute sorrow that characterizes 2 Baruch, it reflects a kind of doubt and skepticism that is reminiscent of the Book of Ecclesiastes. This doubt and, at times, resentful challenge to God's justice and love are not the author's final word, however. Like his colleague "Baruch," this author anticipates the restoration of the Torah—much like the restoration accomplished by his namesake Ezra—and he records a vision of a restored and glorified Jerusalem.

For our present purposes, these Jewish texts of the first century are remarkable in a number of ways. First—their outlook is ultimately hopeful. They testify to the faith and resiliency that enabled the Jews to survive the crisis of the Revolt. Secondly—for reasons whose importance we shall return to, the authors' hopes for the future are bound up in three factors: the ongoing viability of the Torah, the hope of a Messiah who would break the back of Roman power, and the restoration of Jerusalem. Finally—the optimistic viewpoint of these authors could only be articulated after they had given expression to all of the sorrow, grief, doubt, and trauma that followed upon the events of 66–74. Belief in God's ultimate sovereignty over history and creation could not obscure the physical, emotional, social, and religious hurt. These authors could *not* say with the apostle Paul, "I consider that the sufferings of this present time are not worth comparing with the glory that is to be revealed to us" (*Rom.* 8:18). Whatever that glory might be for these authors—and it was there—it did not silence the lament or wholly assuage the hurt. For these Jewish authors, these decades remained, in a real sense, a time to weep.

For Christians—Satisfaction with God's Justice

The situation was altogether different for Christians. Let us return to our comparison. We began by noting the contrasting ways in which two groups of people responded to Jesus of Nazareth. For some Jews and many more gentiles, he was the cause for celebration and joyful anticipation of God's imminent future. For most Jews, Jesus was at worst a cause of trouble and at best, a non-issue. A sharper contrast is evident in Jewish and Christian attitudes about the events of the years 66–74. As we have seen, the aftermath of the Revolt was the cause of severe social and religious disruption and a time of profound sorrow for Jews. For their Christian contemporaries, the Evangelists, who composed the Four Gospels, the situation was altogether different.

As for "Baruch" and "Ezra," the events of the years 66–74 are most noteworthy because of the destruction of Jerusalem and the Temple. The Christian interpretation of the Temple's destruction was, however, vastly different—in two respects. In the first place, the destruction of the Temple was no great loss. For many Christians, even before its destruction, the Temple was no longer a necessity; it had been replaced by the Christian community. Thus its destruction was a visible confirmation of the fact that a religious system which was no longer viable had come to an end.

The second aspect of Christian interpretations of the year 70 relates to the reasons for the destruction. Like Baruch and Ezra, the evangelists believed that the Roman armies were an instrument of divine judgment on a sinful people. Where Matthew, Mark, Luke, and John

differed from their Jewish contemporaries was in their explanation
of the nature of the sin that was being punished. Baruch and Ezra
are vague on this issue. The evangelists are altogether specific. The
people sinned in that they did not acknowledge Jesus as God's Messiah and did not recognize in him and in the resurrection God's
special and final intervention into human affairs. They failed to
understand and believe that in him the promises to Israel were being
fulfilled and the new age had dawned.

The manner in which the evangelists deal with these issues is of
considerable importance for our topic. To state it briefly, the Gospels
are not simple chronicles of the life and deeds of Jesus of Nazareth;
they are interpretive history. This interpretation involves several factors. First, and most obviously, the story of Jesus and his interaction
with the Jews is being interpreted in light of the evangelist's faith
that Jesus is the Messiah. Secondly, the evangelists are looking at
the events of Jesus' life in retrospect, forty to sixty years after the
fact. In doing so, they see these events through a series of screens
or prisms, which are the ongoing history of Jews and Christians in
the years 30 to 90. Thus, they project onto the story of Jesus' interaction with the Jews the story of the subsequent interaction of Christians and Jews. Historical revisionism is at work, and this revisionistic
interpretation of the Jesus story involves at least two issues: the ongoing validity of the Torah, the Jewish Law; and the causes of the
death of Jesus.

The place of the Jewish Law was a cause of serious dispute even
among Christians in the first century. As the writings of Paul indicate, a significant and influential sector of early Christianity believed
that the coming of Jesus had not nullified the validity of this central institution of Judaism. They claimed that Christians, as heirs of
Abraham, were still bound to observe at least parts of the Mosaic
Torah. For others, like Paul, the Torah was passe, at least for gentile Christians. This debate about the Torah was carried on not only
within Christian circles, but also between Christians and Jews. The
debate is reflected in the Gospel stories about the interaction between
Jesus and the Pharisees. These stories were preserved and transmitted by the church of the mid-first century because the church and
the Jewish community were locked in debate over the validity of the
Jewish law. Moreover, as this controversy escalated, the Pharisees
were increasingly perceived as superreligious people, whose hypocrisy
constituted false religion. Thus, in the Gospels, written in the late

first century, the story of Jesus and the Pharisees reflects the bitter facts of a religious standoff between Christians and Jews.

The second aspect of the Gospels' revisionist history involves their interpretation of the causes of Jesus' death. A careful sifting of the evidence in Mark, our earliest Gospel, makes it clear that, in point of historical fact, Jesus was executed because he was convicted of a crime of rebellion against the Empire. The involvement of the Roman governor, the mode of execution, and the charge nailed to the cross all indicate that Jesus was seen as a political threat or a potential political threat to Rome. But here is how Mark interprets the story. For him, the real issue was Jesus' religious authority. When Jesus challenged the Temple establishment and called the sanctuary a cave of robbers, the chief priests and elders concocted a death plot, and to see it to its end, they trumped up charges of revolt and twisted Pilate's arm into an execution.

Mark's revisionist history is taken a step further by Matthew, who used Mark as a source for the writing of his own Gospel. Although the chief priests and other Jewish authorities are instrumental in the plot that leads to the death of Jesus, in the final analysis, it is the Jewish people as a whole who bear the responsibility for the crucifixion. This is portrayed dramatically in the scene at Pilate's court (*Matt.* 27:11–26). Both Pilate and his wife, informed by a divine revelation, attest Jesus' innocence. In a public gesture, the pagan governor washes his hands of the case and states, "I am innocent of the blood of this just man—you see to it." At this point, the scene switches to the crowd. Only they are not a crowd. Matthew calls them "the people." For him they are stand-ins for the nation of Israel. And all the people cry, "His blood be on us and on our children." Two factors are operative here. First, the people as a whole are responsible for the death of Jesus. Secondly, the people as a whole will suffer the consequences of this act.

These consequences are threefold. First, God will send the Roman army to destroy the people and burn their city (*Matt.* 22:1–7). Secondly, God will disenfranchise Israel as his people; he will take the kingdom from Israel and give it to the largely gentile church (*Matt.* 21:33–43). Third, the curse will be passed on to successive generations of Jews (*Matt.* 27:25).

Once again revisionist history reflects the standoff between Christians and Jews at the end of the first century and reveals a startling difference in their responses to the events of the year 70. Baruch

and Ezra may attribute the destruction to sin, but their account is
explicitly tempered with grief and puzzlement over the extremity of
the punishment. For the evangelists, there is no pause. The Jews
had it coming to them. Nor does it make any difference in the final
analysis. God's redemptive activity will go on without the temple,
and God's covenantal relationship is transferred to the Gentiles.
There are losers, but there are winners, and the winners hardly pause
to think of the losers, except with a certain satisfaction that God's
justice has been enacted.

This last point requires brief elaboration (Stendahl 1984: 222–23).
As we have noted, when the Gospels were written, the church was
largely a gentile community. As a result, the gospels' provide the
sayings of Jesus with a context that these sayings did not originally
have. Historically, Jesus the teacher had spoken as an insider, as a
Jew, within the Jewish community. He was a prophet speaking to
his own people. However, when these sayings became imbedded in
the gospels, they became the property of gentiles who understood
them to be directed to those Jews out there. The sayings of Jesus
no longer retained the anguish of the prophet who spoke to his own,
nor did they reflect the grief of the Jewish apostle Paul, who ago-
nized over his own people. They reflected a gentile Christian judgment on non-Christian Jews.

FROM PAST TO PRESENT—THE TRAGIC LEGACY OF MISUNDERSTANDING

We have taken a glimpse into two separate, coexisting worlds. I have
commented on how two groups of people looked at the same events
through different eyes. It has been a study in contrasts. Christians
rejoiced in the death and resurrection of Jesus, the Messiah; Jews
were indifferent to the man and cherished hopes of a Messiah yet
to come. Jews prized the Torah as the indispensable revelation of
God's will; Christians acclaimed Jesus as the epitome of such a revelation. Christians viewed the destruction of Jerusalem with com-
placency or even vindictiveness; Jews wept over its destruction and
awaited a new Jerusalem and a restored Temple.

The story is a fascinating historical study in its own right. But
there is another dimension. As is often the case, the events of the
past continue to affect the present. This is particularly so with respect
to the events that we have considered—and for a very special reason.

Early Christian attitudes about the Jews are not recounted in some dusty chronicle that has been dug out of an archive, or some worm-eaten scroll, found by chance in a cave. These attitudes are enshrined in writings that have functioned for almost two millennia as the sacred scriptures of the church. What is recounted as events of the past is invested with divine authority, and that authority presents itself to the religious community every time that its members read these documents privately or hear them recited in services of public worship.

This continuing interaction with these ancient traditions has a certain anachronism about it. The Gospels reflect controversies of the first century when Christianity was defining itself over against Judaism by showing, often in bitter and angry debate, that Christians were right and Jews were wrong.

All of this historical contingency has continued to exist in documents which have long moved out of that historical setting. In practice, however, it is difficult to separate the contingency from the perennial authority which the documents continue to hold for the religious community. What the documents said about the Jews back then continues to be said about Jews today, and they continue to affect and govern the attitudes of twentieth century Christians toward their Jewish contemporaries.

Historically, the aftertaste has been bad and the results, tragic. The severe anti-Jewish attitude in Matthew's account of the trial and death of Jesus has had untold effects. It is true that so-called anti-Semitism, racist disdain of the Jews, existed before Christianity came into existence. In the Christian era, however, anti-semitism has been aided and abetted by the anti-Judaism attested in the Gospels. There is little doubt in my mind that the events in Germany in the 1930's, however we might explain their origins, were tolerated by Christians, at least in part, because of attitudes informed by the Gospels' accounts of the trial and death of Jesus. Matthew says that the Jews brought a curse upon themselves. In the view of many, the curse took, and, accordingly, well it should have.

Toward the Future—Reversing the Misunderstanding

Finally, my topic is especially appropriate to the present setting, where the university and the community meet. Most of my observations

are not original with me. They have been forced to our consciousness by the events of the holocaust and by the twentieth century
reexamination of the Bible in academic environments that are detached
from religious communities. It is in the environment of a public university, separated as it is from the religious community, that it is
especially possible honestly to scrutinize the past without the restraints
and special agendas of religious dogma—although we, too, are not
free of dogma. Happily this same scrutiny is taking place in inter-
faith dialogues between Christians and Jews. It needs to continue in
both settings, and with cooperation between the two. To what extent
the results of this historical inquiry and self-reflection are convincing and to what extent they will affect attitudes insides and outside
religious communities is a matter that every person must decide for
himself or herself. In that decision lies the possibility to overcome
the separations of the past and to find understanding and empathy
in the present.

FURTHER READING

PRIMARY SOURCES

Flavius Josephus, The Jewish War: Thackeray, H. St. John, Loeb Classical Library
    (Cambridge, MA; London: Heinemann, 1926–28).
The Book of Biblical Antiquities: Harrington, Daniel J. "Pseudo-Philo," in Charlesworth,
    J.H., ed., *The Old Testament Pseudepigrapha* (Garden City: Doubleday, 1985): 2:297–377.
2 Baruch: Klijn, A.F.J. "2 (Syriac Apocalypse of) Baruch," in ibid., 1:615–52.
4 Ezra: See any modern edition of the Bible with the Apocrypha.

SECONDARY LITERATURE

Horsley, R.A. & Hanson, J.S. 1985. *Bandits, Prophets, and Messiahs: Popular Movements
    at the Time of Jesus.* Minneapolis: Winston.
———. Aspects of the social setting of the first century leading to the Jewish revolt.
Klein, C. 1978. *Anti-Judaism in Christian Theology.* Philadelphia: Fortress.
———. A discussion of anti-Jewish theological biases in Christian discussions of the
    Jewish context of first century Christianity.
Nickelsburg, G.W.E. 1981. *Jewish Literature Between the Bible and the Mishnah.* Philadelphia:
    Fortress.
———. A historical and literary introduction to post-biblical Jewish writings.
Rhoads, D.M. 1976. *Israel in Revolution: 5–742 C.E.* Philadelphia: Fortress.
———. A historical discussion, a companion piece to Horsley and Hanson.
Sayler, G.B. 1983. *Have the Promises Failed? A Literary Analysis of 2 Baruch.* Society of
    Biblical Literature Dissertation Series 72. Chico, CA: Scholars.
Stendahl, K. 1984. *Meanings: The Bible as Document and as Guide.* Philadelphia: Fortress.
Stone, M.E. 1990. *Fourth Ezra.* Philadelphia: Fortress.
———. A critical commentary with an extensive introduction.

RESPONSE TO "THE FIRST CENTURY: A TIME TO REJOICE AND A TIME TO WEEP"

WILLIAM S. GREEN*

Perhaps no contemporary American scholar has done more than George Nickelsburg to advance our understanding of intertestamental literature, the Apocrypha and Pseudepigrapha in particular. His careful, thorough, and persistent scholarship has opened this literature to students and scholars alike and shown in fresh ways its pertinence to the history of early Judaism. The responses to his work gathered in this volume are ample testimony to the durability and significance of his contributions to learning.

Nickelsburg's brief study, "The First Century: A Time to Rejoice and a Time to Weep," attempts to bring clarity—primarily for a lay audience—to the historical origins of the separation of Judaism and Christianity. The article was written in 1986 and published with just slight changes eight years later. It is a sensitive and thoughtful effort to epitomize the crisis in first-century Palestinian Judaism that led to the formation of a new religion, Christianity. The piece casts the events of the first century in tragic terms and attempts to account for what it sees as the broken communication between Jews and the earliest Christians. In Nickelsburg's words, ". . . the two sides, governed by their mutually exclusive beliefs and experiences, found it impossible to sympathize and difficult to communicate with one another." The poles of this systemic incomprehensibility are "the death and resurrection of Jesus of Nazareth" and the "destruction of the Temple."

In Nickelsburg's historical epitome, these two components generated two religious worlds essentially closed to one another. One was a new world of victory and optimism, the other a world of "doubt and despair." The sides read the two events very differently. Most Jews ignored Jesus, and the Gospel writers saw the destruction of the Temple as a just punishment for the Jews' refusal to accept Jesus as Messiah. The result of these divergent understandings is a tragic

---

* University of Rochester.

history of alienation and recrimination. Nickelsburg explains the stakes
with characteristically unadorned clarity:

> There is no doubt in my mind that the events in Germany in the
> 1930s, however we might explain their origins, were tolerated by
> Christians, at least in part, because of attitudes informed by the Gospels'
> accounts of the trial and death of Jesus. Matthew says that the Jews
> brought a curse upon themselves. In the view of many, the curse took,
> and, accordingly, well it should have.

This is not a typical sentence for a scholar of biblical and related
literature, and it took conviction and fortitude to write it.

In all scholarship—but perhaps especially in the humanities—
images are everything. They shape a sense of importance and priority; they are lenses for classification and therefore understanding.
Nickelsburg's images of competition and contest, rejoicing and weeping, cast the separation of Christianity from Judaism in primarily
theological terms and in categories of winners and losers. My guess
is that if he were to write this article today, its range of images
would be more nuanced, and expansive. Although belief in Jesus'
resurrection and the destruction of the Temple are not exactly comparable entities, they surely are important variables in the emergence
of Christianity. But the early stories of both communities are more
balanced and complex than the dichotomy suggests.

In his description of the land of Israel in the first century, Nickelsburg
emphasizes "tension between the religious and cultural traditions of
their [the Jews'] past and the concrete realities of their contemporary life." This focus almost makes ancient Judaism appear as a religion of failed or failing expectations, a religion that did not or could
not deliver on its promises. As Nickelsburg's own scholarship has
taught us, it is wise to place these concerns—and the texts that
express them—in context and not see them as either unique or
broadly representative. Readers of Job, Ecclesiastes, II Isaiah, and
Jeremiah for instance, know that the problems of unjust suffering, a
lost Temple, and imperial domination were not new to either Judaism
or to the Jews. These canonical books suggest that Judaism's covenantal canopy had already been stretched to encompass the necessary
complexities of monotheism's theodicy. The literature designated as
Apocrypha and Pseudepigrapha, and the Dead Sea Scrolls, show
that the same extension took place outside the canon. To be sure,
some Jews may have despaired after the second Temple's disap-

pearance (as some followers of Jesus despaired after his death), perhaps even more after the Bar Kokhba revolt than after 70. But
Nickelsburg's own textual examples shows that even apocalyptists
retained hope. The evidence suggests that, as once before, Jews after
the destruction of the second Temple found ways to adapt their basic
religious system to altered conditions and circumstances.

The religion we now label as ancient or early Judaism is a Levitical
religion. It is grounded in a priestly vision of reality, as expressed
in the Pentateuch, itself edited by priests. According to the Pentateuch,
the central institution of covenant maintenance was the Temple cult.
Levitical religion aims to create an order on earth—ethical, social,
and physical—that is congenial to God's presence. It supposes that
because human beings must build that order, there will be breaks
in it. Israel and Israelites will transgress against God's commandments, either deliberately or unintentionally. In addition, there are
other ruptures, which are not classified as sin but as uncleanness or
ritual impurity. The theory behind the cult is that Israel and Israelites
by themselves can take concrete action—through repentance and ritual—to maintain and reconstitute their covenant relationship with
God. They do not require an intermediary or savior to perform that
religious function. The institution of the cult supposes that through
acts of conscience and conscious labor human beings can repair a
ruptured covenant with God, but that God does not initiate a breach
without purpose. God's alienation from Israel, in principle, is not
capricious, and Israel possesses the means to keep and make things
right.

It is clear that Rabbinic Judaism, which ultimately dominated late
antique Jewish religious life, adapted and altered the Levitical system described in Scripture. Rabbinism's system of religious praxis—
halakhah, the "way" of doing things—emerges from the religious
worldview of the Israelite priests and modifies and extends the
Temple's structures of holiness into the life of the community. Rabbinism's religious practice is built around the Levitical binaries of
sacred and profane, clean and unclean, life and death, and the priestly
values of monotheism, covenant, justice, righteousness, and social
responsibility. Its liturgy follows the pattern of the sacrificial cult.
After the destruction of the Temple in 70, Rabbinism began to
shift Judaism's religious focus from the altar to the Torah. Along
with prayer, piety, and acts of morality and social responsibility, it

came to emphasize the study of Torah—both as text and Rabbinic teaching—as a primary religious activity. It understood critical intellectual inquiry as a religious action.

This is not to claim that Rabbinism was the norm in Judaic religious practice after the Temple was destroyed. To the contrary, both Rabbinic literature and archaeological evidence indicate that Rabbinic domination of Jewish communities was slow in coming. It is clear that after 70 Jews inside and outside the land of Israel found ways to accommodate to the dominant pagan culture in the absence of a fully developed post-destruction Levitical ideology and professional religious leadership. But the evidence of synagogues—both literary and archaeological—shows that Torah reading and Sabbath observance were conventional aspects of Jewish life. And, as Nickelsburg himself suggests, "neither in the first century nor thereafter" did Jews in large numbers become Christian. For various reasons, even without the Temple, Christianity's gospel did not address Jews' religious concerns. It is difficult to account for the ultimate emergence of Rabbinism as the principal form of ancient Judaism on the assumption that Jews in large numbers abandoned the basic Levitical system outlined in the Torah. Thus, although one legitimate Judaic response to the Temple's destruction was "doubt" and "despair," as Nickelsburg suggests, an equally important response was the capacity of the Levitical system to adapt to dramatically challenging circumstances and to address them effectively. The persistence of this system in the face of such massive forces of opposition and destruction is at least as interesting a phenomenon as—and in some ways more surprising than—the emergence of a new religion in a period of political and cultural change and instability.

Christianity's response to the crucifixion and resurrection also was not wholly one-sided. In a theological sense, belief "that God had raised the crucified Jesus from the dead . . . made . . . Jews into Christians" and may have been a "liberating, transforming experience" that marked a "time for rejoicing" for early Christians. But socially, politically, and institutionally Christianity's early years were anything but an unqualified success. The "excitement and joy" of which Nickelsburg speaks were tempered by almost immediate strife within the early church itself as well as a series of harsh persecutions by a succession of Roman emperors. Martyrdom was a conventional feature of early Christian life, and bitter schisms marked the Church's establishment throughout its early centuries. The Council of Nicaea shows that divided opinions of Christianity's basic theological doctrines was a persistent trait of the Church's institutional development.

Nickelsburg observes that early Christian writers regarded the destruction of the Temple not as a tragedy but as a vindication. It was a punishment the Jews deserved for their failure to acknowledge Jesus of Nazareth as messiah. In Nickelsburg's account, for many early Christians, belief in Jesus' resurrection brought with it a new conception of how the covenant was to be maintained in particular and, in the last analysis, how humans would relate to God. Not surprisingly, those who understood Jesus' resurrection to create a new foundation for the divine-human relationship would regard the Levitical system of Temple and Torah with skepticism, if not outright hostility. As some suggest, Paul's preoccupation with the problem of "the Law" initially may have been more of an internal Christian matter than a critique of Judaism itself. Nevertheless, it is the first expression of what became a longstanding issue between Judaism and Christianity. Paul appears to have judged that if the Levitical system remained effective in maintaining the covenant and repairing ruptures in it—that is, in preserving Israel's right relationship to God—the salvific meaning he attached to Jesus' resurrection could not be persuasive. Hence his claim in Galatians 2:21, "If righteousness comes through the Law, then Christ died for nothing." Paul's criticism implicitly acknowledges the impact and force of the Levitical system. He did not expend rhetorical and intellectual energy attacking a system his audiences construed to be trivial or useless. Hence, the Temple's destruction also affected Christianity by propelling it towards a non-Jewish audience and undermining potential Christian alternatives to Paul's teaching on "the Law."

To his credit, Nickelsburg does not shy away from assessing the long-term implications of the evangelists' claims that the destruction of the Temple was a punishment the Jews deserved and a sign of divine rejection of the Levitical system. For a lay audience in particular, his explanation of how the Gospel writers recast Jesus' life, and especially his death, in terms of later beliefs, is particularly effective. He allows his readers to see how historical scholarship can help us understand the motives that underlay these dangerous texts.

This is an important move because it helps to explain to a non-scholarly audience the contemporary consequences of biblical scholarship. As Nickelsburg observes, "What the documents said about the Jews back then continues to be said about Jews today, and they continue to affect and govern the attitudes of twentieth-century Christians toward their Jewish contemporaries." This observation is as valid today as when it was written in 1986. But it is important to underscore that historical study cannot in itself undo or overcome theological difference. Paul certainly recognized that the religious movement and perspective he advocated and represented could not be neutral about the system from which it emerged and which it claimed to surpass. Judaism has the theological luxury of having no internal theological need to have an opinion about Christianity, or any other religion. Judaism's religious system does not require other religions to be wrong in order for it to be right. As a variant of Judaism, however, Christianity must know what necessitated its emergence, and that inevitably entails a negative judgment about Judaism's correctness and the effectiveness of the Levitical system in particular. Whether or not this judgment illustrates "misunderstanding" or too much understanding is something scholars and theologians will continue to debate. To be sure, forms of Christianity can affirm Judaism's religious efficacy, but they blunt their own claims of universal urgency in doing so.

Nickelsburg ends his piece with the hope that critical biblical scholarship can help bridge centuries of alienation between Jews and Christians. His judgment that public universities, "separated . . . from the religious community," may provide a particularly effective locus for such an examination is especially apposite. Because American higher education pioneered a system of both public and private institutions—a pattern other national educational systems are beginning to adopt—it allows public universities to play a distinctive role in the study of religion. Because of the First Amendment to the Constitution, American culture perceives religious pluralism as a positive form of difference, an enrichment of American social life. Therefore, American education endorses religiously sponsored institutions, in part to preserve that pluralism and the freedom to believe. Recent Supreme Court decisions are likely to strengthen religious schools and universities. Public universities—because they belong to us all—preserve American pluralism in the classroom and confront it on a daily basis. The department at the University of Iowa, to which George Nickelsburg brought so much distinction, is a model of what the study of religion in a public university can accomplish. His article is a superb illustration of how much good can be done in this important setting of American learning.

RESPONSE TO WILLIAM GREEN

Of all my papers gathered in this volume, this one alone was written for a mixed audience—of lay people and scholars, and of Jews
and Christians who had been in dialogue with one another. I presented the paper a second time, again to a mixed university-lay group
in South Africa, just as apartheid was being dismantled. Its propri-
ety in that setting and the reception it received indicated that very
old problems can remain perennial problems worthy of examination
in the context of the humanities.

Although I sought a broad application for my historical study, my
focus was narrow: a few decades in the first century C.E. The texts
I treated allowed me to deal with the issue of perceptions and how
diverse points of view on the same event can lead to a lack of communication at the best, and to bitter antagonism at the worse.

As William Green rightly points out, my point of focus needs to
be put onto the broader horizon that was its historical context. I
sought to develop that context in some detail in my article, "Jews
and Christians in the First Century: The Struggle for Identity," a
companion paper to this one that was written for a New Testament
congress in South Africa (see below, 613–641). The Jews and Christians
who saw things in very different ways at the end of the first century
were, in a figurative sense, and to some considerable degree in a
real sense, children of the same mother. And while Judaism of the
early first century was, as Jacob Neusner puts it, a complex of "Judaisms," first century Jews and Christians shared much in common—
deep and long-lived traditions, religious and social institutions, faith
in one God. However, as I argue in the other paper, the diversity
among these Judaisms was partly responsible for the split vision and
schism that developed between Jews and Christians around the end
of the first century. Out of the many diverse opinions, Christianity
adopted a set that would be unacceptable to many other Jews.

Following my homely image of an athletic contest, my analysis of
the texts focused on the emotions of the people concerned. Actually,
it was the explicit expressions of emotion in the texts themselves that
gave rise to the opening illustration. Pseudo-Philo, Second Baruch,
and Fourth Ezra are marked, respectively, by a sense of uncertainty,

profound grief, and deep intellectual puzzlement. A notion of joy runs like a thread through many New Testament documents, and a motif of self-satisfied vengeance is all too present at times. But there are exceptions. In Romans 9–11, Paul expresses deep anguish about his fellow Israelites. Matthew is perhaps more complex than I allow in my paper (see below, pp. 655–656). In Pseudo-Philo, 2 Baruch, and 4 Ezra, a ray of hope provides the final word. According to Pseudo-Philo, the covenant will endure as long as the creation. In 4 Ezra the scribe sees the vision of a new Jerusalem and once more receives the Torah. Second Baruch ends optimistically anticipating the exposition of the Torah that would very soon to emerge in Rabbinic Judaism.[1]

As Green notes, the religion of Israel provided a broad, resilient canopy that allowed one to deal with times of tragedy and grief. I hint at that in my article. Two of the works under consideration were composed in the name of ancients (Baruch and Ezra) who dealt with the problem of the first Temple's destruction and the reconstruction that followed the Babylonian Exile. The dialogical structure of 4 Ezra is reminiscent of the Joban dialogues to which Green alludes. Thus, in a certain sense, the events between 66 and 135 C.E. were not new. They raised issues with which the Jews had already learned to cope. Moreover, as Green notes, Judaism had, in the Temple cult and in the rituals that took its place, religious resources that enabled it to deal with issues of evil and sin without the need of special, divinely sent savior figures like the Messiahs described in the post-70 apocalypses.

Christianity has also had a variegated history after the mid- and late first century. The New Testament itself attests antagonism and division within the early Church (for example, between Paul and his opponents and John and the docetists), and matters became more acerbic in subsequent generations and centuries. In one popular stereotype, Rabbinic Judaism was marked by nitpicking debates over halakhic minutia. Much of this debate was certainly serious, though, occasionally one senses genuine humor and fun in the process. In

---

[1] On Pseudo-Philo, see Nickelsburg, *Jewish Literature*, p. 266; on 4 Ezra, see the exposition by Earl Breech, "The Fragments I have Shored against my Ruins: The Form and Function of 4 Ezra," in *JBL* 92 (1973), pp. 267–274. On 2 Baruch, see Gwendolyn B. Sayler, *Have the Promises Failed: A Literary Analysis of 2 Baruch* (Chico, 1982).

pre-Rabbinic circles, the debating was sometimes bitter, condemnatory in the extreme, and creative of sectarian social exclusion.[2] Christians tended not to specialized in halakhic debates. In keeping with the shape of their religion, the debates centered around theology, and especially Christology. The excommunications, schisms, and inquisitions that followed—spreading as they did across the face of Christendom—make the sectarianism of the Qumran community and the Enochic texts pale in comparison.

So Green rightly presses for a broader context in which to place the historical snapshot that was the focus of my paper. I dealt with a moment in a much broader and variegated history. Yet that human moment was genuine, and in its genuineness, one finds a certain perenniality. Mutual empathy and respect are still a desideratum to be achieved by many Jews and Christians. Each is as difficult to achieve as the other. Particularly striking for me was Green's comment: "The persistence of the Jewish religion against massive forces of opposition and destruction is at least as interesting a phenomenon as—and in some ways more surprising than—the emergence of a new religion in a period of political and cultural change and instability." I doubt if many reflective Christians would think of it this way. They would marvel over *Christianity's* survival through the persecutions it faced. So the lack of understanding and communication that characterized the first century are still issues that need our attention and energy.

Finally, I want to parse my two sentences about the Holocaust to which Green calls attention. As the context states, I do not think that Christian anti-Judaic theology *caused* the *Shoah*. Anti-Semitism is a deeper and more complex phenomenon than anti-Jewish theology, as is attested by Gordon W. Allport's landmark study on *The Nature of Prejudice*.[3] Furthermore, as the historical record attests, some of the strongest advocates of the Lutheran Law-Gospel theology that is so compatible with this reading of first century Judaism and Christianity[4] were among the strongest opponents of the Third Reich. Having said that, however, it seems to me that the anti-Jewish theology that

---

[2] See my articles, "The Epistle of Enoch" (below, pp. 105–122) and "Religious Exclusivism" (below, pp. 139–161).

[3] Gordon W. Allport, *The Nature of Prejudice* (Garden City, 1958).

[4] See my review of Charlotte Klein's *Anti-Judaism in Christian Theology*, in *RelStRev* 4 (1978), p. 164.

was informed by the Gospel accounts of the ministry and the trial and death of Jesus was both symptomatic of, and contributory to the atmosphere that pervaded Germany in the 1930s and early 1940s. When we consider another to be religiously inferior, we run the serious risk of demeaning that person's humanity *as a whole*. That is a first and dangerous step toward worse things to come. Like all aspects of human life, we need to looked closely at religion, both for the immense good it does, but also for its potential to destroy what is good and of priceless value.

Anti-Judaism theology in the name of high religion (Christianity supercedes Judaism and is God's final word) is both dangerous and contradictory to the values it espouses. Green has it right: Judaism can have its own identity without finding a foil in Christianity. The universalistic claim of Christianity, however, requires as a foil those religions that it is not, and compromise on this issue blunts its claim to universality. Yet, I wonder, if Christianity is a child of the long-lived Jewish religion, can it find in its mother's genes a more empathic and tolerant strain that it can integrate into its religious world view?

PART TWO

JEWISH APOCALYPTIC LITERATURE
IN ITS CONTEXTS

CHAPTER TWO

THE APOCALYPTIC CONSTRUCTION
OF REALITY IN *1 ENOCH*

George W.E. Nickelsburg

The collection of texts known as *1 Enoch* is universally considered to be an 'apocalyptic' work.[1] In *Semeia* 14, the members of the SBL Genres Project accept this description, and place the different components of the collection in particular categories of texts in which otherworldly revelation of various sorts was mediated in a variety of ways.[2] In this essay I shall not dwell on the issue of genre as such. I agree that the different parts of *1 Enoch* embody the notion of revelation in different, somewhat stereotyped, literary forms or subforms. I am concerned, rather, to demonstrate that, in the variety of Enochic texts, the claim to revelation plays an essential role in a common world-view or construction of reality. Specifically, in a world that people perceive as the locus of alienation, oppression, and injustice, the seer presents evidence of salvation by transmitting a revelation about the future or the remote places in the cosmos, where the reality and promise of salvation lie hidden. Because revelation is an inextricable part of this world-view, we may justifiably and meaningfully speak of it as an apocalyptic world-view.

It may seem ill-advised to search for an overarching unity in a literary collection as lengthy, diverse, and complex as *1 Enoch*.[3] The multiplicity of its component parts (created by many anonymous 'authors' over a period of more than three centuries), its variety of literary forms and genres, and the diversity of its subject matter all

---

[1] It is mentioned in a list of apocalypses in a work as critical as that of K. Koch, *The Rediscovery of Apocalyptic* (trans. M. Kohl; SBT 2/22; Naperville, IL, 1972), p. 23.

[2] See J.J. Collins, 'The Jewish Apocalypses', *Semeia* 14 (1979), pp. 22–28, 37, 40, 45.

[3] On literary issues, date, and related matters pertaining to *1 Enoch*, see G.W.E. Nickelsburg, *Jewish Literature Between the Bible and the Mishnah* (Philadelphia, 1981), pp. 46–55, 90–94, 145–51, 214–23; and J.J. Collins, *The Apocalyptic Imagination* (New York, 1984), pp. 36–63, 142–54.

militate against easy systematization and synthesis. Nonetheless, *1 Enoch* is a consciously shaped compilation of traditions and texts, and it is appropriate to search for internal points of commonality (apart from Enochic attribution in most cases) in which the compilers and editors saw the potential for a unity comprised of diversity. More fundamentally, because successive parts of the tradition developed from and built on one another, some significant unity is to be expected. In fact, comparative analysis indicates that certain motifs, emphases, and interests are repeatedly expressed throughout the collection and are often structured into its diverse literary forms. From these we may extract a set of unifying factors.

1. The Focal Point: The Coming Judgment

The oracle that introduces the collection sets the tone for what follows, announcing God's coming judgment and its consequences: blessings for the righteous and curses for the sinners (chs. 1–5). In one way or another, all the major sections of *1 Enoch* and many of their subsections or component parts either provide background for this theme or elaborate on it and give it prominence.

The mythic materials conflated in chs. 6–11 constitute a narrative that begins with an explanation of the origins of major evil in the world and ends with the anticipation of its eradication on a purified earth among a righteous humanity.[4]

The same counterposition of evil and judgment is evident in the account of Enoch's call (chs. 12–16), which focuses on the nature of the angelic sin and announces the divine verdict three times.[5] The myth of angelic rebellion and a companion myth about rebel stars are focal in the account of Enoch's first journey (chs. 17–19), where the goal of the journey and the climax of the narrative are the places of punishment for angels and stars.[6]

The account of Enoch's second journey also structures the notion of sin and punishment into its literary form, but extends it to include

---

[4] On these chapters, see Nickelsburg, 'Apocalyptic and Myth in 1 Enoch 6–11', *JBL* 96 (1977), pp. 383–89.

[5] See Nickelsburg, 'Enoch, Levi, and Peter: Recipients of Revelation in Upper Galilee', *JBL* 100 (1981), pp. 575–82.

[6] See Nickelsburg, *Jewish Literature*, p. 54.

the human as well as the divine realm (chs. 21–32). At each station of the journey, Enoch has an interpreted vision that relates to angelic sin or to human sin or righteousness, and their consequences in the judgment[7] (cf. also ch. 108). Chapter 33 alludes to Enoch's celestial journeys, which have been recounted in the astronomical material now summarized in the *Book of the Luminaries* (chs. 72–82). While this material is presented in chs. 33–36 and 72–82 almost exclusively in factual form, it is also used as a point of reference for human error (2.1–5.4; 80.2–8) and divine punishment (100.10–101.9).

Human activity and its modes, consequences, and judgment are the exclusive subject matter of chs. 92–105. The counterposition of sin or righteousness, and punishment or reward, is structured into the literary forms that constitute the section.[8] For the most part, the author focuses on sin and its punishment in the great judgment. The admonitions to righteous conduct and promises of reward are set largely in the context of their alternatives. The righteous are either depicted as the victims of sinners, or they are warned to avoid sinful ways.

The temporal dimension of sin (mainly) and righteous conduct, as well as the results of such behavior, are recounted from creation to the judgment, in long and short form, in the *Animal Vision* (chs. 85–90) and the *Apocalypse of Weeks* (93.1–10; 91.11–17). Chapters 83–84 and 106–107 are narratives about humanity's sin and Noah's righteousness and their judgment at the time of the Flood.

The *Parables of Enoch* (chs. 37–71) are a separate compilation of major elements of the Enochic tradition: tours of the celestial phenomena; journeys to the terrestrial places of punishment; stories about Noah and the Flood. However, the judgment motif is set forth mainly in Enoch's heavenly visions of the Elect One who will vindicate the righteous elect and execute judgment on their powerful royal oppressors.

In summary, there is scarcely a page in *1 Enoch* that is not in some sense related to the expectation of an impending divine judgment that will deal with human sin and righteousness, and the angelic rebellions that are in one way or another related to them.

---

[7] See J.T. Milik, *The Books of Enoch: Aramaic Fragments of Qumrân Cave 4* (Oxford, 1976), p. 35; Nickelsburg, *Jewish Literature*, pp. 54–55.

[8] See Nickelsburg, 'The Apocalyptic Message of 1 Enoch 92–105', *CBQ* 39 (1977), pp. 310–15.

2. THE TEMPORAL AND SPATIAL DIMENSIONS
IN 1 ENOCH'S WORLD-VIEW

1 Enoch's view of reality, with its focus on the coming judgment, has both a temporal and a spatial dimension. It views the present situation in terms of the past and the future; and, alternatively, it sets the locus of human activity in relationship to the heavenly realm and the rest of the cosmos.

The temporal dimension

The temporal dimension in *1 Enoch* is perhaps the most obvious to the reader of biblical literature. The activity attributed to God, the angels, and human beings takes place in past, present, and future. Major angelic rebellions occurred in primordial time, but they impinge upon the world as the authors know it in their own time. For the author of the *Animal Vision*, other angelic sin is presently underway and is evident in Israel's oppression by the nations. Human actions have present and future consequences. The righteous are suffering now at the hands of the wicked. The present actions and attitudes of the righteous and wicked will be subject to scrutiny and retribution at God's future judgment, as will the actions of the rebellious angels. The juxtaposition of present and future is so frequent in *1 Enoch* as to be commonplace. The temporal dimension is most obvious, however, in the *Animal Vision* and the *Apocalypse of Weeks*. These texts arrange events along an explicit temporal continuum that stretches from creation to the eschaton, and each author has a specific notion of when the judgment will occur.

This temporal dimension notwithstanding, the texts in *1 Enoch* devote relatively little space to speculations about the *time* of the end. It may be the case that many of the Enochic authors expected the judgment imminently. The *Epistle*, in particular, expresses the idea explicitly at a number of points.[9] But the calculation and periodization that may undergird such an expectation are explicit only in the *Animal Vision* and *Apocalypse of Weeks*, which constitute a mere 13 percent of the text of *1 Enoch*. Clearly, the authors of the various parts of *1 Enoch* had other interests as they composed their texts.

---

[9] See 94.1, 6, 7; 95.6; 96.1, 6; 97.10; 98.16.

The spatial and material dimension

The authors of *1 Enoch* depict human and divine activity taking place in a spatial dimension that is far more explicit and emphatically evident than the temporal dimension. What is obvious in *1 Enoch*, once one sees it, is the authors' preoccupation with a world that is described in spatial and material terms, a world that can be experienced, at least in principle, by the five senses.

This spatial dimension, however, is rarely spelled out with reference to specific geographic locations, and place names are used only of sacred sites: Sinai (1.4; cf. 89.29); Hermon and its environs (6.5; 13.7, 9); Jerusalem, though not by name (26–27; cf. 25.5; 56.7; 89.50, 54–56, 66, 72–73; 90.26–36; 93.7–8, 13). Certainly the authors think of events as occurring in particular places, but it is mainly in the *Animal Vision* and the *Apocalypse of Weeks*, with their recitation of Israelite history, that one can clearly perceive the actions of identifiable people and nations.

The pervasive spatial dimension in *1 Enoch* is present, rather, in the authors' cosmology and mythic geography, and in their references to the nonaminate aspects of creation. It is mainly the places and things in these realms that Enoch sees, smells, hears, tastes, and feels, or to which the readers' attention is called. And to no small extent, the authors emphasize the orderliness and obedience that prevail in this spatial and material realm.

Cosmology is most evident in the *Book of Luminaries* (chs. 72–82). Here Enoch records what he saw when he visited the heavens and traveled across the vast extents of the terrestrial disk: the portals through which the sun, moon, and stars rise and set; the gates of the winds; the four quarters of the earth; its seven great mountains, rivers, and islands. Throughout, the account emphasizes the order of the creation. The cosmic and meteorological phenomena take place in the way they do because God has structured into the cosmos the places and devices that make possible their orderly functioning.

The cosmological traditions selectively gathered in chs. 72–82 are presupposed and sometimes complemented elsewhere in *1 Enoch*, especially in chs. 1–36. Here the Enochic authors refer back to the cosmological and astronomical traditions, enhance them with accounts of Enoch's journeys, and appeal to the readers' senses by elaborating the narratives with references to the spatial dimension and its components.

The introduction to the *Book of the Watchers* (chs. 1–5) contrasts humanity's faithless disobedience with the orderly obedience that prevails among the heavenly bodies and in the changing of earth's seasons. The repeated introductory words, 'observe' and 'see', are an appeal to the empirical experience of nature. The luminaries in heaven, the clouds, dew, and rain, earth's heat and cold, and the foliage of its trees are the exemplary basis of the author's admonition.

The story of the watchers' rebellion makes both negative and positive references to the components of the created realm (chs. 6–11). The watchers revealed forbidden information about the terrestrial world of plants and minerals, and taught prognostication that was based on the movements of the celestial bodies. The deeds of the giants wreaked havoc on the whole terrestrial realm: human beings, birds, beasts, creeping things, fish, and agricultural produce. In consequence, the earth lay polluted and moribund. Conversely, the author's picture of the future envisions a purified earth, with woods and fields, where a renewed and multiplying humanity will be nourished by the fabulous fertility of wine, grain, and oil.

The mythic account of Enoch's heavenly ascent and call is heavily embellished with references to the concrete, material, and experiential (especially 14.8–18). He hears the summons of the clouds and winds, and is sped on his way by shooting stars, lightning flashes, and winds. He sees and enters a heavenly palace constructed of the elements— fire and lightning flashes, hailstones and snow—and he experiences the heat and cold that emanate from them.[10] These components of the call story, combined with references to the seer's emotional state and physical reactions, constitute a powerfully sensual expression of a religious belief.

Chapters 17–19 reiterate and elaborate on the message of chs. 12–16: the rebel watchers (and the disobedient stars) are doomed to eternal punishment. But here this message is tied to the author's cosmology. The temporal dimension (judgment will take place) is reinforced by reference to the spatial dimension: Enoch travels to the edge of the earth, where he views the fiery places of punishment. Moreover, although the point of the journey account is the pair of interpreted visions that bring it to a climax, the seer cannot bypass

---

[10] See Nickelsburg, 'Enoch, Levi, and Peter', pp. 580–81.

the opportunity to document his journey with a string of references to the terrestrial and celestial loci and phenomena that marked the course of the journey. Although the *point* of the section is eschatological, the *medium* of its expression is cosmological. Enoch's second journey account makes roughly the same point in the same way (chs. 21–32); cosmology undergirds eschatology. Places structured into the cosmos that guarantee the coming reality of judgment and the consequent rewards and punishments. God's creation anticipated God's judgment and serves as its instrument. More than in previous sections, however, one finds an appeal to the senses. Enoch sees the cosmic places and realia in detail and marvels over them. He smells the fragrance of the tree of life and the tree of wisdom, and he alludes to the eating of their fruit. The description of the journey to the Far East (chs. 28–31) is a counterpart to ch. 17, but is recounted in botanical rather than cosmological detail. The *Book of the Watchers* ends with summarizing reference to the broader lore about Enoch's journeys through the heavenly sphere (chs. 33–36).

Taken as a whole, the Book expounds a message about the coming judgment. It does so through a variety of literary forms: prophetic oracle, mythic narrative, prophetic call story, journey accounts. In all of these, however, one finds reference not simply to the future when judgment will happen, or to the past when rebellion took place. The temporality of the message is reinforced by repeated reference to the spatial realm and to the things that can be experienced by the senses.

This spatial dimension is also integral to the *Book of Parables* (chs. 37–71). The first and third parables include accounts of Enoch's celestial journeys (chs. 41–44; 60). In the second parable, the book's central message of judgment—carried primarily by the heavenly tableaux which feature the Elect One—is reinforced by accounts of journeys to the terrestrial places associated with judgment and punishment. Running through the book, moreover, are references to the 'earth' or 'land', which is now possessed by the kings and the mighty, but which will be renewed and become locus of salvation after the judgment. This element is reminiscent of chs. 6–11.

Enoch's epistle is composed primarily of the seer's alternating words of doom and promise, which juxtapose the present deeds of the sinners and the present circumstances of the righteous with their future punishment and reward. At one point in particular, however, the cosmic dimension breaks through (100.10–102.3). The elements witness humanity's deeds and enact God's judgment, and heaven and earth will quake and tremble at the final theophany.

Significantly, the concluding chapter of the corpus blends the temporal and spatial dimensions of the Enochic message of judgment (ch. 108). A pair of paragraphs about the doom of the sinners and the blessedness of the righteous (vv. 2–3, 7–10) enclose a brief account of Enoch's vision of the fiery place of punishment. The section and the corpus as a whole conclude with the promise of the judgment, which will send the wicked to the place 'where the days and times are written for them' (vv. 11–15).

3. Dualism in 1 Enoch

1 Enoch's construction of reality, with its temporal and spatial dimensions and its populations of divine and human characters, is characterized by several complementary kinds of dualism.

Temporal dualism

The temporal axis in *1 Enoch* is sharply divided between the present time, which will end with the judgment, and a new age that follows. In many different ways, the authors contrast the present time, which is evil or deficient, with the future, which will bring healing and renewal. A plagued, polluted, and ravaged world will be healed, cleansed, and re-sown (chs. 6–11). The time of demonic domination will come to and end (chs. 12–16; 19.1). Those who have suffered or been murdered will be sustained by the fruit of the tree of life (25.5–6). The Israelite flock, devoured and dispersed by gentile beasts and birds of prey, will be restored and gathered, and humanity, divided at the beginning, will be reunited as one people (chs. 85–90). Most pervasively, this temporal dualism is concerned with the issue of divine justice. Life in the present time is marked by injustice, but this will be adjudicated in the future, at the time of the great judgment (see part 1 above). This concern is worked out most explicitly and in greatest detail in the *Epistle* (chs. 92–105), which is dominated by what are effectively descriptions of human sin and suffering. In the present time, the righteous are unjustly victimized by the sinners, who go unpunished. In the grave, both experience the same fate. All that will be overcome, however, when God rewards the righteous for their piety and compensates them for their suffering, and the sinners receive their just deserts. The *Parables* make the same point but focus on the judgment itself and the events related to it.

Cosmic dualism

The spatial dimension in *1 Enoch* is marked by a sharp dualism that has both vertical and horizontal aspects. Heaven is the realm of the divine and earth the habitation of humans. Disaster occurs when the realms are confounded (chs. 6–16). The descent of the watchers results in the pollution of the earth, which now becomes the habitation of malevolent and destructive demons. Conversely, the decimated earth and the remnants of humanity will be delivered when the divine Judge and his faithful entourage descend from heaven to earth to execute judgment. In the meantime, the mechanisms that will facilitate that judgment exist in the heavenly realms and are operative (esp. 89.59–90.19; 92–105 *passim*). Angels record human deeds and act as mediators and advocates in the divine throne room. The books containing the names of the righteous and their rewards are a prominent reality in God's presence. The Elect One stands before God and receives his commission as the agent of judgment (chs. 37–71). Heaven is also the place of the luminaries and the elements. In contrast to most of earthbound humanity, they faithfully follow the commands that God instituted at creation, and when asked, they execute judgment on the wicked (esp. chs. 2; 72–82).

1 Enoch's cosmic dualism has a horizontal aspect. Enoch's journeys carry him across the face of earth's disk. In places uninhabited by living mortals, God's will is carried out, or at least, the apparatus that will execute God's will stands ready (chs. 17–36). On the mountain of the dead, a distinction is made between the souls of the righteous and the sinners. Beyond it, to the northwest, stands the mountain on which the divine Judge will descend and where presently the tree of life waits to be transplanted to the sanctuary. To the extreme northwest are the pits where the rebellious divine beings already suffer punishment. Far to the east is the original paradise, where wisdom is hidden. All in all, Enoch's journeys carry him to places in the cosmos that are removed from human habitation or hidden from human access, where God's created intent is potential or actualized.

Ontological dualism between divine and human

Related to *1 Enoch*'s spatial dualism is the absolute distinction between
divine beings and humans. In the case of God, this distinction is
emphasized throughout the book by names that denote God's unique-
ness and absolute transcendence (the Great One, the Holy One, the
Great Holy One, the Lord or God of the Ages, etc.). This transcendence is underscored in a special way in the descriptions of the
heavenly throne room in the accounts of Enoch's call (ch. 14) and
ascent (ch. 71) and in the references to the eschatological theophany
(chs. 1; 102.1–3).

The heavenly entourage shares in God's separateness from humanity, as is indicated by their most frequent title, 'the holy ones'.[11]
According to 15.1–16.1, the sin of the watchers consisted precisely
in their violation of the absolute distinction between spirit and flesh
and their defilement of their holiness.

The disastrous consequences of this angelic rebellion are an integral part of a special aspect of the human-divine dualism, viz. the
'demonic' victimization of humanity. According to ch. 8, angelic revelations lead human beings astray. In chs. 12–16 the ghosts of the
dead giants, which are not eradicated because they are spirit, constitute a realm of evil spirits who prey on humanity in a variety of
ways. The *Animal Vision* adds an additional nuance: the angelic shepherds are responsible for Israel's victimization at the hands of the
nations. Through all of this runs the notion that sin and evil, at
least in many of their guises, are functions of a spirit realm that is
at war with humanity.

The disaster of human life here and now: at the intersection of several dualisms

According to *1 Enoch*'s world-view, then, humanity exists at the intersection of three kinds of dualism. The human situation is defined
both as it is and in terms of what it is not. The present age is evil
and awaits the time of adjudication, deliverance, and renewal. This
world is the scene of sin, violence, victimization, and pollution, and
is separated from the heavenly and cosmic spheres, where God's will

---

[11] There is no place in *1 Enoch* where we can be certain that the original text
used the term 'angels'. The Aramaic texts from Qumran indicate that the ordinary
term for these heavenly creatures was 'watchers' (ʿîrîn) and, in their unfallen state,
'watchers and holy ones' (ʿîrîn uᵉqadîšîn), i.e. 'holy watchers'.

is done. Humanity here and now is the prey of evil spirits who oppose God and are contrasted with the holy ones in God's heavenly entourage. Thus, the disastrous character of human existence is emphasized by means of dualistic comparisons that are made in temporal, spatial, and ontological terms.

4. Salvation in 1 Enoch: The Resolution of its Dualism

By its very structure, *1 Enoch*'s dualism optimistically allows for deliverance or salvation from the situation that is pessimistically described from a number of converging perspectives. Opposed to present injustice and disaster here are the future judgment and salvation that are poised in the beyond.

Salvation in the future, when God intervenes

Most obvious, that deliverance lies in the future, at the time of the judgment and thereafter. To begin with, the conflict in the divine realm will be resolved, as only it can be, through direct divine intervention; God and God's holy ones will exterminate their malevolent counterparts: the rebel watchers, the evil spirits, and the angelic shepherds. Additionally, the wicked human perpetrators of sin and oppression will be judged, removed from this world, and destroyed. Equally important, the defiled and moribund earth will be cleansed and revived. Above all, the new state of affairs will be universal and permanent. All evil, sin, and impurity will be removed from the whole earth, and all the children of the whole earth will be righteous for all the generations of eternity (10.20–11.1; 91.16–17).

Salvation in the present: bridging the dualism through revelation given to the community of the righteous and chosen

Although definitive salvation lies in the future, revelation transmitted in the present time effects a significant resolution of the book's temporal, spatial, and ontological dualism. Such revelation is a pervasive concept in *1 Enoch*, and, in one guise or another, the notion is present in all of the book's component parts, whether it is ascribed to the ancient seer or to those living in the author's own times.[12]

---

[12] On the literary forms that embody this notion, see the citations in J.J. Collins, 'The Jewish Apocalypses'.

In chs. 1–5, Enoch cites his visions and their angelic interpretations (1.2), and the whole section is presented in the form of a prophetic oracle. Although the narrative in chs. 6–11 is not presented as a revelation, in 10.1–3 God commissions the angel Sariel to teach Noah about the coming judgment and the means that will save him from its destruction. In chs. 12–16 the purpose of Enoch's ascent is to receive an oracle of doom which he is to bring to earth. In chs. 17–19, 20–36, and 108, the function of Enoch's journeys is to receive revelation about the hidden world, and the *Book of Parables* as a whole is the revelation of such heavenly and cosmic journeys. Revelation takes a special form in chs. 83–90, where Enoch's knowledge of the future, which he transmits to Methuselah, has come to him through dreams. In chs. 33–36, astronomical lore is gained in journeys through the cosmos in the company of an interpreting angel. The *Epistle*, alone of the major sections of *1 Enoch*, does not describe Enoch receiving revealed knowledge; however, at several points Enoch explicitly, or implicitly, bases his admonitions on the things he has seen during his journey (93.2, 11–14; 97.2, 7; 98.6; 103.1–2; 104.1, 7–8; cf. 81.1–4).

The salvific function of revelation is explicit in several key texts in *1 Enoch*. In the *Animal Vision* the opening of the eyes of the blind lambs is a first step toward salvation (90.6). Both 5.8 and 93.10 foresee that 'wisdom will be given to the chosen' of the end time, and in 104.12–13, this is identified with the Enochic books. In each case the reception of wisdom is constitutive of salvation or life.[13]

Revelation bridges the book's dualism in several ways. Enoch's revelation about the celestial structures and the movements of the heavenly bodies are a torah that is foundational for correct calendrical observance (chs. 72–82). His cosmological revelations in chs. 17–19 and 21–32 present evidence that judgment is already being exacted and that the places of future judgment are ready for their tasks. His viewing of the heavenly tablets (81.1–4), his witnessing of angelic advocacy (89.59–90.19), and his visions of events in the heavenly courtroom (chs. 37–71) are assurance that the apparatus for the

---

[13] See Nickelsburg, 'Revealed Wisdom as a Criterion for Inclusion and Exclusion: From Jewish Sectarianism to Early Christianity' in *'To See Ourselves as Others See Us': Christians, Jews, 'Others' in Late Antiquity* (ed. J. Neusner E.S. Frerichs; Chico, CA, 1985), pp. 74–79.

future judgment is already in operation. These revelations are salvific in function because they provide a means of hope in what is, by all appearances, a hopeless world, and because they encourage the righteous to stand fast against apostasy. This exhortative function is explicit in the *Epistle*, where Enoch's revelations are cited as the basis for his repeated admonitions that the righteous should not fear, but be hopeful of vindication.[14] Similarly, in the oracle that introduces the corpus, Enoch's revelations support his promise of future blessing.

Thus the books of Enoch are a corpus of texts that guarantee future salvation on the basis of a present reality to which the seer has been privy and which he now reveals. That seer—in the Book's fiction, Enoch of old, in reality the complement of authors who stand behind these texts—is the bridge between opposing worlds: present and future, earthly and cosmic, human and divine. His revelations, written down, transmitted, and interpreted, are constitutive of the community of the chosen and righteous. Although allegedly received in primordial antiquity, these revelations are promulgated in a present that stands on the threshold of the end time. Functionally, they are eschatological revelation. As the *Animal Vision* and *Apocalypse of Weeks* indicate, they are given at the end of the age (just as Noah received revelation before the first judgment), and this eschatological character further enhances the assurance that the revelations offer. Definitive deliverance will take place soon.

In summary: we may properly use the term 'apocalyptic' to characterize the texts in *1 Enoch*, because the claim to revelation or, indeed, the literary form that presents this claim, is not accidental to the text, but is essential to its world-view, or construction of reality. The authors' revelations are the salvific means by which the readers bridge and overcome the dualisms that are the very nature of reality as they understand and experience it.[15]

---

[14] On these admonitions in 96.1–3; 97.1–2; 102.4–5; 104.2–6, see Nickelsburg, 'Apocalyptic Message', pp. 315–18.

[15] For a similar approach, see the extension of the *Semeia* 14 definition of 'apocalypse' in A. Yarbro Collins, 'Introduction: Early Christian Apocalypticism', *Semeia* 36 (1986), p. 7.

5. The Enochic Writings in their Context

It remains briefly to place the Enochic texts in their context in the
history of Israelite religious thought, as it is attested in the post-exilic
biblical texts. I have emphasized that the Enochic authors locate
human existence at the intersection of a set of dualisms. Temporally
and spatially, humanity is placed at a point where it is bereft of
divine justice and blessing and where it is victimized by malevolent
spirit forces. Earth is not heaven; now is not the age to come. This
heaping up of dualisms underscores humanity's pitiful state.

One can make a case for speaking of a developing dualistic eschatology in post-exilic prophecy.[16] Already in Jeremiah and Ezekiel,
and increasingly in Second and Third Isaiah, the present is qualitatively contrasted with the future, which is often depicted as a return
to first beginnings, whether the Exodus, the covenant, or creation
itself.[17] In addition, of course, the prophets think of God as dwelling
in heaven with the divine entourage. What the biblical texts lack,
however, is the mutual reinforcing of dualisms, which underscores
humanity's inaccessibility of divine blessing and salvation. In *1 Enoch*,
by contrast, the future—which is not yet—is overlaid by the 'there'
that is not here. The Enochic authors provide this spatial axis, in
large part, by using material from the 'wisdom tradition' and shaping and nuancing it to serve the eschatological character and purpose of the temporal axis. Moreover, they endow this wisdom material
with the authority that derives from revelation. Enoch travels to and
sees, and has explained to him, the places and realia of the cosmos
which were inaccessible to humans according to authors like Job.[18]
It is this combination of dualisms, mediated by repeated claims to
revelation, that sets the Enochic texts off from their prophetic counterparts and earns for them the term 'apocalyptic dualism' or 'dualistic apocalypticism'. This set of dualisms is further enhanced by the
dualistic myths about the origins of evil in chs. 6–11, which are the
presupposition for much of the corpus.

---

[16] See George W.E. Nickelsburg, "Eschatology," in *Anchor Bible Dictionary*, vol. 2,
pp. 581–582.

[17] In the case of Second Isaiah, one can really speak of a qualitative difference
between the past and the present, which is the moment of salvation.

[18] On Enoch's place in the diversity of Persian/Hellenistic Judaism, see M.E.
Stone, 'The Book of Enoch and Judaism in the Third Century B.C.E.', *CBQ* 40
(1978), pp. 479–92.

It is a topic worthy of investigation to ask what the driving forces were that fused the prophetic temporal dualism, the spatial dimension of interest to the sages, and the ontological dualism of the myths into a single, mutually reinforcing dualistic construction of reality. Surely experience played a role; people felt alienated and victimized. From the point of view of intellectual and religious history, what is interesting is the fact that they expressed this experience in the dualistic synthesis that we find in *1 Enoch*.

Furthermore, it is noteworthy that the experience which I attribute to the Enochic authors and their communities is widely attributed to the non-Judaic peoples of the Hellenistic age.[19] It would be worth comparing the structure of *1 Enoch*'s thought with that in other texts of the late Persian and early Hellenistic period. Are there dualisms, and how do they work? Does one appeal to revelation as a means to bridge the dualisms?

Whatever the findings of such a comparative investigation, *1 Enoch* is evidence of a vatershed in the history of Israelite thought. The coincidence and heaping of temporal, spatial, and ontological dualisms, and their resolution in the claim of revelation, parallel and presage essential elements in the rise of gnosticism and Christianity and in a kind of spirituality that continued through the middle ages and that is still present in substantial sectors of the Christian church.

---

[19] For a classical expression of this analysis, see R. Bultmann, *Primitive Christianity in its Contemporary Setting* (trans. R.H. Fuller; New York, 1956).

RESPONSE TO "THE APOCALYPTIC CONSTRUCTION OF REALITY IN *1 ENOCH*"

Klaus Koch*

In the last decades no one has done more research than George Nickelsburg on the riddles of the curious apocalypse that is now extant as the Ethiopic Book of First Enoch, but that was probably written in Aramaic and its main parts published before the turn of the era. Nickelsburg has made sophisticated investigations into both the philological questions of each chapter and verse, as well as into the origins and developments of its diverse traditions. He has been not only interested in exegetical details, but at the same time he has searched for the specific groups that stood behind the production of this kind of apocalyptic literature and, especially, their kind of religion and worldview. In addition, he has always had an open eye for the broader environment of this kind of late Israelite literature, which grew up outside of any normative Judaism but which later sometimes had a substantial influence on movements like the *yahad* of Qumran and particular wings of early Christianity.[1] The results of all his work appear in his Hermeneia commentary on the first and last parts of 1 Enoch.[2]

A good witness of Nickelsburg's endeavor for deeper understanding is his article "The Apocalyptic Construction of Reality," first published in 1991 and now, with some revisions, taken over into the commentary as the first part of a comprehensive section on "Worldview and Religious Thought" (above, pp. 29–43, *1 Enoch 1*, pp. 37–34). Motivated by the sociological theory that a determination of "reality" is always a cultural construct of the language of a particular society, Nickelsburg looks for an overarching unified worldview that runs through the various and diverse parts of the Enochic collec-

---

* University of Hamburg.

* University of Hamburg.

[1] George W.E. Nickelsburg, "Eschatology (Early Judaism)," in *ABD* 2, pp. 575–594.
[2] Idem, *1 Enoch 1: A Commentary on the Book of 1 Enoch, Chapters 1–365; 81–108* (Minneapolis, 2001). Aramaic terms are quoted according to J.T. Milik, *The Books of Enoch: Aramaic Fragments* (Oxford, 1976). For the Ethiopic text and English translation, see Michael A. Knibb, *The Ethiopic Book of Enoch* (2 vols.; Oxford, 1978).

tion. He concludes that all of these parts present a similar claim to revelation that will be essential for human salvation. They presuppose a view of the present world as a realm of sin, oppression, alienation and inescapable suffering. Therefore the focus of the revealed message is the imminent universal judgment, which will condemn all sinners forever and bring eternal reward to the righteous. "There is scarcely a page in 1 Enoch that is not in some sense related to the expectation of an impending divine judgment that will deal with human sin and righteousness, and the angelic rebellions that are in one way or another related to them" (above, p. 31; *1 Enoch 1*, p. 37).

The belief in a revelation that was necessary for salvation has as its background a worldview marked by three antagonistic dimensions. In *1 Enoch* there is first a *temporal* one: a sharp division is presupposed between the present epoch of sin and injustice—which is dealt with in the coming judgment over human and supernatural beings—and a subsequent age of eternal justice. Then the downtrodden Israel will be restored forever, and the rest of humanity will become one people under one God. According to Nickelsburg, a second and more explicit dimension is the *spatial and material* one, which has both a horizontal and vertical perspective. The earth below is thought of in the framework of a mythic geography. During his marvelous journey through space, Enoch has seen mysterious places at the ends of the earth, where God's will is already carried out in preparation for the coming judgment. He becomes aware of a paradise for the righteous and terrible pit for fallen angels and stars. The midst of the earth, however, inhabited by humans, is now polluted and moribund because of the evil deeds of the fallen angels, their offspring the giants, and their human followers. Over against this world, the heaven above (thus the vertical perspective) has a totally different quality; it is the realm of the divine and the holy ones. However, it is not a purely spiritual realm. Supernatural books are stored there, in which are recorded the deeds and destinies of humans and angels, and these books are continuously updated. In the heavenly courtroom "the apparatus for the coming judgment is already in operation" (above, pp. 40–41; *1 Enoch 1*, p. 42), and from there divine interventions in earthly events are repeatedly initiated. Because these antagonisms are so clearly articulated, Nickelsburg uses the terms temporal and cosmic dualism.

A third dimension in this worldview Nickelsburg calls "*Ontological* dualism between divine and human." (The adjective "ontological" seems to follow an American use of this term; the Europeans would prefer to call it "anthropological," because the notion apparently does not include the non-human beings). Its content is "the absolute distinction between divine beings and humans," between "spirit and flesh" (above, p. 38; *1 Enoch*, p. 40). God's separateness from humanity is underscored by his names, the "Great One" and the "Holy One," and those of his entourage, "the holy ones."

At the intersection of these three kinds of dualism humankind must exist, weak in itself and tempted by demons. The antagonism will remain until the eschatological consummation. However, before that, revelation occurs, which is represented especially by Enoch's message, which bridges the dualistic gaps in a certain manner and effects a significant resolution even now.

In the 1991 article, Nickelsburg concluded his description with a view of the historical roots and subsequent effects. According to him such a dualistic eschatology had been developing since post-exilic prophecy, but it reached its apex in this apocalyptic literature. Subsequently it influenced movements like Gnosticism and some sectors of Christianity. "1 Enoch is evidence of a watershed in the history of Israelite thought" (above, p. 43). These developments are treated later in the commentary (*1 Enoch*, pp. 82–100). The three antagonistic dimensions that Nickelsburg has elaborated are doubtless to be found in the parts of 1 Enoch on which he has commented. But are those dimensions "dualistic" in an exclusive sense" moreover, does their appearance justify the term "ontological dualism" with respect to the worldview of the apocalypse?

The crucial characteristic of a possible dualism in a religion and its significance is the place of *creation* in the mythological system. If there is really a dualistic ontology in it, as in Zoroastrianism or Gnosticism, then the notion of a good creation that endures to the present time is lacking. Even if one supposes that it existed before all time, it does not determine the structure of the presently existing world, which is ruled by darkness and delusion. What is the case with the Enochic collection?

Several times Enoch is described praising his God, who is still ruling everything he has created, and who is powerfully present over all the earth in spite of human sin and punishment. Thus, in chapter 84, after a vision with the message that "upon the earth there will be a great destruction" (83:9) he looks at the stars above and confesses:

> Blessed are you, O Lord, King . . .
> King of Kings and God of all eternity.
> Your power and your reign and your majesty abide forever and for-
> ever and ever
> and to all generations, your dominion.
> All the heavens are your throne forever,
> and all the earth is your footstool forever and forever and ever.
> For you have made and you rule all things (84:2–3).

Such a hymn is similar to the praise of creation in some of the Psalms. However, Enoch continues on another track and mentions powers that oppose the divine rule.

> And now the angels of your heaven are doing wrong,
> and upon human flesh is your wrath until the great day of judgment . . .
> And now, my Lord, remove from the earth the flesh that has aroused your wrath,
> but the righteous and true flesh raise up as a seed-bearing plant for-
> ever (84:4–6).

These ideas find no analogy in the psalter and are signs of a later period. In the belief of these authors, even the heavenly realm is in bad shape, and the majority of humankind on earth is completely evil flesh and full of sins. The worldview has darkened in compar-ison to the older Scriptures. Nevertheless, below there is still a flesh that is able to bear salvific fruits. This seems to result from the deci-sion of its free will. There is no mention of extra-human forces that cause the good or evil intentions mentioned—contrary to the notion of two supernatural spirits of light and darkness in 1QS 3:13–4:14, where the prince of light and the angel of darkness predetermine the ways of their sons, i.e., the two different kinds of human beings. Enoch, morever, swears to the sinners: "lawlessness was not sent upon the earth, but men created it by themselves, and those who do it will come to a great curse" (98:4). Does the passage quoted above not give the impression that creation is indeed disturbed, but by no means destroyed?

The introductory chapters of the collection express an even more optimistic view of the created world, although they are primarily looking forward to the coming universal judgment. Nevertheless, before that event, "nothing on earth changes, but all the works of God are manifest to you" (2:1–2). Concerning beings that possess spirit, human or angelic ones, the world is indeed divided. Many of them have fallen; so an antagonism has developed between good and evil deeds and destinies, between salvation and destruction. But does this mean regarding humankind that there is a clear-cut and enduring ontological division between the genres of these beings?

To answer these question, it may be illuminating to go into the detail and examine items such as the characterization of Israel and her place in creation, the evaluation of the earth as the home of life, and the ʿalam terminology that refers to God's association with the present aeon and the future ones.

What is the place of *Israel* as God's elect people in the worldview of 1 Enoch? Surprisingly, this name is used nowhere in the entire book, nor are the oft-mentioned elect righteous ever referred to as a kind of nation. The addressees are the righteous in the plural, imagined, rather, as autonomous individuals.

The prehistory and history of Israel, from creation to the end of the world, is recounted in the Animal Vision as the backbone of human history. In the symbolic form of the Vision, the nations are depicted as animals. Here one easily recognizes that the righteous (as a rule) are the descendants of Jacob, who is the founder of the race of sheep. (ʿn' is properly small cattle including goats), whereas the other parts of humankind are depicted mainly as wild animals. The righteous, however, are nowhere collectiely referred to as "the sheep" in the singular, and the neighboring peoples are imagined as pluralities (wolves, boars, etc.) and are not incorporated in one single figure (different from the imagery of Daniel 7). The righteous are sheep, but the sheep are not necessarily righteous. Many are often blinded (89:32, 41, 54, 74; 90:6, *1 Enoch 1*, p. 380), and the majority of them appear to remain godless until the end of days. Nevertheless, God maintains his special relationship to all of them, leading and pasturing them, but also punishing them when necessary. In most cases the Lord deals with all of them in the same manner—the righteous as well as the wicked. Thus they appear as an ontological unity. Thus God is called "the Lord of the Sheep" (mrʾ ʿn') around thirty times, and this is nearly the only title applied to him in this vision. His only house on earth is among them (89:48, 54). In order to pasture the sheep, but also to destroy them when they disobey, the Lord summons seventy other-worldly shepherds, each for its respective time (90:1). All of them refuse to do their duty in the right manner and therefore must be judged and destroyed in the fiery abyss, where the unrighteous sheep and fallen stars will be thrown after the end of the world (90:20–26). Nonetheless, they were appointed by the Lord and could not have been evil from the outset—even though God had foreseen their failure.

The division of the people into two classes of moral conduct, the righteous and the wicked, was inherited from older Israelite cultic and sapiential traditions, as is evident from the psalter, Proverbs, and sometimes, the Prophets. Thus came conviction that each human being can belong only to one side or the other and is characterized by the persistence of good or evil deeds and destinies. This may be called ethical dualism, although, according to the older sources, for every individual there always remains the opportunity during his lifetime to convert from one side to the other (Ezek. 18). Indeed in apocalyptic literature the division is sharpened and eschatologized: one's affiliation with one of these classes will become finalized and decide the person's eternal destiny. Should, therefore, the Enochic differentiation between righteous and unrighteous deeds and the destinies of individuals during the course of history be called ontological dualism? How, then, can divine actions be arranged under this topic, because God is often engaged in the care of the apostates as well?

The author might have imagined the gap between the sheep (the Israelite community) and the gentiles nations as wider than that between the faithful and the wicked in God's own people. But was it conceived of as so radical that it had an ontological relevance for the author of the Animal Vision? As the wild animals, the symbols of the other, mainly hostile nations, are begotten by older, sometimes righteous ancestors according to the content of the Vision (cf., e.g., the descendants of Noah, 89:9–10), their origin could scarcely have been thought to have happened without divine intention. Or will the author keep the nature of their origin in question? In every case their remnant will finally be rescued like the remnant of Israel.

Why is the image of the sheep chosen for the Israelites? According to the economic circumstances in ancient Palestine, small cattle were the common domestic animal for the majority of people, which felt a close and emotional relationship especially with this animal (e.g., 2 Sam 12:3–6). So the divine title presumably expresses not only a juridical, but also a kind of familiar connection. Moreover, the image reflects long time religious use in Israel: "Sheep are a common biblical metaphor for Israel" (*1 Enoch 1*, p. 377).

So it is rather astonishing that according to the Animal Vision, the status of sheep is not the appropriate image for the final destiny of righteous human beings. As the famous forefathers from Adam to Isaac were already depicted as bulls, so, at the eschatological fulfillment, the surviving righteous will be transformed into this species—into white cattle. Just before that there appears a white bull with long horns, which has not been begotten by an animal (i.e., a human father), and the transmutation of all the righteous, including the gentiles, occurs after his pattern (90:37–38).

This white (and wild?, Aram.: *r'm'*) bull is generally interpreted as the future Messiah according to a prophetic tradition. However, as Nickelsburg rightly remarks, this figure should be born from the house of David, who was depicted as a sheep (89:45–46), but none of the typically messianic functions, as promised in Isa. 9, etc., are mentioned here. Moreover, some passages earlier in this Vision describe as one of the last events on earth before the great judgment, the coming of special sheep with long horns, who open the eyes of the other sheep and repulse their enemies. Perhaps there is a hint of Judas Maccabeus (*1 Enoch*, 396), who is pictured in messianic colors. The bull, however, which will appear after the turn of the aeons, will be the prototype of a new humanity and its eternal life. Like the first man Adam he seems, as a white bull, to have come forth from the earth. "He might be seen as a new Adam, who with the transformation of all the animals becomes the head of a new human race" (*1 Enoch 1*, p. 407) in correspondence to the Son of Man in Daniel 7 (translated in Hebrew as *ben 'adam*).[3]

The comparison of the eschatological humankind, as well as the primeval one, with cattle has no basis in the Scriptures, as far as I can see. Only in the book of Hosea is Ephraim twice described as God's heifer; but he is a stubborn one (4:16; 10:11–13); certainly there was no exegetical reason to actualize the metaphor in later times. So it is difficult to explain why the image of sheep—sufficient as the symbol for the people of God as it is later as the New Testament—was reduced to the characterization of a preliminary stage before the real unveiling of the true nature of the righteous. Was the background simply the agricultural experience that cattle are stronger and more autonomous than sheep? In the Hebrew Bible the bull often "illustrates the invincible power and might."[4] Or was

---

[3] For my own interpretation of that passage, see Klaus Koch, "Messias und Menschensohn," in idem, *Vor der Wende der Zeiten, Beiträge zur apokalyptischen Literatur, Gesammelte Aufsätze* 3 (Neukirchen, 1996), pp. 235–266, especially pp. 247–250.

[4] H.J. Zobel, *shor*, ThWAT 7, p. 1203.

the author possibly influenced by a Zoroastrian mythology in which the *Urrind*, "the Uniquely created bull" was seen as the first living creature from which all animals have come?[5]

Is this passage an example of temporal dualism? The transmutation of sheep into cattle may be seen as a change of the ontological order that will take place at the turn of the aeons. But the primeval time of humankind from Adam to Isaac has also been imagined as a period of bulls, so he phenomenon will not be totally new on earth. Thus, the *Urzeit-Endzeit* correspondence would be a better pattern for the interpretation.

According to Nickelsburg, a *spatial dualism* dominates in *1 Enoch*. "Heaven is the realm of the divine and earth the habitation of humans. "Disaster occurs when the realms are confounded" (above, p. 37; *1 Enoch 1*, p. 40). No doubt many passages seem to support the statement. The whole earth was made desolate and defiled by Asael (10:8). So there is now much godlessness on her (8:2); she is ruled by lawless kings (46:4–5; 62:1–5), whereas the heavenly creatures have remained faithful to their creator and will testify against the sinners on earth at the final judgment (100:11). As often as God is obliged to intervene on earth to punish the wicked, "the earth will be wholly rent asunder and everything on the earth will perish" (1:7, cf., 83:8); the earth will be shaken but the heavens as well (102:2).

However, when seen in the context of the Enochic collection as a whole, these utterances are poetic exaggerations. According to other passages the earth is a vivid, although not divine being and has kept her sound contact with her creator. So she "raises the voice of their (the oppressed righteous) cries to the gates of heaven (9:2; *1 Enoch 1*, pp. 202 f.; cf. 7:6). From this lower part of the universe Adam with his wife and sons has come forth (85:3), and "from the beginning until the consummation . . . nothing on earth changes, but all the works of God are manifest to you (2:2). Regarding the vertical perspective there is no thoroughgoing antagonism between the above and the below; and this is valid already for the present. Of course, "Nature's Obedience and Humanity's Disobedience" (*1 Enoch 1*, 152) are discerned, and nature remains in some respects—though not in all regards—"nearer" to God than human civilization, although it

---

[5] Mary Boyce, *A History of Zoroastrianism*, HO 1 8,2,2A (1975), pp. 138–139.

belongs to the earth and not to heaven. Yet both realms of reality are still in close touch with one another.

A similar reservation pertains to the horizontal perspective. Certainly, during his airborne journey at the ends of the earth, Enoch becomes aware of "places uninhabited by living mortals," the regions where the apparatus for the execution of the final judgment is already installed—the tree of life for the righteous, the pits for the condemned, paradise. Thus "God's creation anticipated God's judgment and serves as its instrument" (above, pp. 59, 56; *1 Enoch 1*, pp. 40, 39). But this discovery does not contradict the fact that the inhabited earth also has regions that possess a special relationship to the Most High, which have kept the original value they received by divine creation, and so will have their significance in the coming aeon. Nickelsburg himself stresses that chapters 6–16 describe a sacred geography around Mount Hermon, where God chooses to utter revelations (*1 Enoch 1*, pp. 238–247). In addition, Sinai in the far South appears as a place where God likes to descend to intervene on earth (1:4; 77:1). Much more important is a city in the midst of the earth, Jerusalem, although the name is not used, with a holy mountain where a throne is erected for the great Holy One, who will descend upon it in goodness for the future renewal of humanity (chaps. 24–26; *1 Enoch 1*, p. 19). Nearby is a deep, cursed valley destined for those cursed persons who have, in hubris, uttered words against the Lord. As a "pleasant and glorious land," the whole country to which this city belongs, is distinguished from other parts of the earth. These places are, as far as I can see, the only this-worldly places that Enoch mentions. No normal settlement of Palestine or any other country and no region or capital of hostile people and kings is explicitly localized. The book confines itself to a sacred geography, reserved for the essence of God's purpose for his creation, which must be intentionally distinguished from an empirical geography. However, is a category like dualism not too far-fetched for this kind of conception?

Some remarks concerning the *temporal* dimension. "The temporal axis in 1 Enoch is sharply divided between the present time, which will end with the judgment, and a new age that follows" (above, p. 36; *1 Enoch 1*, p. 40). A linguistic example that illuminates the division and that has not been mentioned by Nickelsburg, may be the uses of the term *ʿalam* (Aramaic and Ethiopic, parallel to the Greek *aiôn*) with characteristic differences between the meaning of the singular and that of the plural (and the determinate versus the indeterminate state). The commentators offer very conflicting renderings. Thus, for the singular, J.T. Milik and Siegbert Uhlig prefer the rendering "world/*Welt*," whereas Nickelsburg and Klaus Beyer choose "eternity/*Ewigkeit*" or the corresponding adjectives. Such different translations are confusing for the reader, because according to our modern understanding, "world" and "eternity" are mutually exclusive; the world has a beginning and is determined by ongoing changes and an often feared transitoriness, whereas eternity contains unperturbable uniformity and a transcendence from the disturbance of this world.

Some semantic remarks. In biblical Hebrew the corresponding *ôlam* has, indeed, primarily a temporal significance, including two types of time, both thought of as remote from the present speaker. The first refers to a past, but fundamental *Urzeit*, the second, to an endurance that lasts into the vast future.[6] Only in the very late layers of the Hebrew Bible can both aspects be combined and express the totality of the time of this world (e.g., Qoh. 3:11).

Later in Mishnaic Hebrew and the later apocalypses (also in the Greek *aiôn* of the New Testament) is the connotation of "world" accentuated and the present *ôlam ha-zeh* differentiated from *ôlam ha-ba'* in the eschatological future. But a temporal perspective remains because the ancients presuppose an inseparable connection between time and world. There is no time for them without the movement of objects, and there are no this-worldly objects without progression in time. That the lexeme means "eternity," absolute time independent of the material world, is nowhere evident in these Hebrew and Aramaic texts.

Seen against this background, to translate the Aramaic singular *'alam* as "eternity" in 1 Enoch becomes questionable, because it frequently alternates with the plural, referring to the endless *aiôn*s of eschatological salvation (9:4; 51:5, etc.). In the last cases Nickelsburg translates "the ages" instead of eternities. However, as a rule the plural of a lexeme refers to a wider realm of the signified phenomenon than the singular. Thus, if the plural is translated "the ages," the singular should mean a part of these, an age, and not an overarching totality like "eternity."

---

[6] H.D. Preuss, *ôlam/'alam*, *TDOT* 10, pp. 530–545.

Some passages underscore that the singular *'alam* is limited to the totality of this time and world that has grown up with creation. When it is said that the chief demon Asael was cast into a dark hole in Dudael after the Flood *eis tên aiôna* (10:4–5 Gk^s), the meaning must be "for this time-world" and not "forever" (*1 Enoch 1*, p. 215), because the next verse predicts that he will be led to the burning conflagration on the day of the great judgment. The connection *dîn 'alma'* in 91:15 surely should be understood as "judgment about the inhabitants of the (now past) time world" and not as "the eternal judgment" (*1 Enoch 1*, p. 435). because it occurs once forever and has no timeless endurance.

Thus *1 Enoch* wants to counterpose the present corrupt world and time with the future aeons of salvation. But the division is not an absolute one because the first was the result of a divine creation, which cannot be totally annihilated. A certain continuity will remain in spite of the major turn of the era. It is not limited to nature. It is also accentuated with regard to human election, which is understood as another mode of creation appearing during history, when its subject is symbolized by the "plant of righteousness," which is analogous to the righteous sheep in the Animal Vision. In Noah it has grown up bearing seed and enduring for all the generations of the *aiôn* (10:3). The proper content of the teaching of the so-called Apocalypse of Weeks is the destiny of the humans who have grown up from the plant of truth (93:1). According to this section, God started the plant with Abraham (*1 Enoch 1*, p. 444) in the third "week." In the seventh "week" the witnesses of the plant of righteousness of the time-world (*'alma'*) will receive sevenfold wisdom and knowledge. In the ninth "week" all humankind will convert to their path of righteousness (cf., also, 10:16–21). The "firmly rooted plant" will have a long history in this time and world and will continue, albeit in a changed and extended manner, into the world to come. In my opinion, this image, which is the basic one for the Enochic collection, does not agree with a notion of a consequent temporal dualism.

The different parts of the Enochic collection do not present a worldview that is consistent throughout. Nevertheless, there seems to be nowhere a denial of the value and endurance of creation, in spite of all the deprivations that fallen angels and human may produce. After the judgment a new creation will certainly grow up, but as renewal and completion of the divine plan, not as quite another world.

No doubt, Nickelsburg's commentary presents an important work that opens new doors for the understanding of the elusive apocalyptic literature before the turn of the era and its aftermath in Judaism and, even more, in Christianity. It may, however be that he goes one step too far in his assertion of an ontological dualism in *1 Enoch*.

RESPONSE TO KLAUS KOCH

Klaus Koch's response to my article and its counterpart in my commentary presses my argument at all the right places and offers me an opportunity to clarify what may be obscure and refine what inclines toward generalization.

I use "dualism" for want of a better term. I might have said "polarity." I wanted to make the point that on several levels, especially the temporal and spatial, the Enochic texts set certain things in opposition to one another or in distinction from one another. My use of "ontological dualism" refers to the qualitative distinction between the divine and the human—a distinction that is violated when the watchers mate with human beings. It should not be confused with anthropological dualism in the sense of an essential distinction between two types of people (as in 1QS 3–4), nor do I intend the expression as an umbrella term that comprises also the temporal and spatial dualisms that I find in parts of *1 Enoch*. In no sense do I imply that creation is ontologically evil. To the contrary, the evil that pervades this world is due to the watchers' primordial revolt, which occurred *after* the world was created. In this sense. *1 Enoch* differs from Gnosticism, which posits a primordial fall in the *pleroma* that *resulted in* the creation of the world.

Koch correctly notes that there is some ambiguity in *1 Enoch* regarding the created world. Chapters 2–5 cite the obedience of the created world. By my own acknowledgment, the region around Mount Hermon is sacred, and Sinai is the same. I take Enoch's vision in chapters 26–27 to be idealized, in particular reflecting the place as it shall be. In any case, there is no reference to any inhabitants. Yet the world *as a place where people live and interact with one another* is in disarray and chaos and defies God's requirement for justice. As chapters 6–11 depict it, humanity lives in a kind of prediluvian condition, awaiting the judgment that will be the counterpart to the Flood. I do not see this or the many other passages that describe the dark side of humanity as "poetic exaggeration" but as reflecting the heart of the apocalypticists' experience of phenomenal reality.

As further relates to my ontological dualism, the authors' experience leads them to posit a supernatural source for evil. According to the double strand of the myth in chapters 6–11, the watchers bring into the world various kinds of evil that victimize humanity. Nonetheless, in the 'Asael myth, angelic revelation also leads to human sin (8:1).[1] Nonetheless, when I say that there is "a realm of evil spirits who prey on humanity" (above, p. 38), I do not include temptation to sin as a major demonic activity, as Koch seems to interpret me. Indeed, I agree with him that the Enochic tradition nowhere approaches the powerful dualism of 1QS 3–4. Moreover, as the tradition evolves, e.g., in chapters 20–32 and 85–90, and 92–105, divine judgment has as its principle object the sins for which humans are responsible. (Here Boccaccini's distinction is apposite, see above, pp. 127–128). This is most clearly articulated in chapters 92–105, where the author employs woes in order to hurl threats of divine judgment against the sinners for actions that are spelled out in considerable specificity.

Koch's observations about the absence of references to the nation of Israel are especially noteworthy. Although the Apocalypse of Weeks refers to Abraham as the righteous plant from whom the plant of righteousness will sprout, things go awry, and in the seventh week, the chosen are a remnant from, or a subgroup of the plant. Thus, election is applied to the righteous community. I do think that the Animal Vision may at times construe "the sheep" in a collective sense, but by and large they are depicted as blind and straying from the path. Of importance for the author, however, are those young lambs whose eyes are opened and who struggle in vain to convince their elders of their sin (89:54). The Epistle also sets the righteous and sinners in contradistinction to one another and emphasizes the polarity between the wise and the lying teachers who lead many astray. Even more radical is the notion that salvation is possible for "all the sons of the whole earth." Moreover in both chapter 10 and the Animal Vision, these gentiles are linked not to the nation of Israel, by whatever name, but to the righteous (10:17–21; 90:30–38).

My understanding of temporal and spatial dualism requires some clarification. There is, in my view, a qualitative difference between this time and world and that which will exist after the judgment.

---

[1] In the Book of Jubilees, the myth explains both the presence of evil and the existence of a demonic realm that leads humans into sin; see Nickelsburg, *I Enoch 1*, p. 73.

Indeed the new age (by whatever name) will reverse conditions as they now exist. This is not to deny the notion of a renewed, rather than a totally new creation. It is the conditions that will change.

The translation of the Aramaic ʿalam and its Greek and Ethiopic equivalents into consistent and good English is a problem. I have rendered the expression variously as "eternity," "eternal," "forever (and ever)," and "age(s)." Nowhere do I give a systematic account of my understanding of the expression, and I should do this in volume 2 of the commentary.[2] My use of "eternity" or "eternal," does not mean a timeless dimension. One might paraphrase the word: "into the distant future, as far as one can conceive of it." "Everlasting" might better catch the nuances of Koch's reference to "duration," but as he points out, the expression need not mean "forever." For example, ʿAsael will lie in the pit *eis aiôna* (presumably *lʿlm*) until the day of judgment (10:5–6), which is some seventy generations in the future (10:13). So there is a terminus here. Koch rightly notes that ʿalam is attested in both the singular and plural in the Aramaic fragments and suggests a consistent English translation in the singular and plural.[3] How might that look in 5:1: *ʾlhh dy ḥy] hwʾ lʿlm dʿlmyn?* Does one translate: "the God who lives for the age (that comprises) the ages? Perhaps the overall evidence suggests that these authors thought of a future age (distinct from the present), that consisted of many, many ages and used the singular or plural (or both together) as they saw fit. This notion of *e pluribus unum* may also be indicated in the expression "all the generations of the age" (e.g., 10:22; 103:4, 8, as well as 10:5–6, 13 cited above). The Enochic authors do not use the term ʿalam frequently to refer to the past. (For an exception, see 9:4: *lkl dr dryʾ dy mn ʿlm[ʾ* (God's throne exists "for every generation of the generations that are from of old"). For the author of the Animal Vision, things begin with the creation of humanity. In the Book of Watchers, with the exception of one reference to the sin of the first parents (32:6), the revolt of the Watchers is the first event of recorded history. In contrast to these specifics about a past that has a beginning, these authors think of an indefinitely extended future of many ages.

Koch rightly notes that I paint with a broad brush when I refer to a construction of reality that runs through all the parts of *1 Enoch.*

---

[2] Preuss's article, "ʿôlam, ʿalam," unfortunately, does not deal with the Qumran Aramaic evidence.

[3] For the relevant passages, see Milik, *Books of Enoch*, p. 388.

My own wording suggests some reservation about the claim: "It may seem ill-advised to search for an overarching unity in a literary collection as lengthy, diverse, and complex as *1 Enoch* (above, p. 29). In fact, the various kinds of dualism that I posit are especially evident in the parts of *1 Enoch* to which they are appropriate. The myth of the watchers dwells on the distinction between the divine and the human and the manner in which it is breached (chaps. 6–18). The account of Enoch's call emphasizes the total otherness of the heavenly sanctuary (chap. 14). Enoch's journeys across the cosmos emphasize the otherworldliness of those realms (chaps. 17–36). The Animal Vision is particularly striking, however, because it imposes an otherworldly dimension onto a recitation of human history. (chaps. 85–90) The watchers of heaven invade the earth. The events from the late pre-exilic period to the Hellenistic period are read in light of the actions of the seventy angelic shepherds and the activity that takes place in the heavenly throne room. The end comes when God descends from heaven to execute judgment on earth.

Yet if all of my dualisms do not pervade all the sections of the Enochic collection, one element in my scheme does, namely the notion of revelation. Enoch sees into the future that lies in and beyond the judgment, he travels through those parts of the universe that are inaccessible to other mortals, and he receives instruction about hidden things from God and members of the divine entourage. Thus revelation is pivotal and integral to the theology and world view of these authors, and it is explicit throughout the corpus.[4] In 1970, as the discussion of "apocalyptic" wandered here and there and got nowhere, Klaus Koch proposed that we might find a point of leverage by studying texts that a consensus would define as apocalypses.[5] In this study of one of those texts, I have argued that the term is justified because revelation is of the essence of the book's world view, theology, and soteriology.[6] It is that which makes the book what it is.

---

[4] The exception is chapters 6–11, where it is mentioned only in Sariel's instruction to Noah.

[5] Klaus Koch, *Ratlos vor der Apokalyptik* (Gütersloh, 1970). Translated as *The Rediscovery of Apocalyptic* (Naperville, 1972).

[6] The work of the Society of Biblical Literature Genres Project, published in *Semeia* 14, laid out in detail the literary structure of a large groups of apocalypses, showing that revelation was constitutive of that structure. The present study supplemented that work by demonstrating that revelation is logically or thematically integral to the content and purpose of this apocalyptic work.

CHAPTER THREE

SALVATION WITHOUT AND WITH A MESSIAH: DEVELOPING BELIEFS IN WRITINGS ASCRIBED TO ENOCH

GEORGE W.E. NICKELSBURG

It is axiomatic in modern biblical studies that variety was a salient feature of early Jewish eschatology. As a probe into this variety, I shall discuss the corpus known as 1 Enoch. In this self-contained body of literature we can trace the development and transformation of certain eschatological traditions over the course of perhaps 350 years. In keeping with the theme of this volume, my focus will be on the Messiah. The topic is not to be taken for granted since this figure is explicitly mentioned only in the latest stratum of the Enochic tradition, the Book of Parables (Chaps. 37–71). My intention, however, is to show how the messianic figure of the Parables assumes functions the earlier strata attribute to other figures.

Dominating the action in the Book of Parables is a transcendent figure, who is the agent of eschatological judgment and salvation. He is known variously as "the Chosen One," "the Righteous One," "the Son of Man," and, on two occasions, "the Anointed One." In the first part of the paper, I shall take up the themes of judgment and salvation in the earlier strata of 1 Enoch, focusing on the following issues: What are the authors' circumstances? That is, what is the nature of the predicament that calls forth judgment and salvation? Who is the agent of judgment and salvation? What is this agent's relationship to God? What is the specific function of the agent and how does the agent mediate judgment and salvation? Against this background, I shall turn in the second part to the messianic soteriology in the Book of Parables.

AGENTS OF JUDGMENT AND SALVATION IN THE EARLY STRATA OF 1 ENOCH

Two myths dominate the Enochic corpus, both of which are set in primordial times but are also closely related to the end-time. The

first myth recounts how the patriarch Enoch was escorted through
the cosmos, where he learned the secrets of heaven and earth, which
he wrote down for the benefit of his children who would be living
in the end-time. The second myth describes the fall of the heavenly
watchers in ancient times and its consequences in the Deluge. The
actions of the watchers and their sons, the giants, as well as the
Deluge, have counterparts in the evil of the end-time and its eradication in the great judgment.

The Astronomical Book (Chapters 72–82)

Chapters 72 ff. are probably the oldest stratum in the Enochic corpus.[1]
Here Enoch recounts how the angel Uriel escorted him through the
heavens, showing him the created order in the activity of the heavenly bodies. Although the compositional history of this section is
uncertain,[2] we can draw several tentative conclusions about the earlier form of the tradition. The alleged author was Enoch, who transmitted his writing to his son, Methuselah. It is uncertain whether
the text was composed as a polemic against people who disagreed
with the author's astronomical and calendrical observations and speculations.[3] The use of the apocalyptic form and its claim of revealed
authority may imply such a polemic. In any case, as parts of Chapters
80–82 indicate, and as the Book of Jubilees confirms, the Astronomical
Book came to be used for such polemical purposes. In that context,
the Enochic writing served a salvific function. It transmitted cosmic
revelations that had been given to Enoch for the benefit and salvation of the latter generations. The astronomical laws were a torah
that governed the proper observance of the religious calendar.

---

[1] See J.T. Milik, *The Books of Enoch: Aramaic Fragments of Qumran Cave 4* (Oxford:
Clarendon, 1976), pp. 7–8, and in much more detail, James C. VanderKam, *Enoch
and the Growth of an Apocalyptic Tradition* (Catholic Biblical Quarterly Monograph Series
16, Washington, D.C.: The Catholic Biblical Association of America, 1984), pp.
79–88.

[2] The Qumran Aramaic fragments of this section indicate that the Ethiopic ver-
sion is a compilation of several documents that have been severely abbreviated by
a later editor. See Milik, *Enoch*, pp. 271–97; and Otto Neugebauer, "The 'Astronomical'
Chapters of the Ethiopic Book of Enoch (72–82). With Additional Notes on the
Aramaic Fragments by Matthew Black," in Matthew Black, *The Book of Enoch or 1
Enoch: A New English Edition with Commentary and Textual Notes*, Studia in Veteris
Testamenti Pseudepigrapha 7 (Leiden: E.J. Brill, 1985), p. 386. See also VanderKam,
Enoch, pp. 76–79.

[3] VanderKam, *Enoch*, pp. 90–1.

Myths about the Rebellion of the Watchers (Chapters 6–11)

Chapters 6–11 are the next oldest stratum in the corpus. They tell the story of the rebellion of the heavenly watchers and its consequences. Actually, two myths are recounted and there is probably another level of redaction.[4] The first myth is an interpretation of the cryptic verses in Genesis 6:1–4 about the mating of the sons of God and the daughters of men.[5] In the Enochic version, the angelic chieftain, Šemiḥazah, and his companions, marry mortal women and beget belligerent giants, who devastate the earth and obliterate life. According to the second myth, the angelic chieftain ʿAśaʾel reveals heavenly secrets about metallurgy and mining, which enable men to forge the weapons that devastate the earth and to make the jewelry and cosmetics that facilitate sexual seduction. In yet another version, the watchers reveal the magical arts an astrological forecasting.

In the present composite form of the story, the angelic intercessors hear the prayer of dying humanity and plead its case before God, who commissions these angels to enact judgment. Although the story is set in primordial times, the description of the salvation that follows the judgment transcends the account in Genesis 9 and takes on the character of an eschatological scenario. Thus, the whole story presumes an Urzeit/Endzeit typology. The primordial giants are prototypes of warriors in the author's own time. In my view, these were the Diadochoi, who claimed divine parentage and waged continual warfare, as they battled for Alexander's crown.[6] Certain of the demonic revelations correspond to aspects of contemporary culture.

---

[4] For the various options, see Paul D. Hanson, "Rebellion in Heaven, Azazel, and Euhemeristic Heroes in 1 Enoch 6–11," *Journal of Biblical Literature* 96 (1977): 195–233; George W.E. Nickelsburg," "Apocalyptic and Myth in 1 Enoch 6–11," *Journal of Biblical Literature* 96 (1977): 383–405; John J. Collins, "Methodological Issues in the Study of 1 Enoch: Reflections on the Articles of P.D. Hanson and G.W. Nickelsburg," in Paul J. Achtemeier, ed., *Society of Biblical Literature 1978 Seminar Papers* 1, pp. 315–22; Hanson, "A Response to John Collins' Methodological Issues in the Study of 1 Enoch," in Achtemeier, *1987 Seminar Papers*, pp. 307–9; Nickelsburg, "Reflections upon Reflections: A Response to John Collins' 'Methodical Issues in the Study of 1 Enoch,'" in Achtemeier, *1978 Seminar Papers*, pp. 311–14; Devorah Dimant, "1 Enoch 6–11: A Methodological Perspective," in Achtemeier, *1978 Seminar Papers*, pp. 323–39; Carol A. Newsom, "The Development of 1 Enoch 6–19: Cosmology and Judgment," *Catholic Biblical Quarterly* 42 (1980): 310–29.

[5] Although the author of this section reflects Genesis 6, this does not exclude the possibility that he also knew an older and fuller form of the tradition that appears in evidently compressed form in Genesis.

[6] See Nickelsburg, "Apocalyptic and Myth," pp. 389–91; see also Rüdiger Bartelmus, *Heroentum in Israel und seiner Umwelt* (Abhandlungen zur Theologie des Alten und Neuen Testaments 65; Zürich: Theologischer Verlag, 1979): 174–87.

In these myths, the evils of the author's own time are not simply
the accumulation of the evil deeds of human beings. They derive
from a radical evil, which came into being through an act of rebellion that took place in a realm beyond human access. The real perpetrators of evil are not flesh and blood, but principalities and powers.
The warrior kings are the personification of an evil that the watchers bred into the world. Magicians and soothsayers are possessors of
forbidden knowledge and the agents of malevolent spirits. And the
human race, as a whole, is their helpless victim.

Since evil derives from supernatural sources, it must be overcome
by divine intervention. Different from Genesis 6–9, this heavenly
deliverance is enacted by angelic agents of judgment and salvation.

The words of commissioning and the specific functions of the
angels are pertinent to our topic. The son of Lamech is the prototype of the righteous person in the end-time. In words reminiscent
of a prophetic commissioning, God dispatches Śariel: "Go to Noah
and say to him in my name, 'Hide yourself'" (10:2–3). The angel is
the revealer, the teacher, who warns of the coming judgment, from
which Noah must flee and hide if he is to be preserved (cf. Isa.
26:20–21) as the plant whose seed will provide a new start for the
human race. Salvation results when Noah obeys the revealed word
of the divinely commissioned messenger. We shall meet this motif
frequently in 1 Enoch.

Raphael, the second angel, is sent against 'Aśa'el. The demon who
has revealed how to bind with spells is himself bound and cast into
the pit, and God's healer cures the earth from the plague that has
afflicted it.

Representing the divine Warrior, Gabriel is dispatched against the
gibborîm, whom he sends against one another in a war of mutual
extermination.

Michael's tasks parallel those of Raphael and Gabriel. He is to
destroy the giants and restore the earth. But at least one nuance is
different. He does not heal the earth; he "cleanses" it. The term has
priestly connotations, and the action is reminiscent of Noah's sacrifice.

To summarize, a myth set in primordial times explains the demonic
origins of evil in the present time and promises its extermination.
The agents of that judgment and the salvation that will follow are
transcendent figures from the heavenly realm, who are commissioned
with functions that parallel those of human agents: prophet, healer,

warrior, high priest. Each of these roles reflects a particular model of salvation, which is here construed in eschatological dimensions.

Enoch's Ascent to Heaven (Chapters 12–16)

The myths in Chapters 6–11 never mention Enoch or suggest that he is their author. Chapters 12–16, on the other hand, are a first person account in which Enoch describes his ascent to the heavenly throneroom and his subsequent interaction with the rebellious watchers. This section does not *narrate* the events in Chapters 6–11, but it does presuppose the story and makes repeated reference to it. Nevertheless, although the judgment of the watchers and the giants is often in focus, the angelic agents of this judgment, who are so prominent in Chapters 6–11, are never mentioned.

The silence is a reflex of Enoch's centrality in the narrative, which, in turn, is related to the genre of these chapters. They recount a series of commissionings, preeminently Enoch's prophetic commissioning.[7] First, Enoch is commissioned by angels to indict the rebel watchers and announce their coming judgment. Then the watchers commission Enoch to intercede for them. When he does so, he is summoned to the heavenly throneroom, where God commissions him to repeat the verdict of the heavenly court. Enoch does this by writing down the indictment and verdict and reading them in the presence of the rebel watchers.

Thus these chapters mirror Chapters 6–11 in some interesting ways. The heavenly intercessors, who plead for humanity in Chapters 6–11, are replaced by Enoch, who pleads ineffectively for the rebel watchers—the fallen heavenly priests.[8] The heavenly agents of judgment have also been replaced by Enoch, who is the agent of judgment because as a prophet of doom he bears the irreversible message of that judgment. Thus these chapters focus not on the actual events of judgment and punishment in primordial and eschatological times, but on the message and the messenger who announces that judgment and the punishment that follow it. When God speaks and God's word is conveyed, the act has, in effect, taken place.

---

[7] H. Ludin Jansen, *Die Henochgestalt* (Oslo: Dybwad, 1939), pp. 114–17; George W.E. Nickelsburg, "Enoch, Levi, and Peter: Recipients of Revelation in Upper Galilee," *Journal of Biblical Literature* 100 (1981): 576–82.

[8] Nickelsburg, "Enoch, Levi, and Peter," 584–7.

The relationship between primordial and eschatological time is essential here. The words of heavenly judgment that Enoch wrote down in ancient times are the words of the text of the book of Enoch. Chapter 14 begins with this superscription, "The Book of the Words of Truth and the Reprimand of the Watchers who were from Eternity." Enoch is important in his role as prophet and scribe, and he describes how God created him and destined him (yᶜhab, 14:2, 3) to be the revealer of the heavenly reprimand. Thus, judgment is bound up with the word that reveals that judgment. The author of these chapters is an agent of judgment in that he reveals the irrevocable sentence of condemnation.

The Journeys of Enoch (Chapters 17–19 and 20–36)

Chapters 17–19 and 20–33 provide a locative affirmation of the message of the previous sections. They recount two cosmic journeys to the places where the judgment already spoken of will be dispensed to the fallen watchers and to the righteous and sinners of the human race.[9] We learn little about the agents of this judgment, although God is mentioned once (25:3). As in Chapters 12–16, revelation is central here. The mediators of this revelation are the angels, who escort Enoch and interpret the meaning of his visions, as well as Enoch himself, who reveals what has been revealed to him.

The Oracular Introduction to 1 Enoch (Chapters 1–5)

Chapters 6–36 are introduced by a prophetic oracle that announces the eschatological theophany and the final judgment and its consequences. In the superscription, Enoch introduces his book with language drawn from the Blessing of Moses and the prophecies of Balaam (1:1–2; Deut. 33; Num. 24).[10] The theophany is described in 1:3c–9. The heavenly warrior will appear with the myriads of his angelic army. The rebel watchers will quake, and the whole cosmos will react. Judgment will be executed on the human race. The wicked will be punished for their impious deeds and blasphemous words. The final section of the oracle contrasts the blessings and curses that will come to the righteous and the wicked (5:6–9). The righteous

---

[9] George W.E. Nickelsburg, *Jewish Literature Between the Bible and the Mishnah* (Philadelphia: Fortress, 1981), p. 54.
[10] VanderKam, *Enoch*, pp. 115–19.

and chosen will be forgiven and receive mercy and peace. They will be the recipients of wisdom, which will enable them not to sin in word and deed and thus to avoid divine judgment.

Different from the previous sections, here the eschatological appearance of God is central, and God, not his angels, is the primary agent of judgment. As in Chapters 12 and following, Enoch remains an important figure; he is the revealer of the coming judgment, and he speaks in the idiom of biblical prophecy. The wisdom that will lead to the salvation of the righteous is possibly related to the Enochic revelation of the judgment (see the next section).

The Epistle of Enoch (Chapters 92–105)

Chapters 92–105 of 1 Enoch purport to be an Epistle from Enoch to his spiritual descendants who would live in the last days. Its primary themes are familiar: righteousness and sin and their reward and punishment in God's judgment. The Epistle differs from Chapters 6–9 in that it makes almost no reference to the primordial angelic rebellion. Like Chapters 20–33 and especially 1–5, it focuses on the judgment of the righteous and the sinners who live in the latter days.[11]

Two types of sin parallel their counterparts in the early chapters. Parallel to the blasphemies and hard and proud words in 1:9, 5:4; 27:2 are idolatry and deceit and false teaching (especially in 98:9–99:10).[12] The wicked *deeds* of the rich and powerful sinners include preeminently their oppression and murder of the righteous (cf. 22:5–7 and the sin of the giants).[13]

The Epistle consists primarily of alternating series of admonitions and woes. Enoch admonishes the righteous to endure in the face of oppression and to resist the temptation to sin, promising them the rewards that are written on the heavenly tablets that he has inspected. In the woes he threatens the sinners with damnation for their sins of word and deed.

---

[11] George W.E. Nickelsburg, "The Apocalyptic Message of 1 Enoch 92–105," *Catholic Biblical Quarterly* 39 (1977): 309–28.

[12] George W.E. Nickelsburg, "The Epistle of Enoch and the Qumran Literature," *Journal of Jewish Studies* 33 (1982: *Essays in honour of Yigael Yadin*): 334–40.

[13] Nickelsburg, "Riches, the Rich, and God's Judgment in 1 Enoch 92–105 and the Gospel according to Luke," *New Testament Studies* 25 (1978–79): 324–32.

Intermingled with the admonitions and woes are several passages that describe aspects of the judgment, employing motifs familiar from the early chapters of 1 Enoch. These and a few other passages provide some information on the nature of the judgment and the divine agents who will execute it. As in Chapter 9, the prayer of the righteous will reach the angelic intercessors, whose intervention will catalyze the judgment (97:3–6; 99:3; 103:14–104:3). One aspect of the judgment will be a familial war of mutual self-destruction reminiscent of the *gigantomachia* (10:9–10). Two descriptions of the judgment allude to the theophany described in Chapter 1 (100:4–5; cf. 1:7, 9; 102:1–3). God's angelic entourage will serve as his agents, dragging the wicked from their hiding places and keeping the righteous and pious safe until the divine fury has spent itself.

But the executors of the judgment are not limited to God and his angels. Two new motifs enter the picture. The heavenly bodies and cosmic forces, mentioned in 2:1–5:3 as paragons of obedience to God's commandments, function in the Epistle as witnesses of human sin and agents of the judgment (100:10–101:9). Moreover, the righteous themselves—whose previous participation in the judgment has been through the prayer for vengeance—will take part in a holy warfare against the wicked (95:3; 96:1; 98:12; cf. 93:10; 91:11–12).[14]

Our discussion of the earlier parts of 1 Enoch noted the important salvific role played by revealer figures: Śariel the angel sent to Noah; Enoch the seer; and the real author of these revelatory texts. This divine activity, which prepares one for the judgment, is crucial in the Epistle. According to the Apocalypse of Weeks (93:9–91:11), the seventh week will be characterized by a generation that perverts truth into falsehood. It will be overcome when the chosen are given the sevenfold wisdom and knowledge that will undermine the violence and falsehood of the perverse generation (cf. also 94:1–2). In 104:12–13 this wisdom and knowledge is identified, at least significantly, with the Enochic literature, which will be the property of the righteous community of the end-time. They, in turn, will instruct the sons of the earth in this salvific wisdom.[15]

These texts direct us to the premise that governs the literary genre of the Epistle and endows it with divine authority. This is a book

---

[14] Nickelsburg, "Apocalyptic Message": 317.
[15] Nickelsburg, "Epistle": 340–5.

of divinely revealed wisdom, mediated through the anonymous sage who has taken the name of the primordial seer, Enoch. The revelatory aspect extends to the corpus as a whole. The descriptions of primordial sin and punishment and Enoch's revelations of the cosmos and of the future are the presupposition for the message of the Epistle. The corpus as a whole is a deposit of revealed wisdom directed to the people of the end-time, providing the divine means to endure judgment and receive salvation. Thus, through his book the sage functions as the indispensable divine agent of salvation.[16]

The Animal Apocalypse (Chapters 85–90)

1 Enoch 85–90 is an apocalypse that recounts in allegorical form the history of the world from Adam to the end-time. Human beings are depicted as animals, the rebel watchers are fallen stars, and the seven archangels are human beings.

This extended allegory has many points of similarity with the earlier strata of 1 Enoch. Angels function as agents of judgment and as mediators between beleaguered humanity and its God. In the end-time Judas, the champion of the pious, leads them in a holy war against the wicked, mainly the gentiles. Final judgment takes place in connection with a theophany.

Idiosyncratic to this text is the figure of the great while bull of the eschaton. Scholars have often identified him as the Davidic Messiah—mainly because they suppose that an eschatological scenario demanded a Davidic Messiah.[17] While this great eschatological beast may, indeed, be a symbol for such a Messiah, several points are worth noting. The only identifiable eschatological human agent of judgment is the ram, Judas Maccabeus. He, if anyone, corresponds to a militant Messiah. The great bull of the eschaton is important not for what he does, but for what (or who) he is. He is born after the judgment has taken place and is a reversion to the white bulls of primordial times—the Sethite line from Seth himself to Isaac. He is, moreover, the first fruits of a humanity returned to primordial

---

[16] On this issue, see Nickelsburg, "Revealed Wisdom as a Criterion for Inclusion and Exclusion: From Sectarian Judaism to Early Christianity," in J. Neusner and E.S. Frerichs, eds., *"To See Ourselves as Others See Us": Christians, Jews, "Others" in Late Antiquity* (Chico, Calif.: Scholars Press, 1985), pp. 73–91.

[17] E.g., R.H. Charles, *The Book of Enoch or 1 Enoch* (Oxford: Clarendon, 1912), pp. 215–16.

purity and vitality.[18] His importance lies in this patriarchal status and not in any explicit messianic function. Indeed, different from all the divine agents we have discussed, this figure receives no commission or delegation of authority, nor is he the recipient of revelation.

THE BOOK OF PARABLES (CHAPTERS 37–71)

For explicit reference to the idea of a Messiah, we must turn to the latest stratum in 1 Enoch, Chapters 37–71, the so-called Book of Parables. Here, motifs previously ascribed to men, angels, and God are attributed to a figure whom the texts described as "the Lord's anointed." However, as we shall see, he is not the kind of Messiah described in texts that await a Davidic king or a Levitic priest. He is a transcendent heavenly figure with titles and functions drawn from several biblical eschatological scenarios.

Relationship to the Enochic Corpus

The Parables are a creative reformulation of the Enochic tradition. Its contents are an account of Enoch's ascent to heaven and his journeys across the earth, where, guided by interpreting angels, he sees in a series of tableaux the events related to the final judgment.

Two related features distinguish the book from the rest of the extant Enochic literature, and they constitute the core of the book's soteriology and theology of judgment. First, the book centers on events in the divine throneroom, where God is preparing his judgment. Second, the agent of this judgment appears nowhere else in the extant Enochic tradition; his pedigree is to be found in non-Enochic texts. Thus a tradent of the Enochic tradition or a group of such sages have drawn materials from outside this tradition and created a composite figure to serve the judicial and salvific functions that the earlier Enochic traditions ascribed to men, angels, and God.

---

[18] George W.E. Nickelsburg, *1 Enoch: A Commentary on the Book of 1 Enoch 1–36; 81–108* (Hermencia; Minneapolis: Fortress Press, 2001), pp. 406–407.

The Setting

The Sinners

Before turning to this figure and the judgment that he executes, we must look at the circumstances that precipitate the judgment. Two groups of villains dominate the scene in the Parables. Between them they divide the sins ascribed to the watchers in Chapters 6–11. The rebel angels in the Parables, whose leader is Azazel, are uniformly accused of the sin that chapters 6–11 attribute to the angelic chieftain ʿAśaʾel.[19] They have revealed forbidden secrets to humanity (Chap. 64) and thus led them astray (54:5–6; 56:1–4; 64; 65:6–11; cf. Chap. 8).

The second, more prominent group of villains in the Parables are "the kings and the mighty who possess the earth (*or* the Land)." Their violent and bloody oppression of the righteous is reminiscent of the activity of the giants in Chapters 6–11 and the deeds of the rich and powerful sinners in the Epistle.

Several factors characterize the conduct of the kings and the mighty (46:5–8). They refuse to acknowledge that they have received their kingship from the Lord of Spirits. Conversely, their faith is in the gods that they have made with their hands (i.e., their idols), and thus they deny the name of the Lord of Spirits.[20] Moreover, they persecute the houses of his congregations, the faithful who depend on the name of the Lord of Spirits. The author refers to gentile kings and rulers who are persecuting pious Jews. Their sin is characterized by means of the myth about the arrogant rulers who are the agents of the demon who storms heaven and assaults the divine throne.[21] To persecute the righteous clients of the Lord of Spirits is to assault God and deny God's ultimate sovereignty.

---

[19] The Parables are extant only in Ethiopic. In Chapters 6–11 this same name occurs in the Ethiopic text, where the Aramaic reads ʿAśaʾel. On the relationship, see Nickelsburg, "Apocalyptic and Myth," pp. 401–4.

[20] It is uncertain whether the author has other opponents in mind when he refers to undefined sinners who deny the dwelling place of the holy and the name of the Lord of Spirits. Possibly he has in mind other persons who deny divine retribution or in other ways disagree with the theology of the author and his group. However that may be, the focus and emphasis is clearly on the gentile kings and rulers whose opposition to the righteous is construed as an act of hubris that demands the divine retribution that will affirm God's ultimate sovereignty. See the next note.

[21] George W.E. Nickelsburg, *Resurrection, Immortality, and Eternal Life in Intertestamental Judaism* (Harvard Theological Studies 26; Cambridge/London: Harvard University Press/Oxford University Press, 1972), pp. 74–5.

The Righteous

The counterparts to the sinful kings and the mighty are "the right-eous" and "the chosen" and "the holy." These three titles appear sometimes singly and sometimes in various combinations, but they are never explicitly defined. The text never states why they have been chosen or what deeds or characteristics make them righteous or holy. We are told only that they "have hated and despised this unrighteous age . . . and all its deeds and ways" (48:7). Nonetheless, the author does mention a few characteristics of the righteous.

Of primary importance is their sad lot in life. The kings and the mighty persecute them (46:8). For this reason, presumably, they grieve (48:4), their faces are downcast (62:15), and they await their rest (53:7). Persecution, moreover, has led to the death of the righteous (47:1, 2, 4).

Repeatedly mentioned is the faith of the righteous. If the nature of their righteous deeds is not described, we are told that these deeds are dependent (lit., "hang on") the Lord of Spirits (38:2), and they themselves are "the faithful, who depend on the Lord of Spirits" (40:5, 46:8; cf. 58:5). In a similar idiom, they rely on (lit., "lean on") God and the "staff" that is the Son of Man (48:4; 61:3, 5; cf. "hope," 48:4).

Central and constitutive to the faith of the righteous and chosen is their knowledge of the heavenly realm and specifically the Son of Man.[22] God chose the Son of Man and hid him in his presence, but he has revealed him to the holy and righteous and chosen (48:6–7; 61:13; 62:7; 69:26). In a formal sense this revelation is a defining characteristic that distinguishes the righteous from the sinners. As we shall see, the Son of Man is the vindicator and savior of the righteous, and, in that capacity, he is the judge of the kings and the mighty who persecute them. With respect to this issue, the author estab-lishes a specific contrast between the two groups. To the righteous has been revealed the one who will enact God's righteous judgment in their behalf. The sinners and the kings and mighty, who perse-cute the righteous, deny God's sovereignty and the possibility of his retributive justice.

---

[22] See the discussion by John J. Collins, "The Heavenly Representative: The 'Son of Man' in the Similitudes of Enoch," in John J. Collins and George W.E. Nickelsburg, eds., *Ideal Figures in Ancient Judaism* (Society of Biblical Literature Septuagint and Cognate Studies 12; Chico, Calif.: Scholars Press, 1980), pp. 111–33.

Whether the righteous and chosen represent a particular, socio-logically and religious defined group of Jews is uncertain. The terms "righteous," "chosen," and "holy" are generic expressions that need not imply that certain other Jews are not part of the community of the saved. Similarly, the expression "the houses of his (God's) con-gregation" (46:8; cf. 53:6) indicates only that they gathered in groups and not that they did so in intentional separation from other Jews.

The Messianic Figure in the Parables

The messianic figure in the Parables, who is to be the executor of divine judgment against the rebel angels and the kings and the mighty, is designated by four names: most frequently "the Chosen One"; twice "the Righteous One"; twice "the Anointed One."[23] Sev-eral times he is called "Son of Man." However, since this term is almost always qualified ("this Son of Man," "that Son of Man," "the Son of Man who . . ."), we must be cautious in calling it a title.[24] The names of the exalted one are derived ultimately from three types of scriptural texts. "Son of Man" has been drawn from Daniel 7.[25] "Chosen One" and "Righteous One" are titles of the Deutero-Isaianic Servant of the Lord. "Anointed One" is a messianic title strictly speaking.

The major references to the exalted one occur in a series of heav-enly tableaux that describe events leading to the enthronement of the Chosen One. In addition to these scenes of dramatic action, there are a number of anticipatory allusions to the functions of the Chosen One. My discussion will draw mainly on the tableaux.

The first major text is Chapter 46. In form it is typical of a certain kind of revealed vision: vision, seers' question, answer by the inter-preting angel. Enoch's vision is based on Daniel 7:9, 13:

---

[23] "Chosen One": 39:6; 40:5; 45:3, 4; 49:4; 51:3, 5; 52:6, 9; 55:4; 61:5, 8, 10; 62:1. "Righteous One": 38:2; 53:6. "Anointed One": 48:10; 52:4.

[24] The term occurs in: 46:2, 3, 4; 48:2; 62:5, 7, 9, 14; 63:11; 69:26, 27, 29; 70:1. It occurs in absolute form only in 62:7 and 69:27. The literature on this figure is, of course, legion. For a good discussion and bibliography, see Carsten Colpe, *"ho huios tou anthropou,"* *Theological Dictionary of the New Testament* 8 (1972) and for an updated bibliography, Gerhard Friedrich, ed., *Theologisches Wörterbuch zum Neuen Testament* 10:2 (1979), pp. 1283–6.

[25] See Johannes Theisohn, *Der auserwählte Richter* (Studien zur Umwelt des Neuen Testaments 12; Göttingen: Vandenhoeck & Ruprecht, 1975), pp. 14–23, who argues that the author of the Parables is dependent on Daniel 7 rather than on a source behind that text.

> And I saw there one who had a head of days
>   and his head was like white wool.
> And with him was another, whose face was like the
>   appearance of a man;
>   and his face was full of graciousness like one of the holy
>   angels.
> (1 Enoch 46:1)

The author introduces the two principal figures from the Danielic vision. The second of these is clearly a transcendent figure. His humanlike face is glorious like that of an angel.

When Enoch inquires about "that Son of Man," the interpreting angel responds:

> This is the son of man who has righteousness,
>   and righteous dwells with him.
> And all the treasuries of what is hidden he will reveal;
>   for the Lord of Spirits has chosen him,
>   and his lot has surpassed all before the Lord of Spirits in
>   truth forever.
> (1 Enoch 46:3)

This explanation uses or implies three of the descriptive terms applied to the transcendent figure. He is "Son of Man." His "righteousness" implies the title "the Righteous One." As the one whom the Lord of Spirits has chosen, he is "the Chosen One." Moreover, he is the highest functionary in the heavenly court—thus surpassing in rank even the four archangels, Michael, Raphael, Gabriel, and Phanuel. The righteousness of this Son of Man is the quality by which he will judge (cf. e.g., 62:3; 63:3, 8–9). The hidden treasuries he will reveal most likely contain the hidden sins of those whom he will judge (cf. 49:4; 50:2; 68:5). The rest of Chapter 46 anticipates the judgment scene in Chapter 62 (see below).

Chapter 47 returns to the Danielic source (7:9, 10, 22): The Head of Days is seated on his glorious throne in the midst of his angelic court, and the books of the living are opened. Judgment will be executed on behalf of the righteous. The event that catalyzes this session of the heavenly court is extraneous to Daniel and is typically Enochic: It is the intercession of the angels, who relay to God the prayer of the righteous whose blood has been shed (47:1, 2, 4; cf. Chap. 9).

Although the session of the heavenly court, described in Danielic language, leads us to expect that God will exact judgment on the kings and the mighty, as the Ancient of Days does in Daniel 7, here this judgment does not happen straightaway. Instead, the author recounts the commissioning of that Son of Man, which in Daniel takes place only after the judgment.

This commissioning is described in two lengthy poetic stanzas (Chaps. 48–49), which draw their imagery and language from the call and presentation of the Servant in Isaiah 49 and 42 and from royal passages in Psalm 2 and Isaiah 11.[26] According to 48:2–3, at this moment in the session of the court, that Son of Man is named in the presence of the Lord of Spirits. Actually, the text goes on, his name was named before creation, and he was chosen and hidden in God's presence at the time (v. 6). In contrast to the Deutero-Isaianic Servant, the naming and hiding of the servant figure precede not a human birth, but the creation of the universe. The functions of this Son of Man are described in language from Isaiah 49:

> He will be a staff to the righteous,
>   that they may lean on him and not fall.
> He will be a light to the nations,
>   and he will be a hope to those who grieve in their hearts.
> (1 Enoch 48:4)

Moreover, he has preserved the portion of the righteous, and he is the vindicator of their lives (48:7).

The narrative switches to an anticipation of the coming judgment. In those days, the faces of "the kings of the earth" will be cast down (48:8). This title for the kings, which occurs in the Parables only here, introduces an allusion to Psalm 2:2: These kings will be judged "because they have denied the Lord of Spirits and his Anointed One" (48:10). Although this judgment is a function of the Chosen One, it will be executed against the kings also by the chosen ones.

The second stanza of this pericope brings us back to the scene in the heavenly court (Chap. 49). The Chosen One has taken his stand before the Lord of Spirits. His qualifications are divine wisdom and righteousness:

> He is mighty in all the secrets of righteousness . . .
> And in him dwell the spirit of wisdom and the spirit of
>   insight,

---

[26] For the best exposition of the messianic material in the Parables, see ibid., pp. 68–99.

> and the spirit of instruction and might,
>   and the spirit of those who have fallen asleep in
>   righteousness.
> And he will judge the things that are secret,
>   and no one will be able to speak a lying word in his
>   presence.
> (1 Enoch 49:2–4)

This passage draws its motifs from Isaiah 11:2–5, which stresses the judicial functions of the Davidic king, primarily the divinely given wisdom that enables him to penetrate the human facade and judge human deeds righteously and with equity. Into this allusion is added reference to the persecuted righteous, whose vindicator the Chosen One is.

The motif continues in the final lines of the Enochic stanza. He can so judge, "because he is the Chosen One in the presence of the Lord of Spirits, according to his good pleasure."

Here the allusion is to the presentation of the Servant in Isaiah:

> Behold my servant, whom I uphold,
>   my Chosen One in whom my soul delights;
> I have put my spirit upon him,
>   he will bring forth justice to the nations.
> (Isaiah 42:1)

This Deutero-Isaianic text itself parallels the passage in Isaiah 11.

The unfolding drama of judgment reaches its climax in Chapters 61–63. In 61:6–13, we are again in the heavenly courtroom, among the angelic hosts. God now seats the Chosen One on his glorious throne. First, he judges the angels.

Then, in Chapters 62–63, he judges the kings and the mighty. This lengthy scene reflects a traditional reworking of the last Servant Song of Second Isaiah, which is attested also in Wisdom of Solomon 4–5.[27] Crucial to this interpretation of Isaiah is the conflation of the Servant Song with the description of the fall of the King of Babylon in Isaiah 14.[28] Through this conflation, the kings and the nations of Isaiah 52–53, who have been neutral spectators of the Servant's suffering, are now identified with the demonic anti-God figure, who strives to storm heaven and is thrown down to Sheol. In Wisdom

---

[27] Nickelsburg, *Resurrection*, pp. 70–74, and the literature cited in nn. 87, 88. See also Theisohn, *Richter*, pp. 114–26.

[28] See Nickelsburg, *Resurrection*, pp. 62–78.

4–5, these royal figures (or at least the wealthy ungodly) are judged by the Servant figure himself, the righteous one whom they have persecuted. In 1 Enoch 62–63, they are judged by the Chosen One, who is the heavenly champion of the chosen ones whom they have persecuted.

This close relationship between the Chosen One and the chosen ones is expressed in two ways in this passage. First, it is a special quality of the chosen ones that the Chosen One who had been hidden was revealed to them (62:6–7; cf. 48:6–7). In contrast to this, the kings and the mighty face their judgment with astonishment. Implied from the parallel in Wisdom of Solomon 4–5 is an element of unexpected recognition: In the exalted Chosen One they recognize the chosen ones whom they have persecuted. Moreover, in their confession (Chap. 63) they acknowledge what they had previously refused to acknowledge: the sovereignty of the God whose chosen they have persecuted. There is a second aspect in the relationship of the Chosen One and the chosen. This relationship does not end with the judgment. The Chosen One is not only their heavenly champion and vindicator. He will be their companion in the eternal life that is now bestowed on them.

We have seen how the Parables describe the exalted one as the agent of divine judgment. One final set of passages describes this figure in language reserved elsewhere in 1 Enoch for God. After the superscription and introduction in Chapter 37, which correspond to 1:1–3b, the text of the Parables opens with reference to an epiphany (37:1–5), which corresponds to 1:3c–6. However, different from Chapter 1, which describes how God will appear to judge, the Parables speak of the appearance of "the Righteous One." A further reference to this epiphany occurs in Chapter 52. The mountains and hills will melt like wax at the appearance not of God (cf. 1:6–7), but of the Anointed One and Chosen One (cf. also 53:6–7) for the appearance of the Righteous and Chosen One).

The Transformation of Traditions in the Parables

The Parables make use of a number of Enochic motifs of significance to us. 1) The author's principal concern is the persecution of the righteous by kings and rulers who are the embodiment of demonic forces. 2) As judge God will adjudicate this gross inequity. 3) Angels will be agents of this judgment. 4) The persecuted righteous also share the prerogative of executing this judgment. 5) The author of the Parables describes his book as revealed wisdom that Enoch received and transmitted for the benefit and salvation of those who will live in the end-time (Chap. 37).[29]

The Parables are remarkable, however, for their transformations of these traditional motifs. These transformations are bound up with the figure of the Chosen One, which itself represents a transformation of other, non-Enochic traditions about divine judgment.

The transformations of the Enochic materials are as follows. 1) Theophany is replace by "huiophany." The righteous Son of Man appears to judge and is seated on God's glorious throne. Corresponding to the royal status of the persecutors, he is God's own king. His relationship to God is denoted both by the messianic term, "Anointed," and the servant term, "the Chosen One." 2) Although the angels carry out punishment on the hosts of Azazel who have led humanity astray and the kings and the mighty who have persecuted the righteous and chosen, their presence is much less dominating than in Chapters 6–11. The preeminent agent of judgment is the high functionary of the heavenly court, whose face shines like an angel, but who surpasses all others in the heavenly court. 3) The participation of the persecuted righteous in the judgment of their enemies is primarily through the activity of the champion of the righteous and the chosen, the Righteous One and Chosen One. 4) The focus of this author's revelation is on visions of the Chosen One, the heavenly figure whom God had hidden but has now revealed to the righteous and chosen.

The other side of the issue is the Enochic transformation and fusing of non-Enochic traditions. Three traditional figures of exalted status have become one figure who is both similar to, and notably different from, the prototypes. The Danielic Son of Man, the angelic patron of the people of the holy ones of the Most High,[30] here appears in the heavenly court not after the judgment, but in order to enact that judgment. The counterpart to the exalted Servant figure of the Wisdom of Solomon is not the vindicated righteous one him-

---

[29] See Collins, "Son of Man."
[30] For the Danielic Son of Man as the archangel Michael, see John J. Collins, *The Apocalyptic Vision of the Book of Daniel* (Harvard Semitic Monographs 16; Missoula: Scholars, 1977), p. 146.

self, but the transcendent heavenly patron of the righteous and chosen. The Anointed One of the Lord, who will execute God's justice on the kings and rulers of the earth, is not a human king born of the line of David, but a member of the heavenly court.

This last point relates in particular to the theme of this volume and requires a little more elaboration. During the Greco-Roman period, when the Davidic throne was vacant, earlier royal texts from the prophets and the Psalms were read as prophecies of a ruler yet to come. Psalms of Solomon 17 employs a remarkable pastiche of language drawn from Psalm 2, Isaiah 11, and Ezekiel 34 to describe the future son of David who will oppose the unrighteous Roman rulers who have overrun the land. A fragmentary *pesher* on Isaiah from Qumran Cave 4 interprets Isaiah 11 (4QpIs[a]). The Florilegium from Cave 4 quotes both the oracle of 2 Samuel 7 and Psalm 2. The Testimonium quotes the Balaam oracle (Num. 24:15–17) with reference to the Davidic king. Running through all these texts is the king's function as the exector of God's judgment. The Testament of Levi 18, which I take to be pre-Christian in essential points,[31] ascribes to the eschatological priest attributes appropriate to the Davidic king.[32]

These texts, among others, testify to a live messianic hope in the two centuries B.C.E. The theologies that informed that hope anticipated variously a Davidic king, an anointed priest, or both. Some even ascribed quasi-divine attributes to these human figures. However, what distinguishes the Parables from these texts is the Parables' identification of the messianic figure with traditional transcendent exalted figures. The central figure of the Parables is God's *heavenly* vice-regent. For whatever reason, the author of the Parables believed that the biblical promises about the future king and the traditional messianic function of the judgment had to be fulfilled by a transcendent savior—one he found described in other traditions. Furthermore, in conflating these traditions, the author allowed the Servant title, "the Chosen One," to dominate the messianic title, "the Anointed One." Later texts from around the year 100 C.E., which also make use of Daniel 7, change this emphasis and designate the transcendent

---

[31] See George W.E. Nickelsburg and Michael E. Stone, *Faith and Piety in Early Judaism* (Philadelphia: Fortress, 1983), p. 199, nn. 2, 3.

[32] Jonas C. Greenfield and Michael E. Stone, "Remarks on the Aramaic Testament of Levi from the Geniza," *Revue Biblique* 86 (1979): 223–4.

judge of the kings and rulers and the savior of the righteous primarily as "the Anointed One."[33]

Although I have stressed the transcendent character of the Chosen
One, it has often been argued that this heavenly figure is an exalted
persecuted righteous man. Two data appear to support this position.
First, the present conclusion to the Parables identifies the Chosen
One with the exalted Enoch (cf. especially 71:14 with 46:3). Secondly,
the Servant traditions in the Parables are most closely paralleled
in the Wisdom of Solomon, which cites Enoch as the example of
the righteous one par excellence (4:10–15) and uses language from
Psalm 2 to describe the interaction between the righteous one and
his rich and royal persecutors (4:18; 6:1). This impressive evidence
gives one pause, but it falls short of certain proof. Chapter 71 may
well be a later appendix to the book. In such a case, the original
form of the Parables construed the relationship between the Chosen
One/Righteous One and the chosen and righteous ones as that of
patron and clients rather than as a one-for-one identification. Nevertheless, the form of the Parables that identifies the exalted figure
with Enoch and the closely related tradition in the Wisdom of Solomon testify to a situation in Judaism that may well have facilitated
the claim of primitive Christianity that a particular persecuted righteous one had been exalted as the unique Chosen One, Son of Man,
and Messiah.

SUMMARY

In the first part of this chapter we worked through the early strata
of 1 Enoch, looking at texts that describe God's judgment, its agents,
and their functions. In the earliest narrative strata (Chaps. 6–11),
angels, described first as heavenly intercessors, are commissioned var-

---

[33] 2 Apoc. Bar. 39–40 interprets the Danielic vision about the four kingdoms.
Chap. 72 bears interesting resemblances to the judgment scene described in Matt.
25:31–46, which, in turn, is related to 1 Enoch 62–63; see David R. Catchpole,
"The Poor on Earth and the Son of Man in Heaven: A Reappraisal of Matthew
xxv.31–46," *Bulletin of the John Rylands University Library of Manchester* 61 (1979): 378–83.
4 Ezra 12–13 is a reinterpretation of Daniel 7. On the complex history of tradi-
tions, see Michael E. Stone, "The Concept of the Messiah in IV Ezra," in Jacob
Neusner, ed., *Religions in Antiquity. Essays in Memory of Erwin Ramsdell Goodenough*
(Supplements to Numen 14; Leiden: Brill, 1968), pp. 303–10; see further, Stone,
"The Question of Messiah in 4 Ezra," in Jacob Neusner, William S. Green, and
Ernest Frerichs, eds., *Judaisms and Their Messiahs at the Turn of the Christian Era*
(Cambridge, 1987), pp. 209–224.

iously as eschatological revealer, healer, warrior, and high priest. Later they will continue to appear as intercessors and as members of the entourage of the Divine Warrior, whose theophany precipitates the judgment. In Chapters 12–16, Enoch assumes functions ascribed earlier to angels: intercessor for the defunct intercessors and the prophet who announces doom on the watchers. This revelatory function underlies the whole of the Enochic corpus. One's salvation or damnation at the judgment hinges on one's response to the revelations mediated by Pseudo-Enoch, the anonymous seer. Finally, functions of divine judgment are given to the elements of nature and to the righteous of the end-time, including Judas Maccabeus. In perhaps one of these texts we may have a single reference to a Davidic king; in none of them does the word "anoint" appear.

In the Parables of Enoch, the subject of the second part of this study, the execution of judgment is partly in the hands of the angels and the persecuted righteous. For the most part, however, the agent of judgment is a transcendent heavenly figure, who assumes functions that the other strata in 1 Enoch attributed to the angels, the righteous, the elements of nature, and God. The author of the Parables describes his protagonist through the use of biblical traditions that originally described the "one like a Son of Man" in Daniel, the Servant/Chosen One of Second Isaiah, and the Davidic king in Isaiah 11 and Psalm 2. In this reformulation of the tradition, two things are noteworthy. First, the messianic traditions are subordinated to those about the Son of Man and, especially, the Chosen One. The title "Anointed One" occurs only twice. Second, by conflating the messianic tradition with the other two, the author depicts the Messiah not as the human son of David, but as a transcendent figure. This type of Messiah continued to appear in Jewish works written shortly after the fall of Jerusalem in 70 c.e.

Finally, we have seen in the Parables the continued importance of the role of revelation. The reality of the Chosen One and the judgment that he will execute are revealed to the righteous, but hidden from their enemies. The book of Parables is the embodiment of this revelation, and through it the author calls the righteous to the faith and faithfulness that will enable them to be saved at the time of the judgment. In this sense, the apocalyptist and his apocalypse play a key role in the drama of judgment and salvation.

The findings of this paper have at least two general implications for the study of early postbiblical Judaism. First, belief in a Messiah was not a *sine qua non* for Jewish theology in the Second Temple

Period. Other savior figures of nonroyal status had ascribed to them attributes and functions that are traditionally called "messianic." In such cases, however, the use of this adjective may be deceptive, because it may wrongly imply that these attributes and functions derived from speculation about a divinely appointed king. Second, speculations about such a king, where they do occur, often differ greatly from one another. The king is not always thought of as a human being descended from the Davidic line.[34] He may be an exalted transcendent figure. He may be described in language drawn from speculation about nonroyal figures. The title "Anointed One" may or may not be prominent in the descriptions of the figure.

These findings are also of crucial significance for the study of Christian Origins, both with respect to our understanding of the development of christology and our interpretation of the early interaction of Christianity and Judaism. But that is the subject of another paper.

---

[34] The complexity of this situation is illustrated by the Qumran text about "The Chosen One of God." For a lengthy discussion, see Joseph A. Fitzmyer, "The Aramaic 'Elect of God' Text from Qumran Cave 4," *Catholic Biblical Quarterly* 27 (1965): 348–72; reprinted in Joseph A. Fitzmyer, *Essays on the Semitic Background of the New Testament* (London: Chapman, 1977; reissued as Society of Biblical Literature Sources for Biblical Study 5; Missoula: Scholars Press, 1974), pp. 127–60. 1:1–4 suggests that this "Chosen One" would be a human being. However, certain of his characteristics mentioned in 1:5–10 are reminiscent of parts of 1 Enoch 49 and 63 that draw on Isa. 11. This may be of special significance, since no manuscript evidence for the Parables has been found at Qumran. Fitzmyer (ibid., pp. 149–50) minimizes the possibility of Isaianic influence on the Qumran text, noting rightly that the latter (very fragmentary) text gives no indication that its protagonist was a scion of David. However, the force of this argument is considerably lessened by the certain Isaianic influence of the Parables, a complete text that certainly does not envision a Davidic origin for the Son of Man/Chosen One/Anointed One.

RESPONSE TO "SALVATION WITHOUT AND WITH A MESSIAH: DEVELOPING BELIEFS IN WRITINGS ASCRIBED TO ENOCH"

WIARD POPKES*

The title of Nickelsburg's article is as cautious as indicative. In terms of contents, the constitutive element is "salvation," the variant being "Messiah." In terms of sources and whom they represent, Nickelsburg speaks of "developing beliefs" within a group of writings assembled under the name of Enoch, usually called 1 Enoch or Ethiopian Enoch (in distinction to 2 Enoch or Slavonic Enoch).[1] The contribution is a part of the collection of articles under the challenging and ground-breaking heading "Judaisms and Their Messiahs at the Turn of the Christian Era." Both key terms, Judaism and Messiah, stand in the plural form. The article itself discusses the question to what an extent "Messiah" is an adequate category to describe the salvific figures mentioned in these writings. Also the other question needs to be raised: Does 1 Enoch, or rather: this Corpus Enochicum encompass one Judaism or several? Our major attention though will be directed to the question of what is understood by "salvation," i.e., the issue of soteriology.

In his analysis, Nickelsburg follows the different parts of 1 Enoch which represent different literary strata in relation to their time and circumstances of origin.[2] The latest part, the Book of the Parables/

---

* University of Hamburg.

[1] George W.E. Nickelsburg, *Jewish Literature between the Bible and the Mishnah. A Historical and Literary Introduction*, pp. 185 ff.; idem, *1 Enoch 1. A Commentary on the Book of Enoch Chapters 1–38*, pp. 82–108.

[2] In his *Jewish Literature*, Nickelsburg locates the parts as follows: 1 Enoch 72–82 and 1–36 under "Palestine in the Wake of Alexander the Great;" 83–90 under "Reform—Repression—Revolt;" 92–105 under "The Hasmoneans and Their Opponents" (followed by a section on "Stages in the Literary Development of 1 Enoch"); 37–71 under "The Romans and the House of Herod." Cf., "Commentary," pp. 21 ff. (1 Enoch as a Literary Composition). In his article ("Salvation"), Nickelsburg is even more differentiated, treating 1 Enoch 72–82; 6–11; 12–16; 17–19 and 20–36; 1–5; 92–105; 85–90; 37–71. Siegbert Uhlig, *Das äthiopische Henochbuch* (Gütersloh, 1984), p. 494, dates the parts as follows: 1 Enoch 1–36 "between the end of the third and the middle of the second century B.C.," 72–92 "in the third or second

Similitudes (37–71), is of particular importance for Nickelsburg's article,[3] because only here the term "messiah" occurs (no more than
twice: 48:10 and 52:4). The precise date of this part is difficult to
ascertain,[4] in particular due to its absence in the Dead Sea material,[5]
but also in view of some kinships with early Christian motifs.[6] There
is little doubt today, however, that there is no need to leave the
Jewish environment for the origin of the Similitudes and 1 Enoch
as a whole. The Parables are in Nickelsburg's focus the more, because
his intention "is to show how the messianic figure of the Parables
assumes functions the earlier strata attribute to other figures" (p. 49).
The terminology, using "messianic figure," goes beyond the traditional term "Messiah," integrating other names or titles, viz. "the

century B.C.," 85–91 "in the second century B.C.," 92–105 and 106–108 "in the
first century B.C.," 37–71 "partially towards the end of the pre-Christian era, essential passages though after the turn of the eras." In general, there is no basic disagreement about the sections and their sequence, in particular about placing 37–71
(the Similitudes or Parables) last. In Qumran Aramaic fragments of most of the
parts were found, with the very exception of the Similitudes. Cf., details in Uhlig,
op. cit., pp. 470–483; Nickelsburg, *Commentary*, pp. 9 ff.

  [3] As well as for other investigations, e.g., John J. Collins, The Heavenly Repre-
sentative: The 'Son of Man' in the Similitudes of Enoch, in John J. Collins and
George W.E. Nickelsburg, eds., *Ideal Figures in Ancient Judaism: Profiles and Paradigms*
(Chico, 1980), pp. 111–133.

  [4] Details on the history of research in Uhlig, op. cit., pp. 574 f., who himself
holds to an earlier date: some parts originate from Maccabean times, "others in
the second half of the first century B.C. and some then after the turn of the eras;
the final redaction took place in the first century A.D., when also LXX f. was added
to the corpus" (p. 575). Further discussion of the evidence in Michael A. Knibb,
"The Date of the Parables of Enoch. A Critical Review," in *NTS* 25 (1978/79),
pp. 345–359; G.L. Mearns, "Dating the Similitudes of Enoch," in ibid., pp. 360–369;
David Winston Suter, *Tradition and Composition in the Parables of Enoch* (Missoula, 1979),
pp. 23 ff., who concludes "that the work was composed sometime between the last
quarter of the first century B.C. and the fall of Jerusalem in A.D. 70." Cf., also
Gerbern S. Oegema, *The Anointed and His People. Messianic Expectations from the Maccabees
to Bar Kochba* (Sheffield, 1998), pp. 140 f. and 146, who argues for "the first century
C.E." as "probable" (p. 140); E. Isaac, "1 (Ethiopic Apocalypse of) ENOCH," in
James H. Charlesworth, ed., *The Old Testament Pseudepigrapha* (London, 1983), vol. 1,
p. 7: "1 Enoch already contained the Similitudes by the end of the first century A.D."

  [5] Johannes Zimmermann, *Messianische Texte aus Qumran. Königliche, priesterliche und
prophetische Messiasvorstellungen in den Schriftfunden von Qumran* (Tübingen, 1998), p. 199,
regards 4Q534 as "ein 'missing link' zwischen den Qumrantexten und den (dort
nicht gefundenen) BR, das möglicherweise auch für die Datierung der BR . . . von
Bedeutung sein könnte." Cf., his entire treatment of 4Q534 under the heading Der
"Erwählte Gottes," pp. 170–204. The "three books" mentioned in 4Q534 line 5
probably refer to the writings of Enoch (pp. 177 f.).

  [6] The most important of all is, of course, the Christological title "Son of Man."
Suter (op. cit., pp. 25 ff.) argues that the Gospel of Matthew likely used the Parables.
On "salvation by faith," cf., Collins, op. cit., pp. 116–119.

Chosen One," "the Righteous One," "the Son of Man," into one
figure which is described phenomenologically, i.e. in terms of its/his
function. Salvation thus is brought about by a "functionary." This
seems to point towards a thought pattern of problem and solution.
We shall try to assess whether this model does justice to the figure
as such. The issue receives further urgency by Nickelsburg's statement that the figure "assumes functions" of other, earlier figures.
The subtitle of his article indicates the assumption that there occurred
a development in belief in various figures. All of this results in a
blending of expectations related to the functions of a variety of figures.
How much of a character of their own do the figures retain, or are
they variable entities? Do they simply represent essential aspects of
the divine-human relationship in terms of "salvation," which is after
all, as Nickelsburg formulates, the decisive element? A functionary
approach is also pursued by Oegema, who gives the definition: "A
Messiah is a priestly, royal or otherwise characterized figure, who
will play a liberating role at the end of time."[7] Oegema thus interprets "salvation" more precisely as "liberation." Moreover, he emphasizes the eschatological frame. Now, both soteriology and eschatology
underwent a significant development during the time represented in
the Corpus Enochicum. What then is the message of 1 Enoch to its
time? "Salvation" is a manifold term; in any case it brings up the
social scientific question of the relevance as well as the contents of
being saved. What does 1 Enoch tell us about the situation, the
desires and hopes of Second Temple Israel towards the very end of
that period? Nickelsburg provides a helpful summary of his results
at the end of his article (pp. 64 f.; it is even easier to read his article starting with its end). With regard to the Parables the dominance
of the titles "Son of Man" and "the Chosen One" is underlined.
Moreover, the messianic figure is a transcendent one, not the human
son of David. And in general, the role of revelation (as conveyed to
and by Enoch) requires attention. On the basis of these results we
shall further dive into the material, with the primary goal to better

---

[7] Oegema, op. cit., p. 26. He also formulates: "the latter-day liberator (the
Messiah)," p. 69, in relation to the figures in 90:20–42. A similar direction is followed by Martin Hengel and Anna Maria Schwemer, *Der messianische Anspruch Jesu
und die Anfänge der Christologie. Vier Studien* (Tübingen, 2001), p. XIII: "Wir verstehen
daher unter dem 'Gesalbten' den von Gott erwählten und gesandten *eschatologischen
Heilbringer und Erlöser....*"

understand which hopes of salvation the people represented in these writings had.

ENOCH—THE DOCUMENT AND THE PERSON

Any interpretation of 1 Enoch evokes a number of methodological questions. After all, we are dealing with a composite work, a collection of various parts of literature that originated at different stages. This poses the literary question of how the parts were assembled and woven together into a whole. What were the inner dynamics behind or within this corpus? How is the intratextuality of 1 Enoch to be assessed?[8] Furthermore and closely related, what is going on intertextually? 1 Enoch picks up several basic ideas from Daniel and is also related to some prophets and to some apocryphal writings.[9] With Qumran there is even more than a kinship of ideas, as most of the material was transmitted by the Dead Sea community—with the very exception of the Similitudes. Parallel to the literary history of the Corpus Enochicum there is the historical setting of the various parts which span a period of more than two, if not up to three centuries. It is one thing to relate the parts to the situations where they originated, at least as far as some clarity about it can be achieved. This is what we usually meet in the studies on 1 Enoch, viz. connections to the Seleucid and/or later circumstances as reflected in the documents. Another thing, however, is to read 1 Enoch as a whole, as an end product in its own shape and capacity. This means interpreting 1 Enoch from a redaction-critical vantage point, not just as a series of separate events and texts. 1 Enoch presents itself as an accumulation of experiences throughout a critical phase of Israel's history, worth of being assembled at a certain point of that history for future insight. Raising such questions is, of course, easier than answering them. We simply know hardly anything about the genesis of 1 Enoch as a literary product, in general or its redaction, its final author, compiler or editor and the circumstances.

---

[8] This is what stands behind Nickelsburg's formulation that "the messianic figure of the Parables assumes functions . . ." (above, p. 61).

[9] Cf., on a range of motifs: George W.E. Nickelsburg, *Resurrection, Immortality, and Eternal Life in Intertestamental Judaism* (Cambridge, 1972); on the relation to Dan. 7; Isa. (11; 42; 52–53) and SapSal 4–5, Nickelsburg in "Salvation," pp. 58–61. Suter, op. cit., emphasizes the (as he argues, oral) influence of Isa. 24:17–23 upon the Parables.

Nevertheless, two rather general vantage points can be established. One is the probable time of the final redaction, taking us sometime into the later first century c.e. It has been a matter of scholarly debate whether 1 Enoch presupposes the destruction of Jerusalem and the temple in 70 c.e. In any case, there is a difference from writings as 4 Ezra and 2 Baruch (or SyrBaruch). They are clearly "apocalyptic responses to the fall of Jerusalem."[10] They are troubled by the questions of why and whither, in particular that of theodicy: how could God possibly permit the destruction of what was dearest to his covenant people?[11] The burning question in 1 Enoch is not theodicy, trying to tackle evil experiences attributed to divine permission or even action. 1 Enoch as a whole is a product of late Second Temple Judaism, reflecting Israel's problems inside and outside. 1 Enoch mirrors the strife for identity and survival which Israel had to face ever since the rise of Hellenism as a cultural power,[12] soon joined by political domination, in particular from the Seleucids and the Romans. It was a period of uncertainties and unrest,[13] with a number of internal frictions and groups. 1 Enoch, having its historical roots in virtually all the phases of that development, thus encompasses a whole tradition of oppression and resistance, of despair and hope. A redaction-critical reading then takes the text as a deliberately collected record of experience and advice. Such an interpretation will try to pay adequate attention to the social implications, reading the text as a manifest of Israel's heritage and hope in a time of crisis.

The second vantage point is the figure of Enoch himself. It is he that unites the different parts;[14] his name is the common denominator of the material. What does Enoch stand for in Jewish tradition of

---

[10] As Nickelsburg puts it (*Jewish Literature*, pp. 280 ff.).

[11] Cf., ibid., p. 280; Egon Brandenburger, *Die Verborgenheit Gottes im Weltgeschehen. Das literarische und theologische Problem des 4. Esrabuches* (Zurich, 1981, especially pp. 148 ff. (and the critical comments by Eckhard Rau, "Kosmologie, Eschatologie und die Lehrautorität Henochs. Traditions- und formgeschichtliche Untersuchungen zum äth. Henochbuch und zu verwandten Schriften" [Diss. Hamburg] 1974, pp. 28 f.).

[12] Cf., Nickelsburg, *Commentary*, pp. 62 ff.: Social contexts, starting with "Antipathy to Hellenistic Culture."

[13] This certainly holds true also for the years leading up to the Jewish Revolt in 66 c.e., even if Josephus in his account of what led to the war is one-sided in giving his own interpretation, as James S. McLaren presumes: *Turbulent Times? Josephus and Scholarship on Judaea in the First Century c.e.* (Sheffield, 1998).

[14] This pertains also to the sections where his name is not directly mentioned.

that time? According to the basic biblical text, Gen. 5:24, the aspects of Enoch's righteousness, i.e. his conduct of life, and of his being taken up to heaven make him outstanding.[15] A closer look shows that, for 1 Enoch, it is actually not Enoch's proper life on earth, but his virtually angelic status that account for his importance.[16] He is not a paradigm for human behavior. Rather, his very being indicates a higher dimension; and this is what makes him, together with his (alleged) literary heritage, significant for Israel.

1 Enoch's Situation of Origin

1 Enoch originated in a time when Israel found itself torn into different directions. Israel's very identity was at stake. The challenge of Hellenistic culture threatened to up-root the religious, educational, ethical and social traditions.[17] One of the remarkable phenomena is the rise of quite a few "sects," reflecting the general strife for and uncertainty of orientation.[18] Several groups actually withdrew from the rest of Israel, claiming to lead the right direction. Among them we find the Qumranites, Enoch's kinship after all.[19] The Early Christian period put the issues even sharper. Who was the legitimate heir of the sacred history and its promises?[20] Who represented the "true" Israel, implying the notion of an "untrue" or even fallen Israel? Since early Maccabean times the Jerusalem temple cult and personnel had

---

[15] Cf., Uhlig, op. cit., pp. 466 f.: "Die Henochgestalt wird in der jüdischen Literatur zum Typus des Gerechten, der gemeinsam mit anderen Erzvätern bei der Offenbarung des eschatologischen Heils vom Himmel her erscheint, ja häufig wird ihm als Prototyp des Himmelsbewohners eine singuläre, quasi engelgleiche Stellung zuerkannt . . ." (p. 466); Collins, op. cit., p. 124.

[16] Cf., Collins, op. cit., pp. 123 f.

[17] Cf., Martin Hengel, *Judentum und Hellenismus. Studien zu ihrer Begegnung unter besonderer Berücksichtigung Palästinas bis zur Mitte des 2. Jh.s v. Chr.* (Tübingen, 1988).

[18] Albert I. Baumgarten, *The Flourishing of Jewish Sects in the Maccabean Era: An Interpretation* Leiden, 1997), draws attention to the astonishing fact that, unusual in Israel's history, so many "sects" (on the term cf., pp. 5 ff.)—"Sadducees, Pharisees, Qumran, Fourth Philosophy, and the followers of John the Baptist or of Bannus" (11)—came up. Baumgarten himself pursues the lines into the first century C.E.; hence we may well add "the followers of Jesus" to his enumeration.

[19] Some desert-theology (cf., Isa. 40) evidently played a role as well, as in the case of John the Baptist.

[20] This question became vital not only between Jews and Christians (e.g., in Paul and Matthew), but even in Qumran's position over against those not in the "true covenant" (cf., 1 QS et al.).

fallen into discredit for some. Even as early as Daniel the impacts of such insights were felt.[21] "Israel" as such seemed no longer to be a clear marker of salvation history. Moreover, Israel's role over against the nations had been blurred. With Daniel a completely new phase of expectations began, different from what had been believed so far; hope now lies beyond, not within, history. Salvation receives a transcendent dimension.[22] A renewed interest in prophecy[23] and wisdom "from above" arose in the apocalyptic movement, which came up in that period and characterized it to a large extent.[24] The hardships and trials (as they were understood) of the time necessitated a re-interpretation of history.

1 Enoch mirrors these developments in several regards. The distinction between Jews and Gentiles is not a topic of importance for him.[25] The lines of distinction can no longer been drawn neatly. Moreover, apocalypticism widens the perspective towards the world in its entirety, not just the traditional, visible world, but creation in its manifold dimension. There is more to say about world and history; there is a more important, decisive dimension, a transcendent world. The real music is played in heaven, as it were. Enoch himself is/became a part of that transcendent world, being able to communicate what otherwise remains invisible and a secret.

It is conspicuous that in the apocalyptic movement the great figures of the very early history receive supreme significance. History as such has to be revisited and reviewed from its very beginnings.[26] The scope of history reaches beyond the here and now into the eschaton.[27] The secrets of the future are connected with those of the beginnings, indicating the correlation between Urzeit and Endzeit. This implies, e.g., that the problem of sin and the scope of judgment can be uncovered adequately only by receiving insight into the primordial

---

[21] Karlheinz Müller, "Erlösung im Judentum," in Ingo Broer and Jürgen Werbick, eds., *"Auf Hoffnung hin sind wir erlöst" (Röm 8,24). Biblische und systematische Beiträge zum Erlösungsverständnis heute* (Stuttgart, 1987), pp. 11–41, especially 19.

[22] Müller, op. cit., pp. 15 ff.

[23] Cf., Rau, op. cit., pp. 452 f.

[24] Cf., Uhlig, op. cit., pp. 491 f., on the "Trägerkreise" of 1 Enoch's tradition.

[25] Cf., Collins, op. cit., p. 117.

[26] So, e.g., in the Animal Apocalypse 85–100 (Nickelsburg, *Salvation*, above, p. 69). Cf., Uhlig, op. cit., pp. 492 f. on "Geschichtsdeutung."

[27] Cf., Müller, op. cit., pp. 20 f.: for the first time we observe "eschatology" (strictly spoken) in Israel.

time which becomes transparent for the eschaton.[28] The present aeon
will be ended and followed by a new one of supreme quality. The
decisive question becomes now how to gain a share in the coming
world/aeon (which is identical with hope for "eternal life"). 1 Enoch
provides an impressive example of this mentality. Since history and
future appear in a new light, the way to salvation, to a blissful future
becomes a new issue. Apparently it is not just (or no longer) sufficient
to "listen to Moses and the prophets"; rather, "if someone of the
dead would come to them, they would repent" (as Luke 16:29 f. puts
it). Revelation, orientation from above and beyond is deemed necessary. It seems that adhering to the Mosaic covenantal law is no
longer a safe enough ground for the future.[29] The cultic performance
at the Jerusalem temple had long become insufficient in the eyes of
some "true believers." What hope then is there for Israel? Who
would show the way? "Wisdom" receives a new notion during this
time; the focus lies on divine, transcendent, revealed wisdom.[30] It is
no wonder that Enoch's revelatory role fills a great deal of the writings.[31] "Seers" such as Enoch provide the wisdom, the transcendent
insight necessary to find the way towards salvation, in times of oppression as well as of confusion and irritation.[32] All of this results in a
qualitative shift both regarding the problems and the solution.

Righteousness and the Role of the Exalted Figure as Judge

The understanding of righteousness and the transcendent figures
(including their mutual relation and their function) have been the
focus of several studies—by Nickelsburg and by others. It will suffice
here to summarize the salient observations, in order to provide a
basis for our own conclusions.

---

[28] Nickelsburg, *Salvation*, above, pp. 65–66 on 1 Enoch 12–16.
[29] Remarkably enough, the Similitudes make no reference to keeping the law:
Collins, op. cit., pp. 117, 124 f. Moreover, the equation between wisdom and law
is not discernible; ibid., p. 118.
[30] Cf., 1 Cor. 2:6 ff.; James 3:17 f.
[31] Cf., Nickelsburg, *Salvation*, above, p. 81; Zimmermann, op. cit., pp. 179 f. (in
connection with 4Q534 line 8).
[32] Cf., Nickelsburg, *Salvation*, above, p. 69: "The corpus as a whole is a deposit
of revealed wisdom directed to the people of the end-time, providing the divine
means to endure judgment and to receive salvation."

(1)   As John Collins points out, "the picture of the righteous ones can be filled out from the frequent descriptions of their opponents."[33] Righteousness thus is primarily conceived of via negativa. Viewed from a social scientific perspective, the urgent problem is unrighteousness. The pervasive focus on judgment in 1 Enoch (to which we shall return) testifies to this assessment. Evil seems to prevail; it manifests itself in all kinds of wickedness, most of all though in violent oppression. Not only the character of evil is of interest for 1 Enoch, but also its origin; only the two together reveal the nature of evil and hence also that of salvation and, by contrast, of righteousness. The origin of evil is uncovered by references to Gen. 6:1 ff. (1 Enoch 1 ff., especially 6–16;[34] 86–87). Evil's source is the in-breaking of transcendent powers into the human world; hence it is beyond human capacity to resolve it.[35] The root of evil is rebellion against God.[36] Evil manifests itself very much as "oppression and murder of the righteous."[37] "The primordial giants are prototypes of warriors in the author's time."[38] Righteousness then, on the other hand, has its core in an attitude of belief and trust.[39] Such an attitude is based in and supported by wisdom as revealed from above, including "belief in a heavenly world and eschatological judgment."[40] The righteous people are thus identical with the faithful and insightful.

(2)   There are several names given to the transcendent figure (in the Similitudes):[41] "the Chosen One" (39:6; 40:5, et al.),[42] "Son of Man/One like a Man" (46:2–4, et al., in absolute form 62:7; 69:27), "the Righteous One" (38:2; 53:6) and "the Anointed One" (48:10;

---

[33] Collins, op. cit., p. 117. Cf., 116 ff. (on "righteousness and faith") in connection with the "Son of Man" in the Similitudes. Neither the statements about the righteousness of the Son of Man nor about the human righteous ones "provide a clear model of conduct" (p. 116).

[34] Cf., Uhlig, op. cit., p. 506.

[35] Cf., Nickelsburg, *Salvation*, above, p. 64: "The real perpetrators of evil are not flesh and blood, but principalities and powers . . . Since evil derives from supernatural sources, it must be overcome by divine intervention."

[36] Cf., Collins, op. cit., p. 117.

[37] Nickelsburg, *Salvation*, above, p. 67 on 22:5–7.

[38] Nickelsburg, *Salvation*, above, p. 63 with reference to chaps. 6–11.

[39] Collins, op. cit., pp. 118 f.

[40] Ibid., p. 119.

[41] Full information is found in Nickelsburg, *Salvation*, above, p. 73, n. 23.

[42] Cf., Zimmermann, op. cit., pp. 195–199, on election. 203: The 'Chosen One' in 4Q534 is "als zukünftige messianische Gestalt . . . gewissermaßen *Henoch redivivus*. . . ."

52:4). The names/titles are derived from Daniel 7 (Son of Man) and
Deutero-Isaiah (the Chosen/Righteous One).[43] In 1 Enoch the names
are used interchangeably,[44] although they never occur in combination.[45] "On the level of function we are dealing with one latter-day
figure or with one messiah."[46] Oegema follows Theisohn's analysis
that this figure is "the Judge sitting on the/his throne of glory" and
"will punish the wicked and reward the righteous."[47] The primary
function of that "figure" is judging.[48] With regard to 1 Enoch as a
whole, the agents of judgment are rather wide-spread: Judgment can
happen by self-destruction (10:9.12; 100:1 f.), heavenly means and
agents (10:13; 103:5 ff.), in particular angels (88:1–3; 62:11; 90:20 ff.;
100:4a; 102:3), even by the righteous ones (in a holy warfare 95:3
et al.;[49] the mighty ones and other sinners will be delivered into the
hands of the righteous 38:5; 48:9; 91:12), but also by God himself
(1–5; 90:13 ff.; 100:4b; 102:1). In parts other than the Similitudes,
Enoch himself is commissioned to announce judgment upon the evil
watchers (12–16). Enoch's relation to the exalted "figure" of the
Similitudes has been a long debated issue anyway.[50] 70:1 and 71:24
suggest an identification, although this might be secondary.[51] In any
case, "it is clear that 'that son of man' refers to Enoch in his exalted
state. . . . For all practical purposes he is treated as a heavenly being."[52] This is totally in line with what we noted about Enoch's role

---

[43] Cf., Nickelsburg, *Salvation*, above, p. 73; Oegema, op. cit., pp. 114 f.

[44] Nickelsburg, *Salvation*, above, p. 79 speaks of a "conflation."

[45] Oegema, op. cit., p. 142. Attempts made in former times, to conclude from
the different titles to a distinction of sources, are no longer pursued today; cf., Uhlig,
op. cit., p. 573.

[46] Oegema, op. cit., p. 142; similarly Collins, op. cit., pp. 112 f.

[47] Oegema, op. cit., p. 141. Johannes Theisohn, *Der auserwählte Richter. Untersuchungen
zum traditionsgeschichtlichen Ort der Menschensohngestalt der Bilderreden des äthiopischen Henoch*
(Göttingen, 1975).

[48] Collins, op. cit., p. 113; Oegema, op. cit., p. 142; Zimmermann, op. cit., pp.
198 f. (on 4Q534).

[49] Cf., Nickelsburg, *Salvation*, above, p. 68.

[50] See the discussion in Collins, op. cit., pp. 119–124. Stefan Schreiber, "Henoch
als Menschensohn. Zur problematischen Schlußidentifikation in den Bilderreden des
äthiopischen Henochbuches (äthHen 71,14)," in *ZNW* 91 (2000), pp. 1–17.

[51] Collins, op. cit., pp. 122 f., because chap. 71, an "epilogue," seems to be a
later addition. Matthew Black, *The Book of Enoch or 1 Enoch* (Leiden, 1985), p. 250,
asks: "Do chapters 70–71 come from a different source, perhaps an even older
tradition?"

[52] Collins, op. cit., p. 123.

in general.[53] The exalted, transcendent figure thus stands in a double allegiance. On the one hand, he participates virtually in God's
prerogatives as the final judge. The scenery is predominantly that of
the heavenly throne-/court-room and council.[54] On the other hand,
the righteous ones, i.e. human beings, function as agents of judgment as well. This position "in between" has caused quite some discussion and reflection.[55]

THE RELATIONAL POSITION OF THE EXALTED FIGURE

What is the relation of the exalted figure to the people (the righteous, the "true" Israel)? This question cannot be separated, of course,
from the other relation, viz. to God. How is the double allegiance
best explained? Several categories have been suggested and discussed.
"Corporate personality" does not do enough justice to the distinction between the exalted figure and the earthly community.[56] An
important aspect of that difference, as emphasized by Collins et al.,
is the fact that, although the exalted figure (the Son of Man) "stands
parallel to the persecuted community," "there is no suggestion that
he suffers or dies."[57] Nickelsburg used the category "champion of
the righteous," who in "a single judgment of a broader scope . . . judges
their enemies."[58] Later he added: "The Chosen One is not only their
heavenly champion and vindicator. He will be their companion in
the eternal life that is now bestowed on them."[59] In this perception,
the relation between the exalted figure and the people exceeds a
certain decisive act and moment (i.e., judgment); rather, it receives
a lasting and quite personal character. The exalted figure renders
more than resolving a problem (i.e., evil); he appears to be something like a friend in personal terms. His very presence is of importance. Oegema's description is more oriented towards the relation
of the exalted figure to God. He quotes and adopts Colpe's view:

---

[53] See above, above, p. 88.
[54] Oegema op. cit., pp. 140 ff.; Nickelsburg, *Salvation*, above, p. 70.
[55] An overview is found in Collins, op. cit., pp. 112–116.
[56] Ibid., pp. 113 f.; cf., p. 120.
[57] Ibid., p. 115. Likewise Nickelsburg, *Resurrection*, p. 86: "References to the past
suffering of the exalted one are deleted."
[58] Nickelsburg, *Resurrection*, p. 83, concerning the Similitudes.
[59] Nickelsburg, *Salvation*, above, p. 77.

"'One Like a Man' symbolizes . . . a personified idea of an eschato-logical and liberating act of God in history." As an analogy he refers to vassal kings; "the 'One Like a Man' and his relation to the Most High as a representative might thus have been modeled on the reli-gio-political balance of power."[60] The term "representative" is used also by Collins, in both directions though (to God and to the people), which is more to the point. He adopts the category "repre-sentative unity" from Mowinckel, but then moves on: "A closer analogy is found with the patron deities of nations in Near Eastern mythology." He then binds the two concepts together as follows: "These deities have a representative unity with their peoples, although they are distinguished from them."[61] Collins further speaks of "heav-enly counterparts" and "Doppelgänger."[62] The Son of Man "sym-bolizes the destiny of the righteous community both in its present hiddenness and future manifestation." Moreover, "the fact that he is preserved from their sufferings makes him a figure of pure power and glory and an ideal embodiment of the hopes of the persecuted righteous."[63]

All these observations and deliberations indicate that the triangle relationship between God, the exalted figure and the people is both an important and touchy issue. There is a "parallelism of action, or 'structural homologue' between the earthly and heavenly counter-parts."[64] On the one hand, the exalted figure is closely related to the righteous people. "His entire function is defined in relation to the human righteous ones."[65] There need not be such a figure unless righteous people were suffering from oppression and similar evils. No judgment would be necessary without the existence of evil. The exalted figure as such, however, is beyond the reach of evil. He is untouched and untouchable by sin as well as by persecution, suffering and death. He is a transcendent figure, after all. On the other hand, he shares in divine power and status, as he belongs to the heavenly throne- and court-room. He represents God's concern for the peo-ple. God as such could do without such a representative. The most

---

[60] Oegema, op. cit., p. 71.
[61] Collins, op. cit., p. 114.
[62] Ibid., pp. 114, 116.
[63] Ibid., p. 116.
[64] Ibid., p. 115.
[65] Ibid., p. 113, quoting 48:4 f.; 62:14.

appropriate category for the double allegiance thus seems to be "representation" including the element of "mediation." The exalted figure represents the righteous community on high as well as God to the people, primarily conveying the hopes in one direction and the promises in the other. One is almost inclined to use later Christian terminology in Christology, speaking of a two-natures-doctrine.[66] Differing from Christology, however, the exalted figure in Enoch does not participate in "flesh and blood" and suffering (to use the language of Heb. 2; 4–5). He is a superior figure throughout. He is a figure of identification, to some extent. For the righteous ones, he is a kind of higher ego, human existence beyond evil and tribulation. At the same time he is identified as the saving power of God; the predominant frequency of the title "the Chosen One" indicates the divine initiative. The exalted figure then is indeed primarily a functionary.[67] He is not really a person of his own. Even the virtual identification with Enoch of old does not provide him a human face. He is not a paradigm for conduct on earth. Enoch's significance is that he went "beyond," that he became a transcendent figure, revealing heavenly insights to the righteous.

Salvation

What then is salvation according to 1 Enoch?[68] Two aspects seem to be decisive in my understanding.

(1) Judgment is a central element from the very first parts (12–16) onward. We noticed already that evil is located in a transcendent dimension, beyond human reach. This means that the world, as it is, is in disorder; a foreign element (viz. evil) entered it and makes it a *mixtum compositum*. Creation is no longer "good" throughout, as it was at the beginning. It needs a transcendent initiative and act to

---

[66] Cf., also the Christology in Hebrews: Christ became the leader of his "brothers" on earth (probably Moses typology); but he remained free from sin. As a sinless high priest he is able to offer sacrifices once for all. Thus he is taking care of his people and he is above them at the same time.

[67] Cf., above, p. 85.

[68] Nickelsburg, *Commentary*, pp. 41 f., describes salvation according to 1 Enoch as "The Resolution of its Dualisms," both "in the Future; When God Intervenes" and "in the Present: Bridging the Dualisms through Revelation to the Community of the Righteous and Chosen."

overcome evil and to restore righteousness itself and the conditions
for a righteous existence, without being attacked by sin and sinners
all the time. The very fact of evil makes judgment inevitable, in
order to remove it. Judgment in 1 Enoch moves in the direction of
a clear separation between right and wrong, good and evil. This is
the decisive factor. It is not in the first place the element of relief,
reward or liberation (we shall take this up later). Rather, judgment
means having the world set straight again, cleansing it from all that
restrains righteousness.[69]

A peculiar re-occurring notion is the rejection of intercession for
sinners (13:1–14:7; 38:6), from whomsoever it may come, possibly
even from angels (14:4).[70] The judgment is irreversible (91:19; 94:7–10;
100:1 ff.; 103:8)[71] and needs to be so. Hence a clear separation from
the wicked is imperative for the righteous (104:5).[72] A stern rigorism
is Enoch's program in this regard. In terms of social science, it
appears as though all attempts of practical compromises with wickedness and wicked people were to be blocked on the readers' side.
The righteous will be able to live without sin. "And then the chosen ones will receive wisdom, and they will live and sin no more,
neither because of forgetting their duties nor of conceit; rather, those
who are wise will be humble" (5:8).[73] "They will not be condemned
throughout their lives, and they will not die . . ." (5:9). Salvation thus
is the removal of evil from the world, brought about by the inex-
orable judgment. Righteousness will be restored unhindered to its
fullness. The world will no longer be a *mixtum compositum*; rather, it
will be purified and thoroughly good.

---

[69] Nickelsburg, *Commentary*, pp. 49 f.: "What is important and central is that God
does act as judge to set the world right." Similarly Zimmermann, op. cit., p. 198,
on 4Q534: The 'Chosen One' is exalted on a heavenly throne, in order to exert
then—as the personified wisdom—the eschatological judgment on the world, "die
Gerechtigkeit Gottes im gesamten Kosmos durchzusetzen und dadurch die Ordnung
der (in Weisheit geschaffenen) Schöpfung wiederherzustellen."

[70] Cf., Uhlig, op. cit., p. 537, note on v. 4b; on the text Black, op. cit., p. 145.
Nickelsburg, *Commentary*, p. 253: "The finality and eternal duration of the heavenly
verdict is emphasized by threefold repetition."

[71] Cf., Uhlig, op. cit, p. 493.

[72] Nickelsburg, *Commentary*, pp. 529 f. on vv. 4–5 refers to the "juxtaposition of
the exhortative formula [scil. Take courage] and the reference to hopelessness."

[73] Nickelsburg, *Commentary*, p. 159, translates 5:8a: "Then wisdom will be given
to all the chosen; and they will all live, And they will sin no more through godlessness or pride. In the enlightened man there will be light, and in the wise man,
understanding."

(2) What else is said in 1 Enoch about salvation? The book says surprisingly little about the resurrection of the dead. The issue is intimately connected with that of judgment.[74] The section 50:1–51:5[75] indicates only that earth and underworld (and even hell) will give back what they received. "And he (the Lord of the Spirits) will select the righteous and holy ones from among them . . . that they be saved" (51:1f.). Resurrection in this case is a prerequisite to the final judgment.[76] Such a "neutral" concept of resurrection comes close to Dan. 12. "For Daniel, resurrection has a judicial function. Daniel 12:1 foretells the coming judgment, in which . . . will be . . . a division made between the righteous and wicked of Israel."[77] But there is another aspect to resurrection as well. Daniel also knows of the particular problem of the unjust deaths of the righteous; the solution was taken from Isaiah 26: God's creative power would bring about new conditions in which the faithful would live in the bliss of paradise.[78] Likewise, 1 Enoch 102:6–11 (a passage that reminds of 1 Cor. 15:14 ff., especially v. 32)[79] refutes the unbelievers' skepticism about the fate of the righteous, as expressed in the question "And how will they rise, and what shall they see forever?" (102:8).[80] In this case, resurrection is a reward for the righteous, different from 52:1 where it is a neutral pre-stage for the judgment. With regard to the resurrection of the righteous, a difference from Daniel should be noted. In 1 Enoch 94–104 (the Book of Visions) resurrection is an answer "to

---

[74] Nickelsburg, *Commentary*, p. 49: "Resurrection is an aspect and function of the great judgment in all the major sections of 1 Enoch," with reference to chaps. 22, 25, 51, 61, 90:32, 102:4–103:8, 108: "the righteous and pious who grieve in Sheol over the unjust circumstances of their deaths [more on 102:4–5, cf., pp. 518 f., comment WP] will be raised to divine blessing, while the wicked who died unrequited will descend to fiery torment."

[75] Uhlig, op. cit., p. 592, superscribes it "Wandlung, Auferstehung und Trennung im Gericht."

[76] Cf., also the phrase "who do not sleep" in 39:12 f.; 40:2; 41:12.

[77] Nickelsburg, *Resurrection*, p. 23. "This resurrection is in the service of judgment."

[78] Ibid., pp. 22 f.

[79] Nickelsburg, ibid., p. 144, entitles 102:4–104:8 "Judgment and Resurrection."

[80] According to the text given by Uhlig, op. cit., p. 735. Nickelsburg, Resurrection 117 follows a variant reading: "From now on will they rise and be saved?" In Commentary 511 he translates 102:8a: "Henceforth let them arise and be saved, and they shall forever see <the light>." Cf., Uhlig's 735 note on v. 8a. Isaac, op. cit., renders: "What will they receive or what will they see forever?" Black, op. cit., p. 96: "Hereafter shall they be saved and rise from the dead, and see (the light) for ever'?" The translation by Michael A. Knibb, "1 Enoch," in H.F.D. Sparks, ed., *The Apocryphal Old Testament* (Oxford, 1984), pp. 169–319, was not at my disposal.

the problem of suffering and oppression, even when it has not resulted
in death" (as is the case in Daniel).[81] 1 Enoch thus treats the issue
on a more general level, not directly on that of martyrology. This
indicates a change in his community's experience and outlook. He
does know the aspects of relief, reward and liberation (as we noticed
before). The "holy book" contains "that everything good and the joy
and honor for your spirits that died in righteousness . . . will be given
to you as a recompense for your travail" (103:2 f.). The righteous
"will shine like the light of heaven" and "will have joy like the angels
in heaven" (104:2–4); they will be free from eternal judgment (104:5).
They will even participate in the judgment upon the oppressors, as
we recorded. The general emphasis in 1 Enoch though is not on these
aspects, even not on resurrection as a reward. Resurrection is more
a transition. Its setting is, in any case, the problem of evil, whether
it enables the judgment of all or the liberation of the righteous.

The main promise for the righteous ones, and hence the primary
content of salvation, in 1 Enoch is that an eternal dwelling place
will be given to them.[82] The evidence is abundant. "And I saw
another vision: the dwelling places of the holy ones and the resting
places for the righteous. Here my eyes saw their dwelling places with
the angels of his righteousness and their resting places with the holy
ones . . ." (39:4 f.). "And I saw a dwelling place underneath the wings
of the Lord of the Spirits . . . There I wanted to dwell . . ." (39:7 f.).
Similarly 41:2, where Enoch again sees the "dwelling places of the
chosen ones and the homes[83] of the holy." The second Similitude is
about those "who denied the name of the dwelling place of the holy
ones and the Lord of the Spirits . . . On that day my Chosen One
will sit on the throne of glory, and he will choose from their works,
and their places of rest will be numerous . . ."[84] (45:1–3). "And they
will shine in the times that will be numerous, for the judgment of

---

[81] Nickelsburg, *Resurrection*, p. 124.

[82] Philo knows of the motif as well, although with a quite different reference:
The souls long for their heavenly home, the city of God, now being foreigners in
the world of senses. Cf., Herbert Braun, "Das himmlische Vaterland bei Philo und
im Hebräerbrief," in Otto Böcher and Klaus Haacker, eds., *Verborum Veritas* (Wuppertal,
1970), pp. 319–327.

[83] Isaac, op. cit., "the company of the holy ones," Black, op. cit., p. 45: "the
congregations of the godly."

[84] Following Uhlig's text. Black, op. cit., p. 47 (v. 3b–c): "And he shall bring
their works to the test, There shall be no place of rest for them."

God is righteousness, because he will be faithful to the faithful in the resting place and in the paths of truth"[85] (108:13). "And they will, with that Son of Man, abide and eat and lie down and rise up forever and ever" (62:14).[86] They will be safe from the oppression of the sinners (53:7; 62:13). The wicked, on the other hand, will have no dwelling place to live (38:2), just as they made it impossible for wisdom to dwell on earth; it had to return to heaven (42:1–3). They will be pulled away from their places of rest (46:4–6). The motif of "dwelling" is pervasive both with regard to time and space. Enoch is shown the place of the chosen and righteous ones where the patriarchs and the righteous have been dwelling since ages (70:3 f.). At the eschaton the righteous ones will dwell on earth (51:5); the holy ones who dwell in the heavens will pray with one voice . . . (47:2). The "lord of the sheep" will bring "a new house, greater and loftier than the first . . . that had been removed" (90:29); that house will be a meeting place for all who "returned to the house" (90:33). Even if this last instance refers to Jerusalem,[87] the emphasis is not on the sanctuary but on the place to live in (like in Revelation 21:2 ff.).[88] Whether or not Jerusalem and the temple had been destroyed already at the time of 1 Enoch's redaction, the issue is the place where to live, to settle, to dwell, to have rest and to be free from oppression. This could indeed mirror the situation towards the end of the first century C.E., when many Jews were dispersed, exiled, expelled and enslaved. But in Israel's mentality this has been a perennial issue: the longing for Erez Yisrael. This is the hope and promise par excellence for the eschaton, as 1 Enoch conceives it. This is salvation. In this sense 1 Enoch is reflecting one Judaism, not several.

---

[85] Cf., Isaac's note, op. cit.: "He will give faith to the faithful ones in the resting place of the paths of truth." Nickelsburg *Commentary*, p. 551: ". . . and to the faithful he shows faithfulness, because they abide in the paths of truth."

[86] Isaac, op. cit.: "The Lord of the Spirits will abide over them; they shall eat and rest and rise with the Son of Man forever and ever." Cf., Collins, op. cit., p. 113.

[87] Cf., Nickelsburg, Commentary, pp. 404–406: "Reference to the house in v. 26 prepares for a major set of events that center in Jerusalem."

[88] Cf., the contributions in Beate Ego, et al., eds., *Gemeinde ohne Tempel. Community without Temple. Zur Substituierung und Transformation des Jerusalmer Tempels und seines Kults im Alten Testaments, antiken Judentum und frühen Christentum* (Tübingen, 1999).

SOME PERSPECTIVES ON EARLY CHRISTIANITY

Traditionally 1 Enoch, in particular the Parables, has been regarded as an important background, if not source, for some Early Christian motifs, most of all the concept of the "Son of Man"; also e.g. for the Epistle of Jude.[89] From our present investigation some other lines deserve attention, simply because of their affinity. They were mentioned in passing by so far and will be assembled here again.

(1)   With regard to Pauline theology, the concept of wisdom in 1 Cor. 2:6 ff. may be comparable to that in 1 Enoch, i.e., wisdom as a "mysterious" insight into history and what has to be known about the future, especially the end of times. Furthermore, as Collins suggested with great care and caution,[90] to a certain extent 1 Enoch follows a concept of salvation by faith, although not brought up as an antithesis. Similar to the discussion in 1 Cor. 15 about the "if and how" of resurrection, we registered skepticism refuted by 1 Enoch.

(2)   The element of "dwelling place" is important for the Gospel of John (especially 14:2 ff.) as well as for Rev. 21. In Heb. 3:7 ff.; 4:1 ff. the emphasis is similar, though more on the "place of rest," including Sabbath terminology (4:9).

(3)   The role of Enoch comes close to the request expressed and refuted in Luke 16:29 f. Is this enough an indication that in the Jesus tradition such writings like 1 Enoch, pretending to be "messages from beyond," found resistance and rejection?

All of these aspects are in one way or another relevant for the question of salvation, which has been the key issue in Nickelsburg's article and in this study.

---

[89] Cf., Isaac, op. cit., p. 8.
[90] Collins, op. cit., pp. 117–119.

RESPONSE TO WIARD POPKES

In responding to my paper, Wiard Popkes draws on a wide range of literature relating to many aspects of 1 Enoch, including, remarkably, my commentary, which appeared only a few months before Popkes wrote his response. He notes that "salvation" is the "constitutive element" in my paper, and "Messiah," the variant, and his purpose is to focus on what I understand by "salvation." In fact he touches on many other issues.

Popkes rightly understands (and agrees with) my position that theological formulations should be interpreted in the context of their historical situations, and he agrees that the constitutive parts of 1 Enoch were generated in a variety of historical contexts that stretched over several centuries. I agree with him that the corpus as a whole may have been assembled in the first century c.e., though, in my commentary I assign no date to this final redaction, and there is no hard evidence that the whole of 1 Enoch existed as a single corpus before the Ethiopic translation was made between the fourth to sixth centuries. The turn of the era, with the composition of the Book of Parables, offers a *terminus a quo* for the composition that that book. Since it indicates no knowledge of the events of 70, this may indicate a *terminus ad quem*.

Popkes emphasizes that the various components of 1 Enoch originated at a time when Hellenistic culture threatened to uproot Israel's religious, educational, ethical, and social traditions, and that these circumstances gave rise of a number of religious "sects" that sought to maintain the nation's identity and orientation. As a consequence, he suggests, "the distinction between Jews and gentiles is not a topic of importance for him" (the final redactor?). I would want to nuance that statement in two ways, at least as it relates to the authors of the various components of 1 Enoch. "Distinction" as such, perhaps not, but antagonism, hostility, and tension between Jews and gentiles, yes. I read the myth of Shemihazah and his rebel hosts as a reflection of the violence of the Diadochan wars. The allegory of the Animal Vision turns on the victimization of the Israelite flock by their gentile enemies. In the Book of Parables, which is the focus of my paper, the chief villains are the oppressors of the congregations

of the righteous and chosen—"the kings and the mighty," idol-wor-
shiping gentiles, probably Roman rulers and generals. Each of these
cases resembles a central concern in the Book of Daniel. This should
not obscure the fact, however, that some of the Enochic texts, in
particular, and the collection as a whole, reflect sectarian division
and are very much concerned with the question of who is the true
Israelite and what is true revelation and right Law (see below, "The
Epistle of Enoch" (pp. 000–000) and "Religious Exclusivism" (pp.
000–000). To what extent sectarian division is itself a reaction against
assimilation to Hellenism is an issue that is difficult to determine,
given the vagueness of the texts.

In re-reading my paper, I realize that though salvation is its "constitutive element," I left this word undefined—though its meaning is
implicit throughout. Gerbern Oegema, whom Popkes cites, defines
salvation as (eschatological in our texts) liberation. In similar fashion, I restrict its usage to situations in which one is saved or delivered from some evil or undesirable entity or situation; I prefer not
to use it to refer to divine beneficent action in general.[1] This usage
fits well with the various Enochic texts that I treat in the paper.
One is delivered from (demonically caused) sickness, death, oppression, cultic impurity, and the damnation that results from not living
according to revealed divine Law. In various of these respects, salvation is a function of divine judgment, which vindicates the righteous for their behavior or vis-a-vis their unjust situation and punishes
their enemies. This places the son of man/Chosen One at the center of the salvific scenario that dominates the Book of Parables.

I want to reiterate the major point of my article: the son of
man/Chosen One/Righteous One of the Parables is a heavenly figure, who assumes salvific and judicial functions that other sections
of *1 Enoch* ascribe to angelic figures and to Enoch himself. Moreover,
the Parables' description of him draws on elements found in three
sources: (1) biblical Davidic texts, (2) the Servant texts of Second
Isaiah, (3) the vision of "one like a son of man" in Daniel 7. In
addition, as I have come to see more clearly since writing this paper,
the royal messianic texts of this period (e.g., Psalms of Solomon, 2
Baruch, 4 Ezra, and some Qumran texts) and the Parables are

---

[1] I pursue this distinction in detail in chapter three of my book, *Ancient Judaism
and Christian Origins: Diversity, Continuity, and Transformation* (Minneapolis, 2003).

directed almost exclusively to situations in which the messianic figure opposes a figure of political power. This is an important consideration for any study of the highly variegated forms of NT Christology, which to not limit themselves to military scenarios and enemies who are kings and governors.

Finally, I suggest two possible modifications to my article. First, to the sources of the Parable's portrayal of its central figure, we might add the figure of heavenly Wisdom with its positing of an existence prior to the creation of the world (e.g., Prov. 8:22–31; Sir. 24:1–4; cf., 1 Enoch 48:3, 6) Second, rather than supposing that the conflation in the Parables is the work of an Enochic author or authors (above, p. 70), we might consider whether the author(s) of the Parables took over an extant conflated exegetical tradition, to which we have no prior attestation.

CHAPTER FOUR

THE EPISTLE OF ENOCH AND
THE QUMRAN LITERATURE

George W.E. Nickelsburg

The "library" of Qumran, like many literary collections, is marked by wide variety in its contents: biblical texts; previously known works of the Apocrypha and Pseudepigrapha; hitherto unknown works, both sectarian writings of Essene provenance as well as sectarian, quasi-sectarian, and non-sectarian writings of unknown provenance. These works differ, moreover, in their literary genre and their theological character (e.g., sapiential, apocalyptic). Wherein lie the principles for the assembling of such a collection? Assuming that we can identify a fair number of Essene works, why did the Qumran sectarians collect and copy the other writings found in the eleven caves? What aspects of the contents of these works made them appealing to the Qumranites? Do these aspects indicate an historical relationship between the authors and the Qumran community, or might they in some cases even indicate that these writings were of Essene provenance? Answers to these questions are complicated for many reasons. Not least, even the writings that are assuredly Essene differ in their emphases and interests and reveals considerable complexity and development in the theology and organization of the sect. Moreover, the discovery of the scrolls has demonstrated that second temple Judaism as a whole was vastly more intricate than previous constructs have allowed, and that many of the contours of that intricacy are hidden from our twentieth century vision.

These problems notwithstanding, I shall attempt here to plot some possible relationships between a writing of unknown provenance found at Qumran, and some of the Qumran Essene literature. The writing is the Epistle of Enoch (*1 Enoch* 92–105). It has long been known to us, and now we have fragments of it from two Cave 4 manuscripts.[1] In the main part of this paper I shall discuss the author of

---

[1] 4QEn^c evidently contained at least 1 Enoch 1–36; 85 (or perhaps 83)–90; the

the Epistle, his group and their religious conflict with other Jews, and the author's purpose in writing. Then I shall draw comparisons with some of the Essene Scrolls and make some suggestions about the reasons for the Epistle's inclusion in the Qumran library.

In previous studies of the Epistle, I have stressed the author's concern with socio-economic tensions between rich and poor, powerful and weak.[2] Although this opposition is the dominating and pervading one in the book, a second polarity, more purely religious in nature, is also evident. Its significance is indicated by literary considerations. Indictments of religious error and references to the wisdom of the wise are not simply sprinkled throughout the work as one of several types of criticism or praise. They occur almost exclusively in three places. They are the primary focus of one major section (98:9–99:10), where they are repeated and emphasized and belaboured. Moreover, they occur at the end of the book (104:9–105:2). Finally, the giving of wisdom to the wise is celebrated as the major eschatological event in the seventh week in the Apocalypse of Weeks (93:10; 91:11).

A. The Wise and their Erring Opponents
in the Epistle of Enoch

1. 98:9–99:10

The first passage, 98:9–99:10, is one of a series of addresses, directed to the righteous and sinners, which constitute the body of the Epistle.[3] Two factors define it as a separate unit. Different from the other addresses in the Epistle, it is concerned almost exclusively with reli-

---

Epistle; and 106–107; see J.T. Milik, *The Books of Enoch* (Oxford: Clarendon, 1976), 178–217. Of the Epistle we have only a couple of words from chs. 104–105, followed after a *vacat* by fragments of chs. 106–107. Milik asserts (ibid., 246) that 4QEn^g contained only the epistle. Problematic for this hypothesis is the fact that the preserved fragments begin in ch. 91, before the superscription of the Epistle (ch. 92) in material that, in the Ethiopic Enoch, binds the Epistle to the Dream Visions that precede it. The fragments also contain parts of chs. 92–94.

[2] 'The Apocalyptic Message of 1 Enoch 92–105,' *CBQ* 39 (1977): 309–28; 'Riches, the Rich, and God's Judgment in 1 Enoch 92–105 and the Gospel According to Luke,' *NTS* 25 (1978–79): 324–44.

[3] My determination of the limits of these units is based on features of structure and content that must await documentation in my *Hermeneia* commentary on *1 Enoch*.

gious matters rather than social issues. This content is emphasized by a pair of complementary passages that bracket the section:

Woe to you fools,
   for you will perish because of your folly.
And you do not listen to the wise;
   and good things will not happen to you,
   but evils will surround you.[4]
   ... do not hope to be saved, O sinners;
   you will depart and die. (98:9–10)

And then blessed will be all who listen to the words of the wise,
   and learn to do the commandments of the Most High;
and walk in the paths of his righteousness,
   and do not go astray with those who are straying;
for they will be saved. (99:10)

These two passages, a Woe and a Beatitude, are directed respectively to those who do *not* listen to the wise and will *not* be saved and those who *do* listen to the words of the wise and *will* be saved. The antithesis is sustained throughout the section.

Although "the wise" (*ṭabibān, phronimoi* [98:9 Gk.]; 99:10) are not identified explicitly, they are obviously of the author's own persuasion and perhaps members of his community or group or sect, if there was such. The appellative occurs seldom in chapters 92–105, although it is often implied in the term "wisdom". Here the stress is not on their wisdom *qua* righteousness (cf. 98:1), a traditional usage in wisdom literature. In focus is the fact that their words are to be listened to; they are teachers of preachers of some sort. Moreover, not to listen to them constitutes folly and results in damnation (98:9–10). The content of their teaching or preaching is in some sense necessary for salvation, i.e., deliverance from the coming judgment.[5]

The second Woe in the section explicates an aspect of the conflict between the wise and the fools (98:11). It is addressed to "the

---

[4] The text of the Epistle is preserved in the many Ethiopic mss. of *1 Enoch* [see Michael A. Knibb, *The Ethiopic Book of Enoch* (2 vols.; Oxford: Clarendon, 1978)] and in Greek in a Chester Beatty papyrus [see Campbell Bonner, *The Last Chapters of Enoch in Greek* (London: Chatto and Windus, 1937)], which begins, after several lost leaves, with 97:6. Translations here are my own and follow the Greek, where possible, with some modification based on the Ethiopic. Problematic readings are foot-noted, usually with reference to my article, 'Enoch 97–104: A Study of the Greek and Ethiopic Texts,' in Michael E. Stone, ed., *Armenian and Biblical Studies* (Sion Supp. 1; Jerusalem: St. James Press, 1976), 90–156. They are cited by reading number in that article. Here see no. 46.

[5] See Nickelsburg, 'Apocalyptic Message.'

stiff-necked and hard of heart,[6] who do evil and consume blood".
The terms "stiff-necked and hard of heart" are applied in our literature almost always to Israelites as distinguished from Gentiles.[7]
In what way or under what circumstances the addressees of this Woe
were consuming blood, or where thought to be doing so, is not clear.
Possibly the author is expressing his idiosyncratic views about what
may be eaten or under what circumstances it may be eaten. He may
be alluding to peculiar laws about slaughtering. The language of
v. 11cd may indicate a contrast between the eating of meat and a
vegetarianism that is seen to be more consonant with the divine
dispensation:

> Whence do you have good things to eat and drink and be satisfied?
> From all the good things which the Lord, the Most High, has
>   abundantly provided upon the earth.[8]

In any case, a passage like *Jubilees* 7:27–33 (cf. also *Jub.* 6:12–14;
21–6), with its elaboration of Genesis 9, indicates that the present
verse does not reflect an isolated concern.

The next two Woes, which echo the social tensions spoken of so
frequently in the body of the Epistle, are, however, the exception in
this section (98:12–13).[9]

In 98:14 the author returns, with some variations, to the theme
of his first Woe and again anticipates the concluding Beatitude:

> Woe to you who annul[10] the words of the righteous;
>   you will have no hope of salvation.

Here "(the words of) the wise" ([99:10]; 98:10) are called "the words
of the righteous". Moreover, it is not a question of *not listening* to,
but of *annulling* these words. In our literature, the verb *akuroō* occurs
with the following objects: "the word of God; covenant; commandments; ordinance",[11] and it is a legal technical term that denotes the

---

[6] See Nickelsburg, 'Texts', no. 48.

[7] Cf., e.g., Exod. 33:3, 5; 34:9; Deut. 9:6, 13: Deut. 10:16; cf. Acts 7:51.

[8] The author writes in the name of a prediluvian patriarch who lived when flesh
was forbidden to humanity. One of the sins of the giants was that they consumed
blood; cf. *1 Enoch* 7:5.

[9] The social disruptions mentioned in 99:4–5 are more a part of the tribulation
associated with the judgment than its cause.

[10] Gk attempts to soften the text and reads, "who wish to annul . . ."; see
Nickelsburg, "Texts", no. 50.

[11] Mark 7:13; Gal 3:17; Jos. *Ant.* 14.10.8 § 216. See Johannes Behm, "*kuroō*",
TDNT 3 (1965): 1099–1100.

nullification of a covenant or the disobeying or disregarding of laws and commandments. The parallel structure and wording in 98:9–10, the expression "the words of the wise" in 99:10, and other passages yet to be discussed, indicate that the author here refers to those who (teach others to) contravene the righteous ones' interpretations of the Torah, which according to the righteous themselves have the force of divine law. For this reason, the author reiterates his sentence of damnation, "you will have no hope of salvation" (cf. 98:10).

The next Woe sheds further light on the opponents:

> Woe to those who write lying words and words of error;
>> they write and lead many astray with their lies, when they hear them.
> You yourselves go astray;[12]
>> and you will have no peace but will quickly perish. (98:15–16)

Particularly noteworthy in this passage is the fourfold occurrence of vocabulary denoting falsehood: "lying words"; "words of error"; "they lead many astray with their lies"; "you yourselves go astray". This complex of expressions has a long history that runs from the Hebrew scriptures through the New Testament.

> The closest biblical parallel to the present passage occurs in Jeremiah 23:32: "Behold I am against the prophets of lying dreams, says the Lord, and they recount them and lead my people astray by their lies and their recklessness . . ." This verse is part of a long indictment against the prophets whose lies are false not only in their content but also because the prophets wrongly claim YHWH as the source of their oracles.
>
> Especially important in the Qumran Scrolls are those passages that combine the expression, "lead many astray", with references to lying and falsehood. According to 4QpNah 2:8, the interpretation of Nahum 3:4 concerns "those who lead Ephraim astray, who by their false teaching, their lying tongue, and their deceitful lips lead many astray". The context before and after this passage indicates that these seducers of Ephraim are the infamous "facile interpreters" of the Scrolls (cf. esp. 2:2). Their interpretation and teaching here almost certainly concern the Torah.[13] A second passage occurs in 4QPs[a] 1:18–19, where the interpretation of Psalm 37:7 "concerns the Man of Lies who led many astray by the words of falsehood, because they followed after vanity and did not lis[ten] to the Interpreter of Knowledge". Again, the interpretation of the Torah appears to be the issue.[14]

---

[12] Nickelsburg, "Texts", no. 30.
[13] This is supported by the frequent identification of this group with the Pharisees.
[14] Cf. especially 2:2–3 and its reference to those "who turn back to the Torah."

The apocalypses in the Synoptic Gospels employ similar terminology. In Mark 13:5–6 (//Matt 24:4–5), Jesus warns the disciples, "Beware
lest anyone lead you astray. Many will come in my name, saying, 'It
is I', and they will lead many astray". In Matthew 24:11 (//Mark
13:22),[15] he predicts that "Many false prophets will arise and lead many
astray". Here the usage is closer to Jeremiah 23:32 than to the Scrolls.
False messiahs and false prophets will speak fraudulently in the name
of God or of Jesus the Christ.

There is, then, in early Jewish and Christian literature a fixed usage
of *t*ʿ*h* and *planaō* in combination with words denoting lies and false
claims. The deceivers are of two kinds. Some wrongly claim to present the right interpretation of the Torah—sometimes in opposition
to the "true" interpretation expounded by the author's protagonist.
Others claim to be prophets who act and speak in God's name. In
both cases the essence of their erroristic activities is the false claim
that they are divinely appointed (and in the case of the prophets,
inspired) spokesmen and agents. In both the Synoptic apocalypses
and the Qumran commentaries, they are phenomena of the end-time.

In the light of these passages, the references to lies and errors in
1 Enoch 98:15–16 are open to two interpretations. The parallels in
Jeremiah and Mark and Matthew may indicate that these propaga-
tors of error claimed to be prophets. The texts from Qumran suggest that the author refers to false exegesis of the Torah. The two
interpretations need not be mutually exclusive. The opponents could
be claiming an inspired interpretation of the Torah. In any case,
the present passage refers to a written and not simply an oral phenomenon; the false teachers write down their lies. Moreover, following the typical form of the Woe, the author utters a word of
damnation against his opponents. Thus he distinguishes not between
right and wrong opinions, but between truth and falsehood that lead
either to salvation or to damnation.

The third Woe in this string (99:1) also makes reference to error
and lying, and we shall return to it below. The final Woe is especially significant and enlightening.

> Woe to you who alter the true words
>   and pervert the eternal covenant

---

[15] The verse, without precise parallel in Mark, appears to be a secondary reformulation, based on Mark 13:22, which Matthew reproduces almost verbatim in 24:24.

> and consider themselves to be without sin;[16]
> they will be swallowed up in the earth.[17] (99:2)

Here the author accuses his opponents of tampering with the Torah, "the true words" of "the eternal covenant".[18] Striking in these lines is the repetition of the idea that the opponents are attempting to alter the inalterable, words that are true or steadfast, the covenant that is eternal. This is not, moreover, a case of outright apostasy (e.g., full-blown Hellenization). The errorists do not disregard, and are not indifferent to, the Law; they claim to be guiltless. In their view, their conduct—i.e., their teaching which the author thinks *alters* the words of the Law—is *in consonance* with the Law. Thus, the wording of this passage supports our hypothesis that the author and his opponents are locked in a dispute over the interpretation of the Torah. Since he views these alternative interpretations as truthful adherence to the eternal Law and erroneous perversion of it, he announces that the erring interpreters face the same judgment that befell the sons of Korah, who rebelled against the divine ordinance that determined the structure of the Aaronite priesthood (cf. Num. 16).

Following this sequence of Woes, the author addresses the righteous, encouraging them to raise those prayers that will trigger the judgment and describing in part the social upheavals that will accompany it (99:3–5). Then he turns his attention once again to the sinners (99:6–9). Here the object of his indictment is not false teaching, but idolatry. Noteworthy is the vocabulary with which he describes idols and their worship: "errors" (v. 7); "straying" and "being led astray" (v. 8); "folly" (v. 8; cf. 98:9); and "false works" (v. 9). The terminology is traditional[19] but it is worthy of attention here because the author has used this same language to describe the false teachers. That is, their religious sin is tantamount to the mortal sin of idolatry.

The close connection between false teaching and idolatry is evident also in the Woe we previously bypassed:

---

[16] On this reading, see Nickelsburg, "Texts", 94 n. 23.

[17] Ibid., no. 31.

[18] A tendency to speak of the eternity of the Mosaic covenant and laws is evident in a number of texts from the Hellenistic period; cf. e.g., Sir 17:12; Tob 1:16; *Pss. Sol.* 10:4; *Jub.* 16:29–30; 33:16; 49:8. Cf. also *Test. Gad* 3:1 and *Test. Asher* 5:4, which appear to be interpretations of this passage and/or 104:9.

[19] See, e.g., the passages cited by Herbert Braun, "*planaō*", *TDNT* 6 (1968): 234. Also noteworthy is the tendency in the Targumim to substitute *ṭ'* and *ṭw* for other biblical words denoting idolatry; see the numerous examples cited by Jacob Levy, *Chaldäisches Wörterbuch über die Targumim* (Darmstadt: Melzer, 1966 reprint) I, 311–12.

> Woe to you who commit erring acts
>   and who by (or for) false works receive honour and glory;
> you will perish, you will have no salvation for good. (99:1)

The use of the concrete nouns, *planēmata* and *erga pseudē* (cf. 99:9),
and the cultic overtones of "honor and glory"[20] suggest that this Woe
originally referred to the making and worshipping of idols. The
author employs it here in a context that uses similar language to
describe false teaching, because such teaching is, in his view, idolatrous.

We are now in a position to understand the thrust of the Beatitude
that concludes this section (99:10). It is a blessing on those who, by
attending to the words of the wise (the Torah as this author understands it), learn what are truly "the commandments of the Most
High". Such persons do not go astray with the false teachers, but
walk in the righteous paths that God has revealed; thus they will be
saved. The contrast with 98:9–10 is clear.

This section, then, presents a full cast of characters. On the one
side are the wise, the expositors of the words of truth—the Torah
as God intended it to be interpreted and practiced. Their adherents
are the righteous. On the other side are the false teachers, whose
lying interpretations lead many astray. These teachers and those who
err with them are compared with the Gentiles who go astray after
idols. The destinies of the two groups are as different as their status and conduct and are described in the Woe and the Beatitude
that frame the section.

2. *99:12,14*

As we noted at the beginning, references to the religious infractions
of the author's opponents are not limited to 98:9–99:10. One such
reference occurs at the beginning of the next section (99:11–100:6).
Three consecutive Woes speak of people who build; two of these
use the language metaphorically (99:12,14; cf. 94:6–7). They indict
those who "lay the foundations[21] of sin and deceit" (*gweḥlut*, probably = *dolia*), and "those who reject the foundation and eternal inheritance of their fathers" and whom "a spirit of error pursues". The
foundation and eternal inheritance of the fathers is the Torah, the

---

[20] For the use of the words with respect to divine figures, cf. Ps 29:1; Dan 7:14;
1 Tim 1:17; 2 Pet 1:17, etc.
[21] See Nickelsburg, "Texts", no. 13.

eternal covenant mentioned in 99:2.[22] Rejection of this inherited con-
venantal Law is in error because it is inspired by "a spirit of error".
However, as in 99:2, the author does not refer to outright apostasy,
for in the place of the foundation of the fathers, the errorists lay
foundations of sin and deceit. Once again, in the context of allusion
to the Torah, the author sets in opposition the truth that is eternal,
and falsehood that deceives by making a pretence of being foundational for true religion.

3. *The Apocalypse of Weeks—A Scenario*

Other passages shed more light on the author and his group, as well
as the function of his writing. The theoretical framework is laid out
in the Apocalypse of Weeks (93:1–10; 91:11–17), which is most likely
a traditional piece re-used by this author.[23] Juxtaposed throughout
this sketchy recitation of history are the protagonists of good and
evil. Of interest to us here are two sets of parallels between ancient
times and end-time. The first of these past ages is the second week,
when "falsehood and violence spring up" *šqr' wḥms' ymṣḥ* 93:4). This
word-pair probably has its counterparts in the social and religious
sins portrayed so vividly in the body of the Epistle. The falsehood
and violence are judged and punished in the flood, from which the
one righteous man (Noah) is saved. The second prototypical age is
the third week, the time of Abraham (93:5). He is "chosen as a plant
of righteous law (*kwenanē ṣedeq* = *dyn qšṭ*)[24] and after him will go forth
the plant of righteousness forever". The reference is to Abraham's
election as the patriarch of God's chosen people, the eternal plant
of righteousness. The antitype of these two past ages is the author's
own time, the seventh week (93:9–10; 91:11). A completely perverse
generation arises. However,

---

[22] Cf. the same usage in CD 1:13–18, also in the context of falsehood and
straying.

[23] The idea has often been suggested. See most recently, Ferdinand Dexinger,
Henochs Zehnwochenapokalypse und offene Probleme der Apokalyptikforschung (SPB 29; Leiden:
Brill, 1977), 102. An indication of different authorship may be the absence in the
rest of the Epistle of the concept of election, which is so central to the Apocalypse.

[24] The indicated Ethiopic-Aramaic equivalence occurs in 91:12 (cf. 4QEn^g 1 4:16;
Milik, *Books of Enoch*, 266). The expression is normally translated "righteous judgment", which is correct in 91:12. Dexinger (*Zehnwochenapokalypse*, 178) correctly suggests "rechte Satzung" here. Although his method is flawed by retroversion to
Hebrew *mšpṭ* rather than Aramaic (ibid., 150–64), there is Aramaic evidence to support the translation; cf. Mur 20 ar 3 and, evidently, Tob 7:13.

At its (the week's) conclusion, the elect will be chosen
    as witnessess of righteousness from the eternal plant of righteousness,
    to whom will be given sevenfold wisdom and knowledge.
And they will uproot the foundations of violence (*ḥms'*)
    and the structure of falsehood (*šqr'*) in it,
    to execute judgment.[25] (93:9–10, 91:11)

The parallelism between the end-time and the two previously mentioned ages is clear. The author's own time is marked by "violence
and deceit", as was the generation of the flood. When God's judgment comes, the righteous will be saved, as Noah was saved. They
will be chosen, as Abraham was (from the midst of idolatrous
Babylon?).[26] Their status as the chosen parallels that of Abraham
and designates them as the true Israel. The means to their salvation
is their endowment with full wisdom and knowledge, however the
author of the Apocalypse understood these terms. The purpose of
this wisdom is to equip the elect as witnesses of righteousness or
truth (*qšṭ*). In this capacity they will uproot the violence of the wicked
and the falsehood of those who deceive.

    This judgment is followed in the eighth week by a second judg-
ment, in which "all the righteous" will wield the sword of the Lord
against "all the wicked". Then the eschatological temple will be built
(91:12–13). In the ninth week the scope widens. "Righteous law[27]
will be revealed to all the sons of the whole earth", all wickedness
will vanish from the whole earth, "and all humankind will look to
the path of eternal righteousness" (91:14).[28]

4. *104:9–12—A Final Word*

Against the background of this eschatological scenario, we may view
the author's final words on his opponents and his own group. To
the sinners he says,

Do not err in your hearts, nor lie,
    nor alter the words of truth
    nor falsify the words of the Holy One,
    nor give praise to your errors (*ṭa'ot*).[29]

---

[25] Translation follows 4QEn^g 1 4:12–14 (Milik, *Books of Enoch*, 265).
[26] This allusion to Babylonian idolatry is suggested by the pattern evident in
93:4,8; see Nickelsburg, 'Apocalyptic Message', 314.
[27] See above, no. 24.
[28] Translations follow 4QEn^g 1 4:19–22 (Milik, *Books of Enoch*).
[29] Gk is fragmented here and in the rest of the verse. For the equivalence of

> For not to righteousness do all your lies lead,
> and all your errors, but to great sin. (104:9)

The wording of this passage closely parallels that of 99:2, although "the words of truth" are here identified with "the words of the Holy One" rather than the eternal covenant. But the point is the same: the false teachers are tampering with divine truth. Moreover, as in the earlier passages, this error is spoken of as if it were idolatry (cf. 99:1). The end result is "great sin", either blasphemy of God's truth or the equivalence of idolatry.

Pseudo-Enoch, the prediluvian patriarch, issues this warning precisely because he knows the divine "mystery" of what will happen in the end-time:

> that sinners will alter and copy the words of truth,
> and pervert many and lie and invent great fabrications,
> and compose writings in their names. (104:10)

The interpretation of this passage is open to debate, in part because of the state of the text. Milik suggests a reference to the Hellenistic historians who rewrote biblical history.[30] The present translation takes its cue from our previous interpretations of parallel passages in the Epistle. The author may be making reference to some kind of tendentious rewriting of the Torah—*similar to* the Temple Scroll or *Jubilees*—in which the errorists place in the mouth of God or his angel or Moses their own interpretation of the Torah, an exegesis that contradicts our author's interpretation and is therefore the epitome of falsehood.[31]

Pseudo-Enoch knows a second secret about the end-time, which completes the opposition familiar to us:

> that to the righteous and pious and wise
> my books *will be given* for the joy of truth and much *wisdom*;

ṭaʿot and *planēsis*, cf. 99:14. Although the Ethiopic word normally denotes an idol (see August Dillmann, *Lexicon Linguae Aethiopicae* [New York: Ungar, 1955 reprint] 1243; see also e.g., R.H. Charles, *APOT* 2, *ad. loc.*), the translation given above is suggested by the many parallels already discussed and by the occurrence of *resʿān* (= *planē*, see Nickelsburg, "Texts", 99, n. 45) at the end of the verse. The ambiguity between the two kinds of religious error led the translator to use the word for idol here.

[30] Milik, *Books of Enoch*, 50.

[31] For this interpretation of "in their names" (i.e., employing the name of God, but writing in one's own authority), see Hans Bietenhard, "*onoma*", *TDNT* 5 (1967): 259.

> yea, to them the books *will be given,*
>> and they will believe in them,
>> and in them all the righteous will rejoice and be glad,
>> *to learn* from them all *the paths of righteousness.* (104:12–13)

Over against the lying writings stand the books of Enoch, the embodiment of truth. As in the case of the Epistle, they will be a source of joy to the righteous through their message of comfort regarding vindication in the coming judgment.[32] They will also provide instruction in the paths of righteousness. Perhaps the author refers to his own exhortations to righteousness in general, or to other Enochic books about the right calendar for the observance of feasts, or to yet other Enochic literature that we no longer possess. Perhaps he refers to all of these. In any case, he sees his group as the possessors of books of wisdom and of the exposition of righteousness which offer the promise of salvation to those who accept them. Furthermore, the author has finally dropped the mask. The sevenfold "wisdom" that "will be given" to the elect in the seventh week is to be found in the books of Enoch, and in them one will "learn" to walk in "the paths of righteousness" (cf. 99:10). Thus, in the closing lines of the Epistle, the author incorporates his writing activity, and probably that of others into the eschatological scheme and predictions made earlier in the Epistle. In typical apocalyptic fashion, a pseudonymous writing attributed to the past is given a crucial function in the time of the real author, which is construed as the eschaton (cf. Dan 12:9; *Test. Mos.* 1:17).

B. The Epistle as an Appeal to Outsiders

Concerning that function, the author has a final, surprising word:

> In those days, says the Lord, they (i.e., the righteous) will summon and testify to *the sons of earth* in their *wisdom.* Instruct them, for you are their leaders and ... rewards over *all the earth.* For I and my son will join ourselves with them forever in *the paths of righteousness* in their life.[33] (105:1–2)

---

[32] See below, n. 34.

[33] The text of this passage is problematic. It is completely missing in the Chester Beatty papyrus, though probably due to homoioteleuton. The very meager evidence of 4QEn^c 5 1:20–23 indicates that it was present in the Aramaic between chs. 104

The books of Enoch, the present Epistle included, are not the private, secret property of a close group. They are part of the words of the wise which are to be listened to because they guide the hearer on the paths of righteousness that lead to salvation (cf. 99:10). When the author and his friends summon the sons of earth and testify to them in their wisdom, they fulfil the universalistic part of the eschatological scenario foretold for the ninth week, when "all the sons of the whole earth" will have "righteous law revealed to them" and will "look to the path of eternal righteousness" (91:14).

In an earlier study I argued that the Epistle was composed to exhort the righteous to faith and courage and joy in the midst of oppression.[34] The superscription of the book (92:1), and the many Exhortations sprinkled throughout, point in that direction. Nonetheless, the closing words of the Epistle suggest that the Woes against the wicked may also have been intended in part for those to whom they are actually addressed. Two other passages support this interpretation; both are related to the author's indictments of the rich sinners. The first makes self-conscious reference to the Epistle and its function:

> And the wise among men will see the truth,[35]
>> and *the sons of the earth* will contemplate these words of this epistle,
>> and they will recognize that their wealth cannot save them when iniquity collapses. (100:6)

The author expects the Epistle to be read by "the sons of the earth" (cf. 91:14; 105:1). Its message of damnation for the oppressive rich will strike home among those wise enough to perceive that they cannot take their wealth with them. Thus they will be saved from the judgment that will coincide with the collapse of the structure of wickedness erected by false teachers and violent men (cf. 91:11; 99:12–14). This same openness to the outsider is evident in chapter 101. Setting aside the form of the Woe and its announcement of swift and sudden judgment, the author appeals to the sinners:

---

and 106; see Milik, *Books of Enoch*, 206–7. Milik (ibid., 208) argues that the text was considerably shorter than the Ethiopic version translated above. His reconstruction, however, is completely hypothetical. Reference to "my son" need not be Christian, but may be an allusion to Methuselah, the tradent of Enoch's works (cf. 82:1–91:2).

[34] Nickelsburg, 'Apocalyptic Message', 325–26.
[35] Nickelsburg, "Texts", no. 18.

> So contemplate, O sons of men, the deeds of the Most High;
> and fear to do evil in his presence.[36] (101:1)

The rest of the chapter implicitly contrasts the sailors who pitch their cargo overboard to save their lives, with the sinners who tenaciously hold on to their goods and refuse to fear the wrath of the divine Judge.

In summary: the author speaks for a group of Jews who make exclusive claims for their interpretation of the Torah and who perceive as revealed wisdom the belief that an imminent judgment will separate them from those whose interpretation of the Law differs from theirs, as well as from the violent rich who oppress them. These exclusive claims notwithstanding, this is not a closed group who simply gather to comfort one another and to hurl curses on their enemies and opponents. The wise speak where they can be heard, and they testify to the truth in the hope that their message will be heeded and met with repentance. The Epistle of Enoch is part of this message and testimony and appeal.

C. Parallels in the Qumran Literature

The most obvious literary parallels between the Epistle and the Qumran literature occur in the description of the seventh week in the Apocalypse of Weeks and the descriptions of the rise of the community in CD 1 and 1QS 8. In CD 1:7–9 the repentant community, called a "planting", are the recipients of revealed knowledge and stand in opposition to the apostates, who are "blind" (cf. *1 Enoch* 93:10; 91:11; cf. 94:2). Even closer is the language of 1QS 8:4–10.

> It shall be an *eternal planting*, a house of holiness for Israel, an assembly of supreme holiness for Aaron. They shall be *witnesses to the truth* at the judgment and shall be *the elect* of good will who shall atone for the land and pay to the wicked their reward. They shall be that tried wall, that precious cornerstone (Isa. 28:16), whose foundations shall neither rock nor sway in their place . . .[37]

---

[36] Ibid., no. 55.
[37] Translation from Geza Vermes, *The Dead Sea Scrolls in English* (Harmondsworth: Penguin, ²1975), 85, slightly modified.

In addition to the italicized parallels, the building imagery is note-worthy. The quotation of Isaiah 28:16 suggests a complementarity between the Qumran community as a building and the counter-structure of violence and deceit in the Apocalypse. Isaiah 28 describes two such counterpoised structures.[38] Almost certainly we have three testimonies to a common tradition about the rise of the righteous community in the end-time. The Apocalypse differs from the two other passages in its expressed ideology. It does not use the con-version language of the Damascus Document or the priestly and cul-tic imagery of the Manual.

This last point is connected with another parallel between the Apocalypse and the Scrolls. Although the Apocalypse makes promi-nent mention of the tabernacle and Solomon's temple and its coun-terpart, the eschatological temple (93:6–8; 91:13), it is completely silent on the second temple. Instead it describes the post-Exilic period as a totally perverse generation. This strongly suggests a polemic against the second temple. Different from the Scrolls, however, the Apocalypse and the rest of the Epistle are silent on the critiques of priesthood and cult that characterize the Scrolls. Nonetheless, both the Apocalypse and the Scrolls may reflect a common, older polemic against temple and cult.[39]

Finally, as a broad terminological similarity with the Scrolls, one should note the frequent use of the concept of election (93:2,5,8,100).[40]

Because the Apocalypse of Weeks is widely viewed as a traditional piece composed independently of the Epistle, we must also seek par-allels to the Qumran literature in the body of the Epistle. Most strik-ing are the conflicts over Torah discovered in one major section of the Epistle, and the terminological resemblances with similar polemics in the Scrolls. Although this language may be traditional, the Epistle does reflect here concerns similar to those in the Scrolls.[41] Moreover, the consequences of salvation and damnation that follow from one's interpretation of the Law are reminiscent of Qumran ideology, as is

---

[38] See George W.E. Nickelsburg, 'Enoch, Levi, and Peter: Recipients of Revelation in Upper Galilee', *JBL* 100 (1981): 596.

[39] See Martin Hengel, *Judaism and Hellenism* (Philadelphia: Fortress, 1974), I, 180.

[40] Cf., e.g., 1QpHab 10:13, 1QS 8:6; and 1QH 2:13, which uses the term "the Elect of Righteousness", which parallels the similar word-pair in 93:2,10.

[41] Cf., e.g., 1QS 5:8–9; CD 1:13–18.

the expectation of an imminent judgment that will bring these rewards and punishment to pass.

Does the author of the Epistle represent a specific group constituted and organized as *the* community of the righteous? The Apocalypse of Weeks strongly suggests such an idea (93:10), but it is less clear in the rest of the Epistle. The end (104:12) appears to be an interpretation of the Apocalypse, but here and throughout, we hear nothing of "the elect" (see below). Whatever the specific constitution of the author's group, it is marked by an openness to outsiders (105:1–2 and 100:6). Such an openness parallels an early stage in the development of the Qumran community (cf. 1QS 8 and CD 4:9–12), but contrasts strikingly with commands to silence and concealment in a passage such as 1QS 9:16–17.

The militant ideology expressed both in the Apocalypse of Weeks (91:12) and in the body of the Epistle (95:3; 96:1; 98:12) provides yet another point of contact with one Qumran document, the War Scroll. Finally, the Epistle's many references to the oppression of the righteous and the abuse of riches find parallels in the opening columns of the Damascus Document (CD 1:20; 4:17).

Taken together, these similarities provide an answer to our first question. The Epistle of Enoch is in many ways compatible with the specific interests, emphases, and viewpoints expressed in various writings of Essene or proto-Essene provenance. Its presence in the Qumran library is not at all surprising.

D. The Question of Provenance

The provenance of the writing is more difficult to determine. Terminological similarities suggest common tradition,[42] although we do not know how far back these go. More important, in the Apocalypse of Weeks, the implicit attitude towards the temple and the description of the rise of the community are strong evidence for a historical connection between the author of this text and the authors of the relevant Qumran writings.

This historical connection might be described in one of three ways. Least likely, the Epistle was written in circles contemporary to the

---

[42] In addition to those discussed in the text above, see also n. 22.

Essenes. Such a hypothesis posits that a sect like the Essenes, with its emphasis on the differences that divide it from the rest of Judaism, would accept and use a writing from a similar and, hence, rival group.

A second possibility is that the Epistle is an Essene composition. This option is problematic for me because I have found in the Epistle neither the specific exegetical traditions nor the specific polemics against temple, cult, and priesthood characteristic of Qumran, nor the heightened dualism which would confirm Essene authorship.[43]

Such an argument from silence does not, of course, falsify a hypothesis of Essene authorship, but it may well point to a third possibility, viz., that the Epistle was composed in circles ancestral to the Essenes. One possibility is that the Epistle was written among the *Ḥasidim*. Such an origin might be indicated by the occurrence of the word-pair, "the righteous and the pious" (*dikaioi kai hosioi*, 103:9; 104:12; and *dikaioi/eusebeis*, 100:4–5; 102:4 Gk.).[44] The militant ideology of the Apocalypse and the Epistle could also indicate Hasidic origin.[45] Unfortunately, we know precious little about a specific group called *Ḥasidim*.[46] Some texts often identified as products of the *Ḥasidim* may well be using the term in a broadly descriptive way, rather than as the title of a specifically constituted group.[47] Quite possibly, that is the meaning of the term in the Epistle.

If the Epistle is pre-Essene,[48] it is a valuable piece of evidence from a period still very much in the twilight of historical uncertainty.[49]

---

[43] Pierre Grelot ("L'eschatologie des Esséniens et le Livre d'Hénoch", *RQ* 1 [1958–59] 118–21) finds Essene eschatology in the Epistle, but his evidence is not decisive.

[44] Cf. also 92:3,4; 91:17, where the Ethiopic probably translates related terms.

[45] See my comments in 'Social Aspects of Palestinian Jewish Apocalypticism', in David Hellholm, ed., *Apocalypticism in the Mediterranean World* (Tübingen: Mohr, 1982), 3.1.1 and 5.4.

[46] Philip Davies, 'Hasidim in the Maccabean Period', *JJS* 28 (1977): 127–40; John J. Collins, *The Apocalyptic Vision of the Book of Daniel* (HSM 16; Missoula: Scholars Press, 1977), 201–5; Nickelsburg, 'Social Aspects', 3.1–3.1.3.

[47] Ibid., 3.1.3.

[48] I have sketched elsewhere some external evidence and some internal literary evidence that may support such an early date; see my book, *Jewish Literature between the Bible and the Mishnah* (Philadelphia: Fortress, London: SCM, 1981), 150–51. On the possible problems with a Hasmonean date, often proposed, see Nickelsburg, 'Social Aspects', 5.1.1–5.1.2.

[49] On the problem of drawing a social map of this period see my article, 'Social Aspects'.

It testifies in this time to a sense of religious awakening, to dissatisfaction with the temple establishment, and to an emerging schismatic definition and interpretation of the Torah heightened by a sense of apocalyptic immediacy. Moreover, it belies the theory that early apocalyptic literature apart from Daniel was the product of closed conventicles.[50]

---

[50] The first draft of this paper was prepared during a fellowship year at the Netherlands Institute for Advance Study. It was read at a colloquium at N.I.A.S. and at the Universities of Munich and Hamburg, at King's College, London, and the Oriental Institute at Oxford. I have profited from the discussions at these presentations and from comments and suggestions by my colleague, Jonathan Goldstein. Final responsibility is, of course, my own.

ENOCH, QUMRAN, AND THE ESSENES:
THE REDISCOVERY OF A FORGOTTEN CONNECTION:
A RESPONSE TO "THE EPISTLE OF ENOCH AND
THE QUMRAN LITERATURE"

GABRIELE BOCCACCINI*

1. ENOCH AND QUMRAN: CONTINUITY AND DISCONTINUITY
ACCORDING TO GEORGE W.E. NICKELSBURG

George W.E. Nickelsburg's article, "The Epistle of Enoch and the Qumran Literature," published in 1982 in the *Journal of Jewish Studies*, is a landmark in contemporary research on the relationship between Enoch literature and Qumran. The article is still as fresh and topical as it was twenty years ago.

Nickelsburg's methodology already belongs to the twenty-first century with its emphasis on Jewish diversity. It fully recognizes the complexity of Second Temple Judaism ("the discovery of the scrolls has demonstrated that Second Temple Judaism as a whole was vastly more intricate than previous constructs have allowed," p. 105). Nickelsburg himself seems to be aware of writing for the next generation ("many of the contours of that intricacy are hidden from our twentieth century vision," p. 105). The article came just one year after the publication of his *Jewish Literature between the Bible and the Mishnah*— the first introduction to Second Temple literature to overcome the canonical boundaries that still so largely and unfortunately characterize even the modern scholarly approach, hiding the original relations among documents.[1] It would take years, however, before the recent works of Paolo Sacchi and Lester Grabbe would make us fully appreciate all the implications of Nickelsburg's methodology for an understanding of the diversity of Jewish thought in the Second Temple period.[2]

---

* University of Michigan.

[1] G.W.E. Nickelsburg, *Jewish Literature between the Bible and the Mishnah* (Philadelphia, 1981).

[2] P. Sacchi, *The History of the Second Temple Period* (Sheffield, 2000); L.L. Grabbe, *Judaic Religion in the Second Temple Period: Belief and Practice from the Exile to Yavneh*

In his 1982 article, Nickelsburg recognized the existence of an ideological connection between Enoch literature and the community of
Qumran. Frank M. Cross had already noticed it in 1958: "The concrete contacts in theology, terminology, calendrical peculiarities, and
priestly interests, between the editions of Enoch . . . on the one hand,
and the demonstrably sectarian works of Qumran on the other, are
so systematic and detailed that we must place the composition of
these works within a single line of tradition."[3] To this intuition, Nickelsburg was now for the first time providing solid evidence through
a detailed analysis of that section of Enoch literature that is chronologically the closest to the origins of the Qumran community—the
Epistle of Enoch. Nickelsburg had no reservations: "The Epistle of
Enoch is in many ways compatible with the specific interests, emphases, and viewpoints expressed in various writings of Essene or
proto-Essene provenance. Its presence in the Qumran library is not
at all surprising" (p. 120). Among the closest parallels between Enoch
and the Scrolls, Nickelsburg mentioned in particular, "the polemic
against the second temple," "the militant ideology" of the literature,
the common denunciation of "the oppression of the righteous and
the abuse of riches" (p. 120), and "the description of the rise of the
community" (p. 120).

At the same time Nickelsburg recognized the major differences
that separate the Enoch literature from the sectarian literature of
Qumran. "The books of Enoch, the present Epistle included, are
not the private, secret property of a closed group. They are part of
the words of the wise which are to be listened to because they guide
the hearer on the paths of righteousness that lead to salvation"
(p. 117). In the Epistle, Nickelsburg found "an openness the outsider" which "parallels an early stage in the development of the
Qumran community but contrasts strikingly with commands to silence
and concealment in a passage such as 1QS 9:16–17" (p. 120). Even
the attitude toward the Temple, in spite of any criticism, was far
from being as radical as in the Qumran literature: "the Apocalypse
and the rest of the Epistle are silent on the critiques of priesthood
and cult that characterize the Scrolls" (p. 119). The Epistle "does

---

(London, 2000). See also G. Boccaccini, *Roots of Rabbinic Judaism: An Intellectual History
from Ezekiel to Daniel* (Grand Rapids, 2002).

[3] F.M. Cross, *The Ancient Library of Qumran* (Garden City, 1958), p. 144.

not use the conversion language of the Damascus Document or the priestly and cultic imagery of the Manual" (p. 119).

Having found strong evidence of both continuity and discontinuity between Enoch texts and the Scrolls, Nickelsburg's conclusion was that "the Epistle was composed in circles ancestral to the Essenes" (p. 121). As a "pre-Essene" text, the Epistle "testifies . . . to a sense of religious awakening, to dissatisfaction with the temple establishment, and to an emerging schismatic definition and interpretation of the Torah heightened by a sense of apocalyptic immediacy. Moreover, it belies the theory that early apocalyptic literature apart from Daniel was the product of closed conventicles" (p. 122).

2. Nickelsburg's Theses Revisited

Contemporary research has confirmed the substance of Nickelsburg's arguments. Enoch literature testifies to the existence of a forgotten, yet fundamental variety of Second Temple Judaism and there is a strong connection between Enoch literature and Qumran. The early apocalyptic literature was not the bizarre product of isolated thinkers but the literary expression of a popular and influential movement that would play an essential role in both Qumran and Christian origins. The rediscovery of Enochic Judaism is in fact one of the major achievements of contemporary research. The "Enoch Seminar," of which Nickelsburg is one of the promoters, is presently exploring in a series of biennial international seminars the history of the Enoch movement from its pre-Maccabean origins (Florence, 2001) to its contribution to Qumran origins (Venice, 2003) to its pre-Christian developments (2005) and its connections with Christian origins (2007) up to its legacy in both Christianity and Rabbinic Judaism (2009). The enthusiasm with which the most distinguished Enoch specialists from all over the world have joined the seminar proves the centrality of the movement for an understanding of the diversity of Second Temple Judaism.[4]

As so often happens to the most brilliant of scholarship, Nickelsburg's article has gloriously aged not for internal failure but for the deepening of the new paths which it has itself contributed to opening,

---

[4] G. Boccaccini, ed., *The Origins of Enochic Judaism: Proceedings of the First Enoch Seminar (Sesto Fiorentino, 2001)* (Turin, 2002).

namely a clearer distinction (a) between the Apocalypse of Weeks and the Epistle, and (b) between Qumran and the larger Essene movement.

(a)   Nickelsburg was aware that the Epistle of Enoch is a composite document made of two major parts: the Apocalypse of Weeks and the core of the Epistle (94:6–104:6). "The Apocalypse of Weeks . . . is most likely a traditional piece reused by this author" (p. 113). He also pointed out a different concept of election as the major ideological difference between the two parts. "An indication of different authorship may be the absence in the rest of the Epistle of the concept of election, which is so central to the Apocalypse" (p. 113, n. 23). Addressing the question, whether "the Epistle represents a specific group constituted and organized as *the* community of the righteous," Nickelsburg found that while "the Apocalypse of Weeks strongly suggests such an idea . . . it is less clear in the rest of the Epistle" (p. 120).

However, Nickelsburg accepted Milik's assertion that the entire Epistle was known at Qumran[5] and therefore concluded that both documents were "pre-Essene." It would be unthinkable that "a sect like the Essenes, with its emphasis on the differences that divide it from the rest of Judaism, would accept and use a writing from a similar and, hence, rival group" (p. 121). But the evidence that the Epistle as we know it from the Greek and Ethiopic versions was known at Qumran is far from conclusive.

All the fragments of the Epistle found at Qumran belong to the Apocalypse of Weeks and related appendixes, while no fragment has been recovered of the much longer section 94:6–104:6, which constitutes the body of the Epistle and appears to be a later addition.[6] Recently Emile Puech has reiterated the claim that some tiny fragments found in Cave 7 (the very same that for some time were incorrectly believed to belong to the Gospel of Mark) should be identified as fragments of a Greek version of the Epistle of Enoch.[7]

---

[5] J.T. Milik, *The Books of Enoch: Aramaic Fragments of Qumran Cave 4* (Oxford, 1976).

[6] See G. Boccaccini, *Beyond the Essene Hypothesis: The Parting of the Ways between Qumran and Enochic Judaism* (Grand Rapids, 1998). Nickelsburg has reached the same conclusion in his recent commentary on 1 Enoch: G.W.E. Nickelsburg, *1 Enoch: A Commentary* (Minneapolis, 2002).

[7] E. Puech, "Des fragments Grecs de la Grotte 7 et le Nouveau Testament?," in *RB* 102 (1995), pp. 570–584; Idem, "Notes sur les fragments grecs du manuscript 7Q4 = 1 Henoch 103 et 105," in *RB* 103 (1996), pp. 592–600.

The fragments are so small and the arguments so fragile from both the philological and the literary point of view that the identification has been dismissed by the majority of Enoch specialists, including Nickelsburg.[8]

The thesis that the body of the Epistle was absent at Qumran is more than an argument from silence. An analysis of the very structure of the Enoch collection preserved among the Dead Sea Scrolls supports such a conclusion. The Aramaic fragments show that the sectarians knew an ensemble of Enoch books that included the Book of the Watchers, the Book of Astronomy, the Book of the Giants, Dream Visions, the Apocalypse of Weeks, and had chaps. 106–107 as its ending. Garcia Martinez has demonstrated that the compiler took these last two chapters from the lost Book of Noah and turned them into a sort of general summary of the entire Enoch collection by supplementing them with an interpolation (106:19–107:1).[9] The very fact that the theology of the interpolation is very close to the doctrine of election in the Apocalypse of Weeks ("a generation of righteous ones shall arise," 107:1) with no reference to the content of the body of the Epistle, makes it likely that the latter was not known at Qumran. The last part of Enoch that the compiler knew and summarized was the Apocalypse of Weeks.[10]

Moreover, the Epistle does not simply lack specific sectarian elements—it has specific anti-sectarian elements. The most obvious is 1 En. 98:4. The passage explicitly condemns those who state that since human beings are victims of a corrupted universe, they are not responsible for the sins they commit, and they blame others (God or the evil angels) for having exported "sin" into the world. "I have sworn unto you, sinners In the same manner that a mountain has never turned into a servant, nor shall a hill (ever) become a maidservant of a woman; likewise, neither has sin been exported into the world. It is people who have themselves invented it. And those who commit it shall come under a great curse" (1 En. 98:4).

Interpreters, like Sacchi and Collins, understand the passage as a reaction against the early Enochic doctrine of the fallen angels, and

---

[8] Nickelsburg, *1 Enoch: A Commentary.*
[9] F. Garcia Martinez, *Qumran and Apocalyptic: Studies on the Aramaic Texts from Qumran* (Leiden, 1992), pp. 27–28.
[10] G. Boccaccini, *Beyond the Essene Hypothesis*, pp. 131–138.

to a certain extent, it is.[11] The central point, however, seems to be otherwise. The author does not deny that evil has a superhuman origin, but holds human beings responsible for the sinful actions they commit. What the author aims to introduce is a clearer distinction between evil, which is from the angels, and sin, which is from humans, in order to show that the Enochic doctrine of evil does not contradict the principle of human responsibility. Evil is a contamination that prepares a fertile ground for sin, but it is the individuals themselves who have "invented" sin and therefore are responsible for their own deeds.

As Nickelsburg also has pointed out in his recent contribution in the *Anchor Bible Dictionary*, over the centuries the Enochic authors were persistent and consistent in making "human beings . . . responsible for their own actions. . . . Nonetheless, the Enochic authors attributed a significant part of the evils in this world to a hidden demonic world."[12] In the Enochic system of thought, the two contradictory concepts of human responsibility and human victimization had to coexist between the Scylla of an absolute determinism and the Charybdis of an equally absolute antideterminism. Accept either of these extremes and the entire Enochic system would collapse into the condemnation of God as the unmerciful source of evil or as the unjust scourge of innocent creatures.

By clarifying that evil is a temptation more than an uncontrollable contamination, the Epistle corrects rather than disowns the position of the earlier Enochic texts. The real opposition is against those who claim that human beings are not responsible because "sin has been exported into the world." The only Jewish group that made such a radical claim was the Qumran community, who must be recognized as the target of the Epistle.

In sum, while the Apocalypse of Enoch was certainly pre-sectarian, there are compelling reasons to believe that the Epistle was post-sectarian, written by a group other than the Qumran sect. As a result, the Epistle remained unknown in the Qumran library, or, if it was known, it was not accepted there. Nickelsburg was right: the sectarians would never have accepted and used a writing from a competing movement.

---

[11] P. Sacchi, *Jewish Apocalyptic and Its History* (Sheffield, 1997), p. 146; J.J. Collins, *Apocalypticism in the Dead Sea Scrolls* (London, 1997), p. 23.
[12] G.W.E. Nickelsburg, "1 Enoch," in *ABD*, vol. 2, p. 514.

(b) The idea that Qumran was not the headquarter of the Essene sect but rather a radical minority group that separated not only from the rest of Jews but also from the members of their parent movement, is one of the most interesting and original developments of Qumran research in the last two decades. In his *Behind the Essenes*, Philip Davies consistently describes Essenism as the parent movement of the Dead Sea sect.[13] Florentino Garcia Martinez' "Groningen Hypothesis" also implies "a split within the actual Essene movement" and locates "the ideological roots of the Qumran community . . . within the Palestinian apocalyptic tradition."[14] In Germany and Italy, scholars, such as Johann Maier and Rainer Riesner, Paolo Sacchi and Sabino Chiala', also agree in describing the Qumran community as a radical group that gradually parted from its original Essene setting and turned out to be, in the first century c.e., a rather insignificant clique.[15] These studies have introduced a fundamental distinction between Essene origins and Qumran origins, a distinction that allows scholars to make more sense of the often conflicting evidence. The implication for both Qumran and Christian origins are monumental. After decades of pan-Qumranism, the history of the Essene movement has ceased to coincide with the history of the Qumran sect, and the Essene origin of Christianity has become a working hypothesis again. As New Testament specialists now say: "Jesus was closer to the non-Qumran Essenes than to the strict and withdrawn Essenes living in the desert of Judah."[16]

Nickelsburg was aware of the complexity of the Essene movement ("even the writings that are assuredly Essene differ in their emphases and interests and reveal considerable complexity and development in the theology and organization of the sect," p. 105). However, he could not go so far as to state a clear ideological difference between

---

[13] P. Davies, *Behind the Essenes: History and Ideology in the Dead Sea Scrolls* (Atlanta, 1987).

[14] F. Garcia Martinez and J. Trebolle Barrera, *The People of the Dead Sea Scrolls* (Leiden, 1995).

[15] J. Maier, *Zwischen den Testamenten: Geschichte und Religion in der Zeit des zweiten Tempels* (Würzburg, 1990); R. Riesner, *Essener und Urgemeinde in Jerusalem: Neu Funde und Quellen* (Giessen, 1998), P. Sacchi, "Bilancio culturale della scoperta dei Manoscritti del Mar Morto," in *Amicizia Ebraico-Cristiana* 38 (2002), pp. 25–37, S. Chiala', *Libro delle Parabole di Enoc* (Brescia, 1997).

[16] J.H. Charlesworth, "The Dead Sea Scrolls and the Historical Jesus," in J.H. Charlesworth, ed., *Jesus and the Dead Sea Scrolls* (New York, 1992), pp. 1–74 (quotation on p. 40).

mainstream Essenism and Qumran, as scholars have begun doing only in more recent years. Facing the question whether the Apocalypse of Weeks and the Epistle had to be seen as "Essene" documents, his answer betrays the limitations of an approach that made the terms "Essene" and "Qumran" virtually interchangeable. "The option [that the Epistle is an Essene composition] is problematic for me because I have found in the Epistle neither the specific exegetical traditions nor the specific polemics against temple, cult, and priesthood characteristic of Qumran, nor the heightened dualism which would confirm Essene authorship" (p. 121). Now, what Nickelsburg singled out as "Essene" features are the generative ideas of the sectarian texts authored at Qumran, not necessarily those of the entire Essene movement. Nickelsburg's overall conclusion, that the ideology of the Epistle does not coincide with the sectarian literature of Qumran, remains valid. Yet, it is not enough to dismiss an Essene origin of the document. The pre-sectarian Apocalypse of Week and the post-sectarian Epistle of Enoch may well be Essene writings, representative of mainstream Essenism. When the equation between "Essene" and "Qumran" is removed, Nickelsburg's description of the ideology and sociology of the Enoch group fits well the ideology and sociology of the larger Essene movement, as described also by Josephus and Philo, with its mixture of separateness and openness that so sharply contrasts with the staunch isolationism of the Qumran community, which so impressed the non-Jewish authors, Pliny and Dio.

> The author [of the Epistle] speaks for a group of Jews who made exclusive claims for their interpretation of the Torah and who perceive as revealed wisdom the belief that an imminent judgement will separate them from those whose interpretation of the Law differs from theirs, as well as from the violent rich who oppress them. These exclusive claims notwithstanding, this is not a closed group who simply gather to comfort one another and to hurl curses on their enemies and opponents. The wise speak where they can be heard, and they testify to the truth in the hope that their message will be heeded and met with repentance. The Epistle of Enoch is part of this message and testimony and appeal (p. 118).

The "Enochic-Essene Hypothesis" I have articulated in my *Beyond the Essene Hypothesis* is exactly an attempt to reconcile the distinction between Essenism and Qurman, introduced by authors such as Davies and Garcia Martinez, with Nickelsburg's intuition of Enochism as the matrix of the Qumran community.

The goal of the Epistle coincided the goal of the Essene movement after the Qumran schism—to correct the message of the Apocalypse of Weeks by developing it according to a different trajectory from that followed by the sectarians of Qumran. The Apocalypse of Weeks had signaled the emergence of a group of chosen among the chosen as the first step toward the eschaton. The followers of the Teacher of Righteousness identified themselves as the only chosen of the last days. The Epistle doctrine of election now marks a systematic demolition of the principle of inaugurated eschatology that the Qumran community had brought to its ultimate conclusion. It did so by reminding its readers that God's gifts of salvation will be fulfilled only at the end, and until that time the righteous and the sinners are condemned to live side by side and the individuals have to struggle for their own salvation. In this world, no individual, no community of people, can claim to possess salvation as a present and permanent gift and profess not to be in need of salvation. It was the Epistle's greatest success: the answer of Qumran was not the only possible answer to the questions raised by the earlier Enochic tradition. Once again, Nickelsburg was right: a different concept of election separated the Epistle from the Apocalypse of Weeks.

3. Conclusion

We may now summarize the results of our analysis in seven points:

(1) The Enochic texts are not the literary product of a closed group, but "the message and testimony and appeal" of a large and influential movement—a component of the rich diversity of Second Temple Judaism.

(2) There is a close relationship between Enochic Judaism and Qumran, so much so that the Qumran community must be seen as an outgrowth of the Enoch group.

(3) The ideology of both the Apocalypse of Weeks and the Epistle are compatible, yet do not coincide with the sectarian literature of Qumran.

(4) The Apocalypse of Weeks predates the emergence of the Qumran community and was written in circles ancestral to the Qumran community.

(5) The ideology of the Epistle of Enoch differs from that of the Apocalypse of Weeks because of a different concept of election.

(6) The Epistle of Enoch is more likely a post- and anti-sectarian document written as a reaction against the sectarian claims of the Qumran community.

(7) Both the Apocalypse of Weeks and the Epistle of Enoch are Essene texts, representative of the mainstream Essene movement immediately before and after the schism of the Qumran community.

The first five points were already explicit in Nickelsburg's article in 1982; the last two are a direct implementation and clarification of the previous ones. We scholars have not yet completed the task of digesting and articulating all the revolutionary ramifications that these points have not only for the study of the relations between Qumran and Enochic Judaism but also for a comprehensive understanding of Second Temple Jewish thought. For twenty years, Nickelsburg's seminal article has been a continuous source of inspiration for all of us and, I foresee, will remain for many years to come.

RESPONSE TO GABRIELE BOCCACCINI

As they relate to the present discussion, my conclusions about the Epistle of Enoch developed in two stages. (1) In the article under consideration, I argued that the author of the Epistle incorporated into his text the Apocalypse of Weeks, an extant piece of tradition that described the history of Israel leading up to the formation of the eschatological community of the chosen. The notion of election, however, was not present in the body of the Epistle. The Epistle as a whole, moreover, was pre-Qumranic, although it was found among the Qumran Scrolls. (2) In my commentary, based on a 1998 article, I reversed myself and stated that the fragments of the relevant Qumran manuscripts (4QEn^cg) contained no part of the *body* of the Epistle (1 Enoch 94:6–104:8).[1] I also argued that the Enochic corpus, in testamentary form, existed at one point without the body of the Epistle.[2] In addition, I stated that there was no evidence that the Epistle as a whole had independent existence prior to the incorporation of this material into the aforementioned testamentary corpus.[3] That is, the Epistle was created when the material that it now comprises was integrated into the corpus.

Also essential for my conclusions in the present article, as Boccaccini notes, was the belief that Qumran and Essene were more to less synonymous. Thus, I spoke about the Epistle as a pre-Essene document. Time and a good deal of historical scholarship has changed that. Pre-Qumran need not mean pre-Essene. In what follows, I will sketch what I consider to be some of the remaining issues relating to the history of Essenism as the Enochic corpus and especially the Epistle of Enoch shed some light on the topic.

Some recent scholarship has argued against an Essene identification for the group that gathered at Qumran and wrote a core set of "sectarian" texts.[4] Moreover, there is a striking omission in the accounts

---

[1] Nickelsburg, "Books of Enoch at Qumran," p. 103.
[2] Idem, *1 Enoch 1*, pp. 24, 336–337.
[3] Ibid., p. 422.
[4] See especially Albert I. Baumgarten, 'The Rule of the Martian as Applied to Qumran," in *Israel Oriental Studies* 14 (1994), pp. 121–142; and in much greater

of Philo, Josephus, and Hippolytus (or the source on which the latter two are based).[5] These texts focus on the daily life and practices
of the Essenes, and one could never extrapolate from them the
priestly-dominated group and the dualistic, eschatological sectarian
world view that are attested in the Community Rule.[6] This omission of the whole *raison d'être* and overall outlook of the Qumran
group is so striking, once one sees it, that one must acknowledge it
and attempt to explain it. Nonetheless, while there are some differences
in detail between the Community Rule and the accounts of Philo,
Josephus, and Hippolytus, the similarities between the Qumran
Community Rule and the other texts are so many and so close that,
in my view, they all but definitively prove an Essene identity for the
Qumran group.[7] I conclude that the omission is due to the ethno-
graphic purpose of the accounts in question. So I agree that the
Qumranites were Essenes of a sort, but that, as Josephus and
Hippolytus attest, the Essene movement was broader and more diverse
than the traditional focus on the Scrolls had tended to emphasize.

If we follow Boccaccini in placing the Apocalypse of Weeks prior
to the founding of the Qumran Community and the body of the
Epistle after it, what features do either or both of these texts have
in common with the Qumran sectarian literature? The Apocalypse
of Weeks, the closing bracket of the Epistle (104:12–105:2), and CD
1:6–11 describe the founding, and (in 1 Enoch 104:12–105:2) the
ongoing existence of a group that construes itself as the eschatological community of the chosen, constituted by revealed wisdom. The
Apocalypse of Weeks (93:8–10) and CD 1:4–11 indicate antipathy
toward the second Temple by totally ignoring it. CD 3:21–6:1 explicitly criticizes the cult. According to 1QS 8:4–10, the Community is,
itself, the Temple. 1 Enoch 93:9–10 may imply the same notion.[8]

detail, idem, *The Flourishing of Jewish Sects in the Maccabean Era: An Interpretation* (Leiden,
1997).
    [5] See Morton Smith, "The Description of the Essenes in Josephus and the
Philosophoumena," in *HUCA* 29 (1958), pp. 273–293.
    [6] Joesphus and Hippolytus discuss briefly some tenets of Essene belief (e.g., immor-
tality), but these are part of a comparison with the beliefs of the Pharisees and
Sadducees, and they do not indicate a context within a dualistic apocalyptic world
view.
    [7] See Todd S. Beall, *Josephus' Description of the Essenes Illustrated by the Dead Sea
Scrolls* (Cambridge, 1988).
    [8] Nickelsburg, *1 Enoch 1*, p. 447.

The body of the Epistle, like a number of Qumran texts (above, pp. 106–109) unleashes bitter invectives against those who pervert divine Law through lies and deceit and threatens them with damnation. The same motif appears at critical points in the Apocalypse of Weeks (1 Enoch 93:4, 10). The Apocalypse of Weeks and the closing bracket of the Epistle anticipate the proclamation of divine revelation to "all the sons of the whole earth," and the same motif is present in the body of the Epistle at 100:6. However, this "universalistic" perspective is notably lacking in the sectarian Scrolls, and in its place is a command to secrecy (1QS 9:16–17). Furthermore, the Community Rule lacks any reference to Enochic revelation and cites as its governing law the Torah of Moses as interpreted by the priests, the sons of Zadok (1 QS 5:8–9). Whether 1 Enoch 99:2, in the body of the Epistle refers to the Mosaic covenant is uncertain. It could indicate in a later stage of the Enochic tradition a warming up to the Mosaic Torah that is explicit in the Book of Jubilees.[9] It is impossible to say whether the reference to "the righteous and pious" in 102:4 (cf. 92:3–4) represents a different conception from "the righteous and chosen" in the Apocalypse of Weeks (93:5, 10).

A comparison of these points with other strata of 1 Enoch is instructive. The Animal Vision (chaps. 85–90) criticizes the cult of the second Temple, describes the founding of the eschatological community through divine revelation, and anticipates the transformation of all humanity to its primordial purity (89:73–74; 90:6–7, 32–38). Chapters 12–16 use language traditional of anti-Temple polemics,[10] and chapters 10–11 await the conversion of the "sons of men" and "all the peoples" (10:21–22). The language of "the righteous and the chosen" appears in the introduction to the corpus (1:1, 3, 8; 5:8). The image of the plant (of righteousness) is common to 1 Enoch 10:16, the Apocalypse of Weeks (93:5, 10), CD 1:7, and 1QS 8:5.[11]

In all of this, I agree with Boccaccini that there is thematic continuity from various strands of the Enochic tradition through the Qumran sectarian texts: an eschatological community of the righteous and chosen, also known as the plant of righteousness, is constituted by revelation. In the beginning, perhaps following Second

---

[9] Ibid., p. 72.
[10] Ibid., pp. 271–272.
[11] But see Patrick A. Tiller, "The 'Eternal Planting' in the Dead Sea Scrolls," in *DSS* 4 (1997), pp. 312–335.

Isaiah, there is a universalistic vision. Righteousness is construed as obedience to a particular understanding of divine Law. Early on Enoch appears to be the revealer, but at Qumran he is supplanted by Moses, though the language of the two ways, which appears in 1 Enoch in the material that surrounds the Apocalypse of Weeks as well as in the body of the Epistle, governs the instruction in 1QS 3–4. In this text, however, the dualism that typifies the early Enochic myths has been considerably sharpened. However, I do not see that the heavy emphasis on predestination excludes human responsibility, as Boccaccini suggests. The very structure of the two ways instruction indicates that humans are rewarded or punished for their righteous conduct or sins.

Finally, there is the question of the "Essene" identity of the various groups in question. As I stated above, I think that the evidence from Philo, Josephus, and Hippolytus, on the one hand, and 1QS, on the other hand, indicates an Essene identity for the Qumranites and for a broader movement of which they are a part. It is possible, but not demonstrable, that the term "pious" in the body of the Epistle indicates such an identity for the parent group of this author's community. However, it is a different issue whether we should employ the term "Essene" with reference to the authors of the earlier Enochic literature, as Boccaccini does. Their own self-designation is "the righteous chosen" and the "plant of righteousness." Of course, the same may be said of the identification of the Qumran Community, but in that case, we have the parallels in Philo and Josephus as controls. These parallels are lacking in the Enochic literature, which does not explicate the specifics of law and life-style.

Thus I raise the possibility that there were a number of anti-Temple protest groups in the third, and even the fourth century B.C.E. that may have had the same self-understanding that is attested in the Qumran sectarian Scrolls and that may or may not have been related to one another theologically and sociologically. Even if there are substantial parallels and points of continuity between the Enochic writings and the Scrolls, given the spotty state of our knowledge, it might be the better part of wisdom to err on the side of caution and not use names (in this case Essene) that suggest that we know more than we presently do. None of this mitigates that fact that the past two decades of research have taught us a great deal about the contours of sectarian Judaism in Hellenistic period and that we stand to learn much more as we sift the evidence with care.

Boccaccini moves out of the Judaic context of the Enochic corpus to suggest that "the Essene origin of Christianity has become a working hypothesis again." Here, too, I believe that we should proceed with great caution. In my commentary, I have suggested that the Enoch pattern of religion offers a certain prototype for the shape of the early Christian community: a group that considered itself to be the eschatological community of the chosen constituted by revelation and intent upon promulgating its revelation to the gentiles.[12] The latest stratum of the Enochic corpus constitutes an additional link. The Book of Parables draws on the earlier corpus and employs the term "the righteous and chosen." Moreover, its major addition to Enochic theology is the figure of the "son of man,' also known as "the righteous one" and, especially, "the chosen one." The links to early Christology are, in my view, demonstrable.[13] This brings at least one wing of the early Jesus movement into proximity with one non-Qumran wing of Enochic apocalyptic Judaism. Under these circumstances, we should re-evaluate early scholarship that saw substantial parallels between the Scrolls and the early church. Having said all of this, we are still a long way from being able to demonstrate the "Essene origin of Christianity," much less the proximity of the historical Jesus to the non-Qumran Essenes.[14] Scholarship has moved a long way since the 1950s. The refinement of our knowledge and our tools should serve both as an encouragement and a caution as we frame new hypotheses and seek to substantiate them with the data.

---

[12] Nickelsburg, *1 Enoch 1*, pp. 86–86.
[13] Idem, "Son of Man."
[14] Note the quotation of James Charlesworth, above, p. 129.

CHAPTER FIVE

RELIGIOUS EXCLUSIVISM
A WORLD VIEW GOVERNING SOME TEXTS FOUND AT QUMRAN

GEORGE W.E. NICKELSBURG

INTRODUCTION

The ready accessibility of the Qumran Cave 4 texts has immensely complicated many truisms from the first forty years of Qumran scholarship which seemed to have the weight of a veritable consensus. Scholars with broadly different approaches and agendas agree now that a good part of the literary material from the eleven caves was not composed by people living at the site we call Qumran,[1] and current scholarship is raising such questions as: What may have came from where? What may have been the relationships between the authors of this material and the people who lived at Qumran? How did these texts get there? Complementing this study of the literary material is a fresh look at the material evidence from the ruins, which will surely refine dating and revise some explanations as to the nature of the activity at Qumran.

The availability of the Cave 4 texts has given rise to the frequent use of the term "sectarian" with reference to a corpus of texts thought to have been authored by members of the group resident at Qumran or, perhaps, a related group—in distinction from texts of a different provenance. But the use of the term "sectarian" should not be taken for granted. The problem of defining the word has been taken up by Carol Ann Newsom.[2] She concludes that it is often

---

[1] See e.g., D. Dimant, *Apocrypha and Pseudepigrapha at Qumran*, Dead Sea Discoveries 1 (1994): 151–59; J.C. VanderKam, *The Dead Sea Scrolls Today*, Grand Rapids, 1994, 29, 34, 43; L.H. Schiffman, *Reclaiming the Dead Sea Scrolls*, Philadelphia, 1994, 181; N. Golb, *Who Wrote the Dead Sea Scrolls?: The Search for the Secret of Qumran*, New York, 1995.

[2] C.A. Newsom, "'Sectually Explicit' Literature from Qumran," in W.H. Propp, B. Halpern, and D.N. Freedman (eds.), *The Hebrew Bible and its Interpreters*, Winona Lake, IN, 1990, 172–79, especially pp. 167–87.

difficult or impossible to determine whether a particular text was, in fact, authored at Qumran. Instead she ties the term to the "rhetorical function of texts."[3]

> A sectarian text would be one that calls upon its readers to understand themselves as set apart within the larger religious community of Israel and as preserving the true values of Israel against the failures of the larger community.

I agree with Newsom that it is often difficult to make a historical judgment about the precise provenance of a given text found at Qumran, and that we need to focus more closely on the text's world view or ideology as a means of making distinctions. My own definition of a "sectarian" text is phrased perhaps more "theologically" than Newsom's and may even denote a subset of the texts she wishes to consider. I refer to texts whose religious world view portrays one's group as the sole and exclusive arena of salvation and thus sees those who are not members of that community as cut off from God' favor and bound for damnation. In this study, I shall discuss a selection of texts found at Qumran that evince such an exclusivistic world view, indicating what issues are at stake, how the authors make their judgments, and, to some degree, what language is used to describe both the community and those who stand outside it. The last point is important because the authors of these texts often view the world in polarities. We are not the others; the others are totally different from us.

Like Newsom, I consider function to be important in the study and definition of these texts. They include: exhortations and liturgical or meditative pieces that invite the reader to tune into, or even articulate an exclusivistic world view; law codes that realize the world view; and allegedly revealed interpretations of Scripture that find the world view hidden in the words of authoritative religious tradition. My survey is not comprehensive; rather I provide some examples that may help in the study of other texts from the Qumran caves.

---

[3] Ibid., 178–79.

A. The Rule of the Community

Because of its self-conscious focus on the notion of community and its explicit regulations for the structuring of community life, the *serek ha-yaḥad* is an appropriate and useful place at which to begin our study. Although I shall note variants in other manuscripts of the *serek*, my survey will be based on 1QS, not least because the manuscript as a whole presents a coherent set of exclusivistic terms, whatever their point of origin may have been in the history of the document's evolution.[4]

Central to the self-understanding of the *yaḥad* is its belief that its members have entered a covenant with the God of Israel. The noun ברית occurs more than thirty times in 1QS 1–6 and 8, not infrequently in conjunction with the verbs עבר, בוא, and שוב.[5] That this expression does not refer to the entering of some sort of general agreement is indicated by the use of the adjective "eternal" (1QS 3,11; 4,22; 5,5–6), by the verb שוב (1QS 5,1.8.14.22), and by the use of the biblical covenantal formulary.[6] The people of the *yaḥad* believed that their community was uniquely the covenantal people of the God of Israel and that to enter the *yaḥad* was to enter a covenantal relationship with that God. Conversely, not to belong to the *yaḥad* was to stand outside the realm of divine blessing. Another way of stating this was to appropriate to themselves the term "the chosen (of his good pleasure)."[7]

An integral part of the covenant between the *yaḥad* and God was, of course, the Mosaic Torah. What is striking about 1QS is the belief that their interpretation of the Torah was *revealed*. More specifically, their communal life was governed by the Torah of Moses, "as it was revealed to the Priests, the sons of Zadok" (1QS 5,8–9; cf.

---

[4] On this evolution, see S. Metso, *The Textual Development of the Qumran Community Rule* (STDJ 21), Leiden, 1997.

[5] The noun ברית occurs in 1QS 1,8.16.18.20.24; 2,10.12.13.16.18; 3,11; 4,22; 5,2.3.5.8.9.10.11.12.18.19.20.22; 6,15.19; 8,9,10,16.

[6] On 1QS 1,18–2,18, see F. Baumgärtel, *Zur Liturgie in der "Sektenrolle" vom Toten Meer*, ZAW 65 (1953): 263–65; K. Baltzer, *The Covenant Formulary*, English Translation by D.E. Green, Philadelphia, 1971, 49; 188–91. On 1QS 3,13–4,26, see ibid., 99–112.

[7] On this and parallel terms, see E. Vogt, "'Peace Among Men of God's Good Pleasure' Lk. 2,14," in K. Stendahl (ed.) *The Scrolls and the New Testament*, New York, 1957, 114–17.

5,2–3).[8] That is, God had shown to them exclusively how, specifically, Torah was to be observed. Since divine blessing depended on the proper observance of Torah, and they alone had the revealed interpretation, they alone could receive that blessing.

This notion, in turn, was dramatized in the covenantal ritual, in which the priests and the levites pronounced, respectively, the blessings and curses of the covenant on the members of the community and those outside it (1QS 1,21–2,18), remarkably employing the priestly blessing of the congregation, given to Aaron, and its imprecatory foil (1QS 2,2–9).[9]

If the *yahad* saw itself exclusively as the covenant people of the God of Israel, who alone had the revealed interpretation of the Torah and stood to benefit from God's blessing, it also defined itself exclusively as the *temple* of God, the exclusive arena of purity and holiness and the sole effective agent of atonement for sin (1QS 8,1–10). The community is God's building, and the deeds of the community effect atonement for the Land. Conversely, the community will act as the agents of divine judgment on the sinners who are not members of it. The same polarity between community and sinners is perhaps implied in this passage's use of language from Isaiah 28,16 (1QS 8,7–8).[10] The biblical passage's image of building and counterbuilding in Jerusalem (28,14–18) may imply a contrast between the status of the *yahad* as God' temple and the identity of the present Jerusalem temple establishment as a counter-temple bound for destruction in God's coming judgment.

The *yahad*'s polarized view of reality has an important corollary. Its members are to separate themselves from the rest of humanity, not least the people who think they are Israelites—for two related reasons. It protects their purity and holiness from outsiders who do

---

[8] Although reference to the priests does not occur in 4Q258 1 1, reference is made to revelation (line 6). On this revelation, see J. Baumgarten, DJD 18, Qumran Cave 4 XIII (1996): 15–16; Metso, *Textual Development*, 80.

[9] See L. Hartman, *Asking for a Meaning: A Study of 1 Enoch 1–5* (CB.NT 12), Lund, 1979, 27–28

[10] See O. Betz, *Offenbarung und Schriftforschung in der Qumrangemeinde*, Tübingen, 1960, 158 ff., cited by A.R.C. Leaney, *The Rule of Qumran and its Meaning*, Philadelphia, 1966, 215–16. See also the comparison of 1QH[a] 14(6),26–27 with Isa 28.16–17 in O. Betz, "Felsenmann und Felsengemeinde: eine Parallele zu Mt 16,17–19," ZNW 48 (1957): 61–63. See also below, n. 26. Column numbers for the Hymn Scroll are given with what is now the commonly accepted enumeration, followed in parentheses by Sukenik's enumeration, which prevails in older editions and discussions.

not share in this status (1QS 8,20–26), and it enables them to practice Torah as it has been revealed to them (1QS 8,12–16).

The two-ways section of 1QS (3,13–4,25) provides a radical theological undergirding for the *yahad*'s exclusivistic self-understanding. Humanity is divided into two groups, the children of light and the children of darkness. One's membership in one or the other of these two groups is a function of a divine decision made in the mists of eternity. In consequence of that decision, one is led along the path of light by the angel of truth or the path of darkness by the spirit of perversity (3,18–25). These two paths constitute the deeds of the righteous and the wicked (4,2–6a. 9–11a), which lead respectively to temporal and eternal blessing and curse (4,6b–8, 11b–14). Thus, the righteous, the children of light (the members of the *yahad*) and the wicked, the children of darkness (the rest of humanity) are actors in the cosmic conflict between the principles of good and evil, God and Satan. The polarized world view of the *yahad* could hardly be written in more black and white terms. Life in the *yahad* and the *yahad*'s place in the world are an integral part of a cosmic struggle that has its beginnings in creation (3,25–4,1) and its consummation at the eschaton, when God will purify the world and rid it permanently of evil (4,16–26). Although, the two ways passage does not provide an explicit time frame for the coming of the end, references elsewhere in the Rule of the Community suggest that the *yahad* sees itself living in the last days, when the dominion of Belial is at it fiercest (1,18.23–24; 2,19). Thus, from a temporal point of view, the *yahad* believes that it is living out its life on the center stage of the cosmos.

In summary, through the use of a variety of terms and metaphors, the Rule of the Community projects a strongly dualistic world view. By virtue of their special election, confirmed by the receipt of revealed Torah (and revelations about the end-time), the members of the *yahad* had the unique, exclusive status as the people of the God of Israel. Separated physically from the rest of humanity, they studied and observed revealed Torah and experienced and anticipated the divine blessings that were the consequences of the covenant. Its segregated status notwithstanding, the *yahad* accepted new members into covenantal status (1,11–2,10; 6,13–23).[11] Entrance into the community involved

---

[11] See the discussion in Schiffman, *Reclaiming the Scrolls*, pp. 104–12.

the passage from darkness to light, from damnation to salvation. Within the *yahad* stringent rules maintained and embodied community and preserved the holy and pure status of the *yahad* (6,24–7,25). Expulsion from the community was, in effect, one's abandonment to the angels of punishment and eternal damnation (2,11–18; 7,22–25).

B. The Visions of Amram (4Q543–48)

This fragmentary document provides a good point of comparison with the Rule of the Community with respect to what one may and may not say about its exclusivistic character.[12] In his vision Amram sees a confrontation between the angel of darkness and the angel of light. Although they are arguing over Amram in particular, this is but an instance of their broader activity. They are in charge of all humanity (4Q544 fg. 1,12) with their responsibilities divided between the children of light and darkness, truth and lying (4Q548). The respective deeds of the children of light and the children of darkness will result in eternal life and eternal destruction (4Q548).

Although the imagery and language is similar to that of 1QS 3–4, there are significant differences. First, and most important, The Visions of Amram is extant only in several very fragmentary manuscripts. Thus, all conclusions about it should be seriously qualified. Having said that, we may note the following. The extant text gives no indication that the children of light are confined to a particular historical community. The *topos* of the conflict of the two angels is well known in Jewish literature of this period.[13] It is noteworthy that one of the closest parallels to this text is the fragment of the Assumption of Moses, which describes the battle between Michael and Satan over the body of the son of Amram.[14] In any case, it is altogether possible that this Aramaic vision account provides background for the heavily dualistic form of the two ways text in 1QS 3–4. It seems

---

[12] On this text, see J.T. Milik, "4Q Visions de 'Amram et une citation d'Origène," *RB* 79 (1972): 77–97; P. Kobelski, *Melchizedek and Melchireša'* (CBQ.MS 10), Washington, D.C., 1981, 23–36.

[13] See G.W.E. Nickelsburg, *Resurrection, Immortality, and Eternal Life in Intertestamental Judaism* (HTS 26), Cambridge MA, 1972, 11–13.

[14] For the extant Greek fragments of the Assumption of Moses, see A.-M. Denis, "Assumptio Mosis," in M. Black and A.-M. Denis (eds.), *Apocalypsis Henochi Graeci et Fragmenta Pseudepigraphorum Quae Supersunt Graeca* (PVTG 3), Leiden, 1970, 63–67.

to me less likely that this text has been created as an apocalyptic reinforcement for the teaching of 1QS 3–4. First, it is written in Aramaic rather than Hebrew. Secondly, it contains no hint of two ways parenesis.[15] Third, it *does* indicate some parallels with 1 Enoch 108,11–15, which constitutes the end of an Enochic vision and makes only one allusion to "the paths of truth" (v. 13).[16]

There is an obvious compatibility between the idea of two angels and the two ways, and these are brought together in texts other than 1QS 3–4.[17] However, the evidence of 4Q543–48 does not allow us to draw any conclusions about a exclusivistic provenance for this text. The most we can say is that the text may have been one of the building blocks, sources, traditions used in the composition of 1QS 3–4, and the number of Cave 4 copies of the text suggests that the text was used to confirm and inform the exclusivistic world view of the people at Qumran.

C. The Damascus Document

The Damascus Document has many of the exclusivistic touches of the Rule of the Community, albeit in a historical setting that is lacking in 1QS. As in the latter, "covenant" is a governing category.[18] Indeed, the third of its exhortatory introductions addresses the readers as "all who have entered the covenant" (כל באי ברית, CD 2,2; 4Q266 fg. 2 2,2).[19] The expression recurs in CD 6,19, which refers to "those who entered the New Covenant (באי הברית החדשה) in the Land of Damascus." The passages that refer or allude to the sojourn in the Land of Damascus are especially pertinent to our discussion, because they focus on the specially revealed Torah that is constitutive of the community of the new covenant.

---

[15] Only in the very fragmentary 4Q548 1,1 is there perhaps a reference to the two-ways construct.

[16] The parallel language of light and darkness and the departure of the sons and light and sons of darkness to their respective places found in both 1 Enoch 108,11–15 and 4Q548 fg. 1,9–15 is striking. The visionary form of both texts underscores the similarity.

[17] Nickelsburg, *Resurrection*, 156–62.

[18] For the numerous occurrences, see K.G. Kuhn, *Konkordanz zu den Qumrantexten*, Göttingen, 1960, 37; S. Pfann, "Concordance," in DJD 18, Qumran Cave 4 XIII, 210.

[19] The expression has not been preserved in 4Q266 fg. 2 2,2, but Baumgarten's reconstruction allows for its presence, DJD 18, Qumran Cave 4 XIII, 36.

According to CD 3,12–4,6, at a time when "all Israel strayed (תעו)," God established his covenant with Israel forever and revealed (נלה) to the remnant the hidden things in which Israel had strayed and enabled them to dig the well of the Torah, by which alone God's people can live. This section alludes to what is spelled out in more detail in CD 6,2–11 (cf. 4Q266 fg. 3 2,10–13; 4Q267 fg. 2, 7–15). The passage is shot through with language related to the notion of revealed Torah. God raised up from Aaron and Israel people who understood (נבונים) and sages (חכמים). Exegeting Num 21,18, the author describes how the converts of Israel (שבי ישראל) had gone out of the Land of Israel into exile in the Land of Damascus, where they sought (דרש) God and dug the well of the Torah through the agency of "the seeker of the Torah" (דורש התורה). The double use of the verb דרש here seems to denote both the repentant seeking of God through prayer and the exegetical searching of Scripture. Finally, we return to 6,14–7,9, where the new covenant in the Land of Damascus is tied to a whole range of commandments. Obedience to them will allow one to live for a thousand generations.

These sections about the exile in Damascus are reminiscent of CD 1, where parallel motifs appear.

	CD 1,3–6; 1,13–2,1	3,10–12.14	5,20–6,2
A time of sin			
God remembers			
covenant	1,4	(3,13)	6,2
A remnant	1,4.7	3,12–13	
A group from Israel			
and Aaron	1,7		6,2–3
They seek God	1,9		6,6–7
God enlightens them	1,8–11	3,13–16	6,2–9
A teacher	1,11–12		6,7–11

Especially noteworthy in CD 1–2 is the recitation of sins in 1,13–21. The "Scoffer" pours over Israel waters of lies (מימי כזב) and makes the people go astray (ויתעם), removing the boundaries (i.e., altering the Torah) and thus bringing on the curses of the covenant. The sinners sought smooth things (דרשו בחלקות), chose illusions (מהתלות), scrutinized loopholes (פרצות) (Isa 30,9–15), acquitted the guilty and sentenced the just, . . . and banded together against the life of the righteous one, and their soul abhorred those who walked in perfection. Thus, among other things, the passage depicts a situation of religious conflict, employing language that will recur in other passages to be considered below. The Scoffer spreads lies. The wicked, different from those who search (דרש) the Torah, search (דרש) smooth things. The sinners abhor those whose conduct is "perfect" (תמים). The allusion to Isaiah 30 is striking also because a few verses later (30,20–21) the prophet promises his people that they will see their teacher (מורה), who will lead them on the right path (cf. CD 1,11).

What emerges from these passages in CD and others, which we may now cite, is a religious world view similar to that in the Rule of the Community. Israel as a whole is in a state of apostasy, here explicitly following the Babylonian Exile. This situation, which is described early in the Damascus Document (CD 1; 4Q266 fg. 2 2), is underscored by the recitation of rebellions against God, whose origins are ascribed to the Watchers (CD 2,17–3,12). The exceptions of Abraham, Isaac, and Jacob (3,2–4) and, by implication, Noah[20] prepare for a reference to the remnant with whom God established his covenant (in Damascus) (3,12–19). Thus, we are thrust into a polarized world—a small covenant community in the midst of a wicked and perverse nation (and world). Typical of this group is their repentance, which enables them to participate in the covenant. Constitutive of that covenant is the revealed Torah that grants life and blessing. The community lives in separation from the rest of the nation and in this respect, 1QS 8,13–16; 9,20–21 are worth noting, with their references to separation in the wilderness in order to live according to the Torah.[21]

The notion of the covenant's revealed Torah is highlighted in the structure of the document itself. Each of its four introductory sections begins with an appeal to listen and see: "And now liste]n to me and I will make known to you" (ואודיעה לכם, 4Q266 fg. 1 1,5); "Now listen all you who know justice, and understand the deeds of God" (CD 1,1–2); "Now listen to me, all you who have entered the covenant, and I will uncover (ואגלה) your ears concerning the ways of the wicked" (CD 2,2); "Now my sons, listen to me, and I will uncover (ואגלה) your eyes to see and understand the deeds of God" (CD 2,14–15). Thus, the document itself embodies the revelation

---

[20] Noah is not mentioned as such, but cf. CD 3,1 and 3,2–4: "The sons of Noah and their families strayed . . ." Abraham, Isaac, and Jacob were friends of God, but "Jacob's sons strayed."

[21] Note the wilderness setting of Num 21,18, cited and interpreted in CD 6,3–7 (4Q266 fg. 3 2,10–16; 4Q267 fg. 2 8–14) with reference to the Damascus sojourn.

that is constitutive of the community. This is especially evident, of course, in the extensive law code that constitutes its second major part.[22]

In section A above, we noted that a cosmic and eschatological dualism undergirds the exclusivistic world view in the Community Rule, notably in 1QS 3–4. Although such a dualism is not as explicit in the Damascus Document as it is in the Community Rule, it is present and informs the document's exclusivistic world view. That the author believed he was living in the last times seems evident in his reference to "the last generation, the congregation of traitors" (CD 1,11–12), who stand in opposition to the community of the new covenant.[23] A reference to God's fixing the ages until eternity appears in CD 2,9–10 in a context that refers to eschatological judgment in a manner reminiscent of 1QS 3–4. While the text does not place a dualistic struggle between two cosmic angelic powers in the foreground, as does 1 QS 3–4, it does allude to the Enochic myth of the watchers (CD 2,17–19), and it refers several times to the early and eschatological activity of Belial (CD 4,12–15; 8,2; 12,2; in 5,17–18, the prince of lights and Belial are, in fact, opposed to one another).

D. The Pesharim

Although the Qumran pesharim offer less detailed information about their origin in a exclusivistic community, they do present a world view akin to that in the Rule of the Community and the Damascus Document. The exegesis in these texts makes clear both their exclusivistic character and their eschatological tendency. The prophets predicted the end-times, and their prophecies relate, especially, to events in the life of the community that has generated the texts. For these authors human history pivots on the events they are experiencing as the faithful, persecuted people of God.

---

[22] On the Qumran evidence for the extensive legal material in the Damascus Document, see Table 2, Baumgarten, DJD 18 Qumran Cave 4 XIII, 4–5.

[23] Whether "the coming of the Teacher of Righteousness at the end of days" (CD 6,10–11) refers to the historical presence of the teacher in the author's own time or immediate past, to a future resurrection appearance, or to a future prophetic figure is a point of dispute; see the extensive discussion by J.J. Collins, *The Scepter and the Star: The Messiahs of the Dead Sea Scrolls and Other Ancient Literature*, New York, 1995, 102–23.

In the Cave 1 Habakkuk pesher, the polarity we have seen in the Rule of the Community and the Damascus Document appears in the repeated references to the antagonism between the Teacher of Righteousness and the Man of the Lie (איש הכוב, 1,13–2,9; 5,9–12; cf. 11,3–8). The sobriquets that designate these characters express absolute religious polarity between true and false religion, or more specifically, true and false religious teaching. The Teacher of Righteousness speaks in behalf of God (2,2–3; 7,4). This teaching comprises both the inspired interpretation of prophecy (7,1–5; cf. also 2,6–11) and the right observance of the Torah (7,10–11; 8,1–3). The members of his community are "the doers of the Torah, who do not desert the service of the truth (אמת)," but show faithfulness (אמנה) to the Teacher of Righteousness. In opposition stands the Man of the Lie and his followers, who "reject (מאס, מאש) the Torah" (5,11–12; 1,11) and "bet[ray the] new [covenant], be[cause they are no]t faithful to the covenant of God" (2,3–4).

The antagonism between the Teacher of Righteousness and the Man of the Lie is central also to the interpretation of Psalm 37 in 4Q171. The Man of the Lie "led many astray with deceptive words" (התעה רבים באמרי שקר) so that they "did not list[en] to the Interpreter of Knowledge" (מליץ דעת, 1,26–27), and he sought to destroy the Teacher (4,8–10). The Teacher, for his part, was chosen by God to create the congregation of the chosen/poor (3,13–17; 2,5,10). They are the ones who have "converted to the Torah" (השבים לתורה, 2,2–3) and "do (God's) will," i.e., "do the Torah" (עושי התורה/עושי רצונו, 2,5.15). This community will inherit the high mountain of Israel, while the wicked will be destroyed by God (3,10–14).

Finally, we note the Nahum pesher (4Q169). The relevant part of this text focuses almost exclusively on a group of false teachers. They are the "facile interpreters," literally "those who seek smooth things" (דורשי החלקות). The technical use of the verb דרש with reference to exegesis, combined with a wordplay on חלקות, indicates that this author is polemicizing against what he perceived to be a false interpretation of the Torah. These interpreters, in turn, are guilty of "leading many astray through their false teaching, lying tongue, and deceptive lips" (בתלמוד שקרם ולשון כזביהם ושפת מרמה יתעו רבים) (fgs. 3–4,2,8; cf. 3,6–7).

What emerges from these passages is a picture similar to what we have seen in the Rule of the Community and, especially, the Damascus Document. The community of the righteous, led by God's appointed

and inspired teacher, observes the Torah as God intends and stands
to receive God's blessing. In opposition to the Teacher of Righteousness,
in the Habakkuk pesher and the Psalms pesher, stands the lying
teacher and his followers, who are bound for divine punishment.
The Nahum pesher focuses on the destructive activity of the false
teachers, who seek to lead others astray with their deceptive interpretations of the Torah. All of this is an integral part of the scenario of the last days. Different from the Rule of the Community
and the Damascus Document, there is no explicit reference to an
overarching antagonism between cosmic forces.

E. The Hodayot

1. *Hymns of Salvation*

The Hodayot offer at least two different kinds of evidence for a
exclusivistic world view. The first appears in two hymns that depict
entrance into the community as resurrection from the dead—as
Heinz-Wolfgang Kuhn was first to note.[24] In 1QH^a 11(3),19–23, the
author thanks God for having raised him from the pit, Sheol, and
Abaddon to an everlasting height, where he takes his place in the
ranks of "the holy ones" and "the sons of heaven." Thus entrance
into the community is likened to the eschatological blessings typically promised in apocalyptic literature (Dan 12,3; 1 Enoch 104,2.6;
cf. Wis 5,5).[25] Communion with the angels is possible because God
has purified the corrupt spirit from a great transgression (רוח נעוה
טהרתה מפשע רב, line 21). Thus, entrance into the community involves
the transition from death to life, from a world dominated by impurity and the power of Belial (1QH^a 11(3),24–36) to heaven. While
the author may have committed what was generally defined as "a
great transgression" (murder, adultery, incest, or idolatry), the heightened language of the passage suggests, rather, that life outside the
community is being construed as existence in mortal, damning sin.

---

[24] H.-W. Kuhn, *Enderwartung und Gegenwärtiges Heil* (SUNT 4), Göttingen, 1966.
Totally independently of his work, I came to the same conclusion in my dissertation in 1965, which was published in 1972, *Resurrection*, 152–56. For a discussion
of the two hymns treated here, see Kuhn, *Enderwartung*, 44–93; and Nickelsburg,
Resurrection, 152–56.

[25] On Dan 12,3, see ibid., 24–26; J.J. Collins, *Daniel*, Minneapolis, 1993, 393–94.
On 1 Enoch 104, see Nickelsburg, *Resurrection*, 120–22. On the parallel between
this passage and Wis 5,5, see ibid., 153.

A second hymn that expresses the same view point occurs in 1QH[a] 19(11),3–14. The author gives thanks to God who has dealt wondrously with dust and mud (line 3) and raised the worm of the dead from the dust into the presence of the angels (lines 11–13). The language of resurrection may well be run together with an idea of new creation (dust and renewal, lines 12–13). The two aspects of this hymn that are especially noteworthy for our purposes are its contrast between past and present and its emphasis on community.

The contrast between past and present runs throughout the hymn. God has dealt marvelously with one who is dust and mud and has allowed uncircumcised lips to sing God's praise (lines 3–5). Lines 9–13 are thick with a description of the contrast. Previously, the author was characterized by transgression (פשׁע), every impure abomination (תועבות נדה), and blameworthy iniquity (אשׁמת מעל), and by a depraved spirit (רוח נעוה), and was a dead worm (lines 10–12). However, God has shown forgiveness and compassion (רחמים, סליחות), purified him (טהר), enabled him to become holy (התקדשׁ), united him with the immortal spirits, and renewed him (התחדשׁ).

The locus of the author's new situation is communal. The root יחד occurs twice in lines 11–14 and the noun סוד, twice. This community, of angels and humans, is characterized by its purity and holiness, but also by the presence of knowledge shared with the angels.

> For you have given them knowledge (הודעתם) on the foundation of your truth,
>> and through your wondrous mysteries (רזי פלאכה), you have made them wise (השׁכלתם)
> (1QH[a] 19[11],9–10; cf. line 4).

Their resurrection is from a depraved spirit to "your knowledge" ([לבינת]כה, line 12), and they are joined with those who know (ידעים) (line 14). This focus is compatible with the emphasis on revelation in the other texts studied above, and although there is no specific reference to Torah here, the purity of the community and the coexistence of humans and angels presume the right observance of the Torah. Finally, knowledge is also tied to the praise of God (lines 4–7, 14).[26]

---

[26] Space does not permit a discussion of 1QH[a] 14(6),22–33, part of another hymn that graphically describes the author's movement from chaos and death into the realm of salvation, described in part with language drawn from Isaiah 28 (see above, n. 10).

2. *A Hymn about a Teacher, his Disciples, and his Opponents*

Among the various hodayot that focus on the activities and experiences of a teacher, 1QH^a 12(4),5–13(5),4 is especially appropriate to our topic. Central to the text is a sharp polarity between true and false teaching. The author of the text provides a first person account of one who claims to be the recipient and dispenser of revelation. The occasion for the hymn of thanksgiving is that fact that the Lord has brightened his face with his covenant. has enlightened him like the perfect dawn (12,1–6), and has made known to him (ידע) the wondrous divine mysteries (12,27). The author, in turn, has his disciples. He enlightened the face of the many (12,27) and poured the drink of knowledge (12,11). The content of revelation is, first of all, the interpretation of the Torah. God has engraved his Torah in the teacher's heart (12,10). Those "who walk in the path of your heart" have listened to him (12,24); they will stand forever in God's presence and will be established forever (12,21–22). The author may also allude to other kinds of revelation. The "vision of knowledge" (חזון דעת, line 18) may refer to eschatological revelation, and God's "wondrous mysteries" (רזי פלאכה, lines 27–28) may refer to the same or imply cosmological secrets.

The author's receipt and dispensing of revealed knowledge is not portrayed in a vacuum, however. It is counterposed to a critical account of the author's opponents, who ridicule and belittle him (12,8–22). They change (מור) the Torah, giving vinegar rather than the drink of knowledge (12,10–11). In addition, they claim to have their own visions (12,20). The text is a veritable compendium of religious polemical terminology that labels one's opponents as deceivers and liars: interpreters of deceit (מליצי רמיה), who lead others astray (ה[תעום], 12,7) and whose actions evidence folly (הולל, 12,8); interpreters of falsehood and seers of deceit (מליצי כזב וחוזי רמיה, 12,9–10), who exchange the Torah for smooth things (חלקות), go astray (תעה, 12,12) in calendrical matters; prophets of falsehood (נביאי כזב), who draw others into error (תעות, 12,15–16); men of deceit and seers of error (אנשי מרמה וחוזי תעות, 12,20–21).

The author's teaching, finally, takes place in the context of a community, described in language reminiscent of several of the texts mentioned above. They are "those who sought me, who were united together in your covenant and listened to me, who walked in the way of your heart and ordered themselves before you in the council of your holy ones" (12,24–25).

In summary, these are the words of a teacher, whose disciples form a covenantal community that is constituted by a revealed interpretation of the Torah and, perhaps, of God's eschatological activity. This teacher and his community, moreover, are seen in polar opposition to other teachers, who are the mouthpieces and expositors of false religion.

F. 1 ENOCH

The Enochic corpus (1 Enoch) offers an important resource for our study. Certain sections of it, found among the Cave 4 scrolls, reflect the religious world view we have been discussing.[27] Yet there is a wide consensus that none of these texts was *composed* at Qumran. Evidently, the people who authored some of the core documents of the *yahad* or its related communities found these texts compatible to their world view.

Two Enochic texts fit well with the historical accounts of the Damascus Document, in particular. The allegorical Animal Vision (1 Enoch 85–90) traces human history from Adam to the eschaton.[28] From the Return on, the sacrifices offered on the Jerusalem altar are considered to be polluted, and the sheep of Israel are blind (apostate) (89,73–74). In time the sheep give birth to lambs who begin to open their eyes and plead with their elders to change their ways, but to no effect (90,6–7). Thus, as in CD 1, in the midst of the sinful post-Exilic age, there is a breakthrough of religious understanding. The Apocalypse of Weeks presents a similar, albeit more radicalized and detailed picture (1 Enoch 93,1–10; 91,11–17).[29] Without making any reference to a Return from Exile or the building of a new temple,[30] the text tells of the existence of a totally perverse generation (93,9). Then

---

[27] For the Aramaic Enoch texts found at Qumran, see J.T. Milik, *The Books of Enoch*, Oxford, 1976, 4–7.

[28] For a brief discussion of this section, see G.W.E. Nickelsburg, *Jewish Literature Between the Bible and the Mishnah*, Philadelphia, 1981, 90–94. For a text, translation, and commentary, see P.A. Tiller, *Animal Vision, A Commentary on the Animal Apocalypse of 1 Enoch* (SBLEJL 2), Atlanta, 1993.

[29] This order of verses, which involves the transposition of a block of the Ethiopic text, is supported by 4QEn^g; see Milik, *Books of Enoch*, 263–69.

[30] The omission of a reference to the Second Temple is remarkable in a text that repeatedly refers to Israelite sanctuaries (tabernacle, 93,6; Solomon's temple, built and burned, 93,7.8; eschatological temple, 91,13).

At its (the period's) conclusion, the chosen will be chosen
  as witnesses of righteousness from the eternal plant of righteousness,
  to whom will be given sevenfold wisdom and knowledge.
And they will uproot the foundations of violence,
  and the structure of deceit in it,
  to execute judgment (93,10; 91,11).[31]

The pattern is familiar. In a sinful age the community of the chosen is constituted by special revelation. The designation of Israel as
the righteous plant is reminiscent of CD 1,7 and 1QS 8, and the
description of evil as a structure with foundations may have in mind
the imagery of Isaiah 28, with its counterposed good and evil structures, implied in 1QS 8.[32]

Especially important for our consideration is 1 Enoch 98,9–99,10,
which lies at the heart of the Epistle of Enoch, the major part of
the Enochic corpus in which the Apocalypse of Weeks is also embed-
ded.[33] The subsection begins with a Woe directed against the "fools,"
who will be destroyed because they "do not listen to the wise" (98,9)
and concludes with a beatitude:

Then blessed will be all who listen to the words of the wise,
  and learn to do the commandments of the Most High,
  and walk in the paths of his righteousness,
    and do not err with the erring;
  for they will be saved (99,10).

Thus is presented the polarized religious world view we have been
discussing. "The wise" are the right expositors of God's commandments. Some will follow them down the right path. Others—fools—
will ignore them and stray from the right path.

However, the polarization is sharper. In counterposition to the
wise are the false teachers.

---

[31] Translation based on the Qumran Aramaic, 4QEn^g fg. 1 4,10–11.
[32] For a detailed and nuanced discussion of the image of the plant, see P.A.
Tiller, *The "Eternal Planting" in the Dead Sea Scrolls*, Dead Sea Discoveries 4 (1997):
312–35.
[33] For this section of 1 Enoch, see Nickelsburg, *Jewish Literature*, 145–50 and the
literature cited on p. 160. Translations here are based on the Ethiopic and Greek,
as discussed in G.W.E. Nickelsburg, "Enoch 97–104: A Study of the Greek and
Ethiopic Texts," in M.E. Stone (ed.) Armenian and Biblical Studies, Suppl. Vol. to
Sion 1, Jerusalem, 1976, 90–156. The analysis that follows summarizes G.W.E.
Nickelsburg, "The Epistle of Enoch and the Qumran Literature," *JJS* 33 (1982) =
Essays in Honour of Yigael Yadin, 334–45 [above, 105–22].

Woe to those who write *lying* words and words of *error* (λόγους ψευδεῖς
    καὶ λόγους πλανήσεως);
    they write and *lead many astray* with their *lies* (ἀποπλανήσουσιν πολλοὺς
    τοῖς ψεύδεσιν), when they hear them.
You yourselves *err* (πλανᾶσθε);
    and you will have no peace but will quickly perish. (98,15–16)
Woe to you who commit *erring acts* (οἱ ποιοῦντες πλανήματα)
    and who by *false deeds* (τοῖς ἔργοις τοῖς ψεύδεσιν) receive honor and
    glory;
    you will perish, you will have no salvation for good. (99,1)
Woe to you who change the true words
    and pervert the eternal covenant
    and consider themselves to be without sin;
    they will be swallowed up in the earth. (99,2)

The italicized words are drawn from the same polemical vocabulary we have seen especially in 1QH^a 12,5–13,4 and the Nahum pesher. The language of 99,1 may well be construing these false teachers as the equivalent of idolatrous priests.[34] Especially striking is 99,2, which accuses the opposing teachers of being revisionists, who claim that their perverse interpretations of the God's commandments are the correct interpretations. Finally, we should note that the form of the Woes and the Beatitudes indicates that observance of right and false teaching results in eternal salvation or damnation.

The framework of the Epistle indicates that the corpus of laws, commandments, and eschatological information that constitutes right teaching is presented under the authority of the patriarch Enoch (92:1; 104:12–13).[35] Long before Moses appeared on the scene, Enoch had ascended to heaven, received his revelations, and written them down to be transmitted to his son Methuselah, who would preserve them so that they could be revealed to the eschatological community of the chosen (82:1–3). Clearly the implied corpus of "Enochic law" comprised a great deal of material that is not present in what we call 1 Enoch. Nonetheless, the body of teaching is said to be

---

[34] I.e., those who seek worship for their gods (see Nickelsburg, Epistle, 339 [above, 112] n. 20). For a related passage that explicitly refers to idolatry, see 1 Enoch 99,7. For the Heb. and Aram. roots העה and שׁטא with reference to idolatry, see H. Braun, Art. πλανάω, TDNT 6 (1968): 233–36; and J. Levy, *Chaldaisches Wörterbuch über die Targumim* 2, Darmstadt, 1966 reprint, 311–12. For the notion that wrong Israelite religion is tantamount to idolatry, cf. 1QS 2,11–12; 4Q166 2,5–6.

[35] Nickelsburg, Epistle, 343 [above, 116]. On the Enochic corpus as authoritative scripture, see G.W.E. Nickelsburg, "Scripture in 1 Enoch and 1 Enoch as Scripture," in T. Fornberg and D. Hellholm (eds.), *Texts and Contexts: Biblical Texts in Their Textual and Situational Contexts* (Fs. Lars Hartman), Oslo, 1995, 343–47.

divine revelation that had been given through Enoch. The full extent of the issues comprised by this revelation is something we cannot determine. Surely it included astronomical and calendrical speculation, which *is* at the heart of the Enochic corpus, and almost certainly it involved concerns about the conduct of the Temple cult, which are also important for the Enochic authors.[36] It is not coincidental that both calendar and cult were issues of concern in some of the texts discussed above.

Finally, it is unclear to what extent the Enochic documents issued from a formally constituted community, like that described in the Rule of the Community. The Enochic texts contain no rules for communal structure and activity. The most we can do is posit a Sitz im Leben in which Enochic law could be effectively observed.

In conclusion, relevant parts of 1 Enoch present a world view in which right and wrong teaching of right and wrong Torah are highlighted as the alternatives that will lead to salvation and damnation. The counterposition of these alternatives is placed in a historical situation that is construed as eschatological, and the insight to recognize the true from the false is identified as primordial revelation received by Enoch and preserved for the end time.

G. The Book of Jubilees

The final text that we shall consider here is the Book of Jubilees, which has been preserved in seven fragmentary manuscripts from Qumran Cave 4 and is cited as an authoritative text in CD 16,3–4.[37] It is generally recognized that this text, like 1 Enoch, was not composed at Qumran.

The heart of the issue of concern to us is presented in a histori-

[36] For the Temple as an issue in 1 Enoch, see, in addition to the Animal Vision and the Apocalypse of Weeks: chapters 6–16, as interpreted by D.W. Suter, "Fallen Angel, Fallen Priest: The Problem of Family Purity in 1 Enoch 6–16," HUCA 50 (1979): 115–35; and chapters 12–16, as interpreted by G.W.E. Nickelsburg, "Enoch, Levi, and Peter: Recipients of Revelation in Upper Galilee," JBL 100 (1981): 582–87 [below, 436–42]; see also B.G. Wright, "Putting the Puzzle Together: Some Suggestions Concerning the Social Location of the Wisdom of Ben Sira," SBL.SP 1996, Atlanta, 1996, 133–49.

[37] For the Qumran manuscripts of Jubilees, see J.C. VanderKam, DJD 13 Qumran Cave 4 VIII (1994): 1–140. For a critical edition and translation of the Ethiopic version of Jubilees, see idem, *The Book of Jubilees* (CSCO.Ae 510, 511), Louvain, 1989.

cal review in Jub. 23,11–32. In the last time, Israel will go astray
and forsake the covenant and the laws, notably those relating to calendrical observance (23,16.19). As a result, God will punish the nation
by sending "the sinners of the gentiles," who will show them no
mercy. Finally,

> In those days the children will begin to search the laws,
>   and to seek the commandments,
>   and return to the path of righteousness (23,26).

In response to this repentance, God's wrath will turn to mercy, and
blessing will return to the nation. Noteworthy in this passage is the
double use of the Ethiopic verb *hašaša*, which doubtless reflects an
original Hebrew דרש and perhaps also, as a variant, בקש. The former appears in several of the Qumran texts with reference to the
interpretation of Scripture.

The laws and commandments which the children search and
observe are, without a doubt, the corpus of law contained in the
Book of Jubilees itself. This work, which is a rewritten form of Genesis 1–Exodus 12, purports to be a transcript of a revelation given to
Moses by the angels of the presence on Mount Sinai.[38] To begin
with, events in the biblical narrative are set within a chronology that
is based on a solar calendar, and the pre-Mosaic patriarchs are portrayed as observing the feasts according to this calendar. In addition, this biblical narrative is interpolated with halakic additions about
calendar and moral issue, which are said to have been recited from
the heavenly tablets. Thus, the rewritten biblical account is presented
explicitly as direct divine revelation of heavenly truth, taken from
the eternal law code itself.[39] In this respect, its claim parallels that
of the Enochic corpus, even though the recipient and transmitter of
the revelation is Moses rather than Enoch and the content is mainly
legal rather than eschatological. The consequences of one's obedience
or disobedience of these laws is clear enough. Israel presently suffers
because it has disobeyed the commandments, and various of the revelations carry with them the threat of damnation for disobedience.

As in 1 Enoch, it is difficult to extrapolate from this text any ref-

---

[38] On the Book of Jubilees, see G.W.E. Nickelsburg, "The Bible Rewritten and
Expanded," in M.E. Stone (ed.), *Jewish Writings of the Second Temple Period*, CRINT
2:2, Assen/Philadelphia, 1983, 97–104.

[39] For some of the relevant texts, see Jub. 1,26–2,1; 3,10; 4,5; 6,17; 15,25; 18,18;
24,33; 28,6; 30,9; 33,10; 50,6–13.

erence to a specific community. The polarity is twofold: between
Israel and the nations; between Israelites who obey right Torah and
those who do not. There are no references to false teachers. Nonetheless, we are presented with a text that claims to be right Torah
directly revealed to Moses and that *really is* the precipitate of an
interpretation of the Torah (cf. the use of דרש in 23,26). As in 1
Enoch one must use one's imagination to envision a Sitz im Leben
in which the calendrical Torah, in particular, could be observed.

H. Conclusions

I have discussed a series of texts, all found in the Qumran caves,
that present an exclusivistic religious world view, with a range of
nuances. Common is the notion that a true Israelite is not simply
one who is ethnically a descendent of the patriarchs. Divine blessing is promised only to those who observe right Torah. This right
Torah, however its contents may be defined, is presented as revealed
truth, however that revelation may have taken place (e.g., through
visions or exegesis of authoritative texts).[40] This right Torah, in addition, is set in stark contrast to wrong, or perverted Torah. In some
cases, this polarity is extended to include bitter polemics against the
teachers of false Torah. Going yet another step, the texts may focus
on the existence of a particular historical community that is the
exclusive locus of salvation. The Community Rule, at the very extreme,
lays out the protocols for the structure and activity of this community. I stop short here of suggesting which of the other texts I have
studied may have issued from communities like the *yahad*. They are
silent at key points and on key issues. Nonetheless, judging from the
number of manuscripts and from some occasional citations, these
texts were useful to the people at Qumran. Put another way, the
site at Qumran drew to it people for whom these texts—some of

---

[40] For a discussion of revelation in these texts, see G.W.E. Nickelsburg, "The
Nature and Function of Revelation in 1 Enoch, Jubilees, and Some Qumranic
Documents," in E.G. Chazon and M.E. Stone (eds.), *Pseudepigraphical Perspectives: The
Apocrypha and Pseudepigrapha in Light of the Dead Sea Scrolls, Proceedings of the Second
International Symposium of the Orion Center for the Study of the Dead Sea Scrolls and Related
Literature, 12–14 January 1997*, Leiden, 1999, 91–119.

which they certainly brought with them—were especially important.

I. Implications

1. *For Qumran Studies*

With the newly revealed texts from Cave 4 at the disposal of the scholarly world, a new generation of exegetes and historians will take up new questions. How do these texts relate to, especially, the Cave 1 texts? Which texts may have been authored at Qumran or communities closely related to it. What may have been the provenance of the other texts? What might we learn about the history of the Qumran community, its ancestors and its siblings? These questions will often not be answered with any finality, but scholars, being what they are, will continue to ask them.

One way to seek an answer is to look for common terminology, or clusters of such terminology. The presence of common or diverse *halakot* offers perhaps more precision (surely more than compatible or conflicting eschatologies).[41] Another approach, which I have begun to take here, is to move out from the most explicit and most radical of these texts—the Rule of the Community—and to trace common or related exclusivistic ideologies. It will be useful to look at other Cave 4 texts for some of the tendencies I have identified here. One excellent candidate for this trajectory is the Aramaic Levi Document (4Q213–214). Conversely, other of the Cave 4 texts, e.g., Sapiential Work A (4Q416–418), wholly lack an exclusivistic world view.[42] Finally, as one places these texts on a broader horizon, it

---

[41] For three discussions on some of the halakic peculiarities of Qumran texts, see: on 4QMMT, E. Qimron, DJD 10 Qumran Cave 4 V (1994): 123–77; and Y. Sussmann, ibid., 179–200; and on the Damascus Document, J. Baumgarten, DJD 18 Qumran Cave 4 XIII, 11–22. Attempts to distinguish texts and parts of texts on the basis of "conflicting" eschatologies have often been governed by anachronistic western rationalistic presuppositions.

[42] See, e.g, T. Elgvin, "Wisdom, Revelation, and Eschatology in an Early Essene Writing," SBL.SP 1995, Atlanta, 1995, 460–63; D.J. Harrington, "Two Early Jewish Approaches to Wisdom: Sirach and Qumran Sapiential Work A," SBL.SP 1996, Atlanta, 1996, 130–31.

[43] In an early article, David Flusser rightly saw significant parallels between the Martyrdom of Isaiah and some of the Qumran texts, "The Apocryphal Book of Ascensio Isaiae and the Dead Sea Sect," IEJ 3 (1953): 30–47. As the social map of pre-Christian Judaism becomes more complex, a Qumranic provenance is less

will be helpful to look at texts from the Apocrypha and Pseudepigrapha which have not been found at Qumran, such as the Martyrdom of Isaiah and the Psalms of Solomon.[43] Short of new evidence,
such comparative study will probably not tie many texts to specific,
known communities. However, we stand to learn a great deal generically about the diversity and proliferation of what has often been
called sectarian or pietistic Judaism in the centuries around the turn
of the era. A step beyond this will be to move backward into the
texts of the Hebrew Bible to seek points of continuity and possible
"trajectories."[44]

2. *Implications for the Study of Christian Origins*

Early Christianity is an integral part of the kind of exclusivistic
Judaism I have attempted to sketch in this study. I cite here only
two texts that require much more detailed study on this matter.

Although Paul sees the Torah as passé, and emphasizes justification
by faith rather than by the deeds of the Law in several of his epistles, he claims that all will be judged on the basis of their deeds.[45]
Indeed, the two fit together. The right life is possible only through
the power of the Spirit of the risen Christ. While he hopes for the
salvation of "all Israel," he sees the Torah as a dead end, because
the Torah has been compromised by the power of sin, which inhab-
its all humans, Jews and gentiles alike.[46] Thus, his claims to have
been a Pharisee notwithstanding, the shape of his exclusivistic religion is akin to some of the Qumran texts we have been discussing.

For Matthew the situation is different, but not totally so. The

---

demonstrable, not least because the text has not been found at Qumran. Nonetheless,
the parallels stand, and the text needs to be discussed in the context of the Cave
4 material. The Psalms of Solomon, with their references to "the congregations of
the pious" (συναγωγαὶ τῶν ὁσίων) need also to be placed in the discussion, albeit
with full recognition that: (a) they were not found at Qumran; and (b) they lack,
e.g., the dualistic features typical of some of the texts discussed above.

[44] Cf., e.g., the use of the term "chosen" in Third Isaiah; Nickelsburg, *Resurrection*,
203; P.D. Hanson, *The Dawn of Apocalyptic*, Philadelphia, 1975, 93, 96, 152–53.

[45] The issue is, of course, massively complex. However, interpretations governed
by a Protestant theological point of view need to take seriously texts like Rom
2,5–11; 1 Cor 3,13–15; 2 Cor 5,10; Gal 5,15–6,8; 1 Thess 5,23, as these are naturally interpreted in the context of first century Judaism.

[46] Again the problem is massively complex. See, however, my brief treatment,
"The Incarnation: Paul's Solution to the Universal Human Predicament," in B.A.
Pearson (ed.), *The Future of Early Christianity: Essays in Honor of Helmut Koester*, Minneapolis,
1991, especially 351–54 [below, 593–96].

Torah is not totally bracketed out (Matt 5,17–20). Nonetheless, salvation turns on obedience to the commands given by the earthly Jesus, whose words are defined as Torah by the risen Christ, who commissions the eleven to "make disciples of all the nations" (28,16–20). That same Christ had previously commissioned Simon as the rock on which he would build his messianic *ekklesia* that was to replace the *qahal yisrael* (16,18–19). Thus, whatever Matthew's attitude toward the Mosaic Torah or any parts of it, he presents an exclusivistic religion that is tied to the messianic identification of the risen Jesus of Nazareth.[47]

These two examples are symptomatic of an exclusivistic religious world view, based on claims of divine revelation, which would seem to have pervaded much of the first century Christian communities,[48] and which was strengthened and developed in the second and following centuries C.E., as the first century Christian texts took on authority as sacred scripture, added to "the Old Testament." It would be interesting to scrutinize these first century texts for the presence and maybe occasionally the absence of such exclusivism.

---

[47] To what extent Matthew sees ethnic Israel as excluded from the Kingdom is a hotly debated point. For two opposed interpretations of the expression *panta ta ethnê* in Matt 28,19, see D.R.A. Hare and D.J. Harrington, "Make Disciples of All the Gentiles (Matthew 28:19)," CBQ 37 (1975): 359–69; and J.P. Meier, "Nations or Gentiles in Matthew 28:19," CBQ 39 (1977): 94–102. However one solves the issue of whether Matthew envisioned Jews in the Church, the christological identification of "the true Israel" seems clear; W. Trilling, *Das Wahre Israel* (StANT 10; 3rd edit.), München, 1964, 154–62.

RESPONSE TO "RELIGIOUS EXCLUSIVISM: A WORLD VIEW GOVERNING SOME TEXTS FOUND AT QUMRAN"

Carol A. Newsom*

In "Religious Exclusivism" Nickelsburg seeks to devise a method of inquiry that will clarify the nature of the relation of the various texts found at Qumran to the *yahad* community and to other similar religious movements and communities (p. 159). He properly recognizes that our ability to make decisive judgments about the provenance of texts is often limited by the nature of the evidence. Nevertheless, the very process of asking the questions in a critically reflective manner helps to clarify and refine the assumptions that guide the inquiry.

Nickelsburg begins his discussion by citing and revising the definition of "sectarian text" that I proposed some years ago, preferring to give a somewhat sharper edge to the oppositional nature of sectarian self-consciousness, namely, as "portray[ing] one's group as the sole and exclusive arena of salvation" (p. 140). Although Nickelsburg is certainly right about Qumran's views on the locus of salvation, I am not certain that I would want to include such a strong formulation in a general definition. In part, of course, how one chooses to define this notoriously slippery term has to do with the kind of inquiry one wishes to make. Even within the world of the social-scientific study of religion, there is no agreed-upon way of defining sects and considerable doubt as to whether a universal definition is possible. Consequently, it may be helpful to see how other recent scholars of Second Temple Judaism with a distinctly sociological bent have defined the term and for what reasons. Albert Baumgarten, for example, opts for a softer-edged definition of a sect as a "voluntary association of protest, which utilizes boundary marking mechanisms— the social means of differentiating between insiders and outsiders— to distinguish between its own members and those otherwise normally

* Emory University.

regarded as belonging to the same national or religious entity."[1] His intent in framing his definition in this fashion is to formulate one that not only fits within the range of accepted usages of social-scientific research but also intentionally allows "considerable room for variation in the degree of separation from other Jews, or opposition to prevailing views."[2] This definition allows him to consider not only Essenes and the Qumran community, but also Sadducees, Pharisees, and several other Jewish movements, differentiating among them by means of Bryan Wilson's typology of sects as "reformist" and "intro-versionist."[3] Thus for his definition a sect need not claim to be the sole arena of salvation, though it does treat others as "outsiders."

Jutta Jokiranta's recent study is more concerned with the problem of definition itself.[4] Her study of the trends in the sociological study of sects leads her to be cautious about essentialist or categorical definitions. She argues instead for the utility of an analysis that measures the degree of certain stances within a text or group. The two variables that form the parameters for sectarianism are the degree of tension with the socio-cultural environment and "the extent to which a religious group considers itself to be uniquely legitimate."[5] Thus Jokiranta argues that "a *sectarian text* should contain clear evidence of a *sectarian stance*—that is, of the self-understanding as uniquely legitimate, and of the negative tension with the social environment."[6] At the same time, she recognizes that these are not all-or-nothing judgments and that a particular text might exhibit these characteristics in varying degrees.

Nickelsburg's definition, with its emphasis on the presence of exclusivistic ideology, is thus closer to Jokiranta's than to Baumgarten's. The reason, I think, is related to his interest in tracing what he calls "trajectories" among the texts that evince these ideologies, identifying not only aspects of similarity but also clarifying the "diversity and proliferation" of sectarian Judaism (p. 160). For this purpose Nickelsburg's definition is appropriate, and he begins his investigation in

---

[1] Albert I. Baumgarten, *The Flourishing of Jewish Sects in the Maccabean Era: An Interpretation* (Leiden, 1997), p. 7.
[2] Baumgarten, p. 12.
[3] Bryan Wilson, *Magic and the Millennium* (London, 1973), pp. 18–26.
[4] Jutta M. Jokiranta, "'Sectarianism' of the Qumran 'Sect': Sociological Notes," in *Revue de Qumran* 20 (2001), pp. 223–239.
[5] Jokiranta, pp. 228, 229.
[6] Jokiranta, p. 237.

the right place and in the right manner, privileging the Community Rule as the fixed point to which other texts can be compared. Here is a text that not only expresses an "exclusivist worldview" but also refers to the organizational structures by which that worldview was embodied in a clearly defined community that set itself apart as the "sole and exclusive arena of salvation" (p. 160).

The implicit logic of Nickelsburg's inquiry is somewhat obscured by the sequence in which he treats the texts. If I may take the liberty of a slight rearrangement, it appears to me that he actually identifies and analyzes four groups of texts. The first consists of the texts that articulate the self-definition of exclusivist communities and refer not only to their worldview but also to their structures of organization (i.e., the Community Rule and the Damascus Document). The second includes two texts that, though they belong to genres that do not concern community organization, nevertheless clearly refer to the same community and worldview as the Community Rule (i.e., the Pesharim and the Hodayot). These, of course, are the easy cases.

Nickelsburg's analysis becomes more interesting with the third group, which consists of two texts that reflect overlapping concerns with the sectarian texts but which do not appear to have been produced by the Qumran community (i.e., portions of 1 Enoch and Jubilees). Most scholars would agree that 1 Enoch reflects some sort of emerging separatist group consciousness, reflected in the polarizing rhetoric to which Nickelsburg draws attention and in such terms of self-reference as "plant of righteousness." But Jubilees is less clearly a candidate for inclusion in a trajectory of sectarian literature, since it largely does not employ the kind of exclusivist rhetoric that marks the other texts. Here, Nickelsburg's analysis is subtle and insightful. Both 1 Enoch and Jubilees, he argues, are concerned with the knowledge that leads to correct understanding of "the commandments of the Most High." Although 1 Enoch employs a polarizing rhetoric that contrasts false teachers with the wise who teach people how to "walk in the paths of righteousness," Jubilees' representation of itself as "a text that claims to be right Torah directly revealed to Moses and that *really* is the precipitate of an interpretation of the Torah" (p. 158). This claim means that its internal logic is also implicitly exclusivistic even if its rhetoric is not. Thus it deserves a place in the trajectory of sectarianism.

Finally, the fourth group, though Nickelsburg treats it earlier in his discussion, consists of a text that employs dualistic rhetoric and angelological lore but which does not seem to make allusion to a particular community or movement (i.e., The Visions of Amram) and may or may not come from an exclusivistic provenance. Nickelsburg defends its inclusion in the study, however, because it appears to have been used "to confirm and inform the exclusivistic world view of the people at Qumran" (p. 145).

It is at this point that I begin to have some reservations about the way in which Nickelsburg has set up the program of research and in particular the role of the exclusivistic worldview in determining the nature of the texts that might be included for comparison. Although sectarian communities are obliged from time to time to engage in the sort of boundary marking rhetoric that differentiates them from other groups, that is not all that they do. They separate from others over particular issues of belief and practice. What gives them the right to see themselves as the exclusive locus of salvation is what they claim to know about things that are matters of concern for the whole community. Nickelsburg himself acutely notes that ways in which the self-understanding of the *yahad* is articulated has to do with covenant, torah, and temple, that is, with core elements of Jewish identity in general. In developing the objects of their special knowledge and the modes of their knowing, sectarian communities engage a variety of texts and discourses from their cultural world, not only those that also exhibit separatist or exclusivist rhetoric. Thus if we are to understand the ways in which sectarian communities develop their distinctive identities, we may need to look closely at materials that in themselves do not have within them implicit or explicit exclusivist tendencies.

A concrete example of how the focus on exclusivistic ideologies may lead to problems is found in Nickelsburg's discussion toward the end of his article on the implications of his inquiry for Qumran studies. As he sketches possible avenues of further investigation he contrasts the Aramaic Levi Document ("an excellent candidate for this trajectory") with Sapiential Work A (now known as 4QInstruction) as a work "wholly lack[ing] an exclusivistic world view" (p. 159). If I understand him properly, he would set aside 4QInstruction as less relevant to the project of tracing "trajectories" of sectarianism and understanding its "diversity and proliferation." While recent scholarship tends to confirm the nonsectarian nature of the text itself,[7] it

---

[7] ". . . the lack of any reference to a sectarian group, community, or practice,

also demonstrates the significant number of literary relationships between 4QInstruction and various Qumran texts that are crucial to the sectarian self-consciousness of the community.[8] The most recent and careful of these studies, that of Eibert Tigchelaar, documents literary connections between 4QInstruction and 1QS III-IV (the Two Spirits discourse) and also between 4QInstruction and 1QH^a V (Sukenik XIII and frags.).[9] Both the Two Spirits discourse and 1QH V, 19–VI, 7 are concerned with topics of anthropology, divine pre-destination, and forms of dualism. Even though the Qumran texts reflect a much more developed form of speculation, the role of 4QInstruction in facilitating the development of these ideas is evi-dent. Elgvin's judgment that 4QInstruction exercised "considerably influence on the development of sectarian theology on these sub-jects"[10] is warranted. In a similar fashion 4QInstruction and sections of the Epistle of Enoch (especially 1 Enoch 91 and 103–104) also have a probable literary relationship, with 4QInstruction most likely influencing the Epistle of Enoch.[11] Thus a nonsectarian, nonexclu-sivist wisdom instruction appears to contribute in significant ways to the articulation of a developing sectarian, exclusivistic ideology in the Enochic and Qumran literatures.

A singular focus on exclusivistic worldviews might also leave aside texts such as the Songs of the Sabbath Sacrifice, many of the cal-endrical texts, the pseudo-Daniel literature, and much else that is in various ways ideologically and sometimes verbally linked to the explic-itly sectarian texts. The privileging of texts with exclusivistic world-views would, I fear, lead to an impoverished and distorted picture of the nature of sectarian discourses and the ways in which they develop into quite differentiated forms.

One way of articulating my hesitation concerning Nickelsburg's proposal is perhaps by scrutinizing his metaphor of trajectory. A tra-

---

suggests that the composition is not sectarian, but of a more general nature, and is in no apparent way critical of the Jerusalem priesthood." Eibert J.C. Tigchelaar, *To Increase Learning for the Understanding Ones: Reading and Reconstructing the Framentary Early Jewish Sapiential Text 4QInstruction* (Leiden, 2001), pp. 247–248.

[8] In addition to the study by Tigchelaar, see also Armin Lange, *Weisheit und Prädestination: Weisheitliche Urordnung und Prädestination in den Textfunden von Qumran* (Leiden, 1995) and Torlief Elgvin, "An Analysis of 4QInstruction" (Ph.D. diss., Hebrew University of Jerusalem, 1998).

[9] Tigchelaar, pp. 194–207.

[10] Elgvin, pp. 163–164.

[11] Tigchelaar, pp. 212–217.

jectory, "the path described by a projectile flying,"[12] suggests a linear relationship in which ideas or texts or movements might be related to one another in a simple fashion. I would like to suggest another metaphor, one that I think could better guide our interest in the "diversity and proliferation" of sectarian Judaism without sacrificing the concern to attend to the crucial role of an exclusivistic worldview. This metaphor is that of the Venn diagram, which "represents . . . logical sets pictorially as circles . . . common elements of the sets being represented by intersections of the circles."[13] Or, to employ a slightly different metaphor, what I would urge is a more detailed and finely grained "mapping" of the discourses that overlap between sectarian texts and those of other, presumably nonsectarian texts.

I am, in fact, inclined to argue for the merits of a revised and chastened version of the old "naive" approach to the analysis of Qumran texts to which Nickelsburg alludes at the beginning of his article. In the 1950s and 1960s scholars often assumed without reflection that all the texts found in the caves were both sectarian and the products of the people who lived at Qumran. Both of those assumptions have been shown to be false, and scholarship is the better for it. Equally unpersuasive, however, are the arguments that the texts found in the cave constitute a purely random collection of Second Temple Jewish literature.[14] Analyses of Qumran orthography and scribal practices[15] and the significance of cryptic scripts[16] have provided something of a profile of texts that were produced or copied by the Qumran community, but such texts account for only a small percentage of the manuscript material. I would not wish to argue that the Qumran "library" was a comprehensively planned

---

[12] *The New Oxford American Dictionary* (New York), p. 1796.

[13] Ibid., p. 1874.

[14] Especially as championed by Norman Golb, *Who Wrote the Dead Sea Scrolls? The Search for the Secret of Qumran* (New York, 1995). See the critique of Florentino García Martínez and A.S. van der Woude, "A 'Groningen' Hypothesis of Qumran Origins and Early History," in *Revue de Qumran* 14 (1990), pp. 521–541.

[15] Emanuel Tov, "The Orthography and Language of the Hebrew Scrolls Found at Qumran and the Origin of These Scrolls," in *Textus* 13 (1986), pp. 32–57. See also William Schniedewind, "Qumran Hebrew as an Antilanguage," in *Journal of Biblical Literature* 118 (1999), pp. 235–252.

[16] Stephen J. Pfann, "The Writings in Esoteric Script from Qumran," in L.H. Schiffman, E. Tov, and J.C. VanderKam, eds., *The Dead Sea Scrolls: Fifty Years After Their Discovery 1947–1997* (Jerusalem, 2000), pp. 177–190.

collection or that all of the texts found there in some way contributed to the formation of the *yahad*'s theologically distinctive stance. I am inclined to assume that the library developed largely from the deposits of personal collections brought by persons who came to live at the at the community as members or prospective members. But the manuscripts found there, especially those that occur in more than one copy, provide an index of the sorts of things that persons attracted to this sectarian community found interesting and helpful to their intellectual and spiritual formation, whether or not these texts were themselves sectarian or proto-sectarian. Although it is not always possible to identify relationships as intriguing as that provided by 4QInstruction, the Community Rule, and the Hodayot, the appropriation and transformation of nonsectarian forms of discourse by the sectarian community is an important element of our understanding of their modes of thought.

While I agree with Nickelsburg that texts like the Community Rule, the Damascus Document, the Hodayot, and the Pesharim form the touchstones for understanding the formation of sectarian consciousness, and while I would agree that the tracking of exclusivistic rhetoric is of great importance, I would urge that this inquiry be part of a much larger (and probably considerably more messy) project. To return to the image of trajectories, what we will eventually need is the tracing out of dozens of trajectories to see how the complex discourses of Second Temple Judaism, both in its sectarian and in its nonsectarian manifestations, intersect and interrelate. Nickelsburg's study makes an important contribution to one of the most significant of these trajectories.

RESPONSE TO CAROL NEWSOM

My article on religious exclusivism had its origins in a undergradu-
ate honors seminar on "The Dead Sea Scrolls and the Media," which
I directed in 1997. We looked at press coverage on the Scrolls and
Scrolls research from 1948 to 1955 and from 1990s in light of some
theoretical writing on the media, and we studied some of the major
Scrolls in translation, in light of sociological studies on sectarianism
by Bryan Wilson and Werner Stark and psychological studies by
T.W. Adorno, et al., and Gordon Allport.[1] The sociological and psychological material provided a framework within which to study the
world view of some of the Scrolls and, in particular, the manner in
which the ancient authors described the relationship between themselves and those outside their group.

In writing the article, I developed my definition of a sect with
several things in mind. First, I wanted to extend the use of the terms
"sect" and "sectarian," so that they did not refer simply to the group
at Qumran and to vocabulary that was typical of documents that
arguably emanated from that group. My own observation, partly
from inductive study and partly on the basis of the theoretical work
cited above, indicated that these texts were characterized not only
by a common religious and social terminology, but also by a world
view that was embodied, in part, in this language and rhetoric. Second, I wanted to broaden the study to include other texts—not written in Qumran—in which I found this same world view and, to
some extent, this same terminology. At the end of the article, I suggested that some early Christian texts share the same world view and,
to some degree, the same attitude toward those outside the group.

Thus while Carol Newsom rightly suggests that the texts I discussed in the article can profitably be studied on a broader continuum that includes other related texts found in the Qumran "collection,"
my purpose was, in fact, to broaden a discussion that I felt was too

---

[1] Bryan R. Wilson, *Religious Sects: A Sociological Study* (London, 1970); Werner Stark,
The Sociology of Religion: A Study of Christendom, Vol. 2: *Sectarian Religion* (5 vols.; London,
1966–72); T.W. Adorno, et al., *The Authoritarian Personality* (New York, 1982); Gordon
Allport, *The Nature of Prejudice* (Garden City, 1958).

narrowly focused on terminology and on literature that was arguably generated within the Qumran "sect."

Critical comments on the collection by Robinson and Koester, *Trajectories through Early Christianity*,[2] should have nudged me away from the use of the term "trajectory." I did not intend to suggest a deterministic view of intellectual and theological discourse. Curiously, before reading Newsom's response and with no knowledge of what a "Venn diagram" is, I used the analogy of a set of overlapping circles in another response in this volume (below, p. 514). One might also think of a bolt of cloth in which the intersecting threads of the warp and woof create a variety of patterns, hues, and shades at a number of intersecting points, or one might think of the repeated confluence of a number of streams in a delta system. However one models the reality, Newsom correctly argues that the texts generated by the Qumran group reflect a complex intermingling of motifs, language, and literary forms that are at home elsewhere in texts that are not marked by what I call the sectarian mentality and world view of the Qumran group.

I also agree that the "collection" of texts found in the Qumran caves doubtless includes personal manuscripts brought there by individuals who came to participate in the community. Thus while we must exercise caution in extrapolating a Qumran theology from these texts, they do provide some insight into the kind of people who were drawn to the community. The place was a magnet for persons who valued certain kinds of literature. Moreover, to the extent that multiple copies of certain texts were actually copied at Qumran, we may suppose where priorities lay and how some of these texts functioned in the life and religious thought of the community.[3]

As to the matter of definitions—in this case the definition of "sect" and "sectarian"—such definitions are necessary for analytic, heuristic purposes. At the same time, they can either confine one's view into the material (my definition of sect), or they can open a very broad view in which one can lose the trees in the midst of the forest (a soft view of sect). It may be useful to work with several definitions. My own definition of a sect is relatively narrow. It parallels closely that of Shaye Cohen, although I did not have his before

---

[2] James M. Robinson and Helmut Koester, *Trajectories through Early Christianity* (Philadelphia, 1971).

[3] Nickelsburg, "The Books of Enoch at Qumran," pp. 109–113.

me: "A sect is a small organized group that separates itself from a larger religious body and asserts that it alone embodies the ideals of the larger group because it alone understands God's will."[4] It also has much in common with Jokiranta's analysis, as Newsom notes. The *narrowness* of my definition allowed me, paradoxically, to find continuities between the texts generated by the Community and a *broader* range of texts created outside, and prior to the founding of the Community. Thus it served a useful function. At the same time, as Newsom notes, this restrictive definition lacks the advantages of Bryan Wilson's range of sectarian phenomena[5] and Albert Baumgarten's "softer" definition, which makes reference to Wilson's.[6] They allow one to place the Qumran group and the authors of the Enoch literature within a broader range of possibilities for context of social organization. Thus, in trying to reconstruct the social realities of the ancient world, it seems to me useful, if not necessary, to work with this variety of definitions. The definitions are not the realities, but provide differing perspectives into those realities.

I describe my definition of sect as more theologically oriented that the definition offered by Newsom, which reflects the sociological orientation of Wilson's typology and Baumgarten's definition. Cohen's definition has theological and sociological features; he speaks of social separation but also of one's view of oneself as alone understanding God's will. The focus on theology or, perhaps more correctly, religious world view, allowed me to find certain commonalities among both texts of the Qumran Community and those imported into it, as well as some early Christian texts.

The relevant theoretical literature cited above provides some interesting insights into this world view. Allport's study of prejudice resonates as one reads the labeling, blaming, and scapegoating terminology of the Qumranites and the author of the Epistle of Enoch. Stark's discussion of "The Origin of Sects" provides a connection between world view and experience.

> The last [sic!] root of all sectarianism lies in the alienation of some group from the inclusive society within which it has to carry on its life. It is a kind of protest movement, distinguished from other similar movements by the basic fact that it experiences and expresses its

---

[4] Shaye J.D. Cohen, *From the Maccabees to the Mishnah* (Philadelphia, 1987), p. 125.
[5] Wilson, *Sects*, pp. 23–47.
[6] Baumgarten, *Sects*, p. 13.

dissatisfactions and strivings in religious (rather than political or generally secular) terms.[7]

He then goes on to catalog in detail what these experiences were in the case of certain known and historically describable groups.[8] In working with ancient texts that are either anonymous or pseudonymous, one's historical description is always tenuous. However, much has been written on the circumstances that gave rise to the Qumran Community and its historical development, and I have made some suggestions about the context of the Epistle of Enoch.[9] The process is worth attempting, and if one cannot be certain of the particular historical context of a text, one can, with caution, extrapolate some information about the *type* of situation that gave rise to a text and thus learn something about the text's possible function(s). This brings us more into the realm of social scientific than of historical method.

Having explained the rationale for my narrow point of entry into the issue of ancient Jewish sectarianism, I do want to second Newsom's call to incorporate this study into a broader perspective, governed, perhaps most usefully, by Wilson's typology of "sects." There are points of similarity and distinctions between the world view and theology of the texts I discussed and those, for example, of the Pharisees, whose name suggests a form of separatism. And there are differences between the aspirations, hopes, and behavior of the Pharisees and the Qumran group. As I have argued and Newsom has noted, the Epistle of Enoch and the Book of Jubilees fall somewhere in the middle of a social continuum. In part, as we note, this reflects the fact that we do not possess a community manual for the Enochians or the group who studied and generated the torah of the book of Jubilees.[10] So, we know really nothing about the community organization of those who generated these texts, and only a little bit about their daily life, as this can be extrapolated from their law: for the Enoch group, their calendrical observance; for those who wrote Jubilees, the same and some other details of halakhic observance.

---

[7] Stark, *Sects*, p. 5.

[8] Ibid., pp. 6–92.

[9] The literature on Qumran is immense. On the Epistle of Enoch, see Nickelsburg, "Riches, the Rich, and God's Judgment," "Social Aspects," "The Epistle of Enoch," "Revisiting the Rich and Poor," "Religious Exclusivism."

[10] On 1 Enoch, see Nickelsburg, *1 Enoch 1*, pp. 64–65. On Jubilees, see idem, *Ancient Judaism*, chapter two.

The relationships between the Qumran Community and those who wrote the Enoch literature, Jubilees, and the Aramaic Levi document are a puzzle to me. First, this pertains to the general content of the texts and the identity of their authors. The number of manuscripts of each of these preserved at Qumran suggests, as I indicated above, that Qumran was a magnet for people whose persuasions are reflected to some degree in these documents. The priestly origin of the Levi document and, at least, the priestly interests of Jubilees indicate compatibility with the priestly orientation and governance of Qumran, although, in the case of Jubilees, the absence of any reference to Aaron in a document ascribed to his brother is striking. Issues of Temple and cult are important to the writers of 1 Enoch, but the priestly identity of the Enochic authors is not proven.[11] The devaluation of the Mosaic tradition in 1 Enoch stands in striking contrast to the Mosaic authorship of Jubilees, which, however, incorporates sizable pieces of Enochic tradition into its texts and celebrates the figure of the patriarch.[12] Mosaic Torah is, of course, central at Qumran.

Second, there is a question of ideology and what Newsom describes as "some sort of emerging separatist group consciousness." Here I simply second her observations about exclusivistic and polarizing rhetoric. But the issue is complex. Especially noteworthy is the "universalistic" language that appears in all the major sections of 1 Enoch except the Book of the Luminaries, where it has no real place. Enochic wisdom is the potential source of salvation for those of "all the sons of earth" (i.e., the gentiles) who will embrace it in the end-time.[13] This notion sits paradoxically, if not uncomfortably in the context of the powerful polarizing rhetoric of the Epistle—though evidently it was not problematic for the author of the Epistle. It also stands in striking contrast to the Jew/gentile polarity that runs through Jubilees. Apart from the War Scroll and some of the *pesharim*, Jew/gentile polarity is not really an issue in texts written at Qumran. To some degree this is to be explained by the circumstances that generated these texts. If the gentiles are the persecutors, or, conversely,

---

[11] Idem, *1 Enoch 1*, p. 67.
[12] On Moses in 1 Enoch, see ibid., pp. 60–61; on Jubilees' use of the Enoch materials, see ibid., pp. 71–76.
[13] Ibid., pp. 52–53.

if relations with them are too close for comfort, one speaks in polarizing terms. If wrong-headed Jews are the problem, then inner-Jewish
polarizing language is front and center. Nonetheless, as Newsom
notes, there are degrees of severity in the way one expresses one's
antagonism. Jubilees lacks the polarizing rhetoric of the Epistle of
Enoch and many of the Qumran texts. Nonetheless, the presupposition and foundation of the whole text is the belief that Israel has
strayed from right Mosaic Torah and that the author of this text
and his colleagues have searched out and now explicate that Torah
(23:16–26)

The sorting out of these issues is, as Newsom rightly observes, a
complex and "messy" project. Its complexity is exacerbated, as she
notes, when we attempt to explain the theological and literary interrelationships between motifs and forms found in non-sectarian (by
whatever definition) texts and texts written in the Qumran Community
that employ these motifs and forms as carriers of the Community's
theology, ideology, and world view.

Symptomatic of this situation is the sapiential text known as
4QInstruction. Its relatively recent appearance in the scholarly spot-
light, moreover, has thrown into the proverbial cocked hat a good
deal of generally accepted scholarship about the distinction between
wisdom and apocalypticism.[14] The text also complicates and makes
more crucial the issue of literary genre and its relationship to the
content of a text. At first glance, 4QInstruction is an innocent looking sapiential text with many of the concerns and modes of expression found in the Wisdom of Ben Sira. Upon closer inspection
problems emerge.[15] To cite just three examples, how do the cosmic
world view implied in language about heavenly books, the allusions
to an eschatological denouement, and the references to the revelatory *raz nihyeh* relate to similar elements in texts that are usually
described as apocalyptic, and where do they place this text in relation to the Wisdom of Ben Sira? When added to the other examples cited by Newsom, and discussed in terms not only of theological
and intellectual development, but also of community origins and

---

[14] On the problems with this scholarship, see Nickelsburg, "Wisdom and Apocalypticism," below, pp. 000–000.

[15] On 4QInstruction, see the excellent edition of the text, together with an introduction and commentary on it, and a bibliography of relevant publications by John
Strugnell and Daniel J. Harrington, *DJD 34*, pp. 1–503.

development, these issues add up to a complex project whose full execution cries out for eschatological clarity.

Finally, I add just a few comments about the concluding section of my article. How does all of this, not least the clarifying comments by Carol Newsom, pertain to our study of Christian origins? What connections might we find between Enochic Judaism and the early church, and how do the parallels between the New Testament and the Qumran literature complicate matters? How does a social scientifically oriented approach, informed by Wilson's typology shed light on the issue, when one works comparatively with both the Jewish and Christian texts? To the extent that we use Stark's insights about alienation and protest as constituents in sectarian origins, what do we learn about the similarities and differences between the Jesus movement and the rise of Christianity, on the one hand, and Jewish sectarianism, by whatever definition? Persecution, alienation from the centers of power, and an apocalyptic world view are readily evident in the Book of Revelation. What about the rest of the New Testament corpus? Some promising forrays into that topic are provided by John Kloppenborg's analysis of Q, Luke, and James (below, pp. 572–585).

CHAPTER SIX

PATRIARCHS WHO WORRY ABOUT
THEIR WIVES: A HAGGADIC TENDENCY
IN THE GENESIS APOCRYPHON*

GEORGE W.E. NICKELSBURG

FOR JONAS GREENFIELD

דכיר לטב

The Genesis Apocryphon (1QapGen) provides an excellent subject
for discussion in a symposium that is devoted to "Early Usage and
Interpretation of the Bible in Light of the Dead Sea Scrolls" and
that is intent upon an analysis of Scroll material in its shared and
unique dimensions. The text was unknown until the discovery of its
sole manuscript in Qumran Cave I. Its relationships to the Enochic
literature and the Book of Jubilees have been noted since its first
publication by Nahman Avigad and Yigael Yadin,[1] and scholars have
discussed and disputed whether it is a product of the Qumran community. Unfortunately, its poor state of preservation has severely limited its interpretation, not least with respect to the issues of interest
to this symposium. This paper will attempt a new look, nevertheless, focusing primarily on the stories of the birth of Noah and
Abram's and Sarai's sojourn in Egypt with a view toward patterns
of narrative technique and questions of social setting. Occasional
appeal will be made to other fragments of text, which are just now
being brought into the discussion, thanks to the work of Jonas
Greenfield, Elisha Qimron, and Matthew Morgenstern.[2]

* I have profited from the discussion of a previous draft of this paper that was
read at the biennial meeting of the Taskforce on Apocalyptic of the Wissenschaftliche
Gesellschaft für Theologie, held in Bethel, Germany in March, 1995.
[1] *A Genesis Apocryphon* (Jerusalem: Magnes, 1956). The major comprehensive study
of the scroll, from which I have learned much, is Joseph A. Fitzmyer, *The Genesis
Apocryphon of Qumran Cave 1* (2nd ed.; BO 18A; Rome: Biblical Institute, 1971).
[2] Jonas C. Greenfield and Elisha Qimron, "The Genesis Apocryphon Col. XII,"

1. LAMECH'S ACCOUNT OF NOAH'S BIRTH: COLS. 1–5

1.1. *The Story in Comparison with 1 Enoch 106–107*

Columns 1–5 contained an extensive account of Noah's birth, narrated in the first person singular by Lamech his father. Since the story is already in progress at the top of column 2, it must have begun somewhere in the lower half of column 1.[3] Thanks to parallels between cols. 2–5 and 1 Enoch 106–107—where Enoch recounts the story of Noah's birth—we can reconstruct the overall content of the story in the Genesis Apocryphon:

1QapGen	1 Enoch
2:19–26	106:4–5a + 7–8
3:3	106:13
5:9–10	106:18
5:18?	106:19
5:20?	107:2
5:24–25	107:3

The story in the Apocryphon seems to have progressed as follows. Lamech marries Bitenosh,[4] who gives birth to Noah (col. 1 ‖ 106:1), whose glorious appearance is then described (col. 1 ‖ 106:2–3). Lamech concludes from the child's appearance that his wife was impregnated by one of the watchers (2:1 ‖ 106:5–6) and is struck with fear at the prospect (2:2–3 ‖ 106:4a). Lamech confronts Bitenosh, demanding that she speak the truth under oath, but she insists that the child is Lamech's (2:3–18 ‖ –). Lamech then runs to Methuselah, asking that he, in turn, request Enoch to query the holy ones (2:19–21a ‖ 106:4–7). Methuselah goes to Enoch, who is at Parvaim, and tells him about the miraculous birth (2:21b–26 + [27–34] ‖ 106:8–12). Enoch responds

Abr-Nahrain Supp. 3 (1992): 70–77. Correspondence about the text with my friend and companion in Enoch studies, Jonas Greenfield, was broken off by his premature and lamented death. In writing the paper, I derived my "first-hand" knowledge of the unpublished parts of the scroll from Emanuel Tov, ed., *The Dead Sea Scrolls on Microfiche: A Comprehensive Facsimile Edition of the Texts from the Judean Desert* (Leiden: Brill, 1993) microfiche 126. For a preliminary edition of new material from 1QapGen, see Matthew Morgenstern, Elisha Qimron and Daniel Sivan, "The Hitherto Unpublished Columns of the Genesis Apocryphon," *Abr-Nahrain* 33 (1995) 30–54. I wish to acknowledge the help I received from Matthew Morgenstein during the writing of the paper.

[3] My estimate is conservative; I am allowing about as much space for the beginning of the story as it occupied in 4QEn[c]; see below n. 5.

[4] On the vocalization see the discussion by Fitzmyer, *Apocryphon*, 82–83.

at great length, describing the sin of the watchers, the judgment that will come through the Flood, and Noah's role in that judgment (columns 3–4 ‖ 106:13–17, signalled by 3:3 ‖ 106:13b). He assures Methuselah that the child is Lamech's (5:3–8) and tells Methuselah to return with that news (5:9±11 ‖ 106:18). He continues his speech with a description of the eschaton (5: ± 11–23 ‖ 106:18–107:2). Methuselah returns to Lamech, conveying Enoch's information (5:24–25 ‖ 107:3). The section concludes with a brief description of Lamech's positive response to the news (5:26–27).

Although the severely damaged condition of columns 1, 3, 4, and 5 of 1QapGen limits our ability to compare this version of the Noah story in detail with 1 Enoch 106–107, some conclusions are possible. First, a comparison of 1QapGen with the Aramaic 4QEn^c and the Greek Chester Beatty papyrus of 1 Enoch indicates that the Apocryphon's version was approximately 3.74 times as long as that in 1 Enoch 106–107.[5] The following table indicates the (estimated) number of lines for each narrative component in the respective versions and the proportion of the whole occupied by each component.

	1 Enoch 106–107			1QapGen	
	lines	%age		lines	%age
	Greek	Aramaic			
1. Beginning	14	5	15	6	4.5
2. Lamech/Bitenosh	–	–	–	15	12
3. Lamech to Methuselah	14	5	15	2.5	2
4. Methuselah to Enoch	23	8.3	24	13.5	10.5
5. Enoch's oracle	38	13.7	40	87	68
6. Methuselah to Lamech	6	2	6	2	1.5
7. Lamech's response	–	–	–	2	1.5
		34	100	128	100

The bar graph presents this information visually.

---

[5] My calculations are based on a comparison of 4QEn^c (J.T. Milik, *The Books of Enoch: Aramaic Fragments of Qumran Cave 4* [Oxford: Clarendon, 1976]), the Chester Beatty Papyrus (Campbell Bonner, *The Last Chapters of Enoch in Greek* [Darmstadt: Wissenschaftliche Buchgesellschaft, 1968 reprint]), and the edition of Avigad and Yadin. 1 Enoch 106:13–107:2, preserved in 4QEn^c 5 2:17–30 (Milik, *Enoch*, 209–210), occupies 14 lines × 55 characters, a total of 770 characters, compared to the Greek (Bonner, *Enoch*) of 39 lines × 30 characters, a total of 1170 characters. Taking this 66% relationship of the Aramaic to the Greek and multiplying it by the total 2850

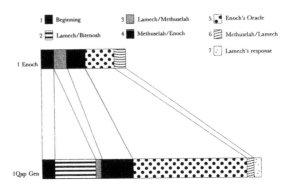

From these estimates and the preserved material in 1QapGen, we note the following. (a) In both cases the first person narrator is the person of immediate concern. In 1QapGen it is Lamech the father; in 1 Enoch, it is Enoch, the author of the corpus. (b) The beginning of the narrative (1) may have been about the same length in 1QapGen as it is in 1 Enoch; however, this estimate and the content of the section are uncertain. (c) Although in 1 Enoch Lamech suspects that Noah's conception was of angelic origin (106:6), the stormy emotional scene between Lamech and his wife in 1QapGen 2 (2) has no counterpart in 1 Enoch 106–107. (d) 1 Enoch stresses the child's miraculous appearance by a double repetition of the initial description (106:2–3 + 5–6 and 10–12), and the child's appearance suggests to Lamech that the child is a portent of things to come (106:6). 1QapGen 1 must have had an initial description of the child, but 2:19 (3) is much shorter than its counterpart to 1 Enoch 106:5–6 and briefly summarizes the action in column 1 without repeating the description. (e) Methuselah's address to Enoch (4) in 1QapGen 2:26–34 was a somewhat longer than its counterpart in 1 Enoch and almost certainly repeated the description of the child in the first part of the story. (f) Enoch's oracle (5) in 1QapGen is more than six times longer than its counterpart in 1 Enoch 106:13–107:1. Some preserved wording at 1QapGen 5:18 indicates that this final section of Enoch's speech contained a prediction of the eschaton similar to 106:19–107:1.

---

characters in the Greek of 106–107 (95 lines × 30 characters), we arrive at an estimated 1881 characters for the Aramaic of 1 Enoch 106–107, which tallies roughly with Milik's estimate that chapters 106:1–107:2 covered 35 lines in 4QEn^c 5:1:26–2:30. I estimate the length of the story in 1QApGen to have been 128 lines (6 lines for col. 1 + 34 lines each for cols. 2–4 + 27 lines for col. 50—a total of 135 lines, reduced to 128 to allow for *vacats*) × 55 characters, a total of 7040 characters, which is 3.74 times as long as the estimated 1881 characters of the Aramaic 1 Enoch 106–107.

The existence of two versions of the same story—such as we have in 1 Enoch 106–107 and 1QapGen 1—naturally raises the question of their relationship to one another. Is 1 Enoch 106–107 dependent on 1QapGen? Is 1QapGen an expansion of 1 Enoch 106–107? Are both dependent on a common source, perhaps to be identified with a Book of Noah? Although I shall not treat this issue in detail, I shall suggest below (4.2) that my findings have some bearing on the matter. My task is, rather, an interpretation of Apocryphon's account of Noah's birth, as we know it from the preserved and fragmentary parts of cols. 1–5 and by inference from 1 Enoch 106–107, and as we can understand it in the context of the rest of the scroll. Part of that context is the story of Abram and Sarai in Egypt, which will be the subject of part 2 of this paper.

1.2. *Interpretive Tendencies in 1QapGen 1–5*

The account of Noah's birth that once stood in 1QapGen was a massive expansion of a brief notice in Gen 5:28–29 whose motifs and tendencies reflect its author's interests and historical setting.

1.2.1. *Reflections of Enochic Traditions*
Traditions preserved in the early strata of 1 Enoch, some of them about Enoch, are a major component in this story's interpretation of Genesis. (1) The versions in both 1 Enoch 106–107 and 1QapGen presume the myth of the watchers and the women recounted in 1 Enoch 6–11. Lamech suspects that the child has been fathered by one of the heavenly beings that were mating with human women, and Enoch summarizes the story and assures Methuselah that Noah is not a child of the watchers. (2) The linkage to Methuselah and Methuselah's association with Enoch point to parts of 1 Enoch (e.g., chaps. 72–82; 83–84; 85–90). (3) Enoch's association with the angels is paralleled in 1 Enoch 12:1–3. (4) The parts of the Apocryphon's story that have no counterpart in 1 Enoch 106–107 contain terms typical of 1 Enoch 6–11, such as "watchers and holy ones" (2:1, 16, 20; cf. 1 Enoch 1:2; 10:1; 12:2), "the sons of heaven" (2:5; 1 Enoch 6:2; "ἄγγελοι" is used in the Greek of 1 Enoch, as is typical in that version),[6] "the Great Holy One" (2:14, 16; 1 Enoch 1:3; 10:1), and "Lord/King of all the ages" (2:4, 7; 1 Enoch 9:4).

---

[6] The Greek of 1 Enoch, and the Ethiopic version following it, use the term "holy angels" throughout chaps. 1–36 and 97–107. Where it exists for the relevant

The story of the watchers and the women was not simply presumed by the author of the Apocryphon. The scroll had at least two
columns preceding the present column 1 (1Q20), which appear to
have actually contained a version of the story of the watchers and
the women similar to that now in 1 Enoch 6–11.[7] References in
1Q20 to God's wrath (1:1, 2) and to certain individuals who are
"bound (אסירין, 1:4) parallel elements in the Enoch story[8] and would
provide the reader with a context for Lamech's suspicion about the
angelic conception of Noah (1QapGen 2). Lines 2–3 of 1QapGen 1
refer to "the mystery (of evil)," which may be identified with the
watchers' revelations in 1 Enoch 8:1–4; 16:3.

1.2.2. *Eschatology*

Because of the badly damaged condition of the Apocryphon and the
fragmentary form of its narrative in columns 1–5, we cannot determine the degree to which the Apocryphon's version of the story of
Noah's birth was driven by an eschatological *Tendenz*. However, we
may note the following. (a) The story of the watchers and the women
in 1 Enoch 6–11 involves an eschatological recasting of Genesis
6:1–4. 1 Enoch 10–11—though it begins with the immediate problem of the pre-diluvian situation and its solution—provides a scenario for the *eschaton* and the final and complete eradication of all
evil from the earth.[9] (b) The story in 1 Enoch 106–107 has a sharply
focused eschatological *Tendenz*. Noah's physical appearance indicates
things to come and reflects his role as the remnant figure at the
time of the Flood. As such, he may portend a similar figure who
will survive the eschatological judgment that will parallel the Flood.
Enoch utters a bipartite oracle to Methuselah—the first half about
the flood (106:15–17), the second half about subsequent history which
concludes with the great judgment (106:18d–107:1). This double
structure and its *Urzeit/Endzeit* typology is paralleled also in 1 Enoch
91:5 and 6–9, as well as in 1 Enoch 93:4, 9–10 + 91:12–17. There
is clearly enough room in 1QapGen 5:9–19 to have contained some
of this material and a few words of it are preserved in 5:18.

---

passages, the Aramaic always uses the term "watcher" or "watcher and holy one";
see Milik, *Enoch*, 387.
   [7] See D. Barthélemy and J.T. Milik, ed., DJD 1, 86–87.
   [8] God's wrath is presumed in references to the judgment (10:6, 12–14; cf., e.g.,
1:9; 10:22). On the binding of the watchers, cf. 10:4, 11, 14.
   [9] George W.E. Nickelsburg, "Apocalyptic and Myth in 1 Enoch 6–11," *JBL* 96
(1977): 388–389.

1.2.3. *Revelation*

Enoch's function as revealer in both versions of the story reflects his traditional role in the earlier strata of 1 Enoch, where he is the recipient and transmitter of revelations. While we cannot be certain of many of the details in the story in the Apocryphon, the extraordinary length of the section that transmitted Enoch's speech is noteworthy, and Enoch's revelatory role was crucial in the resolution of the crisis precipitated at the beginning of the narrative.

1.2.4. *A Psychologizing Focus on the Characters' Emotions*

A major feature in the story of Noah's birth in the Apocryphon is its interest in the psychological dynamics between husband and wife. The lines 3–18 of column 2 recount a bitter dispute between Lamech and Bitenosh—of which there is no hint in 1 Enoch 106–107, let alone Genesis 5. Lamech suspects that his wife has conceived through one of the watchers or sons of heaven, and he puts her under an oath to speak the truth. She denies the allegation by reminding him of her sexual pleasure when they made love. The point is a bit obscure. The issue is not whether Lamech and his wife have been to bed together, but whether this child was conceived under other circumstances. Perhaps Bitenosh appeals to her pleasure in order to affirm her love and thus to deny that she would sleep with someone other than her husband. In any case, Lamech is furious with her response, and so, with great emotion, she again refers to their lovemaking and then employs a double oath to underscore a triple assertion that the Lamech is the father and a triple denial that the child has been conceived by an angel.

> I swear to you by the Great Holy One, by the King of the Heavens:
>   from you is this seed,
> and from you is this conception,
> and from you is the planting of this fruit;
> and not from any stranger,
> and not from any of the watchers,
> and not from any of the sons of heaven (2:14–16)

The situation is serious enough because Lamech suspects adultery; it is exacerbated by his concern that his wife has consorted with a divine being, that is, a kind of demon. Abhorrence of such an unnatural confusion of the heavenly/spiritual and the earthly/human is expressed in the Enochic version of Noah story in 106:14–17 (cf. the divine oracle that Enoch receives in the account of his ascent in 1 Enoch 15:3–7).

The interaction between Lamech and Bitenosh reflects an explicitly psychological interest that has an increasing number of parallels in post-biblical literature. In content, its closest parallel is perhaps in the book of Tobit (2:11–14), where Tobit and his wife Hannah argue about a goat that she has brought home; he accuses her of having stolen it and she denies the allegation and accusing him of hypocrisy. Other examples of this kind of intense psychological interest in scenes that depict male/female interactions appear in Joseph and Aseneth 6–9, the Testament of Job 24–26, and the Testament of Joseph 3–9. These parallels notwithstanding, there is also a major difference between this text and other early Jewish haggadah (Jubilees; parts of the Testament of Job; the Testaments of the 12 Patriarchs, to the extent that it preserves Jewish material). Much in these latter texts focuses on moral vices and virtues *as such* and not on the psychology of the persons who embody these characteristics. Lamech's narrative, however, *presumes* the immorality of the alleged adultery, but *focuses* on the anger and anguish felt both by himself and by his wife, and indeed on the pleasure of their lovemaking.

1.3. *Literary Genre*

1.3.1. *Predecessors in Israelite and Greek Literature*
Our interpretation of this story should place it on its generic horizon.[10] Genesis 17, 21, Judges 13, and 1 Samuel 1 recount stories about the divinely induced conceptions of heroes, persons who would play a positive role in the divine economy. The *present* story also recounts the birth of a hero, but it evokes stories that are alien to the biblical accounts about divinely induced conceptions and that derive from Greek myth.[11] Behind it lie the accounts of the mating of the watchers and the women (1 Enoch 6–11 + 12–16), and behind them stand Greek tales about, and references to sexual encounters between gods and humans. Nonetheless, the Noah story is veiled in ambiguity. Speaking through Lamech, the author recalls the stories of the watchers and women and their divine-human coupling, only to allow Bitenosh and Enoch to deny that the present situation is a case in

---

[10] Here I am indebted, in part, to the doctoral dissertation of my student, Beverly A. Bow, *The Birth of Jesus: A Jewish and Pagan Affair* (The University of Iowa, 1995).

[11] Nickelsburg, "Apocalyptic and Myth," 395–97. On the Samson story, however, see Rüdiger Bartelmus, *Heroentum in Israel und seiner Umwelt* (ATANT 65; Zürich: Theologischer Verlag, 1979), 79–112.

point. Noah's glorious appearance powerfully evokes the imagery of divine epiphany. Little wonder that Lamech suspects that Bitenosh, a "daughter of man" (cf. Gen 6:2,4; 1 Enoch 6:1, 7:1), has slept with a divine being.[12] Nonetheless, what the author gives with one hand he takes away with the other. The telltale similarity to a suspected divine father turns out to be deceptive.[13] Noah's epiphanic glory does not indicate divine conception. It reflects his "divine beauty"[14] and is a sign of his divinely appointed function. The heroes of biblical stories about special conception all have divinely appointed roles to play, but this is never indicated by visible, epiphanic appearance.[15]

1.3.2. *The New Testament*

If we carry the generic discussion one step further, to the New Testament, the ambiguity is heightened. Without explaining what he means, Fitzmyer observes laconically that the account of Noah's birth "is not without its significance for the understanding of the genre of the Lucan and Matthean Infancy Narratives."[16] Wherein lies "its significance"? Like the gospel stories, it recounts the birth of a divinely appointed savior figure. The similarities to the Matthean account are especially close. Matthew 1:18–25, like the Noah story, is told from the husband's point of view and focuses on Joseph's concern about Mary's pregnancy. This concern is alleviated by means of a divine revelation (an angel rather than Enoch), which concludes with the command to give the child a name that signifies his salvific function. The Matthean story has a particular twist that makes it a foil to the Apocryphon's story. Lamech thinks that Bitenosh was impregnated

---

[12] That the author is playing on this word and its relationship to Genesis 6 has been noted by Fitzmyer, *Apocryphon*, 82–83; Gedaliahu A.G. Stroumsa, *Another Seed: Studies in Gnostic Mythology* (Nag Hammadi Studies 24; Leiden: Brill, 1984), 23–24, 58; and James C. VanderKam, *Enoch: A Man for All Generations* (Columbia: University of South Carolina, 1995) 96.

[13] It was suggested to me at the first reading of this paper in Bethel, Germany, that the disjunction in the narrative might indicate a polemic against a tradition that Noah was a divine figure of some sort. The only possible indication that I have found of this is in Philo, *De Praemiis et Poenis* 23, which identifies Noah with Deucalion, who was the son of Prometheus, according to Apollodorus (Library 1.46). For a detailed discussion of Jewish and Gnostic stories about impregnation through rebellious divine beings, see Stroumsa, *Another Seed*.

[14] See Otto Betz, "Geistliche Schönheit: Von Qumran zu Michael Hahn," *Die Leibhaftigkeit des Wortes*, O. Michel and U. Mann, ed. (Fs. Adolf Köberle; Hamburg: Im Furche, 1985), 72–75.

[15] See, however, the account of Jesus' birth in the Protevangelium of James 19.

[16] Fitzmyer, *Apocryphon*, 79.

by a divine being, but the child is his own. Joseph thinks that Mary
has slept with another *man*, but Mary is pregnant through divine
agency—though Matthew gives no indication that the Holy Spirit
(vv. 18, 20) had sexual intercourse with Mary.[17]

In the case in Luke 1:26–35, the story of Jesus' conception is told
from Mary's—rather than Joseph's—point of view, and we hear nothing of the latter's suspicion. Nevertheless, the issue of the conception
is even more complicated than in Matthew, because the language—
though it is not explicitly sexual—employs physical imagery:

> the Holy Spirit will come upon you,
>   and the Most High will overshadow you. (Luke 1:35)

But however one wishes to read this metaphor, the result of this
activity is the conception of a child who is "holy" and "son of God,"
titles for the angels in 1 Enoch and elsewhere.[18] Again, I do not
suggest that Luke posits sexual intercourse between the Holy Spirit
and Mary.[19] Nonetheless, much traditional Christian exegesis of this
text misses the point by raising the possibility that it could refer to
divine human coupling, only to dismiss it. However *Luke* may have
construed the conception process, one must ask how a *gentile reader*
of Luke's gospel might have interpreted this story and whether Luke
phrased his text to allow such an interpretation? Would the story
have evoked mythic tales about intercourse between gods and women?
Might it have reminded one of the subtly phrased story about Zeus
impregnating Danae through a shower of gold (Apollodorus, *Library*
2.4.1)?

In conclusion, the story of the birth of Noah in the Genesis Apocryphon attests a pair of tendencies in the interpretation of Genesis

---

[17] It is beyond the scope of this paper to discuss in detail the account of the
birth of Melchizedek, which is attached to the end of some MSS. of 2 Enoch. Even
the most basic problems are complex: text, date, Jewish or Christian provenance.
The following facts are noteworthy, however. The father of Melchizedek is said to
be Nir, the brother of Noah. Although the story occupies a place in 2 Enoch that
is analogous to chapters 106–107 in 1 Enoch, it contains a stormy scene between
Nir and Sopanim, his wife, which parallels 1QApGen 2 rather than 1 Enoch
106–107. Different from the Noah stories, Sopanim conceives without benefit of
any male partner, although the conception is not virginal as in Matthew. This
single-parent conception, moreover, is due to priestly abstinence from sexual intercourse, of which there is no hint in 1QApGen, or Matthew for that matter.

[18] 1 Enoch 6:1, "sons of heaven"; 1:2; 12:2 and passim, "holy ones." For the
two terms together, cf. Wis Sol 5:5; 1QH 11:22.

[19] On this issue with respect to Matthew and Luke, see Raymond E. Brown, *The
Birth of the Messiah* (Garden City: Doubleday, 1977), 124–25, 290–91.

during the Greco-Roman period. One is derived from Greek myth and from psychologically focused narrative; the other reflects the apocalyptic eschatology of early Enochic traditions. Several questions remain open. What is the import of the emotional interchange between Lamech and Bitenosh in 1QapGen 2? What is the relationship between the psychologizing and eschatological tendencies? A partial answer will be found as we consider a second story in 1QapGen, the sojourn of Abram and Sarai in Egypt.

2. Abram's Account of His Sojourn in Egypt (1QapGen 19:13–20:32)

2.1. *Outline of the Story*

The story of Abram's sojourn in Egypt recounted in Gen 12:10–20 has been expanded in 1QapGen to nine times its original size, from approximately 520 characters in the Hebrew Bible to approximately 4550 in 1QapGen. In this transformation, the tightly written Genesis account has been interpolated with additional narrative details, motifs, and whole genres completely absent in Genesis.

We may summarize the Apocryphon's revision of Genesis as follows. As the story begins, Abram has a dream, which he interprets for Sarai (19:14–19). Then, in the account of Sarai's abduction, the comment in Gen 12:15—that the princes have praised Sarai's beauty— is spelled out in a lengthy *wasf* that dwells in delicious detail on the features of her physical beauty. After Sarai's abduction, Abram's prayer for vindication catalyzes Pharaoh's affliction (20:12–16). Then the account of Pharaoh's affliction and healing is narrated as a contest in which Abram accomplishes what the Egyptian magicians and healers cannot do.

2.2. *Narrative Features*

The Apocryphon's retelling of the Genesis story is shaped by a number of features that are paralleled in its version of the story of Noah's birth and in the sources, traditions, and tendencies that shaped that story.

2.2.1. *First Person Narrator*

As we have seen, the first person singular narrative voice is a striking feature of the scroll's version of the story of Noah's birth. It

recurs here. As the text of the Abram story emerges at the top of
column 19, it is Abram, the major character, who narrates the story.
This first person narrative continues well into column 21—to the
beginning of the section corresponding to Genesis 14.[20]

2.2.2. *Psychologizing Interest*
Like the Apocryphon's version of Noah's birth story, this story is
interested in the characters' emotions and in their expression of these
emotions. When Abram awakes from his dream, he is frightened
(19:18), and when he explains the dream, Sarai weeps and greatly
fears that trouble lies ahead (19:21, 23). The emotional temperature
of the scene involving husband and wife is reminiscent of the interchange between Lamech and Bitenosh, although here there is no
confrontation between the two. When Sarai is taken to Pharaoh's
house, the author adds some narrative tension by having Pharaoh
threaten to kill Abraham (thus fulfilling a non-biblical detail in Abram's
dream, viz., that Pharaoh's princes would attempt to kill Abram
[19:15] and justifying Sarah's ambiguous statement about Abram
being her brother). After Sarai's intervention, Abram weeps—three
times (20:10, 12, 16).

2.2.3. *Eroticism*
In a massive embellishment of Genesis 12:15, the author elaborates
the story of Sarai's abduction through the use of the genre of the
wasf,[21] whose erotic details—totally lacking in Genesis—fit well with
the erotic tone of Bitenosh's double reference to her sexual pleasure.
This lingering on the many fine features of Sarai's beauty then provides explicit motivation for Pharaoh's decision to bring Sarai to his
house. Different from his Genesis counterpart, Pharaoh is said to
have loved her very much (רחם) (20:8). This reference parallels other
emotional elements in the Apocryphon.

2.2.4. *Revelation*
Reference to revelation is another feature that this author has added
to the Genesis account. In Gen 12:11–13 Abram's warning to Sarai

---

[20] For the first person singular, see 19:14; 21:15 and cols. 19–21:21. For a shift
from first person to third person narration, cf. Tobit 1:1–3:6 and 3:7 ff.
[21] On this genre, see M.H. Goshen-Gottstein, "Philologische Miszellen zu den
Qumrantexten," *RQ* 2 (1959): 46–48; Fitzmyer, *Apocryphon*, 119–20.

is straightforward and based on the common sense observation that oriental monarchs do as they please when it comes to beautiful women, and, indeed, Pharaoh's abduction of Sarai follows a report about Sarai's beauty (Gen 12:14). The author of the Apocryphon has a different explanation for Abram's warning and for his request that Sarai state that they are brother and sister. Abram is warned of coming events in "a dream in the night" that predicts that Pharaoh's princes will attempt to kill him and that Sarai will claim that "we are both from one family." Thus Abram is depicted as the recipient and interpreter of revelatory dreams. This has some foundation in Gen 15:12–21, where Abraham sees a vision about his and Israel's future; however, that is very different from this portrayal of him as the dreamer and interpreter. The motif of revelation has already appeared in the figure of Enoch in the story of Noah's birth.

2.2.5. *Demon and Exorcist*

In another departure from Genesis, which reflects contemporary beliefs, the author states that Pharaoh's affliction is caused by an evil spirit, who has been sent by God. This parallels 1 Enoch 15:11–16:1, and especially Jubilees 10:1–13, where evil spirits are the cause of sickness.[22] In that the demon is dispatched by God, this detail differs from texts that depict the evil spirits as a kingdom unto themselves, or as a hoard that is under the power of an arch-demon, e.g., Mastema. The notion that an evil spirit could wreak physical havoc at God's behest recalls 2 Cor 12:7–9, where Paul's thorn in the flesh is "an angel of Satan" that keeps Paul from the sin of arrogance.

2.2.6. *Abram and the Figure of Daniel*

The features in this author's portrayal of Abram mentioned in the previous two paragraphs indicate that this author is recasting the biblical patriarch in the mold of Daniel. He is the recipient and

---

[22] It was suggested in the session that "evil spirit" (רוח באישהא, 20:16, 28, 29) need not refer to a personified spirit, i.e., a demon of sorts. However, cf. Jub. 10:13 in the context of a story about the progeny of the watchers. For the Aramaic expression as a cliche in the exorcism formulae of later amulets and bowls, see Joseph Naveh and Shaul Shaked, *Magic Spells and Formulae: Aramaic Incantations of Late Antiquity* (Jerusalem: Magnes, 1993) amulets 19:24–5, 26, 36–37; 25:5; 26:10; bowls 16:7; 23:3, 10; 25:2; 27:7–8.

interpreter of dreams (Dan 2; 7–12).[23] In addition, his healing of Pharaoh makes him the winner of a contest in which all the healers and sages of Egypt fail (Dan 2, 5; Prayer of Nabonidus).[24]

2.2.7. *Abram, the Enochic Tradition, and the Story of the Watchers*

Finally, we note additions to the Genesis story that tie 1QapGen 19–20 to the Enochic tradition. Although the text is damaged at 19:25, it appears that the author describes Abram reading to the Egyptian princes from "the [book] of the words of [En]och."[25] The key words, חכמתא and קושטא, which appear immediately previous to this narrative detail, are major Enochic expressions for the content of the sage's message.[26] Equally remarkable is the Aramaic formulation וקרית קודמיהון לכתב מלי חנוך. The language is employed in contexts describing the formal reading of a binding document (cf. 1 Enoch 13:10).[27] Thus, this author shows a respect for the Enochic corpus that parallels its usage in the Apocryphon's Noah story and, perhaps, the account of the watchers and the women in 1Q20.

More striking is the way in which the author has reshaped the Genesis 12 story to conform to the story of the watchers and the women. The parallels are the following:

1 Enoch 6–11	1QapGen 20
Sons of Heaven see beauty of the women	Pharaoh sees Sarai's beauty
They desire them	He loves her
They take them as their wives	He takes her as his wife
They have intercourse with them	
The dead, the earth, the holy ones pray	Abram prays
God sends angels for judgment	God sends a spirit
	Pharaoh does not have intercourse with Sarai

---

[23] B. de Handschutter, "La rêve dans l'Apocryphe de la Genèse," W.C. van Unnik, ed., *La Littérature juive entre Tenach et Mischna* (Leiden: Brill, 1974), 52–54.

[24] On the literature about these contests, see John J. Collins, *Daniel* (Minneapolis: Fortress, 1993), 42–47.

[25] See Fitzmyer, *Apocryphon*, 118.

[26] For "wisdom" as a summary of the contents of Enoch's writings, cf. 1 Enoch 1:8; 37:1–4; 82:2–3; 92:1; 93:10; 104:12–13. The Epistle of Enoch makes frequent reference to "the path(s) of righteousness or truth. See also below, n. 39.

[27] In 1 Enoch 13:10, the Aramaic verb is מלל. This expressions, with either verb is the regular targumic translations of the Hebrew קרא/דבר באזני, which appears in biblical contexts describing formal readings; see Harry M. Orlinsky, "The Septuagint as Holy Writ and the Philosophy of the Translators," HUCA 46 (1975): 94–103.

In Gen 12:15 Pharaoh simply hears the princes' report about Sarai's beauty (1QapGen 19?-20:8). Here he witnesses it for himself. His love for her (20:8) parallels the desire ascribed to the watchers (6:2). The reference to Pharaoh's taking her as his wife (Gen 12:19) is drawn into the Apocryphon's narrative much earlier (20:9), at a point that corresponds to 1 Enoch 6:2/7:1. Of necessity, the reference to intercourse is deferred until later in the narrative. Abram's prayer for divine vindication (20:12–15) is spoken in the idiom of the prayer for vindication in 1 Enoch 9. It is specifically in response to this prayer that God exacts justice in behalf of Abram and does so through the agency of a spirit (20:16–20; cf. 1 Enoch 10). The stories differ in that here God's judgment prevents intercourse between Pharaoh and Sarai, whereas in 1 Enoch 6–11 the judgment comes after the divine-human mating has produced the giants, whose devastating activity triggers the prayer.

In summary, the major elaborative features in the Apocryphon's interpretation of Genesis 12 are all consonant with, and similar to features in the Noah story. The story is narrated by the protagonist in the first person singular. The emotions of various of the characters are emphasized. Connections with Danielic and Enochic apocalyptic literature are evident. Revelation plays an important role, and Abram has been cast in the mold of Daniel. Especially important is the common use of the story of the watchers and the women.

2.2.8. *Triangulation in the Plot*

There is, however, another parallel in plot between the story about Abram and the Apocryphon's legend of Noah's birth that is created by means of the Apocryphon's versions of the two stories. At the center of the Noah story in columns 1–5 and the story of Abram's sojourn in Egypt in columns 19–20 is an episode whose major characters are husband and wife. In focus are the husband's concern about the possibility that his wife has had or will have sexual relations with someone other than himself and the alleviation of that concern with the assurance that such extra-marital sex has not taken place. Moreover, when Lamech suspects that Bitenosh has conceived from one of the watchers, she takes an oath that she has not done so. Similarly, Abram prays that Pharaoh will not defile his wife, and after, ironically, an evil spirit keeps Pharaoh from consummating the relationship, the king swears an oath to Abram that he has not had intercourse with her. This striking narrative feature, which the two stories have in common with one another, but not with their sources

or other parallels, requires some consideration, since it may well reveal something about the interests and social world of the Apocryphon's
author.

In both the Lamech episode and the Abram story, the third member of the erotic triangle is a larger than life figure. In the first
instance, the alleged lover is a divine being, one of the "watchers,"
"holy ones," "nephilin," or "sons of heaven" (2:1, 5, 16). For Abram
the cause of anxiety is the Egyptian Pharaoh, at the very least one
whose political and social status was qualitatively different from
Abram's, at the maximum, one who was thought to be a son of
God. Jewish and Christian interpretations of Genesis 6:1–4—the
source of the story of the watchers and the women—understood
"sons of god" to mean, alternatively, divine beings or sons of "nobles,"
"rulers," or "judges."[28] This latter meaning fits well with Pharaoh's
playing out the role of one of the watchers, and it may also relate
to an interpretation of 1 Enoch 6–11 that identifies the giants with
the Diadochoi.[29] Another point of consideration is Bitenosh's use of
the term זר as a synonym for "watchers" and "sons of heaven."
In the logic of the narrative, given the child's appearance, it is hardly
a reference to some other human other than her spouse and must
refer to "a being foreign to this world."[30] Nonetheless, the expression should be noted, since in the Abram story, Pharaoh is a for-
eigner to Abram's race, i.e., an Egyptian rather than an Israelite (to
speak anachronistically).

3. Accounting for the Parallels between the Stories

The author of the Apocryphon has shaped these two stories in a
common direction. First, in both stories, the wife is brought to the
foreground as a viable character, who participates in a conversation
with her husband and whose sexuality is emphasized. Secondly, the
story is told from the husband's point of view and focuses on his
expressed anxiety that his wife has been or will be drawn into a sex-

---

[28] See Philip S. Alexander, "The Targumim and Early Exegesis of 'Sons of God'
in Genesis 6," *JJS* 23 (1972): 60–71.
[29] See Nickelsburg, "Apocalyptic and Myth," 396–97. On the claim that Ptolemy
I was thought to have descended from Dionysus, see ibid., n. 61.
[30] Fitzmyer, *Apocryphon*, 90.
[31] For the range of meanings for the biblical verb זור, see BDB, 266.

ual relationship with a "stranger." Finally, in both cases the anxiety is shown to be unfounded.

From these parallels I conclude that the author of the Apocryphon is concerned about some kind of miscegenation. The sexuality of Israelite women is seen to constitute a danger. The precise nature of this danger is unclear, and the range of possibilities is wide, depending upon how literally one takes the text. It could refer to: adultery in general; intercourse with someone of different social status; intercourse with a non-Israelite; intercourse with a divine being; marriage (of one's daughter) to a non-Israelite.[31] Since we do not have access to the full scroll, we cannot determine whether and how this erotic motif may have been explicated in other stories that would have easily lent themselves to this: Isaac and Rebekah, Jacob and Rachel, Judah and Tamar, Joseph and Potiphar's wife.[32] Possible analogies do appear in other texts, however. In 1 Enoch 12–16, the wording of the story of the watchers and the women suggests a critique of priests who have defiled themselves sexually.[33] A concern about mixed marriages and their defiling consequences occurs repeatedly in the Book of Jubilees (20:4; 22:20; 25:1–9; 27:8–10; 30:7–17; 41:2), which may be of more than passing concern, given the Apocryphon's relationship with that text.[34] One other detail is worth mentioning; the husband's anxiety turns out to be unfounded. This is, of course, due to narrative necessity: Noah cannot have been fathered by a watcher, and the biblical story precludes intercourse between Pharaoh and Sarai. Nonetheless, this outcome takes on significance when it concludes a story in which the anxiety has been introduced. In the one instance, Bitenosh is shown to be faithful; in the other, God is in control. The sexuality of Israelite women is a clear and present danger, but it need not be fatal.

---

[32] It is impossible to determine how long the original scroll was. The extant part consists of four sheets of 4, 5, 7 and 6 columns respectively. The fragments 1Q20 indicate at least two more columns for the first sheet. To the end of the scroll, where the suture marks on column 22 can still be seen, would have been added at least one more sheet of at least five columns. This would have constituted a scroll of roughly 3.3 meters, not a very long scroll in comparison to the great Isaiah scroll (7.34 m.) or the Temple Scroll (8.148+ m.).

[33] See David W. Suter, "Fallen Angel, Fallen Priest: The Problem of Family Purity in 1 Enoch," *HUCA* 50 (1979): 115–135; George W.E. Nickelsburg, "Enoch, Levi, and Peter: Recipients of Revelation in Upper Galilee," *JBL* 100 (1981): 584–587 (below, 438–42).

[34] On the relationship of 1QapGen to the Book of Jubilees, see Fitzmyer, *Apocryphon*, 16–17; and Greenfield and Qimron. "Apocryphon," 76.

The erotic motifs in the Apocryphon are of more than passing interest. Certainly, the text does not evidence a misogynistic or an ascetic, anti-sex bias.[35] To the contrary, the two stories highlight the erotic element. Bitenosh makes two references to her orgasm. The author attributes to the princes an enthusiastic description of Sarai's body. The presence of the motif needs to be considered in relation to other elements in the Scroll and its context. How does one relate the erotic element to the eschatological emphasis in Enoch's oracle? Whatever the author's eschatological horizon and proclivities, these do not preclude the author from an interest in the erotic and a concern about husbands and wives, the humanness of their interactions, and their faithfulness toward one another, or, more broadly, a concern about proper marriage for Israelite women.

This intriguing interest in sex, marriage, and the eschaton can be compared and contrasted with the apostle Paul's instructions to the Corinthian congregation. In 1 Corinthians 7, in the context of his belief that "the appointed time has grown very short" and that "the form of this world is passing away" (7:29, 31), Paul states that "it is well for a man not to touch a woman" (7:1), and he counsels the unmarried remain in that state (7:8, 27), so that they can attend to their religious responsibilities rather than family matters (7:32–35). Having said this, Paul concedes the power of the sex drive. Thus, he counsels against sexual abstinence in marriage and advises those who cannot exercise self-control to marry, since "it is better to marry than to burn" (7:9). Thus, for Paul the imminent eschaton is given priority, and family life is seen as a burden, marriage is permitted by concession, and sex is only to be tolerated.

In the context of this comparison, I suggest that the author of the Apocryphon evidences a much more positive attitude toward sex and marriage, his eschatological viewpoint notwithstanding. To put it bluntly, it is difficult to imagine Paul being very interested in Bitenosh's orgasm or Sarai's breast and legs. The author of the Apocryphon appears to affirm sexuality, even if he recognizes its dangers. Paul also recognizes the dangers of sexuality and his eschatological inten-

---

[35] J.W. Doeve ("Lamechs achterdocht in 1Q Genesis Apocryphon," *NedTTs* 15 [1961] 401–415) suggests that Essene authorship of the story is reflected in Lamech's suspicion of Bitenosh's unfaithfulness, which corresponds to the attitude that Josephus attributes to the Essenes in *JW* 2.8.2 (§ 119–21). If this is the case, why does the author show Lamech's suspicion to be unfounded?

sity notwithstanding, he tolerates concessions, spelling them out in halakic fashion.

Having compared and contrasted the viewpoints of the Apocryphon's author and the apostle Paul, I leave it to others to consider how the viewpoint in the Apocryphon would have played out in a Qumran context. What is this scroll doing in a collection of texts that belonged to a supposedly celibate community? Is the viewpoint espoused in the scroll—with its erotic interests and its focus on husband/wife relationships and interactions—likely to be the expression of a Qumranite? Is the Scroll more likely to have been the composition and, at first, the property of a wing of the Essene movement in which marriage was normal?[36]

4. Implications and Broader Considerations

4.1. *The Stories in the Context of the Scroll*

Our findings about the stories of Noah's birth and Abram's and Sarai's sojourn in Egypt can be brought together now and placed in the broader context of the whole scroll of the Apocryphon, to the extent that the fragments permit this.

4.1.1. *Revelation*
The motif of revelation in Enoch's oracle about the Flood and the eschaton and in Abram's dream about coming events in Egypt recurs in columns 13–15. According to Greenfield and Qimron, these columns "contained a vision about trees and about heavenly matters that affect them."[37] It is the third instance in which a section of Genesis that has no reference to revelation has been substantially elaborated through an appeal to revelation.

4.1.2. *The Enochic Tradition*
Much of the Apocryphon's elaboration of Genesis derives from, or parallel traditions that are connected with the figure of Enoch. The Apocryphon's version of Noah's birth story devotes much more space to Enoch's oracle than its counterpart in 1 Enoch 106–107. The

---

[36] CD 12:1; 19:2–5; 4Q270 101:12–13; 4Q416 2 3:20–4:5.
[37] Greenfield and Qimron, *Apocryphon*, 74.

story of the watchers and the women, which is presumed in the birth story, appears to have been told in the opening columns of the Apocryphon. The Noah portion of the scroll also mentions the "holy ones" intercourse with the daughters of men (6:20) and the blood shed by the Nefilin (6:19),[38] and the title "the Great Holy One" appears in 6:15; 12:17. The story of the watchers and the women has also informed the account of Abram and Sarai in Egypt, which also makes reference to Abram's reading "the Book of the Words of Enoch" in the presence of the Egyptian princes. Perhaps more striking, because it is paralleled in 1 Enoch in the Epistle of Enoch (chaps. 92–105) rather than in the story of the watchers, are Noah's descriptions of his life in terms of the two ways of uprightness/truth and violence/deceit (col. 6).[39]

This substantial influence of Enochic traditions is noteworthy because it is paralleled in the Book of Jubilees 4:15–27; 5:1–12; 7:21–24), which appears to have been, in turn, one of the sources of the Genesis Apocryphon. At the same time, there is no indication that any of the aforementioned examples of Enochic influence on the Apocryphon has been mediated through the Book of Jubilees.[40] Rather, Jubilees and the Apocryphon are two separate, but related instances of the powerful influence that the Enoch traditions exerted on Jewish interpreters who sought to apply the events of primordial history to their own time.

4.1.3. *A Psychologizing Tendency*

We have noted a focus on the characters' emotions in the stories of Lamech and Abram and Sarai in Egypt. The tendency also occurs in the second part of the Lamech story and in the latter part of the material about Abram. At 2:25 in words not paralleled in 1 Enoch 106–107, Methuselah says to Enoch, "Do not be *angry* with me. . . ." At 21:7, Abram states, "it *grieved* me that Lot . . . had parted from me." After Lot is captured, a third person narrator tells us, "Abram *wept* for Lot his nephew; then he *summoned up his courage*, rose up, and chose . . . the best men for war" (22:5) Neither reference to Abram's emotions appears in the Genesis account.

---

[38] See Morgenstern, Qimron and Sivan, "Unpublished Columns," 42–43.

[39] Cf., e.g., 1 Enoch 91:2–4, 18–19; 92:1–5; 94:1–4; 104:13–105:2. On "violence and deceit" as the epitome of sin, cf. 93:4, 91:11.

[40] Note, for example, that the names of God which 1QapGen has in common with 1 Enoch do not appear in Jubilees.

4.1.4. *First Person Accounts and the Structure of the Genesis Apocryphon*

The first person singular narration that we have noted in Lamech's account of Noah's birth and in the main part of the Abram stories appears also in preserved parts of columns 6–12, where Noah recounts his own story (6:2, 6; 7:7; 10:13, 15; 12:3, 8, 10, 13, 15–17, 19). A clue to this usage has been discovered by Richard Steiner, who reconstructs at 5:29 the words, "The Book of the Words of Noah" (כתב מלי נוח) and argues that they served as a superscription to the entire section running from 5:29 to column 17.[41] Thus, we have in succession a set of first person narratives placed in the mouths of Lamech, Noah, and Abram. This suggests that the scroll presented itself as a collection of extracts from a Book of Lamech, a Book of Noah, and a Book of Abram, all of them narrated in the first person voice of their central figure.[42] Another hint of such a notion may be found in 19:25, where Abram is said to have read from "the [book] of the words of Enoch." The material preceding Lamech's account may have been presented as a book of Enoch. Scholars have tended to identify 1 Enoch 6–11 as a Noachic fragment, as it may well have been. However, in the sequence of the present text, a first person account preceding Lamech's story would have to be attributed to Enoch. The author of the Apocryphon may well have had access a form of the Enochic corpus that included chaps. 6–11 and have included material from it as part of the "Book of the Words of Enoch" (cf. 1 Enoch 1:1).

The Apocryphon, then, elaborates the anonymous account in Genesis and casts the material into a first person form, attributed, successively, to various of its major characters: Lamech, Noah, and Abram, with, at least, an implied Book of Enoch. Thus, the events in Genesis are presented to the reader in a new form, recited by the central characters in various sections of its narrative.

This tendency to recast the biblical narratives into the first person singular needs to be related to the Apocryphon's dependence on the Book of Jubilees. Although Jubilees is not narrated as first person singular accounts of its major characters, it is a pseudepigraphic recasting of Genesis (and parts of Exodus). This ascription,

---

[41] Richard C. Steiner, "The Heading of the *Book of the Words of Noah* on a Fragment of the Genesis Apocryphon: New Light on a 'Lost' Work," *DSD* 2 (1995): 66–71.

[42] See Avigad and Yadin, *Apocryphon*, 38.

different from Genesis itself, is explicitly Mosaic—after a fashion. In fact it uses the first person *plural* and founds its authority on the claim that it was dictated to Moses by "us angels of the presence." Thus, the anonymous text of Genesis, believed to be Mosaic in Hellenistic times, is recast into the explicitly Mosaic narrative of Jubilees, ascribed more basically to the angels of the presence. That text, in turn, informs the Genesis Apocryphon, which retells the stories as a series of pseudepigraphic patriarchal narratives. On the one hand the Apocryphon moves away from the angelic revelation of Jubilees (which provides authority for its halakah); on the other hand, it provides reliability for its narrative by placing it on the lips of the characters themselves.

Scanning a broader horizon, we may note the first person singular narrative in the Qumran Aramaic Levi material (4QLevi[a] 1 2; 4Q213) and other patriarchal texts (4Q537, Jacob; 4Q538, Judah?; 4Q215, Naphtali). The parallels to the Levi and Naphtali material in the Testaments of Levi and Naphtali and general use of first person narrative in the Testaments of the 12 Patriarchs and other testaments have led, in the scholarly mind, to an association of first person narrative with the testamentary form. However, the Genesis Apocryphon indicates the existence in the Greco-Roman period of a broader corpus of first person haggadic narrative attributed to the patriarchs.[43] The picture is complicated by the use of the first person narrator in the Book of Tobit and in apocalyptic works like 1 Enoch, because both of these texts have been influenced by the testamentary form. In any case, further work needs to be done on the use of first person narration, its characteristics, the forms in which it occurs, its relationships to other types of "rewritten Bible" and the broader phenomenon of pseudepigraphy, and its possible parallels in contemporary non-Israelite literature.

4.2. *The Source of the Noah Story and the Relationship Between its Two Versions*

I return, finally, to a question raised at the beginning of this paper: what is the relationship between the versions of Noah's birth story in the Apocryphon and 1 Enoch 106–107? Is one dependent on the other, or are both dependent on a common source from a Book of

---

[43] Cf. Steiner ("Heading," 71), who notes that the "Words of Noah" cannot be his testament.

Noah? There is perhaps some consensus that 1 Enoch's version of Noah's birth story is a summary of a longer story that constituted the first part of an older Book of Noah, and that the Genesis Apocryphon's version preserves a fuller form of the old Noachic material.[44] Without discussing the details, I think it probable that 1 Enoch and the Book of Jubilees have preserved parts of a Noachic corpus. Moreover, as we have seen, the Genesis Apocryphon 5–16 claims to contain material from "the Book of the Words of Noah." But what of columns 1–5? Although the fragmentary condition of the scroll qualifies any conclusions about this subject, several considerations suggest to me that the Apocryphon's version of the story is dependent on 1 Enoch 106–107 rather than on a common source in a Book of Noah. (1) The episode between Lamech and Bitenosh in 1QapGen 2 is paralleled in the additions to the story Abram and Sarai in Egypt and by other references to the characters' emotions; this seems to indicate an authorial tendency in the Apocryphon rather than a remnant from earlier tradition in column 2. (2) The first person narration by Lamech fits the technique of the Scroll and need not derive from a source. (3) The Apocryphon devotes more space to Enoch and his activity than does 1 Enoch 106–107; he would have had to be very prominent in any source from which this story was taken. This suggests an Enochic rather than a Noachic source for the Lamech version of the story. (4) If the source of 1QapGen had been a Book of Noah, it is strange that the superscription identifying "The Book of the Words of Noah" follows the Lamech material and precedes the section on Noah's life and activities.

I suggest that a Noah book may have provided source material for 1 Enoch 106–107, whose author enhanced the figure of Enoch and added some eschatological material drawn from other parts of the Enochic corpus. The Apocryphon's author further elaborated the Enochic story with the haggadic motifs that were of interest to him and with Enochic material, which has also influenced other parts of the Apocryphon.[45]

---

[44] See Milik, *Enoch*, 55; Florentino Garcia Martinez, "*4QMessAr* and the *Book of Noah*," ibid., *Qumran and Apocalyptic* (STDJ 9; Leiden: Brill, 1992), 41.

[45] One possible indication that 1QapGen 1–5 is dependent on a source other than 1 Enoch 106–107 is Jub. 2:28, where Lamech's wife is called Betanos. However, since the Apocryphon knows Jubilees and Jubilees indicates no knowledge of the present story, there is no reason to take the name here as evidence of a source other than Jubilees.

RESPONSE TO "PATRIARCHS WHO WORRY ABOUT THEIR WIVES: A HAGGADIC TENDENCY IN THE GENESIS APOCRYPHON"

EILEEN SCHULLER*

The article reviewed here originated in a paper George Nickelsburg presented at the first international symposium of the newly inaugurated Orion Center for the Study of the Dead Sea Scrolls and Associated Literature at the Hebrew University in Jerusalem in May, 1996.[1] As we take up this essay again in the context of this Festschrift, it is fitting to recall that the original was dedicated to the memory of Jonas Greenfield, who contributed so much to the study of Qumran Aramaic and who was actively working on a re-edition of the Genesis Apocryphon at the time of his death.

This is the only published paper that George Nickelsburg has devoted specifically to the Genesis Apocryphon, an Aramaic retelling and expansion of the biblical stories of Lamech, Noah, and Abraham preserved in a single, badly damaged copy from Qumran's Cave 1. In the fifteen years prior to this essay, Nickelsburg had touched briefly on the Genesis Apocryphon in a variety of written contexts, most extensively in *Jewish Literature between the Bible and the Mishnah*, his survey of all the key texts of Second Temple literature.[2] A comparison of this early treatment with his 1996 paper shows that in 1981 Nickelsburg had already begun to formulate some of the key points that would become central in his later article (e.g., the importance of the lengthy "emotionally oriented" scenes between husband

---

* McMaster University.

[1] The paper was subsequently printed in Michael E. Stone and Esther G. Chazon, eds., *Biblical Perspectives: Early Use and Interpretation of the Bible in the Light of the Dead Sea Scrolls: Proceedings of the First International Symposium of the Orion Center, 12–14 May 1996* (Leiden, 1998), pp. 137–158. A previous draft of the paper was read at the Taskforce on Apocalyptic of the Wissenschaftliche Gesselschaft für Theologie, Bethel, Germany.

[2] G. Nickelsburg, *Jewish Literature between the Bible and the Mishnah: A Historical and Literary Introduction* (Philadelphia, 1981), pp. 263–265. A briefer treatment can be found in "The Bible Rewritten and Expanded," in M. Stone, ed., *Jewish Writings of the Second Temple Period: Apocrypha, Pseudepigrapha, Qumran Sectarian Writings, Philo, Josephus* (Philadelphia, 1984), pp. 104–107.

and wife). On the other hand, we can see that over time he abandoned certain ideas or reformulated them, especially as required
when more material from this fragmentary scroll became known (e.g.,
his nuancing of the earlier suggestion that the author of the Genesis
Apocryphon "omitted eschatological material").[3]

Nickelsburg does not purport to present a comprehensive study of
the Genesis Apocryphon but focuses "primarily on the stories of the
birth of Noah and Abram's and Sarai's sojourn in Egypt with a view
toward patterns of narrative technique and questions of social setting"
(p. 177). He points out the surprisingly large number of similarities
in two passages that have usually been treated quite independently.
Both stories are narrated in the first person singular by the protagonist; there is a focus on psychological dynamics and emotional
responses; there is an eschatologizing interest reflective of elements
in the Enochic tradition. In both stories the patriarch is concerned
that his wife may have had sexual relations with a "stranger" and
in both the anxiety is discovered to be unfounded. Clearly the author
of the Genesis Apocryphon has "shaped these two stories in a common direction" (p. 192).

Although the title, "Patriarchs Who Worry about their Wives," is
pithy and catchy, it is somewhat misleading in that it highlights only
one component of this dense, multi-topic article. Indeed the title may
suggest that the essay is to be aligned primarily with that substantial body of scholarship from the last twenty years or so that explores
how biblical women are portrayed—or not portrayed—in biblical
retellings from the Second Temple period.[4] But while this article
remains the most comprehensive study that I know of the women
in the Genesis Apocryphon,[5] its subject matter extends far beyond

---

[3] Nickelsburg, *Jewish Literature*, p. 264.

[4] For example, James L. Bailey, "Josephus' Portrayal of the Matriarchs," in Louis
H. Feldman and Gohei Hata, eds., *Josephus, Judaism and Christianity* (Detroit, 1987),
pp. 154–179; Betsy Halpern Amaru, "Portraits of Biblical Women in Josephus'
Antiquities," in *JJS* 39 (1988), pp. 143–170; Eileen Schuller, "Women of the Exodus
in Biblical Retellings of the Second Temple Period," in Peggy Day, ed., *Gender and
Difference in Ancient Israel* (Philadelphia, 1989), pp. 178–194; Cheryl A. Brown, *No
Longer Be Silent: First Century Jewish Portraits of Biblical Women* (Louisville, 1992); P.W.
van der Horst, "Images of Women in Ancient Judaism," in Ria Kloppenborg and
W.J. Hanegraaff, eds., *Female Stereotypes in Religious Traditions* (Leiden, 1995), pp.
43–60; Betsy H. Amaru, *The Empowerment of Women in the Book of Jubilees* (Leiden, 1999).

[5] For a briefer and very different treatment, see A.K. Blau and I. Sheres, "Women
Anonymous: The Dead Sea Scrolls' Gender Legacy," in *Centennial Review* 39 (1995),
pp. 156–157.

women, even beyond the Genesis Apocryphon per se, and includes
issues in the study of 1 Enoch (especially themes of eschatology and
revelation), narrative theory (specifically the interplay of first person
and third person narration), and cross-cultural comparison of the
birth tales of famous figures. In this response, I take up only three
specific issues raised by Nickelsburg. For each, I try to specify what
is distinctive and original in his approach and to suggest a few places
where further development might be possible.

1. Comparison of 1QapGen 1–5 and 1 Enoch 106–107, particularly the relative length of narrative components

In the first section of the article Nickelsburg makes a detailed comparison between the story of the birth of Noah in the Genesis
Apocryphon in columns 1–4 and the version of the birth story in 1
Enoch 106–107. That these two texts are closely related was recognized already in 1956 in the *editio princeps* of the Genesis Apocryphon
when Avigad and Yadin published the full transcription and translation of those columns that were fairly well preserved (columns 2
and 19–22) and a narrative summary with selected readable phrases
from the other columns.[6] The editors wrote:

> The narrative in the scroll resembles chapter cvi of the *Book of Enoch*
> in most essential points, though there are some significant additions in
> the scroll, such as the dialogue between Lamech and Bat-Enosh and
> Enoch's long reply to Methuselah—some five times as long as the ver-
> sion in the *Book of Enoch*.[7]

Nickelsburg was able to advance the discussion of similarities and
differences because he had access to more material than Avigad and
Yadin did some forty years earlier. With regards to 1 Enoch, in
1967 Milik had published the relevant fragments of 4QEn^c (5 i 26–ii
30) and established that the sparsely preserved Aramaic text was very
similar to the more fully-preserved Greek version found in the Chester

---

[6] N. Avigad and Y. Yadin, *A Genesis Apocryphon: A Scroll from the Wilderness of Judaea: Description and Contents of the Scroll, Facsimiles, Transcription and Translation of Columns II, XIX–XXII* (Jerusalem, 1956). The major commentary by J. Fitzmyer, *The Genesis Apocryphon of Qumran Cave I: A Commentary* (Rome, 1966; revised edition 1971) had the same textual basis.

[7] Avigad and Yadin, *Genesis Apocryphon*, p. 19.

Beatty-Michigan papyrus.[8] With regards to 1QapGen, since 1988 J. Greenfield and E. Qimron had been studying the original infrared photographs from the 1950s in preparation for publishing the still-unpublished columns; new photos were taken by Bruce Zuckerman of the West Semitic Research Project, and in 1994 the scroll was scanned by G. Bearman using advanced infrared technology.[9] Although this project is ongoing and we still await the promised new edition, by the time Nickelsburg was writing his article he had access to new readings for columns 2, 19–22 and a transcription of much more text in columns 1, 3–17, including the decipherment of the key words that begin a new section in 5:29: "[a copy] of the book of the Words of Noah."[10]

Earlier commentators had noted the obvious major differences between the Genesis Apocryphon and 1 Enoch 106–107, especially the stormy dialogue between Lamech and Bitenosh (1QapGen 2:3–18), which has no counterpart in 1 Enoch, and the fact that in 1 Enoch when Lamech goes to Methuselah he describes for a second time the extraordinary appearance of the child (106:10–11), but in the Genesis Apocryphon (1QapGen 2:19b) there is no space for such a description. Nickelsburg goes beyond this to compare, chart, and diagram each subsection in 1 Enoch (Greek and Aramaic texts) versus 1QapGen with particular attention to comparative length (pp. 179–180, especially footnote 5). He is able to establish that the Genesis Apocryphon's account overall was approximately 3.74 times as long as that in 1 Enoch 106–107. This detailed comparison becomes especially interesting in the two specific subsections where there are significant differences, the Beginning and Enoch's oracle.

---

[8] J.T. Milik, *The Books of Enoch: Aramaic Fragments of Qumrân Cave 4* (Oxford, 1976), pp. 206–217.

[9] For a description of the project, see E. Qimron, "Towards a New Edition of the Genesis Apocryphon," in *JSP* 10 (1992), pp. 11–18; and "Toward a New Edition of 1Q*Genesis Apocryphon*," in D. Parry and E. Ulrich, eds., *The Provo International Conference on the Dead Sea Scrolls: Technological Innovations, New Texts, and Reformulated Issues* (Leiden, 1999), pp. 106–109. Also G. Bearman and S. Spiro, "Imaging Clarified," in ibid., pp. 5–12.

[10] M. Morgenstern, E. Qimron, and Daniel Sivan, "The Hitherto Unpublished Columns of the Genesis Apocryphon," in *Abr-Nahrain* 33 (1995), pp. 30–54; R.C. Steiner, "The Heading of the Book of the Words of Noah on a Fragment of the Genesis Apocryphon: New Light on a 'Lost' Work," in *DSD* 2 (1995), pp. 66–69. Also J.C. Greenfield and E. Qimron, "The Genesis Apocryphon Col. XII," in *Abr-Nahrain Supplement* 3 (1992), pp. 70–77, though Nickelsburg did not discuss this column.

Let us look more closely at what Nickelsburg terms the "Beginning."
The narration of Lamech's marriage to Bitenosh, the birth of Noah,
and the description of the extraordinary appearance of the child is
told in 1 Enoch 106:1–3, in 14 lines in Greek, and in 4QEn^c 5 i
26–30 in 5 lines. Nothing from this section is preserved in 1QapGen,
but the corresponding text came at the end of column 1 and the
beginning of column 2; notice that the reference in 2:2 to "this child"
assumes that the child has already been introduced and described.
According to Nickelsburg's chart (p. 139), the "Beginning" section
covered 6 lines in 1QapGen, and if I understand him correctly (for
he does not spell this out exactly) this would be 1QapGen 1:31–34
and 2:1–2.[11] That is, Nickelsburg thinks that 1QapGen 1:25–29 (the
so-called Trever fragment")[12] must have belonged to a previous section, which may have ended with line 29 ("he did for them and also
for all flesh") or may have continued into line 30 (part of line 30
may have been a *vacat*). Thus he concludes that this "Beginning"
section "may have been about the same length in 1QapGen as it is
in 1 Enoch," although he allows that "this estimate and the content
of the section are uncertain" (p. 140). It is possible, however, to
come to a slightly different conclusion.[13] According to Avigad and
Yadin, there were thirty-seven lines in each column on the first
sheet.[14] The "Beginning" section, then, covers 1:31–37 and 2:1–2,
and thus is nine lines in length (possibly even ten, if it starts in 1:30).

---

[11] It is difficult to be sure exactly where Nickelsburg thinks the section he calls
"Beginning" comes in 1QapGen, since he doesn't work it out in exact lines. He
states explicitly in n. 5 that columns 2–4 each have thirty-four lines (contra Avigad,
see my discussion, immediately below), and presumably thinks that column 1 does
also. According to the chart, "Beginning" covers six lines, presumably four lines in
column 1 (1:31–34) and the first two lines of column 2 (2:1–2). Footnote 5, however, talks explicitly of "6 lines [of the story] for col. 1," which would require that
"Beginning" start at 1:29.

[12] The "Trever fragment" appeared in a picture in E. Sukenik, *Megillot Genuzot
II* (Jerusalem, 1950), photo facing p. 32. It was first placed in column 1, tran-
scribed and translated in a paper presented to the SBL in 1991 by Bruce Zuckerman,
"The Trever Fragment: Recovery of an Unstudied Piece of the Genesis Apocryphon."
I am following the reconstruction of column 1 as presented by Morgenstern, Qimron,
and Sivan in "The Hitherto Unpublished Columns," pp. 36–37.

[13] No reconstruction can be offered with certainty since we cannot know exactly
where the previous section ended and "Beginning" started.

[14] Avigad and Yadin, *Genesis Apocryphon*, p. 14. There are thirty-four lines on the
fourth sheet (columns 17–22), that is, the other columns that are the focus of
Nickelsburg's attention, and therefore he seems to have assumed that there were
thirty-four lines on the first sheet.

Thus, this initial section with the description of the extraordinary child might well have been somewhat longer in the Genesis Apocryphon than in 1 Enoch.

Assuming that this section is longer in the Genesis Apocryphon, it is interesting to look at the other two retellings of the description of the child. As noted above already, in 1 Enoch 106:5–6 when Lamech is consulting with Methuselah, he redescribes the child in a passage of virtually the same length as the first description. In 1QapGen 2:19 this is all much abbreviated: "then, I, Lamech, ran to Methuselah, my father and [told] him everything [missing circa ten spaces, Enoch] his father and learn everything . . .;" there is no space for a repetition of the actual description. The third description of the child is in the section "Methuselah to Enoch," 1 Enoch 106:8–12. The corresponding text in 1QapGen is from column 2:21b to the end of the column, or perhaps it extended into the first line of column 3 (by 3:3 the speaker has changed and it is clearly Enoch speaking, "in the days of Jared my father"). That is, this section is considerably longer than in 1 Enoch: 8.3 lines in Aramaic Enoch (as reconstructed) versus 16.5–17.5 lines in 1QapGen (not 13.5 lines as Nickelsburg calculated), and it most likely included an expanded description of the child.[15] Nickelsburg recognized the discrepancy in the second description (its omission in 1QapGen), but I suggest that he could have put more emphasis on the fact that the first description and the third description are longer in the Genesis Apocryphon than in 1 Enoch. Even though we can say nothing about the precise content of the expanded sections since no actual text has been preserved, the author of the Genesis Apocryphon seems to have taken (for whatever reasons) a special interest in the description of this extraordinary child.

There is one other place where differences in comparative length and new readings give information that reveals the *Tendenz* of the author of the Genesis Apocryphon. In his 1981 book, Nickelsburg had suggested that "the author of the Genesis Apocryphon may have omitted eschatological material that was not of interest to him,"[16]

---

[15] Nickelsburg had earlier suggested that the end of the column "may have described the confrontation between Lamech and his wife or the appearance of the child, or it may have contained other discourse between Methuselah and Enoch" (*Jewish Literature*, p. 272 n. 86). Now he is more certain that this section "almost certainly repeated the description of the child" (p. 140).

[16] G. Nickelsburg, *Jewish Literature*, p. 264.

but this no longer seems to be the conclusion to be drawn. From his detailed comparisons, Nickelsburg can now establish that the section "Enoch's oracle" is more than six times longer in 1QapGen 3:2–5:23 than in 1 Enoch 106:13–107:1. In 1 Enoch, half of the oracle is about the flood, and the second half covers history up to and including the final judgment. Although only scattered bits of text have so far been read and published from this section of 1QapGen, it seems clear that the Genesis Apocryphon is dealing with similar themes of eschatological judgment (cf., 4:11 "I/you saw to do judgment"). In particular Nickelsburg draws attention to 5:18, "doing great acts of lawlessness they will do until[" and relates this to 1 Enoch 106:19–107:1 as a prediction of the eschaton (p. 141). Thus, on the basis of both phraseology and length, Nickelsburg now allows that there was an eschatological interest in Genesis Apocryphon, just as in 1 Enoch.

2. Literary Observations

In the opening paragraph of the article, Nickelsburg states that he intends to pay special attention to "patterns of narrative technique and questions of social setting" (p. 177). One of the distinctive narrative techniques that he discusses is the recasting of the biblical narrative into first person form, so that the various incidents are told by Lamech, Noah, and Abram consecutively. Nickelsburg was not the first to call attention to this use of first person narration and to the similarities between the Genesis Apocryphon and Tobit in this respect; a short article by James Miller some years earlier highlighted many of the same points.[17] What Nickelsburg emphasized was that at least one reason for the choice of first person narration is the issue of authority. A book like Jubilees can claim the authority of "us angels of the presence" (Jubilees 1:27; 2:2; 2:18) who dictated divine revelation to Moses. In the Genesis Apocryphon, there is no heavenly speaker, but the fact that the "I" is telling his own story implicitly attests to the reliability of what is being said. Nickelsburg called for further work to be done on the use of first person narration and this was taken up in part by Moshe Bernstein in a paper

---

[17] James E. Miller, "The Redaction of Tobit and the Genesis Apocryphon," in *JSP* 8 (1991), pp. 53–61.

at the next year's Orion Conference. Bernstein cautioned that the situation is rendered more complex since "all three of the extant sections of the Apocryphon employ both first and third person narration."[18] This is one area where more work could still be done.

Perhaps the least satisfying aspect of Nickelsburg's paper is when the attempt is made to move from the literary level to "questions of social setting" (p. 177). Nickelsburg makes a strong case for his claim that the two stories being compared share certain distinctive elements that are not to be found in their sources or other parallels (the emphasis on the sexuality of the wife, anxiety about sexual relations with "the other" [Watchers/Pharaoh], an eventual acknowledgement that there is no sexual impropriety). But what can this tell us about the author and his social setting? On this point Nickelsburg only draws the sketchiest of conclusions: the author is "concerned about some kind of miscegenation" (p. 193); he had a "positive attitude toward sex and marriage, his eschatological viewpoint notwithstanding" (p. 194); he was probably not a celibate Qumranite (even though the scroll was found in the caves) but may have belonged to that wing of the Essene movement that married (p. 195). Nickelsburg is right to be subdued in his claims since, as is so often the case in this type of literature, there is no clear path from even the most detailed literary analysis to social reality.

There is, however, perhaps one other passage in the Genesis Apocryphon that could be brought into this discussion, though its precise significance is equally unclear. In the badly damaged column 12, first deciphered by Greenfield and Qimron,[19] the author of the Genesis Apocryphon introduces genealogical material about Noah's children drawn from Gen. 10; he expands the biblical text to include not only the number of sons born to Shem, Ham, and Japheth but also the number of daughters born to each. James VanderKam has pointed one that that this is yet another instance in which the author of the Genesis Apocryphon has paid special attention to women.[20]

---

[18] M. Bernstein, "Pseudepigraphy in the Qumran Scrolls: Categories and Functions," in E.G. Chazon and M.E. Stone, eds., *Pseudepigraphic Perspectives: The Apocrypha & Pseudepigrapha in Light of the Dead Sea Scrolls: Proceedings of the International Symposium of the Orion Center, 12–14 January 1997* (Leiden, 1999), pp. 15–17.

[19] "The Genesis Apocryphon Col. XII," pp. 70–77.

[20] J. VanderKam, "The Granddaughters and Grandsons of Noah," in *RevQ* 16 (1994), pp. 457–461.

VanderKam goes further and suggests that the precise number of daughters in relation to the number of sons is significant, that is, it is a function of the author's concern with the purity of the line of Abraham. The family of Shem has five daughters and five sons so that there need be no marriage beyond the chosen family, while the four sons and seven daughters of Ham can marry the four daughters and seven sons of Japheth. Given that these matters are treated quite differently in Jubilees, VanderKam suggests that "the numbers of Noah's granddaughters fall into a pattern having a wider significance far surpassing their being just another instance of an interesting characteristic of the *Genesis Apocryphon*,"[21] but again, beyond general statements of concern with purity and familial line, it is difficult to be specific about the concrete social reality that underlies this interest.

Nickelsburg is more successful in using literary analysis to explore the relationship between the Genesis Apocryphon and 1 Enoch. For Nickelsburg, the close comparison of the birth story in the Genesis Apocryphon and 1 Enoch 106–107 contributes to a broader discussion about the interrelationships of these two works and a (hypothetical) Book of Noah. The problem is outlined early in the article (pp. 180–181), and Nickelsburg returns to it for his conclusion (pp. 198–199); more recently, he has taken up the question in his full-length Enoch commentary where the discussion is heavily dependent on this article.[22] Nickelsburg is going against "some consensus" (p. 199) about how the relationship between 1 Enoch 106–107 and the Genesis Apocryphon is to be reconstructed.[23] The tendency has been to see the version of the birth of Noah in the so-called "Book of Noah" as primary, both chronologically (fourth or third century B.C.E.) and in length;[24] the Genesis Apocryphon as a summary of materials in the Book of Noah; and 1 Enoch 106–107 as yet a briefer summary of the Book of Noah. Nickelsburg proposes a different interrelationship: "the Apocryphon's story of the birth of Noah is an expanded

---

[21] Ibid., p. 459.
[22] G. Nickelsburg, *1 Enoch* (Minneapolis, 2001), pp. 541–542.
[23] Milik, *Enoch*, p. 55; F. García Martínez, "4QMessAr and the Book of Noah," in *Qumran and Apocalyptic* (Leiden, 1992), p. 41.
[24] Nickelsburg assumes, without explicit discussion, that there was a "Book of Noah." For problems with this assumption, see Devorah Dimant, "Noah in Early Jewish Literature," in Michael E. Stone and Theodore A. Bergen, eds., *Biblical Figures outside the Bible* (Harrisburg, 1998), pp. 123–150, and C. Werman, "Qumran and the Book of Noah," in *Pseudepigraphic Perspectives*, pp. 171–181.

version of the account in 1 Enoch 106–107 rather than a more complete witness to the Noachic source of 1 Enoch 106–107."[25] In particular the whole conversation between Lamech and Bitenosh with
its unusual focus on psychological dynamics and emotional interaction is not something taken over from the Book of Noah (and omitted in 1 Enoch), but a creative haggadic development by the author
of Genesis Apocryphon. The primary evidence for this understanding of the interrelationship is precisely the fact that the distinctive
psychologizing/emotional approach that marks the episode of Lamech
and Bitenosh is to be found in the Abram/Sarai story in repeated
short references to the emotional/psychological state of various characters (Abram is frightened, 19:18; Sarai weeps, 19:21, 23; Abram
weeps, 20:10, 12, 16; Pharaoh desires her, 20:8).

3. THE PROBLEM OF THE LENGTH OF THE ORIGINAL 1QapGen SCROLL

It is difficult to propose with confidence a statement of the purpose
and *Tendenz* of the Genesis Apocryphon as a whole when neither its
beginning nor its conclusion has been preserved, and we do not
know the quantity of text that is missing at either end. The issue of
length is especially important for Nickelsburg's argument that some
kind of miscegenation was a key concern for the author of the Genesis
Apocryphon. His case would be strengthened if issues related to
women, purity, and sexual relations were evidenced in an embellishment of the story of the Watchers at the beginning of the scroll
or in a retelling of the Garden of Eden and, in the latter part of
the scroll, in stories about Isaac and Rebecca, Jacob and Rachel,
Judah and Tamar, Joseph and Potiphar's wife. Although Nickelsburg
suggests that such materials might have been included, he is forced
to admit that such conjecture is highly speculative since "it is impossible to determine how long the original scroll was" (p. 193, n. 32).

In the years since Nickelsburg's article, a few scholars have taken
up this issue of the length of the original scroll and presented tentative, though at times contradictory, proposals about both its beginning and the end. In terms of material missing at the end, Nickelsburg
recognized that there was originally text beyond column 22: "To the

---

[25] G. Nickelsburg, *1 Enoch*, p. 542.

end of the scroll, where the suture marks on column 22 can still be seen, would have been added at least one more sheet of at least five columns" (p. 193, n. 32). In 2001, in a paper given at the meeting of the International Organization of Qumran Studies in Basel, Daniel Falk argued, on the basis of his calculation of the diameter of the rolled scroll, that the maximum amount of material that could have followed column 22 would have been about 84 cm, approximately the length of sheet 4 (columns 17–22, 82 cm), that is, there would have been one more sheet, but not more.[26] Given the ratio between Genesis text and expansion in the preserved sections, he tried to show that in this final sheet the author could have reached (if the retelling was very abbreviated) to the end of the story of Abraham (Gen. 25:11) but not beyond. In contrast, Stegemann proposes that what has been preserved of 1QapGen is only "roughly the first half of this work" and that a long section has been lost at the end that continued to "at least the conclusion of the story of Abraham in Genesis 25 or even further."[27]

In discussing the beginning of the scroll (the outer part when rolled), Nickelsburg allowed that "the fragments of 1Q20 indicate at least two more columns for the first sheet" (p. 193, n. 32).[28] He highlights a number of phrases in "column 0" (as the text which precedes column 1 is called) and in what can be read of column 1 that suggest that there was some version of the story of the watchers and the women in this section (p. 182), but how extensive the retelling was and whether it played up similar miscegenetic motifs is impossible to determine because so little is preserved. In an article in 1996,

---

[26] I am grateful to Daniel Falk for sharing with me an unpublished written version of this paper.

[27] Stegemann's written comment in *The Library of Qumran: On the Essenes, Qumran, John the Baptist, and Jesus* (Grand Rapids, 1998), p. 98, is very brief, even cryptic. He explained to me recently that this suggestion is based primarily on a hypothetical reconstruction of the content of the composition and that the end of 1QapGen was cut off in antiquity before the scroll was rolled (the cut can be seen on the left side of the sewing seam after the last column). Perhaps the strange white material covering the lower part of columns 10–14, which Avigad had described (*A Genesis Apocryphon*, p. 14), was related somehow to the repair of damage in antiquity. I am grateful to Hartmut Stegemann and Annette Steudel for recent informal discussion of these problems.

[28] Milik had already recognized that eight small fragments (1Q20) recovered from Cave 1 were from the manuscript that he knew as the Lamech Scroll, *Qumran Cave I* (Oxford, 1955), pp. 86–87. A preliminary placement and reading of these fragments was presented by Michael O. Wise and Bruce Zuckerman in an unpublished SBL paper in 1991, "Toward a New Edition of the 1Q20 Fragments."

M. Morgenstern reported that he saw the letters *pê*, *sadê*, and *qôp* on the top right corner of the last three sheets and suggested that these letters served to number the sheets.[29] Morgenstern argued that the section of the scroll that is preserved is sheets 16, 17, 18, and 19 (or perhaps sheets 15–18 if the *waw* was not used) and some 70–105 columns have disappeared so that we have "only the tail-end of an enormously long scroll." In fact his reconstructed scroll would be at least twelve meters,[30] much longer than any preserved scroll (cf., 1QIsa[a] at 7.34 m or 11QT[a] at 8.75 m, though it has been proposed that a few scrolls should be reconstructed as over ten meters).[31] If Morgenstern's reconstruction is correct, many different proposals could be made about the content of all these missing columns: a very expansive rendering of all or parts of Gen. 1–5; a lengthy retelling of the story of the watchers and perhaps a version of other material known from 1 Enoch 6–36; even a completely different work that only was on this scroll by random chance. But all this is highly speculative, and Morgenstern's proposal has been received so far with a certain skepticism or at least suspension of judgment.

There is still much work to be done on this very damaged scroll, using advanced photographic technology to read as much as possible and reconstructing, in so far as possible, the dimensions of the original. Fortunately we can look forward to a new edition and commentary by Moshe Bernstein and Esti Eshel.[32] When first read in the 1950s, the Genesis Apocryphon seemed a deceptively simple,

---

[29] M. Morgenstern, "A New Clue to the Original Length of the Genesis Apocryphon" in *JJS* 47 (1996), pp. 345–347. For other proposed markings to number sheets, see E. Tov, "Scribal Markings in the Texts from the Judaean Desert," in Donald W. Parry and Stephen D. Ricks, eds., *Current Research and Technological Developments on the Dead Sea Scrolls* (Leiden, 1996), pp. 68–69.

[30] Morgenstern ("Clue," p. 347) calculates that the missing section was "some 9 meters long;" the preserved section is 2.53 meters plus the missing columns on sheet 1.

[31] 4QRP, at 22–27 m (E. Tov and S. White, "Reworked Pentateuch," in H.W. Attridge, T. Elgvin, et al., eds., *Qumran Cave 4.VIII. Parabiblical Texts, Part 1* [Oxford, 1994], p. 192); possibly 4QKgs, 20 m (J.T. Barrera, "4QKgs," in E. Ulrich, F.M. Cross, S.W. Crawford, et al., eds., *Qumran Cave 4.IX. Deuteronomy to Kings* [Oxford, 1995], p. 182). See E. Tov, "The Dimensions of the Qumran Scrolls," in *DSD* 5 (1998), pp. 71–72.

[32] M. Bernstein gave notice of this forthcoming commentary at the Orion Conference, 2001. The new edition will include improved readings and the "Trever fragment" and other small fragments that are part of the Schoyen collection, Ms. 1926/2c–e (published preliminarily by M. Lundberg and B. Zuckerman in the *Newsletter for the Comprehensive Aramaic Lexicon*, 12 [1996], pp. 2–5).

pious retelling of favorite Genesis stories. It is now recognized as a complex and nuanced composition that can make an important contribution to our understanding of both biblical interpretation per se and of broader issues in Second Temple Judaism. In this article George Nickelsburg has served scholarship well by paying close attention to the realia of the scroll and its preservation, bringing to bear his vast and comprehensive familiarity with the Enochic literature, and asking fundamental questions about the author's purpose as reflected in the distinctive shaping of these narratives. His essay remains an important contribution to the ongoing study of this badly damaged but fascinating document.

RESPONSE TO EILEEN SCHULLER

My publications about the Genesis Apocryphon interacted with different stages of that document's publication. My initial treatments in *Jewish Literature between the Bible and the Mishnah* (1981) and *Compendia ad Rerum Iudaicarum ad Novum Testamentum 2:2* (1983) were based on the 1956 edition of Avigad and Yadin and its five published columns. The first draft of my 1996 Jerusalem paper made use, additionally, of the microfiche photos of the whole document and profited from some correspondence with Matthew Morgenstern (1996). The paper was revised for publication with the new readings of Morgenstern and Elisha Qimron in hand. Thus my most recent discussion made use of new data, and this forced me to revise earlier conclusions. But as one looks at the first photographs and at Morgenstern's and Qimron's readings based on more technologically sophisticated photography, one sees the many lacunae that remain, and one is (or should be) forced to qualify any general statements made about this text. We have substantially less than half the letters that were first penned on the manuscript.

Had I taken note of Avigad's and Yadin's line count of the first sheet (p. 14), I might have, and certainly should have, emphasized that the Apocryphon's account expands the first and third sections in 1 Enoch that describe the newborn Noah, as Eileen Schuller notes. The second, very brief mention of the child, considerably compressed from 1 Enoch, is not anomalous; it simply sets one up for the lengthy final description, which purports to repeat what Lamech had, in fact, told Methuselah in the second episode. As Schuller notes, the child is the center of attention in the story. When one adds this to the ten or more columns (6–15) that claim to be a transcription of "the Book of the Words of Noah" (5:29), it is clear that the author of this text had an immense interest in the figure of Noah. This fits well with parts of the broader Enochic tradition on which it draws (1 Enoch 6–11, 37–71, and 83–84, in addition to 106–107). Furthermore, the lost sheet that preceded the present column 2, appears to have included a substantial amount of material on the fall of the Watchers, which set up the story of the birth of Noah. While we do not know how many columns were devoted to

Abraham (at least eleven columns), the extensive coverage of primordial, Noah-related material is striking.

This concern with primordial history, moreover, is consonant with the author's interest in eschatology, which in the extant text is evident in the expanded form of Enoch's speech. That I originally suggested that the author of the Apocryphon expunged eschatological material raises a couple of methodological issues. First, my judgment was based on an argument from silence. I observed that the preserved text contained no explicit eschatological material, and I assumed there was no such material in the columns that I knew were there, but that were illegible at that time. Related to this, I suppose, was an assumption that a narrative text with a focus on emotions and sexuality would have no great interest in eschatology. We need to be careful not to place our literary and theological categories in exclusive hermetically sealed compartments.

Bernstein's paper on the phenomenon of pseudepigraphy (Schuller, n. 18) is a very useful step toward sorting out the complex literary phenomenon of texts that recast narratives found in the Bible, and it should be read by anyone interested in the topic. My idea that the first person singular strengthens the reliability of a narrative text does not differ all that much from his suggestion that it increases the vividness of the account. I meant reliability in the mind of the reader. I agree with Bernstein that this kind of pseudepigraphy differs substantially from pseudepigraphy written in the name of a figure of antiquity whose (revelatory) words are authoritative the reader.

My attempt to move from the literary level to the text's social setting was as unsatisfying to me as it is to Schuller. In examining the surface structure of a text, one can identify many elements that persons of good will can agree are present. My comparison of the stories of Noah and Abraham laid out a fair number of these. In what context and to what end the author composed these parallel texts requires a good deal of inference and, with it, uncertainty, especially in a text of which he have only parts. The problem is compounded because an author in the Hellenistic period is making his point by telling a story about antiquity. So my conclusions were sketchy. Sex and (potential) miscegenation are at the center of both the Noah and Abraham stories (as they are in the Enochic texts behind them). But if miscegenation was a concern of this author of the Hellenistic period, of what sort was it? The issue seems to be different from a number of texts in *Jubilees*, for example, with its explicit strictures against marriages between Israelites and gentiles, which are marriages between equals (i.e., human and human characters).

My suggestion about the provenance of the text builds on four facts: (1) the text takes marriage for granted; (2) it was found in a collection of manuscripts belonging to an Essene community; (3) while it is not identifiably an Essene sectarian document, it is saturated with Enochic material, which is very much at home in that manuscript collection; (4) according to Josephus, there were communities of married Essenes. While this is suggestive, it hardly allows an indisputable conclusion.

The debate about the original length of the Scroll perhaps epitomizes the problems related to my paper. How much more might we be able to determine about individual units in the Apocryphon if we had their full literary context? Without that context, we should draw our conclusions—however shrewd—with caution and tentativeness. A comparison helps to make the point. None of our extant manuscripts of the Book of Biblical Antiquities, so-called Pseudo-Philo, takes the book to its original conclusion. However, they present a very long text with few evident lacunae. On this basis, one can draw some solid conclusions about the literary and religious tendencies in the document. The Genesis Apocryphon, by comparison, is a text without some indeterminate amount of its beginning and latter part(s). Of what we do have, as I noted above, perhaps half of its letters are indecipherable. Our conclusions must be much more tenuous. But there is this: technology has brought us substantially more of the text than we had previously, and this has allowed us to be more aware of the whole text and to raise broader issues than we could previously.

Eileen Schuller's response provides an excellent summary of much of the research done on this intriguing, but frustrating, document, and her detailed comments, with which I have no cause to take issue, provide some very helpful contributions to that discussion.

CHAPTER SEVEN

TOBIT AND ENOCH: DISTANT COUSINS WITH A RECOGNIZABLE RESEMBLANCE

George W.E. Nickelsburg

In one of the better known instances of duping in ancient literature, Raphael the archangel, fresh from the heavenly throneroom, shows up on Tobit's doorstep at a moment of crisis, offering his services as a tour guide and bodyguard for young Tobias. When Tobit asks Raphael about his family background, the heavenly messenger produces bogus credentials, claiming to be Azariah the son of the patriarch Hananiah—a relative of Tobit. The scene is played well, and Tobit falls for the line, hook and sinker. With his cover story firmly established, Raphael, alias Azariah, sets out with Tobias on an adventure in which family relationships play an important role and appearances must be deceiving.

In this paper I shall turn Tobit's question back on the author of the Book of Tobit—but with a twist. From what intellectual and religious family does this author hail? Where in the literature of Judaism do we find some look-alikes?

There is an obvious candidate in the Book of Job. Both texts are stories from a wisdom tradition which focus on the problem of theodicy. Their heroes—whose names even sound a bit similar—are wealthy men, introduced as pious and righteous (Job 1:1–3; Tob 1:3–9), who lose both their wealth and their health. After a bitter exchange with his wife, each wishes that he were dead (Job 2:9–10; 3:1–26; Tob 2:11–3:6). Ultimately, however, both are restored to health and obtain new wealth, and the stories end with reference to the heroes' deaths and the inheritance of their goods. In both cases, the story, which is played out on earth, makes explicit reference to the heavenly realm, in which an angelic witness—in Job the accuser, in Tobit, the intercessor—plays a prominent role. Both texts, though in very different proportions—make use of narrative form and poetic wisdom.[1]

---

[1] For the latter, see especially Job 31:13–22, which addresses some of the specific concerns in Tob 4:7–11, 14.

While the book of Tobit is obviously very different from the book of Job, on some basic details there are recognizable similarities.

While these family resemblances suggest some sort of relationship, I shall make a case for a less obvious relationship. Their major difference in appearance notwithstanding, I perceive some resemblance between features in the book of Tobit and parts of 1 Enoch. Is it possible that the author(s) of this wisdom tale and the apocalyptic authors of 1 Enoch are distant intellectual relatives?[2]

The major differences between the two texts are obvious and can be briefly summarized. Enoch is a collection of revelatory texts, in which the primordial patriarch transmits secret information about the hidden recesses of the cosmos and the hidden events of the future, information gathered during journeys through the cosmos and in elaborate eschatological dream visions. Tobit is a narrative tale (albeit pseudepigraphic like 1 Enoch and recounted, in part, in the first person singular) about the trials and tribulations of an exiled Israelite family living in Mesopotamia after the Assyrian Exile. The Enochic texts are heavily mythic in their content and cryptic in their allusion to history; proper names are scarce and limited almost exclusively to angels and demons and to the patriarch and a few members of his family. The story in Tobit, though it is fiction, takes place in a realistic and recognizable historical setting, and its characters are for the most part human beings with names, who live in places with names.

Fully recognizing these substantial differences, which could be elaborated in greater detail, I shall pursue my comparison with reference to four aspects of the two works: their cosmology, angelology, and demonology; their eschatology; their ethical teaching; and their liturgical vocabulary. In my comparison, I shall note details of sim-

---

[2] For a source-critical analysis of Tobit, see Paul Deselaers, *Das Buch Tobit: Studien zu seiner Erstehung Komposition, und Theologie* (Göttingen: Vandenhoeck & Ruprecht, 1982). For the purposes of this paper, I have consulted neither this book nor Deselaer's paper prepared for this session.

My comparison will confine itself in 1 Enoch to chapters 1–36 and 91–105. My text of Tobit is based the longer recension of the Greek (S and some allied MSS, and the Old Latin), now attested in principal by the Qumran Aramaic and Hebrew MSS; see J.T. Milik, "La Patrie de Tobie," *RB* 73 (1966): 522. Occasionally, I have adopted a reading from the S tradition which agrees with the shorter recension when S appears to be defective.

Some points made here briefly have been developed at somewhat greater length in my short commentary on "Tobit," in James L. Mays, ed., *Harper's Bible Commentary* (New York: Harper and Row, 1988).

ilarity, at the same time attempting to sharpen and elaborate the aforementioned differences. On the basis of this analysis, I shall suggest the hypothesis that the two works reflect an older common stock of ideas, traditions, and terminology, not simply to be found in the Hebrew Scriptures, which has developed in different directions in the respective texts.

A. Cosmology, Angelology, and Demonology

1. *1 Enoch*

The Enochic writings presume a well-defined dualism between the empirical world and the hidden recesses of the universe. Lengthy sections of 1 Enoch are devoted to descriptions of these hidden cosmic realia. Chapters 72–82 describe the structures and mechanics of the heavenly bodies and the meteorological phenomena, and chapters 17–19 and 20–36 track Enoch's journeys across the earth. Both sections are presented as the revelation of hidden knowledge, mediated by the seer. In chapters 72–82, the purpose of the revelation is to teach an astronomical torah—the truth about the solar orientation of the universe and the calendar. The accounts of Enoch's journey provide the assurance that God has built into the universe the places where the final judgment will be administered, and thus the factuality of that judgment is guaranteed.

Heaven is not only the place of the luminaries, but also, or preeminently, the dwelling of God. The throneroom of the divine King is located in a celestial palace or temple. Its *temenos* is bounded by a wall built of hailstones and belted by fire. The throneroom itself is an oven of raging fire, whose walls are stone-like slabs of snow. It is roofed with shooting stars and lighting flashes and floored with snow, and access is possible only through doors of blazing flame. Enthroned on a chariot of ice with wheels like the sun is "the Great Glory," who is attended by myriads of courtiers, known as watchers and holy ones. All of this is recounted by the seer, who was granted the unique privilege of being taken up on high to hear the Divine Judge pronounce a sentence of doom on the rebellious watchers (chaps. 14–16).[3]

---

[3] For details supporting my interpretation of chapters 12–16, see George W.E.

The holy ones—by whatever name (see n. 4)—are an essential feature in the Enochic revelations. Their numbers are legion, and their functions are many and varied. In the Astronomical Book, they are in charge of the operation of the heavenly bodies. In chapters 1–5 they appear as a divine army (1:4, 9). In chapters 12–16, they are described as priests in the heavenly sanctuary and as courtiers in the throneroom. Elsewhere they function as agents or messengers of God, although it is uncertain whether or where the original Aramaic ever used the word מלאכא to describe them.[4] Chief among the heavenly entourage is a special group, which is four or seven in number, depending on the tradition.

In chapters 6–11 the four, named Sariel, Raphael, Gabriel, and Michael, intercede with God in behalf of humanity and then are sent as the agents of God's judgment at the time of the Flood and presumably at the eschaton.[5] The names of two of them signify their area of responsibility. Raphael "heals" the earth of the plague brought by the rebellious watchers. Gabriel sends the giants (among them the *gibborîm*) into a war of mutual extermination.

To the four, chapters 20–36 add the names of Uriel, Raguel, and Remiel. In this tradition, the seven are in charge of various parts of the cosmos and the activities that take place there. Uriel presides over the luminaries. Raphael is in charge of the mountain of the dead, where the shades reside. Michael, the protagonist of God's people, looks after Jerusalem. These functions, listed in the ono-masticon in chapter 20, are elaborated in the narrative, as the "holy angels" or "holy watchers" (see n. 4) accompany Enoch on his journey and explain what he sees in their respective areas of responsibility.

Nickelsburg, "Enoch, Levi, and Peter: Recipients of Revelation in Upper Galilee," *JBL* 100 (1981): 575–82 (below, 427–85).

[4] In the Qumran Aramaic fragments of 1 Enoch, in those relatively few places where the text is extant, every occurrences of "holy angel(s)" in the Greek and Ethiopic has for its counterpart "watcher(s) and holy one(s)." This could indicate, though it is by no means certain, that wherever "angel" occurs in the Greek and Ethiopic of 1 Enoch, it translates "watcher" in the original Aramaic. This could be the case also in Tobit.

[5] For my interpretation of chapter 6–11, and particularly the idea that the story reflects aspects of both primordial and eschatological times, see George W.E. Nickelsburg, "Apocalyptic and Myth in 1 Enoch 6–11," *JBL* 96 (1977): 383–405. On other matters relating to these chapters, see Paul D. Hanson, "Rebellion in Heaven, Azazel, and Euhemeristic Heroes in 1 Enoch 6–11," *JBL* 96 (1977): 195–233; and the papers by Hanson, Nickelsburg, John J. Collins, and Devorah Dimant in Paul J. Achtemeier, ed., SBLASP 1978, Vol. 2:309–39.

Chapters 92–105 presume the heavenly world and its activity rather than describe it. Here, too, allusions are made to the functions of the heavenly courtiers, although their number and proper names are not indicated. Their roles closely approximate those of the four in chapters 6–11. As scribes, they keep a daily record of the sins of the wicked. As intercessors they bring memoranda (μνημόσυνον; 97:5–6; 99:3; 103:4) to the attention of the heavenly King and "call to remembrance" (ἀναμιμνήσκουσιν) the contents of the prayers of the righteous "in the presence of the glory of the Great One" (ἐνώπιον τῆς δόξης τοῦ μεγάλου, 104:1).[6] Chief among these prayers are complaints about oppression and injustice and petitions that God intervene as Judge. When the judgment occurs, the heavenly ones will function as God's agents (100:4; 102:3).

Another specially mentioned group among the watchers—though never called *holy* watchers for obvious reasons—are the two hundred who rebelled against God in the time before the Flood. Chapters 6–11 recount the story of this rebellion in three versions, or fragments of three versions (see n. 5). According to the first version, which controls the present shape of the narrative, the heavenly watchers became enamored of the beauty of the daughters of men, and at the behest of their leader Šemiḥazah, descended, took these women as wives, and begat bastard (half-divine, half-human) offspring—giants who ravaged the earth and its inhabitants. In the second version, the watcher chieftain was named ʿAśael (presently he is the lieutenant of Šemiḥazah); he rebelled by revealing the secrets of metallurgy and mining, which made it possible for humans to fashion weapons, as well as the jewelry and cosmetics that facilitate sexual seduction. The third version of the story, if it was a separate version ascribed to the watchers, is the revelation of the secrets of astrological forecasting and of the magical arts.

These myths function to explain the presence of certain kinds of evil in God's world and to promise their extirpation. These evils originated in primordial antiquity, and their cause was the rebellion of divine beings. The violence of war experienced in the present time is not due simply to human intentions and actions. According to the myth about Šemiḥazah, the captains and kings of the earth

[6] See also 103:1. The title "The Great Holy One," occurs in 1 Enoch 1–36 and 91–105 with considerable frequency.

are incarnations of evil bred into the world through the lust of rebellious heavenly beings. In the story of ʿAśael, war has been made
possible by the forbidden revelation of the technology that facilitates
the fabrication of effective weapons. Similarly, occult knowledge about
the future and magical means to manipulate one's world constitute
a body of knowledge that God has proscribed for humanity. The
evils brought by the rebel watchers are dealt with in two stages. In
primordial times, God sent the four holy ones to imprison the villains and kill their offspring. At the end of time, God's agents will
take the rebels to their final punishment and will extirpate the evil
that they brought and will heal and cleanse the creation.

Chapters 12–16 of 1 Enoch recast the old myths in a significant
way. Because the rebellious watchers were spirit, which is not mortal, the death of the giants released their spiritual components, which
now constitute a world of demons which ravage the earth and humanity through acts of violence "against the sons of men and against
the women, because they have come forth from them," through sickness and possession, and, possibly, by tempting humans to sin. This
condition will prevail until God intervenes and exterminates the
demons at the eschaton (15:11–16:1).

2. *Tobit*

On the first reading, the book of Tobit appears to depict a world
that is very different from Enoch's. Its author offers no elaborate
revelations of cosmic phenomena and heavenly secrets, recounts no
myth about the primordial origins of evil, and posits no final angelic
extermination of evil to usher in a renewed and cleansed creation.
These striking differences notwithstanding, the author of Tobit presumes and employs some important elements which we have seen
in 1 Enoch, mixing material that is found in various of 1 Enoch's
sections or strata.

Although the author did not describe or claim to have seen the
heavenly world, he alludes to it. God dwells there in glory, attended
by "holy angels" or "holy ones," evidently a multitude of them (8:15;
11:14).[7] Seven of them, including Raphael, serve as witnesses of

---

[7] See all the references to "the holy ones" in 8:15.

human deeds and as intercessors who bring the memorandum of the prayer of the righteous into the glorious presence of the Great One or Holy One (3:16–17; 12:12–15; ἐγὼ προσήγαγον τὸ μνημόσυνον τῆς προσευχῆς ὑμῶν ἐνώπιον τῆς δόξης τοῦ ἁγίου,[8] and they are sent to earth as God's agents to combat evil and help those in trouble. As in 1 Enoch 10:4–8, Raphael is the divinely sent healer (3:17; 12:14). Like the angels in 1 Enoch 20–36, Raphael also accompanies Tobias on a journey (albeit an earthly journey, Tobit 6–11). When Tobias asks him about the strange pharmacopeia he has been ordered to take with him, Raphael acts as an interpreter (6:6–8). When Tobias cries out for help, Raphael saves him from danger (6:3 S).[9]

The author of Tobit ascribes some forms of evil to the activity of "evil demons." The villain is Asmodeus, whose desire for Sarah causes intense suffering for her and her parents, to say nothing of her seven bridegrooms. The duel between Raphael and Asmodeus concludes with the former binding the latter and removing him from the scene. The wording of Tob 8:3 resembles the description of the duel between ʿAśael and Raphael in 1 Enoch 10:4,[10] although the demon's passion for Sarah is similar the motivation of the sin of Šemiḥazah and his associates (6:2), whose opponent in 1 Enoch 10 is Michael, and its attribution to a demon recalls the statement in 15:11 cited above. In a particular nuance that differentiates Tobit from 1 Enoch (7:1; 8:3; 9:8), the good angel reveals magical information that enables Tobias to combat the demon and cure Tobit (6:1–8).

Against the background of these parallels, the difference between 1 Enoch and Tobit stand out more clearly. Sometimes the righteous do suffer as victims of demonic activity, as in the case of Sarah.[11] They may be oppressed by other human beings (cf. 1 Enoch 92–105) either because they seek to fulfill God's law (as when Tobit buries the dead) or simply in spite of the fact that they act righteously (as

---

[8] The "Great One" is indicated by the B text of 3:16, when compared with S, and "The Holy One" is indicated by 12:15 B, when compared with S.

[9] For angelic response to a human appeal, cf. 1 Enoch 7:3; 8:3 and chapters 9–10.

[10] See especially the reading of Syncellus, which uses two verbs and, in fact, the same roots as does the Greek of Tob 8:3.

[11] On the possibility that the bird in Tob 2:10 is an agent of the devil, see my commentary, ad loc.

when Tobit is taken into exile although he fulfills God's commandments, 1:3–10). But Tobit's chief explanation for his own suffering
is that God chastises even the righteous because of their sin, and
Tobit employs a similar paradigm to explain Israel's exile. God is
smiting his people, so that they may repent and find mercy.[12]

God's mercy for Israel lies in the future (see the next section), as
in 1 Enoch. However, in an emphasis very different from 1 Enoch,
the author of Tobit focuses on the presence of God and the activity of God's healing angel *here and now*. Raphael's mission is placed
neither in primordial times nor at the eschaton; it is in historical
time that he descends to heal the suffering of human beings. In this
sense, the difference in genre between 1 Enoch and Tobit is significant.
Although the book of Tobit is set in past time, its characters are
real human beings with whom the readers can identify. The implication is that God is now present among his people, and God's
angels are active to heal the ills of God's people.

Herein lies the importance of the element of revelation in Tobit
and the significance of its difference from Enoch's revelations. In
Tobit, people do not understand the real meaning of what is happening to them, nor do they perceive the real identity of the heavenly agent who claims to be a long lost cousin. Only at the end of
the story, when Azariah reveals that he is really Raphael, does Tobit
understand that even in his suffering, God was with him. The reader
may deduce that in other cases the suffering of the righteous does
not indicate divine absence or neglect, or the lack or failure of justice. Although the anguish in the prayers of Tobit and Sarah may
elicit the sympathy of the reader who also suffers, the angelic revelation assures the same reader that in reality things are not as they
appear and that help and vindication are on the way. This focus on
God's presence now in the lives of individuals distinguishes Tobit
from 1 Enoch, where God's beneficent, saving will, which is being
done in heaven, will be realized on earth only in an eschatological
denouement.

---

[12] For the formula, "scourge, have mercy," see 11:15 of Tobit and 13:2, 5, 9 of
Israel. On the parallelism between the two stories see George W.E. Nickelsburg,
Jewish Literature Between the Bible and the Mishnah (Philadelphia: Fortress, 1981), 33.

B. Eschatology

1. *1 Enoch*

The eschatological emphasis in 1 Enoch is evident in the first lines of the collection, which announce the coming of a final judgment that will bring blessing to the righteous chosen ones and punishment to the wicked (1:1). This superscription leads into a prophetic oracle, said to be the crystallization of Enoch's heavenly vision. At many other points, in almost all strata of the collection, this eschatological judgment is announced and emphasized. A brief description of the renewed creation forms the climax to the myth about the rebellious watchers (10:17–11:2). Like a prophet Enoch hears God's announcement to this effect in chapters 12–16. In the journey accounts in chapters 17–19 and 20–36, mythic geography and cosmology undergird the eschatological message by describing the places of its enactment. In chapters 92–105 the woes and assurances, again with prophetic analogies, announce, warn, and assure that human deeds are subject to God's future judgment.[13] Only in two instances, however, is the eschatological judgment placed in historical perspective, in a "historical apocalypse." Contrary to some stereotypes of apocalyptic literature, the authors of the Enoch texts do not dwell on the "when" of the judgment and the consummation. The two apocalypses are Enoch's extended dream vision in chapters 85–90 (the Animal Vision) and the Apocalypse of Weeks in 93:1–10; 91:11–17.[14] Both texts—one in great detail, the other in brief schematic form— trace the course of history from creation to the eschaton. The Apocalypse of Weeks is of special importance here, because it has an interesting parallel in the book of Tobit.

The author of this little apocalypse claims to present the contents of a vision which Enoch received in heaven, as well as the contents of the heavenly tablets, which he read (93:1–2). It is introduced twice in language that parallels Enoch's experience to that of Balaam the prophet (93:1, 3: cf. 1:2–3).[15] Speaking from the fictional perspective

---

[13] On these forms, see idem, "The Apocalyptic Message of 1 Enoch 92–105," *CBQ* 39 (1977): 310–13.

[14] This order in the Apocalypse is attested in the Qumran Aramaic fragments; see J.T. Milik, *The Books of Enoch* (Oxford: Clarendon, 1976), 265–66.

[15] On the parallels between chapter 93 and chapter 1, see James C. VanderKam, "Studies in the Apocalypse of Weeks," *CBQ* 46 (1984): 516–17.

of Enoch's time, the author forecasts history from the end of the first "week," the seventh generation from Adam, to the time of the tenth "week" and the many weeks without end that will follow it.

The following features in the Apocalypse are important for our consideration. In the third week, Abraham is "chosen as the plant of righteous judgment" (93:5). The fourth and fifth weeks are marked by the building of the tabernacle and the temple respectively (93:6–7). The sixth week concludes when "the temple of the kingdom is burnt with fire" and "the chosen root is dispersed" (93:8). No mention is made of a return or of the rebuilding of the temple. The seventh week is characterized as totally perverse (93:9), but at its conclusion, "the chosen are chosen as witnesses of righteousness from the eternal plant of righteousness" (93:10).[16] They are given sevenfold knowledge so that they can uproot violence and deceit (91:11), and in the eighth week all the righteous are given a sword to execute judgment against all the wicked. The "the temple of the kingdom of the Great One will be built in the greatness of its glory for all the generations of eternity" (91:12–13). In the ninth week, "righteous judgment (or law) will be revealed to all the sons of the whole earth, and the deeds of wickedness will vanish from the earth and descend into the eternal pit, while all humanity turns to the path of eternal righteousness" (91:14).

2. *Tobit's Eschatology*

Although the story of Tobit's and Sarah's troubles and their alleviation begins and concludes in a past historical time period, the book has a significant orientation toward the future. The story of Tobit's suffering and its alleviation is paralleled by the story of Israel's suffering and its alleviation. Both are interpreted as divine chastisement and mercy (see n. 12). But whereas the healing of Tobit (and Sarah) brings closure to that plot, the story of Israel's suffering remains unfinished. From the time perspective of the alleged author and from the point of view of the real author, God's mercy on Israel will be realized in the future. Tobit's story, with its happy conclusion, is the paradigm for Israel's story, which remains to be concluded.

---

[16] My reconstructions of the text of the Apocalypse of Weeks are based on the Qumran Aramaic, 4QEn^g.

This point is made through the use of two separate literary forms in chapters 13 and 14. Chapter 13 is an eschatologically oriented psalm, set in the land of captivity, where the author anticipates God's mercy, when the people will return from exile and dispersion and Jerusalem will be rebuilt in the glory predicted in the latter chapters of Isaiah. Chapter 14 repeats the point in a section of text that parallels the Apocalypse of Weeks. On his deathbed, the patriarch summons his children so that he can transmit his testament. Its contents are primarily a forecast of the future that closely shadows important features of Enoch's Apocalypse. Since Tobit is speaking during the exile, the forecast picks up at this point, near the conclusion of Enoch's sixth week. Significant events have their counterparts in 1 Enoch.

Tobit's "brethren will be scattered," Jerusalem will be desolate, and the "the house of God . . . will be burned until the time" (14:4; cf. 93:8). "God will return them to the land of Israel, and again they will build the house, but not as the first one, until the time, when the time of the seasons is fulfilled" (14:5; contrast 93:9). "After these things, they will all return from their captivity, and they will build Jerusalem in glory, and the house of God will be built in it as a glorious building for all the generations of eternity, as the prophets of Israel spoke concerning her" (14:5; see 91:13). "And all the nations in the whole earth will all turn and fear the Lord in truth, and they will all discard their idols, which lead them astray . . . and they will bless the God of eternity in righteousness" (14:6–7; see 91:14). "And those who love God in truth will rejoice and those who do sin and iniquity will disappear from the whole earth" (14:7; see 91:14).

A comparison with the Apocalypse of Weeks indicates the following parallels, sometimes expressed in precisely the same words: the scattering of the people and burning of the temple; the building of an eternal, glorious eschatological temple; the conversion of the gentiles; the removal of all the wicked. Of the gentiles destroying their idols, there is nothing explicit in the Apocalypse of Weeks, although they could be referred to as "the deeds of wickedness." However, in 91:9, in a section that parallels the Apocalypse, we are told that "all the idols of the nations will be given up // and the towers will be burned with fire // and they will remove them form all the earth // and they will cast into the fiery judgment."

The parallels are sufficiently close in content, sequence, and at times wording to suggest that the two texts reflect common tradition. In addition, Tobit's time references in 14:5 (see also 14:4, "All the things will happen in their times"), indicates a fixed chronology and sequence that is compatible with the determinism of Enoch's ten weeks. A more finely-tuned determinism, applied to the lives of particular individuals, is evident in Raphael's assertion that Sarah is the bride "destined" for Tobias "from eternity" (6:18: μεμερισμένη πρὸ τοῦ αἰῶνος S; ἡτοιμασμένη ἦν ἀπὸ τοῦ αἰῶνος B).

Against these similarities, there are notable differences between 1 Enoch and Tobit, which should be placed in their respective contexts. Tobit and the Apocalypse of Weeks reflect different assessments of post-exilic Israel and the second temple. The Apocalypse mentions neither the return nor the Zerubbabel's temple. The seventh week is totally perverse until a remnant of Israel is chosen and God gives them the revealed knowledge to be saved and to act as agents of judgment. Subsequent to this, and only then, does Enoch mention a post-exilic temple, which is the glorious eschatological temple. The author of Tobit, on the other hand, acknowledges the fact of the return and the building of Zerubbabel's temple, although the latter is a disappointing replica of the first temple, which will be replaced by the glorious eschatological sanctuary. In addition, by mentioning the return, the author acknowledges the post-Exilic community's status as Israel. Thus it is not necessary to posit a new chosen remnant in that community, whose gift of revealed saving knowledge and an eschatological sword equips them to be God's agents of judgment on their wicked contemporaries.

This element of revealed eschatological wisdom is a significant distinguishing feature between the two texts.[17] In its fictional testamentary context, Tobit's prediction can be read as a revelation, spoken with the divinely given clairvoyance of one about to die.[18] Moreover, this testamentary context parallels the testamentary context of the Apocalypse of Weeks (see 91:1 ff.).[19] Nonetheless, Tobit does not claim to be transmitting a revelation brought from heaven (contrast

---

[17] On the issue of revealed wisdom and religious error in the Epistle, see George W.E. Nickelsburg, "The Epistle of Enoch and the Qumran Literature," *JJS* 33 (1982): 334–45 (above, 106–81).

[18] Revealed forecasts of the future are typical in pseudepigraphic testaments. For a discussion of such forecasts, see Anitra Bingham Kolenkow, "The Genre Testament and Forecasts of the future in the Hellenistic Jewish Milieu," *JSJ* 6 (1975): 57–71.

[19] On the testamentary character of this section, see ibid., 61–62.

1 Enoch 93:2; cf. 91:1). The source and authority for his prediction
lie in the publicly proclaimed words of the prophets of Israel. "I
believe the word of God against Nineveh, the things that Nahum
spoke . . . and whatever the prophets of Israel spoke, whom God sent.
All things will happen, and not one of all these words will fail, and
all things will happen in their times" (14:4; see also 14:5, quoted
above).[20] Thus the author's voice is not that of a fictional primordial patriarch, nor that of a real leader of an eschatological community of the chosen, who are distinguised by their possession of
esoteric, salvific wisdom.

C. Wisdom and Ethical Teaching

In the two previous sections I have argued that the book of Tobit
reflects two major concerns in 1 Enoch and that the author of Tobit
has introduced these matters through the use of traditions or traditional language that he has in common with the Enochic authors.
In this section, I shall reverse the procedure and address a major
facet of the book of Tobit and then compare it with its parallels in
1 Enoch.

1. *Tobit*

Viewed as a literary whole, the book of Tobit can properly be
described as a sapiential story (less a simple tale than a more complex novel)—a narrative text which is governed by a pervasive interest in proper human behavior and which embodies this interest not
simply in its narrative description, but also in literary forms and
specific themes that are at home in such wisdom writings as Proverbs,
Job, and Sirach. The episodes that describe Tobit's activity and fate
in the Assyrian court (1:10–22) remind one of the tales about persecuted sages in Genesis 37 ff., Daniel 1–6, Esther and the Story of
Ahikar (who is, himself a minor figure in the book of Tobit; 1:21–22;
14:10). Tobit's identity as a sage is evident in the traditional proverbial wisdom with which he instructs Tobias (see also Ahikar 2, 8),
when he transmits his first testament in chapter 4. Set mainly in

---

[20] See also 2:1, 6, where Tobit sees Amos 8:10 fulfilled in his own lifetime and
situation.

parallelistic poetic distichs, this instruction treats a number of topics familiar to the reader of Proverbs and Sirach: the obligation to honor one's parents; the evils of sexual immorality and drunkenness; and, preeminently, the importance of using one's wealth responsibly and for the benefit of others. Integral to these proverbs and often structured into their two-line form is the notion that human actions are subject to divine reward and punishment. Punctuating this specific instruction are two generalizing admonitions that employ the traditional wisdom theme of the two ways of righteousness and wickedness and their respective reward and punishment (4:5–6, 19). In addition to this formal wisdom instruction (which is also put on the lips of Raphael 12:6–10), the author makes his didactic point by means of the events that are narrated. Tobit's actions are the embodiment of right conduct toward others. He buries the dead, acts as a responsible husband and father, and is generous in the sharing of his wealth. Above all, the plot line demonstrates that God rewards the righteous, even if they suffer for a time.

Both in the narrative itself and in the formal sections of instruction, wisdom is substantially equated with the Mosaic Torah, and right conduct toward God and one's fellows involves the keeping of the Torah. While he lived in the apostate northern kingdom, Tobit worshiped at the Jerusalem sanctuary and paid the proper tithes (1:3–8). When he was exiled in a gentile environment, he avoided forbidden food (1:10–11). When he became ritually unclean through contact with a corpse, he followed the law about ablutions (2:4–9). His command that Tobias marry a woman from his own tribe is based on the examples of the Genesis patriarchs (4:12).

2. *1 Enoch*

A concern with human conduct and divine retribution is also central to the Enochic corpus, as is readily evident from its repeated references to the final judgment. Herein, of course, lies an important difference. Taken as whole, 1 Enoch focuses on God's response to human actions rather than on the actions themselves, and this response is mainly reserved for the future, which is pervasively the point of reference for Enoch's references to judgment and his descriptions of the cosmos. In spite of this emphasis on eschatology and the cosmology that undergirds it, one section of the corpus does specifically address and describe in detail the human actions that are subject to God's judgment—the so-called Epistle of Enoch (chaps. 92–105) and its redactional preface (chap. 91).

As is the case in Tobit 4, specific human actions and their recompense are given a theoretical framework in the ethical construct of the two ways. Three segments of two ways teaching alternate mainly with two apocalyptic sections to form the introduction to the Epistle.

Two ways instruction	91:1–4
An apocalypse	91:5–9
Two ways instruction	91:18–19
[Introduction to the Epistle	92:1–5]
Apocalypse of Weeks	93:1–10+91:11–17
[The source of Enoch's revelation	93:11–14]
Two ways instruction	94:1–5

The sections of two-ways material are stereotyped and repetitious, but with variations and turns of phrase that provide additional nuances. Analogies to various of these distichs can be found in the book of Proverbs, especially chapter 4, Sirach 2:6, 12, 15, and in Tobit's testament (4:5–6, 19). Literary connections, however, are probably impossible to prove. 1 Enoch 94:1–5 appears to echo some of the language of Proverbs 4 (cf. 94:1; Prov 4:6; 94:3; Prov 4:14–15). However, 94:3 is also paralleled in Tob 4:5–6, and the concluding admonition in 94:5ab, which looks like a paraphrase of Prov 4:5, is, at one point, more closely paralleled by the concluding admonition in Tob 4:19:

Prov 4:4–5:	Let your heart hold fast my words . . .
	Do not forget the words of my mouth
1 Enoch 94:5:	Hold fast in the thought of your heart
	Do not erase my word from your heart
Tob 4:19:	Remember my commandments;
	And let them not be erased from your heart.

Both 1 Enoch and Tobit have an expression that is paralleled only in Proverbs, and a common turn of phrase that does not occur in Proverbs. All three texts place these admonitions in the context of explicit two-ways phraseology. The simplest explanation is that both 1 Enoch and Tobit employ common traditional two-way material which partly reflects Proverbs, but also has its own nuances.

In 1 Enoch 91:1–94:5, the apocalyptic sections that alternate with the two ways instruction provide the latter with a specific temporal reference for the retribution that is announced for those who will walk in the two ways, viz., the final judgment, which will occur at a specific time. Similarly, 94:2, 5ce indicate an eschatological locus for the revelation of saving wisdom and its rejection by those who walk in evil ways.

Taken as a whole, 91:1–94:5 introduce the rest of the Epistle and are explicated in it. Three literary forms treat the issue of human actions and divine judgment. The Woes collectively provide a detailed description of some of the sins of the author's enemies and warn of the consequences. The exhortations encourage the righteous to await the divine vindication of their righteousness and piety. Several descriptive passages provide a scenario for the coming judgment (see n. 13). The sins that are condemned in the Epistle of Enoch are of two major types. One picks up a central theme in Tobit (wealth and the wealthy); the other relates to a point of discontinuity already observed (the possession of special, divinely given wisdom).

The major point of overlap between the ethical teaching in Tobit and its counterpart in 1 Enoch 92–105 is their common assertion that the rich have an obligation to the poor and lowly. Their actual treatments of the subjects stand in sharp contrast to one another. Tobit is depicted as a wealthy man, who uses his riches and possessions for the benefit of others (1:16–17) and admonishes his son to do likewise (Tob 4:7–11, 14; see also 12:8–9; 14:10–11). The author of the Epistle portrays the rich and powerful as guilty of sinful excesses, notably the oppression of the lowly righteous.[21] In keeping with their common emphasis on just divine retribution, the two authors posit diametrically opposing fates for the rich. Consonant with his own expressed beliefs (4:6–11), Tobit's generosity is rewarded when his health is restored, and Tobias, who presumably heeds his father's admonitions, lives a long and fruitful life. According to 1 Enoch 95–105, the oppressive rich are set to receive the divine punishment that their sin deserves.

The time or manner of the reward or punishment differentiates the viewpoints of the two authors and is a function of their respective eschatologies. The author of Tobit, playing on the idea of the

---

[21] For a contrast between 1 Enoch's severe appraisal of the rich and a more optimistic view in Luke that is more consonant with the wisdom tradition in Tobit, see George W.E. Nickelsburg, "Riches, the Rich, and God's Judgment in 1 Enoch 92–105 and the Gospel According to Luke," *NTS* 25 (1979): 324–44.

two ways, states that Tobias's way prospers when he literally makes his way across Mesopotamia to seek his fortune (cf. 4:6, 19; 5:16, 21 [5:17, 22 Grk.] 11:1, 15). Although the idea of "the ways" is basically an ethical construct, Tobias's journey on the road across Mesopotamia is parabolic of the author's belief that one's reward is received during one's lifetime. Tobit's enunciation of this principle in the midst of his disastrous suffering appears to be ironic in context (4:6–11), but it proves to be right when his fortune changes at the end. For the author of Tobit it must be so, because at death one descends permanently to Sheol, "the eternal place" (3:6, 10). The author of the Epistles, on the other hand, admits that it is possible for the righteous not to receive their just deserts in their lifetime but to "descend with grief into Sheol" (102:5). He solves this problem of theodicy, however, by positing a resurrection that will permit the kind of change in fortune that Tobit must experience *before* he dies (103:1–4).[22] For Tobit burial is important because it concludes one's life, and it is appropriate, therefore, that rich poeple like Tobit and Raguel go out in grand style (14:11–13). In the Epistle, the magnificent funerals of the oppressive rich are deceptive. They are not a final reward for righteousness, but stand in marked contrast to the wretched fate that awaits them in the fires of Sheol, where they will receive just retribution for their sinful lifestyles (103:5–8).

In addition to social injustice, the author of the Epistle condemns his opponents for false teaching and perversion of the Torah. The emphasis is a function of his belief that the righteous chosen of the end-time possess a special revealed wisdom, which is necessary for salvation (see n. 17). Although the Animal Vision and the Apocalypse of Weeks both make reference to the Mosaic Torah, the emphasis in the corpus is on the revealed wisdom that Enoch brought from heaven. It includes the solar calendar, knowledge about the coming judgment, and, most likely, particular interpretations of the Mosaic Torah. This viewpoint distinguishes the Enochic authors from the author of Tobit, for whom there is no such esoteric or special eschatological wisdom that defines a chosen remnant as the true Israel, who alone will be saved.

---

[22] For a detailed analysis of the reversal of fortunes indicated in 1 Enoch 102:5–104:8, see Nickelsburg, "Apocalyptic Message," 318–23.

D. Liturgical Vocabulary

Tobit and 1 Enoch share some common liturgical vocabulary. Tobit has a marked liturgical and, mainly, doxological tone. Tobit and Sarah offer prayers of complaint (3:2–6, 11–15), and all that follows is said to have been triggered by their prayers (3:16–17). When Asmodeus is vanquished, Tobias and Sarah and then Raguel offer prayers of thanksgiving and supplication (8:5–8, 15–17). When he is healed, Tobit blesses God, once briefly (11:14–15) and then at length (chap. 13). The latter hymn is in response to Raphael's command that they praise God and write a book that documents God's might deeds (12:17–22). In 1 Enoch, as in Tobit, prayer can trigger God's saving activity (7:6, 8:3; chaps. 9–11; 97:5–6; 98; 3; 103:15–104:1). Two lengthy prayers are recorded in chapters 9 and 84. Enoch is introduced in 12:3 as "blessing the Lord of majesty, the King of the ages," and after various stages of his journey and after his two dream visions, he praises God (22:14; 25:7; 27:5; 36:4; 81:3, 10; 83:11; 90:40). Although one should not make too much of it, there are close parallels in the high and exalted terminology that these texts use to address God: King of the ages; Lord of righteousness; blessed is your holy name. Related to this is the vocabulary used in Tob 4:16; 12:12, 15 and in 1 Enoch 103:1; 104:1, where, in the context of prayer or an oath, reference is made to ther glorious presence of God, the Great One or the Holy One. Both texts appear to know a formal liturgical vocabulary that asserts itself into the presence of a God who is paradoxically addressed in the highest and most exalted terms. It is a view of God that emphasizes the divine righteousness that executes judgment and the majesty and greatness that rules over "all the generations of eternity," which are part of the typical vocabulary of the eschatological passages discussed above.

E. An Attempt to Define Relationships

Although our findings have documented many fundamental and important differences between Tobit and 1 Enoch, we have noted several significant areas of similarity, which is sometimes underscored through the use of (almost) identical wording:

(1) Both texts posit the existence of seven holy ones, perhaps "holy watchers," one of them named "Raphael"—God's Healer—who func-

tion both as witnesses and intercessors in the heavenly throneroom and as divinely sent agents of salvation or judgment. Tobit may also be combining the biblical idea of "the angel who goes with you" with the picture in 1 Enoch of a journey in the company of an interpreting angel.

(2)   Although the story of Sarah and Asmodeus doubtless reflects very old and common folkloristic motifs, the confrontation between Asmodeus and Raphael parallels and combines aspects of the primordial and eschatological conflict between supernatural powers in the mythic complex of 1 Enoch 6–11.

(3)   Tobit's testament in chapter 14 and Enoch's Apocalypse of Weeks posit a common eschatological scenario set in a definite time frame.

(4)   In dealing with ethical issues, both Tobit and Epistle of Enoch construe human behavior and divine retribution within the traditional framework of the two ways and focus on the issue of wealth and the wealthy and their interaction with the poor and lowly.

(5)   Both texts employ some common liturgical vocabulary that indicates similar views of God, whose majestic presence in heaven is accessible through angelic mediation and whose hold on history is sufficiently firm to guarantee the enactment of the respective eschatological visions.

These similarities are significant because the details that document them suggest that they are not easily explicable as the result of independent and coincidental dependence on the Hebrew Scriptures and its idea and vocabulary. They attest either the literary dependence of (parts of) one text on (parts of) the other, a knowledge of oral tradition, or the common dependence of both texts on traditional developments of biblical materials. They could indicate a combination of these.

A choice from among these options requires that one consider the dating of the respective texts. Chapters 1–36 of 1 Enoch can be dated, in various stages between 320 and 200 B.C.E.[23] The Epistle of Enoch and the Apocalypse of Weeks may have been composed as early as the first two decades of the second century B.C.E., but cannot be safely and surely dated prior to this.[24] The book of Tobit

---

[23] For the date of 1–36, see idem, "Apocalyptic Myth," 389–91.
[24] On the date of the Epistle, see idem, *Jewish Literature*, 149–50 and p. 158 n. 153.

certainly antedates the persecution by Antiochus IV and could thus
be contemporary with the earliest dating for the Epistle and Apocalypse
of Weeks. It may have been written in the early part of the Hellenistic
period and have roots in the Persian period.[25]

In light of this dating, it is impossible to prove and unfeasible to
posit that Tobit is simply dependent on various parts of the Enochic
corpus. Even if the complex of materials dicussed in Section A above
indicates knowledge of material in 1 Enoch 1–36, the formulas about
angelic intercession have their verbal parallels in the Epistle, which
cannot be shown to antedate the book of Tobit. In addition, the
considerations discussed in sections B and C indicate parallels in the
Epistle and the Apocalypse of Weeks. It would be a tour de force
to argue that the author of Tobit has employed 1 Enoch 1–36,
90–105, stripping the latter, most problematic part of its peculiar
eschatology and its emphasis on the eschatological community's possession of special revelation. It seems more likely, therefore, that
Tobit and Enoch attest common tradition.

The positing of common tradition raises interesting questions that
have an important bearing on our description of the development
of Judaism in the Persian Hellenistic periods.

(1) Our study indicates that a text like Tobit—which is, by consensus, a sapiential text—can employ traditional material which also
occurs in an apocalyptic collection like 1 Enoch. This is a significant
piece of data for those who have argued that the roots of apocalyptic literature are planted, in part, in the soil of the wisdom tradition. In addition, Tobit breaks the stereotype that wisdom literature
is uninterested in history and eschatology; the integrally related parallel stories of Tobit and Israel and the inclusion of Tobit's testament and psalm manifest precisely such an interest.

(2) Although the Apocalypse of Weeks claims heavenly revelation
as the source of its authority, the wording of Tobit's testament implies
that speculation about the times of eschatological events could occur
in circles that did not posit such a heavenly revelation, but developed such speculations explicitly on the basis of an exegesis of the
prophets. In this respect, Daniel 9, with its interpretation of Jeremiah's
seventy years, and the Testament of Moses, which is de facto an
interpretation of Deuteronomy 28–33, are suggestive analogies to

---

[25] On the date of Tobit, see ibid., 35.

Tobit's testament. Daniel 9 is particularly interesting because it attributes the interpretation to an angel, indeed one of the four and seven listed in 1 Enoch 6–11 and 20–36 respectively.

(3) Although Tobit's insight into the prophets is not ascribed to an angelic revelation, such revelation is, in fact, integral to the book of Tobit. The work as a whole is said to have been commissioned by Raphael (12:20), whose presence and activity are described within the framework of an extensive angelophany (chaps. 3–12) that has a multitude of parallels to biblical angelophanies, but also the revelation in Daniel 9 and 10–12. In Tobit, the form is triggered by Tobit's and Sarah's prayers (3:1–15). It then recounts the sending and appearance of the angel (3:16–17; 5:1–8), his false self-identification (5:9–21), his going along the way with Tobias and his beneficent activity (chaps. 6–11), his function as interpreter (6:6–8), his revelation of his identity and his functions in heaven and on earth (12:12–15), and along with the latter his explanation of events in Tobit's life, the typical terrified reaction tot he self-revelation (12:16), the reassuring "Fear not" (12:17), the commission to praise God and write a book (12:20), his disappearance (12:21), the partial fulfillment of these commands (12:21; 13:1).

Although it would not be helpful to suggest that the book of Tobit is formally an apocalypse,[26] what the book does claim to know about the activity of the heavenly world and the world's impingement on human life is, in fact, ascribed to an angelic revelation. Raphael is primarily intercessor and helper, but the angel is also a revealer of his own activity and God's. This important role played by revelation, even in the received form of the book of Tobit, raises the question of the place of angelic revelation in the sources and traditions behind Tobit. As we have seen, the angelology, descriptions of the heavenly throneroom, and eschatology in 1 Enoch are all integral and functional parts of that work's apocalyptic, i.e., revelatory character. It is possible that angelic revelation played a role in the common traditions attested in Tobit and 1 Enoch. The presence of an angelic guide and/or interpreter is already attested in Ezekiel 40–48 and Zechariah 1–6.[27] On the other hand, we must consider the

---

[26] For a literary definition of apocalypse, see John J. Collins, "the Jewish Apocalypse," *Semeia* 14 (1979): 21–59.

[27] On the relationship of 1 Enoch 12–16 especially to Ezekiel 1–2, but also to

possibility that at least some of these traditions (surely the liturgical material and probably the wisdom material) existed in forms that did not claim revelation as a source of authority.

F. Geographical Considerations: Upper Galilee and Mesopotamia

A curious pair of geographical considerations ties Tobit and 1 Enoch together. Both works are associated with both Upper Galilee and Mesopotamia. It is widely recognized that aspects of the Enochic tradition are most closely paralleled by Babylonian materials.[28] However, the mythic events described in chapters 6–11 and 12–16 are played out in Upper Galilee in the region of Dan and Mount Hermon, and the narrative indicates specific accurate knowledge of the region's geography.[29] The collection in its present form is usually thought to be Palestinian, and certainly the Animal Vision indicates specific knowledge of events in early second-century Palestine.

The explicit setting for most of the book of Tobit is the general region from which some of the Enoch traditions are said to originate, viz., Mesopotamia, albeit its northern part, Ecbatana and Nineveh. The book is so thoroughly oriented to the Dispersion and problems that would be encountered by Israelites in the Dispersion, that a Palestinian origin seems unlikely.[30] Nonetheless the story begins in Upper Galilee, which is said to be the home of Tobit (1:1–6). Perhaps this is casual backdrop, but interestingly, the geographic setting that is the locus of revelation in 1 Enoch is specified as the place of the seductive apostate cult which is a foil to Tobit's Jerusalem-oriented piety.

Ezekiel 40–48, see Nickelsburg, "Enoch, Levi, and Peter," 580–81 (below, 433–34). On the similarities between Enoch's journeys and Ezekiel 40–48 and to Zechariah 1–6, see Martha Himmelfarb, *Tours of Hell* (Philadelphia: University of Pennsylvania, 1983), 56–58.

[28] See, most recently, James C. VanderKam, *Enoch and the Growth of an Apocalyptic Tradition* (CBQMS 16; Washington, DC, 1984).

[29] Nickelsburg, "Enoch, Levi, and Peter," 582–87.

[30] On the Diaspora provenance of Tobit, see George W.E. Nickelsburg, "Stories of Biblical and Post-Biblical Times," in Michael E. Stone, ed., *Jewish Writings of the Second Temple Period* (CRINT 2:2; Assen/Philadelphia: van Gorcum/Fortress, 1984), 45.

Milik has argued that the story of Tobit originated in Samaria and was intended to enhance the prestige of the Tobiad family.[31] Subsequently, a Judean redactor provided an orthodox version in which the primary changes pertained to the Jerusalem cult. The initial action was moved to Galilee, presumably to allow the connection with the Assyrian exile. The hypothesis has a number of difficulties, for all of Milik's ingenious explanation of textual problems and geographical uncertainties. The names Tobi and Tobiah, while they can be related to the Tobiad family, can also find their significance in the story itself, which recounts the Lord's goodness to the protagonists. Jerusalem is a central component in both Tobit's psalm and his testament and hardly a bit of retouching. In addition, if the book was written in Samaria, why would the author be so centrally concerned with the problems raised by living in the diaspora? To attribute this material to a Judean reviser also makes even less sense and would radically change the nature of Milik's understanding of the revision of the text. The parallels between Tobit and 1 Enoch suggest that we reconsider the originality of Tobit's references to Galilee, although the very different appraisal of the religious character of the area of Dan requires an explanation.

---

[31] Milik, "La Patrie," 522–30.

CHAPTER EIGHT

THE SEARCH FOR TOBIT'S MIXED ANCESTRY
A HISTORICAL AND HERMENEUTICAL ODYSSEY

GEORGE W.E. NICKELSBURG

Two Jewish Aramaic texts—the books of *Enoch* and *Tobit*—both found among the fragments in Qumran Cave 4, have been the object of substantial work by Jozef Tadeusz Milik.[1] In an earlier paper, I laid out a set of *similarities* between these two very *different* Jewish texts and suggested that it might be fruitful to attempt to define the possible relationship between these "Distant Cousins with a Recognizable Resemblance."[2] Some members of my audience were skeptical and suggested that I had identified elements that were simply common coinage in Second Temple Judaism. My suspicion remains: some of the parallels between *1 Enoch* and *Tobit* are more than coincidental and indicate contact between these texts and/or the traditions behind them. At the same time I concede that other parallels between *Tobit* and *1 Enoch* reflect common features in Second Temple Judaism, albeit in sectors of Judaism that are often thought to be totally *different* from one another. In my view, we can better understand *Tobit* and *1 Enoch*, and we stand to learn more about early Judaism more broadly construed, if we study these two texts together rather than in isolation from one another. But the situation is more complicated. As a survey of the secondary literature indicates, *Tobit* must be set in the context of a wide array of texts. Even if the author of *Tobit* knew (first or second hand) elements in the Enochic tradition, a balanced interpretation of *Tobit* must relate *Tobit*'s use of these elements to other features that the story shares with other texts and traditions.

---

[1] On *Tobit*, see "La Patrie de Tobie," *RB* 73 (1966): 522–30, and n. 3 below. On *1 Enoch*, see, especially, *The Books of Enoch: Aramaic Fragments of Qumran Cave 4* (Oxford: Clarendon, 1976).

[2] George W.E. Nickelsburg, "Enoch and Tobit: Distant Cousins with a Recognizable Resemblance," *Society of Biblical Literature 1988 Seminar Papers*, David J. Lull, ed. (Atlanta: Scholars Press, 1988), 54–68 (above, 217–39).

Achieving this difficult exegetical goal requires that we pursue new paths and ask new questions along the way. In honor of J.T. Milik's stimulating and "pioneering work" on *1 Enoch* and *Tobit*[3]—often providing a new slant and always provocative—I shall frame a few new questions for the book of *Tobit*. My concern, however, is broader. The book's points of contact with a whole range of texts, traditions, and trajectories and the manner in which scholars tend to discuss these in isolation from one another raise hermeneutical issues that pertain to the study of other ancient texts that we study so hard and understand so little.

In addition to my own appeal to the books of *Enoch*, the literature on *Tobit* has sought to shed light on this rich and variegated narrative by reference to the Pentateuch, the book of *Job*, biblical and non-biblical tales about the persecuted righteous, folkloric parallels, and Homer's *Odyssey*. I shall suggest that we must try to understand *Tobit* as a unique work of art that reflects, blends, and modifies a variety of traditions from diverse cultures and world views. Thus, it is inappropriate to use any single hermeneutical key to unlock this complex text. Like ourselves, ancient Jewish writers lived in a complicated, syncretistic, multi-cultural environment. They dipped their pens in many ink pots and, I would suggest, they wrote at the behest of muses they sometimes did not recognize. Finally, I wish to emphasize that modern scholarly categories that we use to interpret ancient texts (such as wisdom, apocalyptic, eschatology, and folklore) are *our own* inventions; and while they are helpful for heuristic purposes, they should not be conceived of as hermetically sealed and mutually exclusive entities in the ancient cultures that we wish to understand and explicate.[4]

---

[3] Milik's work on the text and context of the Aramaic Enoch (*Books of Enoch*) is foundational, even where one does not agree with him. In his edition of the Qumran texts of *Tobit*, Joseph A. Fitzmyer acknowledges that "What I present here is mostly dependent on his [i.e., Milik's] pioneering work," DJD 19, 1. I am grateful to Prof. Fitzmyer for allowing me to use the proofs from his section of this volume.

[4] George W.E. Nickelsburg, "Wisdom and Apocalypticism in Early Judaism: Some Points for Discussion," *Society of Biblical Literature 1994 Seminar Papers*, Eugene H. Lovering, ed. (Atlanta: Scholars Press, 1994), 729 (below, 267–87).

A. Sources and Resources used by *Tobit*'s Author[5]

1. *The Hebrew Bible*

It is not surprising that the Israelite author of *Tobit* used or alluded to texts that were (in the process of becoming) Israel's sacred scripture. Like other stories from the late Persian and early Hellenistic periods, this tale is set in a past time of Israelite history, in relation to situations and characters known from this history.[6] Although the specific times and locations differ, *Tobits* shares with the Danielic stories and the Book of *Esther* a common setting in the Mesopotamian exile and a related set of problems relating to Israelite identity and safety in an alien world populated by foreign monarchs and courtiers.

In addition, the author has drawn on motifs and narrative details in the patriarchal stories in *Genesis*.[7] Tobias's bride, Sarah, has the name of the nation's ancestress. Like Abraham, Tobit is anxious that his son find a bride from his own family. This marriage takes place as the result of a journey in which Tobias is accompanied by Raphael, whose function as marriage broker resembles that of Eliezer. The marriage is contracted and the rite carried out "in accordance with the Law of Moses" (6:13; 7:13). Given these allusions, it is not surprising to find affinities between *Tobit* and some of the concerns of *Deuteronomy*.[8]

As a story about the unjust suffering of a righteous man, the story of *Tobit* recalls the biblical book of *Job*, and some of its narrative details (particularly those describing the acrimonious interaction between the protagonist and his wife) parallel its older counterpart.[9]

---

[5] On the question of a single or multiple authorship for *Tobit*, see below, part C.

[6] Idem, "Stories of Biblical and Early Post-Biblical Times," *Jewish Writings of the Second Temple Period*, Michael E. Stone, ed. (CRINT 2:2; Assen: Van Gorcum/Philadelphia: Fortress, 1984), 33.

[7] Jonas C. Greenfield, "Ahiqar in the Book of Tobit," *De la Torah au Messie*, Maurice Carrez, Joseph Dore, Pierre Grelot, eds. (Paris: Desclée, 1981), 330. Paul Deselaers, *Das Buch Tobit* (Orbis Biblicus et Orientalis 43; Freiburg: Universitätsverlag, 1982), 292–304.

[8] Alexander di Lella, "The Deuteronomic Background of the Farewell Discourse in Tob 14:3–11, *CBQ* 41 (1979): 380–89; Will Soll, "Misfortune and Exile in Tobit: The Juncture of a Fairy Tale Source and Deuteronomic Theology," *CBQ* 51 (1989): 209–31.

[9] Ibid., 378–79; Nickelsburg, "Enoch and Tobit," 54 (above, 217); Devorah Dimant, "Use and Interpretation of Mikra in the Apocrypha and Pseudepigrapha," *Mikra: Text, Translation, Reading and Interpretation of the Hebrew Bible in Ancient Judaism*

At the same time, the interpretation of Tobit's suffering and its alleviation as divine "scourging" and "mercy" and the application of
this paradigm to Israel's exile and return find their counterparts in
texts as far removed from *Job* as *2 Maccabees* and the *Psalms of
Solomon*.[10]

Finally, the author refers explicitly to the prophets. Not only does
he anticipate a future when the prophet's words will be fulfilled in
their determined times (14:5), he also appeals to *Amos* and *Nahum* by
name in order to explain events in his life and in Nineveh's future
(2:6; 14:4).[11] Additionally, the hymn of praise in chapter 13 (vv. 9–18)
draws on the language of Second and Third *Isaiah*.

In short, material from the Pentateuch, the former and latter
prophets, and the writings provided a resource for the composition
and shaping of the book of *Tobit*, and on occasion the author explicitly referred to these texts.

2. *Folklore*

These biblical parallels, sources, and influences notwithstanding, the
closest parallels to some of the most important elements in *Tobit*
occur in extra-biblical materials of Israelite and non-Israelite provenance. Scholars have long recognized that folkloric motifs are an
essential component of the book of *Tobit*. Pfeiffer cites a number of
older studies that pursued this line of interpretation.[12] The introduction to Zimmermann's edition of *Tobit* also devotes considerable
space to a discussion of folkloric elements.[13] In his lengthy monograph on *Tobit*, Deselaers cites folkloric parallels and concludes that
such an element is present in *Tobit*, although the book cannot be

---

and Early Christianity, Martin Jan Mulder, ed. (CRINT 2:1, Assen: Van Gorcum/
Philadelphia: Fortress, 1988), 417–19.

[10] See George W.E. Nickelsburg, *Jewish Literature Between the Bible and the Mishnah*
(Philadelphia: Fortress, 1981), 33, 40, n. 40; 119, 154, n. 58. It is the motif to
which I point and not the texts themselves, which are later than *Tobit*.

[11] The allusion and reference to prophetic literature is carried a step farther in
6:2 and 14:4, in the shorter and secondary version of the text, where Jonah is the
prophetic book of note. On the two textual traditions of *Tobit*, see Frank Zimmermann,
The Book of Tobit: An English Translation with Introduction and Commentary (New York:
Harper & Brothers, 1958), 127–28, Fitzmyer, DJD 19, 2–4.

[12] Robert H. Pfeiffer, *History of New Testament Times: With an Introduction to the
Apocrypha* (New York: Harper & Brothers, 1949), 269–71.

[13] Zimmermann, *Tobit*, 5–12.

reduced to this generic definition.[14] Most recently Soll has refined this emphasis by adopting the approach of Vladimir Propp.[15] According to Soll, the plot of the *Tobit* story contains a significant number of the functions that Propp identified as typical of the Russian folk tale. For Soll this indicates that a "fairy tale source" stands behind the book of *Tobit*, although he does not attempt to describe how that story may have run. In any case, there is wide agreement that the story of *Tobit* is partly rooted in folk tradition.

3. *Tales about Persecuted Courtiers*

A related point of reference for interpreting *Tobit* is found in tales about the persecution and vindication of an innocent courtier.[16] Stories in this category occur both in the Hebrew Bible and in non-Israelite sources. In the Hebrew Bible the story type has shaped the Joseph cycle (*Gen* 37 ff.), as well as *Daniel* 3 and 6 and the Mordecai material in the book of *Esther*. Among non-biblical material, it is exemplified in the *Story of Ahiqar*. All of these stories except the Joseph story are set in Mesopotamia, as is *Tobit*. Although the plot typical of these tales does not comprise the whole of the book of *Tobit*, it is encapsulated in *Tobit* 1–2: Tobit is a court official, the buyer of provisions of Shalmaneser. After the king's death, Tobit carries out acts of charity during the reign of Sennacherib. When certain "men of Nineveh" inform on him, he must fleee for his life, and eventually his property is confiscated. Later he is delivered from death.

Tobit's connection with this type of story is evident in the book's explicit references to the *Story of Ahiqar*. Not only does the author mention some of the tale's narrative details, it claims that Tobit was a cousin of Ahiqar and makes him a participant in the action of the Tobit story (1:21–22; 2:10; 11:18; 14:10). Different from the general folkloric parallels that scholars have indentified—however convincing

---

[14] Deselaers, *Tobit*, 268–70, 280–92.

[15] William Soll, "Tobit and Folklore Studies, with Emphasis on Propp's Morphology," *Society of Biblical Literature 1988 Seminar Papers*, David J. Lull, ed. (Atlanta: Scholars Press, 1988), 39–53.

[16] These court tales have been the subject of considerable discussion in the past two decades; see G.W.E. Nickelsburg, *Resurrection, Immortality, and Eternal Life in Intertestamental Judaism* (HTS 26; Cambridge: Harvard University, 1972), 48–58; Idem, "The Genre and Function of the Markan Passion Narrative," *HTR* 73 (1980): 155–63 (below, 473–82); and the discussion and literature in John J. Collins, *Daniel: A Commentary on the Book of Daniel* (Minneapolis: Fortress, 1993), 38–50.

they are—the *Story of Ahiqar* is a specific story that our author certainly knew and used. Greenfield goes so far as to claim that the
story of *Tobit* was composed with an eye toward the *Ahiqar* tale. With
its negative picture of Nadan, the disobedient child, the *Story of Ahiqar*
provided a foil for this author's story about Tobit and his obedient
son, Tobias.[17]

4. *Homer's Odyssey*

Around the same time that scholars were identifying folkloric parallels to the book of *Tobit*, Carl Fries wrote an article that laid out
parallels between the book of *Tobit* and the Telemachos cycle in
Books 1–4 of the *Odyssey*.[18] In both stories a young man, whose father
is in distress, sets out on a journey accompanied by a divine figure
(Athena and Raphael), who appears in the form of a known human
being (Mentor/Mentes and Azariah) and advises and otherwise helps
the young man on his quest. The comparison is supported by a
string of verbal similarities and numerous parallels in narrative detail,
some more convincing than others. Fries concludes that *Tobit* and
the Telemachus cycle attest a common mythic kernel, perhaps the
motif of the separated and restored divine twins.

5. *The Enochic Tradition*

With this survey in mind, I return to the findings in my article on
Tobit and *1 Enoch* and note that none of the parallels cited there
occur in the aforementioned texts.[19]

(1)   Both *Tobit* and *1 Enoch* posit the existence of seven holy ones,
one of them named "Raphael" (God's Healer) who function both as
witnesses and intercessors in the heavenly throne room and as divinely
sent agents of salvation or judgment. *Tobit* may also be combining
the biblical idea of "the angel who goes with you" with the picture,
found in *1 Enoch*, of a journey in the company of an interpreting
angel.[20]

---

[17] Greenfield, "Ahiqar" 331–34. Deselaers (*Tobit*, 438–50) sees material from *Ahiqar*
and the Joseph story entering *Tobit* at a second stage of composition.
[18] Carl Fries, "Das Buch Tobit und die Telemachie," *ZWT* 53 (1910–11): 54–87.
[19] "Tobit and Enoch," 66.
[20] On the *biblical* motif in *Tobit*, see Merten Rabenau, *Studien zum Buch Tobit*
(BZAW 220; Berlin: de Gruyter, 1994), 106–15.

(2)   Although the story of Sarah and Asmodeus reflects very old and cross-cultural folkloric motifs, the confrontation between Asmodeus and Raphael combines narrative details of the primordial and eschatological conflict between good and supernatural powers recounted in the mythic complex in *1 Enoch* 6–11.

(3)   Tobit's testament in chapter 14 and Enoch's *Apocalypse of Weeks* present a common eschatological scenario set in a definite time frame.

(4)   In dealing with ethical matters, both *Tobit* and the *Epistle of Enoch* construe human behavior and divine retribution within the traditional wisdom framework of the two ways and focus on the issue of wealth, the wealthy, and their interaction with the poor and lowly.

(5)   Both texts employ a common liturgical vocabulary that expresses a view of God whose majestic presence in heaven is accessible through angelic mediation and whose firm hold on history guarantees the enactment of the respective eschatological issues.

I concluded:[21]

> These similarities are significant because the details that document them suggest that they are not easily explicable as the result of independent and coincidental dependence on the Hebrew Scriptures and its ideas and vocabulary. They attest either the literary dependence of (parts of) one text on (parts of) the other, a knowledge of oral tradition, or the common dependence of both texts on traditional developments of biblical materials. They could indicate a combination of these.

6. *Summary*

A wide variety of texts have been justifiably identified as sources of material in the book of *Tobit*. They include narratives, prophetic books, folk tales, wisdom literature, and an apocalyptic collection— texts of Israelite, Mesopotamian, and Greek provenance. How do we imagine the convergence of all this material of diverse origin, character, and genre in single work like *Tobit*?

This question has two aspects. It seeks a unity in the text's diversity and multi-dimensionality, and it attempts to relate that unity to the text's point of origin and the circumstances of the compositional process. Neither of these issues has been addressed in detail by the literature, in part, I suggest, because of counter-currents in the field of biblical studies.

---

[21] "Tobit and Enoch," 66 (above, 235).

B. A Paradox: Progress also Impedes the Interpretive Process

Events in the history of biblical scholarship over the past half century—which reflect substantial and significant progress in our understanding of antiquity and our interpretation of ancient texts—have,
paradoxically, led in directions that sometimes hinder a reading of
texts as integral parts of the broader world that constituted their
authors' environment. Increased knowledge and the new data, methods, and means that generate it can, in fact, stymie the acquiring
of fuller and more accurate knowledge. Here I can only sketch some
of the problems. In doing so, I readily admit that the reader can
find examples of biblical scholarship that move in exactly the opposite directions—directions I myself will suggest below. Nonetheless,
I press my point particularly with reference to the study of the non-
or deutero-canonical texts of Second Temple Judaism, where, *in comparison with the Hebrew Bible and the New Testament*, relatively little work
is being done and much more is necessary.

1. *The Problem of Reductionism and Focused Interpretation*

New data and new methods create individual and collective agendas that drive our scholarly inquiry. The geometric increase in these
data and methods require us to publish much of our work in focused
studies that appear in the short form of articles and papers that are
often narrow and reductionistic. Our agenda may lead us to read
Tobit as a piece of biblical *Nachgeschichte*, or to view it through filter
of a sub-discipline that is new on our horizon (e.g., folklore studies,
anthropology), or to argue for the wide influence of one's text of
close inquiry (e.g., *1 Enoch*). However, such interpretive studies are
not only a function of the fruitful diversity of modern critical scholarship and the insights born of new data, new methods, and inter-
disciplinary inquiry; they are also *necessary* because we are working
with ancient, often anonymous texts that derive from uncertain prove-
nances in distant generative worlds foreign to our own.

    Nonetheless, focused study of ancient texts—however necessary
and productive it is—can mislead the reader who does not attend
closely to what is happening. A study of "Narration and Comedy
in the Book of Tobit,"[22] or of *Tobit* as folktale, or as an expression

---

[22] David McCracken, "Narration and Comedy in the Book of Tobit," *JBL* 114
(1995): 401–18.

of Deuteronomic theology can give the impression that *Tobit is* a comic narrative, or *is* a folktale, or *is* Deuteronomic or Enochic *Nachgeschichte*. Fortunately articles like Soll's help to discourage such an impression by identifying, in this case, "The Juncture of a Fairy Tale Source and Deuteronomic Theology." Yet the fact remains that the focused character of our scholarship can suggest that its method, repertory of related texts, or pericope or literary aspect under study provides the single hermeneutical key for understanding a particular text.

2. *The Problem of Abandoning Historical Exegesis*

Hermeneutical discussions over the past half-century have made us increasingly conscious of the subjective elements in the interpretive process. On the one hand, an ancient text offers us modern readers a picture of its author's world that is colored by the author's predilections, prejudices, and experiences. Thus, there is no simple, foolproof way back to the world that affected the author's composition of the text and no way at all back to the *totality* of that world. On the other hand, our own reading of a text is colored by *our* experience, culture, and society. Therefore, we have no access to the mind of the author. These insights have radically altered and complicated our work as exegetes and historians, and some would say they have undercut the viability of historically oriented exegesis. Nonetheless, while these critiques need to be heeded, the fact remains that the ancient texts are historical artifacts, and this justifies—I would say demands—the attempt to interpret them with reference to their own generative contexts, however frustrating the process and fragmentary its results.

3. *The Problem of Identifying the Interpreter's World with that of the Author*

Although the hermeneutical revolution and the information explosion have revealed the great distance between the ancient texts and their modern interpreters, ironically, we sometimes act as if the gap were not there. At times we seem to reify the analytic and heuristic categories that we have created to interpret the texts—speaking as if they are the things themselves and implying that an ancient author would have recognized and thought in terms of the genre classifications and other categories that we have distilled from the texts. We may suppose that the patterns and structures that we recognize in texts were the conscious products of ancient authors, who conceived, outlined, and composed texts much as we scholars write articles and books. In fact, conversations with contemporary writers of non-scholarly literature reveal that the poetic process often bubbles up from the unconscious in fits and starts, bits and pieces, developing in unexpected ways without conscious intentionality.[23] In short, our recognition of historical distance and interpretive subjectivity notwithstanding, we sometimes write as if the authors of the ancient texts were tidy, twentieth century scholars.

C. *Tobit*'s Author at Work in His World: Reimagining the Poetic Process and Product[24]

In the first part of this essay I identified a range of ancient texts, generes, and traditions that scholars have suggested as sources for the story of *Tobit* or influences on its author. In the second part I suggested that such lines of individual inquiry are functions of our increased knowledge of antiquity and our methodological progress and that they enrich our understanding of the text in question. At the same time, I asserted, they shift our attention away from a consideration of the text as a whole. I also observed some tendencies toward dehistoricizing ancient texts. In this concluding section, I plead for an interpretation of Jewish texts that complements analysis with synthesis. Such interpretation would place the text of *Tobit* as a whole within the whole of its environment and attempt to understand *Tobit* as the end-product of a poetic process that can be imagined as holistic and integrative. However, "imagine" is the key word, because what we have is a kind of literary fossil from which we can deduce only as much of the whole original as our present evidence, knowledge and wisdom allow.

My intention is not to deprecate narrowly construed and focused studies. They are necessary and, when done well, helpful building blocks toward the reconstruction of the world of antiquity. Alongside

---

[23] For an instructive example, see David Rabe's comments on the writing of his play, *Hurlyburly* (New York: Grove Press, 1985), 161–71.

[24] I assume that *Tobit*'s author was a man rather than a woman; see the discussion of relevant matters in Amy-Jill Levine, "Diaspora as Metaphor: Bodies and Boundaries in the Book of Tobit," *Diaspora Jews and Judaism: Essays in the Honor of, and in Dialogue with, A. Thomas Kraabel*, J. Andrew Overman and Robert S. MacLennan, eds. (South Florida Studies in the History of Judaism 21; Atlanta: Scholars Press, 1992), 105–17.

of them, however, I propose broader, synthetic work. This might take the form of introductory essays on particular texts that seek to find their literary integrity and to discover a unified world view that ties together their variegated thematic threads and social concerns.[25] More ambitiously, we need commentaries on works for which there are none. However, integration can also be a dimension of our focused studies, if we develop methods, rhetoric, and a *modus operandi* that encourage the exposition, or at least the suggestion of some of the broader implications of these focused studies. How does a given theme, tendency, genre, or the influence of a source relate to and affect other elements in the book or, indeed, the whole of the work? As it is, we often make disclaimers that bracket out these questions, leaving them for someone else to ask.

It is also not my desire to minimize the importance of studies on genre and the other analytical categories (e.g., wisdom and eschatology) that have contributed greatly to our understanding of ancient texts. I am concerned, rather, that we recognize these for what they are—mainly our own modern categories and abstractions—and that we seek a better understanding of the ancient realia that created, shaped, embodied, and were affected by these things that we have abstracted and distilled and that we call by names of our own invention. To no small degree this involves a shift—already underway—from the history of ideas to a consideration of social and cultural settings, of offices and institutions. Again, the texts are historical remains, footprints made in the past. What kind of creatures made them, and what were they doing and where were they going when they made them? How, for what purposes, in what settings and in what roles did people create the kind of deterministic predictions that are preserved both in *Tobit*'s testament and in Enoch *Apocalypse of Weeks*? What can we learn about the author's attitude and experience with respect to family life and gender roles?[26] How can we use our categories not only to analyze the texts, but also to reveal the specifics of the *ancient* realities and forces that generated the texts we analyze.

---

[25] For a good example of such an approach, see ibid.
[26] In addition to Levine's article, see Beverly Bow and George W.E. Nickelsburg, "Patriarchy with a Twist: Men and Women in Tobit," *Women Like This: New Perspectives on Jewish Women in the Greco-Roman World*, Amy-Jill Levine, ed. (SBLEJL 1; Atlanta: Scholars Press, 1991), 127–43.

This leads one to the poetics of our text. *Tobit*, with all of its complexity, is a wonderful example to contemplate. In it we find a
plethora of literary genres: prayers, an angelophany, wisdom instruction, two testaments, a historical review. Additionally, we see the
influence of a wide range of texts and traditions of Israelite. Mesopotamian, and Greek provenance. How do we imagine the genetics of
such a text? Is the best answer to be found in a source-critical or
tradition-critical analysis, which emphasized tensions and diverse tendencies in the text?[27] Or can we imagine a single human being dip-
ping his pen in many pots—receiving, synthesizing, reshaping, and
re-presenting the traditional materials that we can identify in this
text? If so, to what degree did this activity involve the conscious use
of recognized traditions and to what degree was it the product of a
fruitful and synthetic unconscious responding to unrecognized muses?
To what extent were some of these mixes and syntheses already
extant in the author's culture?

Careful methodology is critical at this point. What are the strengths
and weaknesses of literary critical analysis that explains diverse sources
and traditions as the result of compositional layers? Can we cite
known examples from our own time in which conscious or unconscious authorial synthesis reproduces and modifies multiple and complex traditions that are in the author's environment and culture? If
the process is unconscious, are there cognitive theories that may
explain it and help us to see whether it might have operated in
antiquity. In any case, in thinking about the poetics of ancient texts,
it is important to distinguish the assimilation, digesting, and compositional integration of traditions that are current in one's own culture from learned analytic processes such as the use of concordances
to texts and indices of folkloric motifs which are not part of one's
own cultural persona.

D. In Conclusion: Reassembling of Fragments

I have phrased much of this last section in the form of questions—
because I do not have the answers. Yet as we ask these questions,
we are on the horns of a dilemma. The very asking of questions

---

[27] See Deselaers, *Das Buch Tobit*, and Rabenau, *Studien zum Buch Tobit*.

appropriately avoids the appearance that the products of our scholarship offer a straightforward representation of the realities of antiquity, but the asking also results in the frustration of partial answers.

I have used a number of metaphors and similes to describe the
evidence we study and the process of study and interpretation: inkpots
and muses, fossils and footprints, search and odyssey. In conclusion,
I suggest that J.T. Milik's work on the scrolls provides an appropriate image. Our evidence comes to us like so many boxes of scroll
fragments. With care, study, imagination, cleverness, and a little bit
of luck we can reconstruct parts of the whole. We will disagree on
the validity of a particular join in the evidence, the placement of
this or that fragment, and the reconstruction of material missing in
the lacunae. And we need to be acutely aware that our diplomatic
transcription and our reconstructed text are not the same as the
original itself, much less the whole of it. For some the reassembling
of a fragmentary manuscript or the reconstruction of bits of history
is not worth the effort, given the paucity and uncertainty of the
results. Yet, in point of fact, we know a great deal more than we
did before 1947, although we know less than we thought we knew
before the discovery of the scrolls. But if we do not give the impression that our knowledge and our interpretation are the real thing—
much less all of it—and we press to learn more about the realia
and the larger pictures, the work and its results will reward the
effort—as we know from a reading of J.T. Milik's oeuvre.

SERIOUS GEORGE, OR THE WISE APOCALYPTICIST— RESPONSE TO "TOBIT AND ENOCH: DISTANT COUSINS WITH A RECOGNIZABLE RESEMBLANCE" AND "THE SEARCH FOR TOBIT'S MIXED ANCESTRY: A HISTORICAL AND HERMENEUTICAL ODYSSEY"

Robert Doran*

George Nickelsburg has constantly prodded his colleagues to be alert to the wealth of Jewish literary activity in the Second Temple period. In his early work, *Jewish Literature between the Bible and Mishnah* (Philadelphia: Fortress, 1982), Nickelsburg provided an excellent introduction to the richness of the material, a richness that has only been augmented by the library of the Qumran Covenanters. But Nickelsburg insisted not only that one be aware of this literary activity, but also that one not keep the respective texts separate from one another. One had to try to see relationships and correspondences between parts of the corpus.

Perhaps one of his more daring suggestions for such interaction between differing works of the corpus was his attempt to link Tobit and 1 Enoch. I have been asked to comment on this suggestion, a task made doubly difficult because Nickelsburg himself reflected on his own paper in "The Search for Tobit's Mixed Ancestry. A Historical and Hermeneutical Odyssey," in *Revue de Qumran* 17 (1996), reproduced above, pp. 241–253. There, with characteristic humor, he noted that his first audience was not too receptive to his suggestion (p. 241) and wryly hinted that scholars should be cautious in arguing "for the wide influence of one's text of close inquiry, e.g., 1 Enoch)" (p. 248). In this wonderful, reflective essay, one can only applaud Nickelsburg's call for methodological sophistication in interpretation and his sensitivity to the role of imagination needed to gain an integrative appreciation of the texts we possess.

* Amherst College.

Wisdom and Apocalyptic

Whatever the merits of the specifics that Nickelsburg found in common between 1 Enoch and Tobit—seven holy ones, the name Raphael, common liturgical vocabulary—his coupling of 1 Enoch and Tobit insightfully showed that both texts, so different in many ways, contained a certain variety of wisdom teaching. Nickelsburg here saw that difference in genre did not automatically mean different author: That the same ancient writer could write in what modern scholars would classify as different genres and that different genres could be found in the same ancient writing. An apocalypse like 1 Enoch could contain material based on the wisdom tradition of the two ways and ethical teachings about the poor, and Tobit, which Nickelsburg called a wisdom novel, could speak of what would happen in the future. The same writer could employ in one work whatever genres, which modern scholars have employed as heuristic categories, he or she wished. With this insight, genre criticism by itself could no longer be used as a means of source criticism. When Nickelsburg later noted that the categories of wisdom and apocalyptic were being used, particularly in studies of Q, to distinguish sources, he formed a group at the annual Society of Biblical Literature Meeting, "Wisdom and Apocalyptic," to debate these issues. The insight obtained by comparing 1 Enoch and Tobit has had far-reaching consequences.

Biblical Sources

In his reflective essay on Tobit, Nickelsburg listed biblical writings that may have shaped the writing of Tobit. (One further reference, perhaps not mentioned because it is so obvious, should be made to the seven eyes of Zech. 4 as a source for the seven angels of 1 Enoch and Tobit.) Nickelsburg also challenged his colleagues to explore themes and larger concerns implicit in the work. This is excellent, but should one not also note where thematic strands in the work are at odds with other writings? A first example might be a comparison with Ezra. While Nickelsburg is rightly suspicious of Milik's suggestion that Tobit provided a genealogy for the Tobiads,[1] it is important to note the insistence in Ezra of the return from exile

---

[1] J.T. Milik "La Patrie de Tobie," in *RB* 73 (1966), pp. 523–530.

"of the heads of families of Judah and Benjamin" (Ezra 1:5). Where does this leave the Ephraimite Tobit and his family? Tobias settled in Ecbatana and Ezra 6:2 claims that it is there that a copy of Cyrus' decree for the return of the exiles is found. Granted that Tobit is fictional, should not the character, the pious Tobias, surely have known of it? Secondly, the last words of the work emphasize that Tobias died happy because Nineveh was destroyed. True, the author had Tobit earlier in his testament look forward to the inclusion of gentiles at the final restoration (13:11). But the work ends on this note of jubilation at the downfall of Nineveh. What a contrast to Jonah! By employing the emotion of revenge, was the author of Tobit using the worst kind of rhetorical ploy to emphasize the distinction from gentiles? Is this why it was popular at Qumran? Finally, Ezra and Tobit have in common an emphasis on endogamy and kosher food, the latter also present in Dan. 1–6, but totally absent in that other writing set in exilic times, Esther. Unless we are to think that *kashrut* is implicit and that Haman was looking forward to a kosher meal with Esther (Est. 5:7–9a), what are we to make of this absence? Should we therefore not only seek themes in common, but themes which show the diversity of opinion in Second Temple writings?

In this connection, the stance of Tobit and 1 Enoch towards the Mosaic Law is of special interest. First, Tobit follows the law of Moses in distributing a third tithe to the widows and orphans in Jerusalem (S 1:8), and Tobias marries Sarah according to the law of Moses (S 6:13; S 7:12; BAS 7:13). However, as Nickelsburg writes of 1 Enoch:

> To judge from what the authors of 1 Enoch have written, the Sinaitic covenant and Torah were not of central importance for them. . . . one looks in vain in 1 Enoch for formal parallels to the specific laws and commandments found in the Mosaic Pentateuch and the *Book of Jubilees*, or for references to issues like Sabbath observance, the honoring of one's parents, the rite of circumcision, and the full range of cultic laws. . . .

> In short, the heart of the religion of 1 Enoch juxtaposes election, revealed wisdom, the right and wrong ways to respond to this wisdom, and God's rewards and punishments for this conduct. Although all of the components of "covenantal nomism" are present in this scheme, the words "covenant" and "law" rarely appear and Enoch takes the place of Moses as the mediator of revelation.[2]

---

[2] George W. Nickelsburg, *1 Enoch 1* (Minneapolis, 2001), pp. 50–51, 53.

Second, both works emphasize the role of the Temple. Tobit visits the Temple in Jerusalem every year for the festivals (1:4–8), and he looks forward to the Temple's restoration, although the first re-building will not be like the First Temple (13:9–17; 14:5). In 1 Enoch, the Apocalypse of Weeks mentions the building of the Temple (93:7), as does the Animal Apocalypse (89:50). But, as Nickelsburg summarizes his findings about Temple and cult in 1 Enoch:

> ... its authors generally take a dim view of the Jerusalem temple and its cult, which are of course crucial to covenantal notions about forgiveness ... According to [the Animal Vision], sacrifices offered at the Second Temple were polluted from the beginning (89:73–74), and the situation persisted to the author's time. More radically, the author of the Apocalypse of Weeks does not even mention the construction of the Second Temple.[3]

Nickelsburg has therefore nudged us to see the variety of attitudes present in Second Temple Judaism towards the Temple and its cult. Tobit would reflect a mainstream attitude, 1 Enoch a more hostile one.

WORLD-VIEW

In comparing 1 Enoch and Tobit, Nickelsburg forced us to ask the big questions: What is the world implicit in a literary work, and what does a similarity in world-view say about the two works?

In his comparison, Nickelsburg carefully noted how different the two works were in style:

> Enoch is a collection of revelatory texts, in which the primordial patriarch transmits secret information about the hidden recesses of the cosmos and the hidden events of the future.... Tobit is a narrative tale ... about the trials and tribulations of an exiled Israelite family living in Mesopotamia after the Assyrian exile. The Enochic texts are heavily mythic in their content and cryptic in their allusion to history.... The story in Tobit, though it is fiction, takes place in a realistic and recognizable historical setting.[4]

Yet, even with this awareness, Nickelsburg found significant similarities between the two works and reaffirmed his conclusions in his later article (p. 247).

---

[3] Nickelsburg, *1 Enoch 1*, p. 54.
[4] George W.E. Nickelsburg, "Tobit and Enoch: Distant Cousins With a Recognizable Resemblance," in David J. Lull, ed., *SBL Seminar 1988 Papers* (Atlanta, 1988), p. 55.

Let me state up front that I find none of Nickelsburg's suggested relationships convincing beyond the fact that, for both authors, God controls history, and there are angels of whom there is a specific group of seven and one of them is called Raphael. The language for the binding of Asmodeus in Tobit 8:3 is common in magical incantations. As for "the common eschatological scenario set in a definite time frame," the differences between Tobit 14 and the Apocalypse of Weeks in 1 Enoch seem to me too striking: I see Tobit 14 as a re-hash of themes in the prophets (Isaiah 45—note in Isaiah 45:14 the rejection of idols by the Gentiles; 60), whereas the Apocalypse of Weeks, with its tenth week of final judgment, its language of 'elect' and righteous," betokens a different world.

However, for all this disagreement, I confess that Nickelsburg has asked the right question: what is the world of the author of Tobit? I would like to make two suggestions. First, it is an oral world. Secondly, it is a world in contact with Greek culture.

The discovery of six copies of Tobit at Qumran, five in Aramaic and one in Hebrew, has evidenced not only the popularity, but also the multiformity of the Tobit story. While it is true that the Qumran fragments of all six copies mostly follow that of the longer Greek text, found in Sinaiticus (S), it is also true that there are variations. One interesting example is found in 4Q200, fragment 7 ii, on Tobit 13:18–14:2. Below is a table of 4Q200 compared with S and the shorter version found in Alexandrinus (A) and Vaticanus (B):

4Q200	S	BA
. . . Jerusalem [shall sing] a psalm of [exultation Blest be] the God wh[o exalts you, and blest] because [in you they will bless his h]oly [name] for[ever]	The gates of Jerusalem shall sing Psalms of exultation, and all her houses will sing, Alleluia, Blest be the God of Israel, and the blessed will bless the holy name for ever and again.	All her streets shall sing Alleluia, and they will sing, saying, Blest be God, who exalts all the ages.
So [were] completed [the words of Tobit's thanksgiving, and he d]ied in peace at the age of [. . .]	And the words of the blessing of Tobit were completed. And he died in peace at the age of 112, and he was buried honorably in Nineveh. He was	And Tobit ceased confessing.

Sixty-two years old
when he saw again,
he lived virtuously.

[H]e was fif[ty]-eight years old [when] his [s]ight, and afterwards[he lived fifty-]fo[ur years.][5]	He was Sixty-two years old when he saw again, he lived virtuously.	He was fifty-eight years old when he lost his sight, and he saw again after eight years.

The table shows how the Qumran Hebrew text contains elements found in both S and BA, but not together in the Greek texts. This is a variation typical of an oral culture, where each telling, either by different tellers or by the same teller at different times, will vary. It betokens a vibrant culture that enjoys telling stories. Tobit has the same delight in wit that Erich Gruen has explored in the works of Judeans written in Greek.[6]

The scene at Tobit 8:9–15, where Raguel has a grave dug while Tobias and Sarah are in their wedding chamber and then, when he finds Tobias is alive, has to be sure the grave is filled in before day-break, would surely have evoked a smile from the listener. Even more mirthful is the contrast between what the hearer knows and what the characters know. For example, when Tobit interviews Raphael/Azariah for the job of taking his son to Media, the hearer knows Raphael is an angel. Yet the teller, at least of S, shows Tobit shrewdly questioning the young man/angel. He first of all laments how pitiful he is (Tobit 5:10), but then quickly asks what the visitor's tribe is. Raphael's retort asking whether Tobit wants a guide to Media or a respected genealogy reveals how cautious Tobit really is: He only trusts those whom he knows, his kinsfolk. In an exilic setting, this is surely wise. But the listener knows that Tobit is being fooled, even when he appears most shrewd. Another striking incongruity is that between the account in the first person that Tobit gives of himself at the beginning of the story, and the details that come out during the story. In his self-aggrandizing account, Tobit insists that he alone went up to the festivals in Jerusalem (Tobit 1:6). Yet,

---

[5] The translation is that of Joseph A. Fitzmyer, "Tobit," in *DJD* 19 (Oxford, 1995), p. 74.

[6] Erich Gruen, *Heritage and Hellenism* (Berkeley, 1998).

in his discussion with Raphael/Azariah at 5:14, Tobit admits that
he went to Jerusalem with Azariah's kinsmen. This incongruity
between word and action is also found in his unjustified anger at
his wife (Tobit 1:11–14).

It is always extremely difficult to judge exactly what would have
been humorous in any particular society. The scene of Asmodeus
the demon being repelled by the stench of days-old fish heart and
liver (Tobit 8:2–3) strikes me as particularly funny—one wonders if
any of the listeners ran out to try to exorcize their wives—but it
may have been a well-known magical remedy, as A.J. Levine tries
to show.[7] The story is thus cleverly told, even if it lacks suspense.
With the long prayer of Tobit in chap. 13 and his testament in
chap. 14, the textual versions of the story emphasize the hope for
future restoration. But this element should not overshadow the well-
told quality of the tale. It is a tale for people who like a good story.
What does this tell us about the culture of the community/com-
munities in which it was told? If we are to use our imaginations to
reconstruct the world in which the tale of Tobit flourished, as
Nickelsburg exhorts us, then I suggest we imagine a vibrant, lively
culture, one in which stories were told and enjoyed.

Second, I would suggest that it is a world in contact with Greek
culture. At the beginning of the twentieth century, Carl Fries provided a detailed, if perhaps overstated, case for the influence of Greek
literature on Tobit.[8] Nickelsburg has seconded Fries' suggestion.[9] But
he has also shown, in his recent commentary on 1 Enoch, how that
work too shows connections with Greek literature. In his introduction to the commentary, Nickelsburg cautiously states:

> Greek mythology appears also to have left its imprint at a number of
> points in 1 Enoch. None of the examples cited here in itself demon-
> strates such influence; however, taken together, they strongly suggest
> contact with material at home in the Greek world. The precise nature

---

[7] A.J. Levine, "Diaspora as Metaphor: Bodies as Boundaries in the Book of
Tobit," in Andrew Overman and Robert S. MacLennan, eds., *Diaspora Jews and
Judaism: Essays in Honor of, and in Dialogue with, A. Thomas Kraabel* (Atlanta, 1992), pp.
105–117, particularly 115–117.

[8] Carl Fries, "Das Buch Tobit und die Telemachie," in *ZWT* 53 (1910–1911),
pp. 54–87.

[9] Nickelsburg, "The Search," p. 343.

of that contact is uncertain, and dependence on material common to Greek and ancient Near Eastern myth is not to be excluded.[10]

Nickelsburg suggests that the Greek Nekyia offers "the best available model for Enoch's journey" in 1 Enoch 17–19, in particular, the passage which deals with the prison of the rebellious angels.[11] Nickelsburg also points to the division between the various types of sinners (1 Enoch 22:8–13) as evidencing a "debt to Greek thought," as well as the influence of Hesiod on the punishment of the rebellious angels at 1 Enoch 88:1–3.[12] The phrase used to describe the rest of the righteous in 1 Enoch 100:5, "sweet sleep," has "precisely the same connotations as its usage and that of its synonyms in Homer."[13]

Nickelsburg has provided the data for further elaboration of Martin Hengel's thesis of the influence of Hellenism in Israel.[14] If these two works do provide evidence of contact and knowledge of Greek writings, one must acknowledge that terms like "Hellenizers" used pejoratively make little sense. For these two works are staunchly patriotic. Many people would have heard Greek performances, and some perhaps been educated to read Greek writings. 2 Macc. 12:29–31 provides an instance of how Scythians and Judeans could live together in harmony in Scythopolis/Beth-Shean (perhaps the nearness to Galilee will intrigue Nickelsburg, as he places 1 Enoch in Galilee, and Tobit is said to come from Galilee), while the behavior of the Gentiles in Joppa and Jamnia is just the opposite (2 Macc. 12:3–9). As John Barclay has argued,[15] one needs to be aware of the huge spectrum of interaction that can be envisaged among Judeans and their neighbors. But, to follow Nickelsburg's advice, we need to imagine Judeans and Greek-speaking peoples living together in Israel, if we are to understand the debate, turned violent in the second century B.C.E., over what it means to be a Judean.

---

[10] Nickelsburg, *1 Enoch 1*, p. 62.

[11] Nickelsburg, *1 Enoch 1*, pp. 280, 286.

[12] Nickelsburg, *1 Enoch 1*, pp. 307, 374.

[13] Nickelsburg, *1 Enoch 1*, p. 501.

[14] Martin Hengel, *Judaism and Hellenism: Studies in Their Encounter in Palestine during the Early Hellenistic Period* (Philadelphia, 1974).

[15] John M.G. Barclay, *Jews in the Mediterranean Diaspora from Alexander to Trajan (323 B.C.E.–117 C.E.)* (Edinburgh, 1996), pp. 82–102.

CONCLUSION

With his comparison of Tobit and 1 Enoch, Nickelsburg opened up
suggestive paths to follow. Particularly significant has been his vision
that wisdom and apocalyptic can co-exist in the same group, even
in the same author, and that a fascinating Mediterranean culture
was forming among Judeans in the third and second centuries B.C.E.

RESPONSE TO ROBERT DORAN

As Robert Doran notes, over the years I have understood the literary and historical interpretation of Jewish literature to be an exercise in comparison and contrast. This comparative instinct appears already in my dissertation (1967), and in the first papers that I wrote (1970–72).[1] In my view, one thing is better understood when it is compared with another, and things are best understood when we consider both their similarities and their differences. Such a comparison of texts, however, does not always develop in a methodologically organized enterprise; it may be triggered as one studies "a" while also thinking about "b." My first pass through Tobit in *Jewish Literature*, written in 1979, made no reference to 1 Enoch. The comparisons emerged in my second pass, in the Compendia article, which was written in 1980/81,[2] when I was also working intensively on my 1 Enoch commentary. Thus our understanding of any given text can be repeatedly enriched as we read the whole corpus of relevant texts over and again.

As I reworked my analysis of Tobit, three elements were struck me, because accepted wisdom would consider them anomalies in a narrative and sapiential text. The first was the manner in which the plot turned on a heaven/earth polarity that involved the intercessory activity of seven high angels—one of them named Raphael, who functioned as God's healer through an antagonistic relationship with a demon. The general set of motifs was more at home in apocalyptic literature, and the specifics and even some of the phraseology had counterparts in 1 Enoch. The second element was the eschatological scenario at the conclusion of Tobit. References to the end time, and indeed to the prophets, were not part of traditional descriptions of sapiential texts. The conclusion of Tobit's prediction of the future was phrased in language that was, again, paralleled in 1 Enoch, specifically the Apocalypse of Weeks. Finally, turning the

---

[1] *Resurrection, Immortality, and Eternal Life* (published in 1972), "1 Maccabees and 2 Maccabees" (1971), "Eschatology in the Testament of Abraham" (1972), "Narrative Traditions" (1973).

[2] "The Bible Rewritten and Expanded" (1983).

comparison in the other direction, I noted that apocalyptic 1 Enoch had a special propensity for the sapiential two-ways construct that appears also in Tobit's instruction to Tobias. These three elements were the genesis of my comparison, which a session of the SBL Pseudpigrapha Group provided me the opportunity to develop in my 1986 article.

In 1996, in a *Festschrift* article for J.T. Milik, who had done foundational work on both Tobit and 1 Enoch, I saw the opportunity to search for more conclusive results to the comparison. Instead I found myself having to deal with the fact that the author of Tobit was beholden to a whole range of traditions that had counterparts in a variety of biblical and non-biblical texts. So I argued that our interpretation of any text so complicated in this fashion, while it may focus on one aspect (in my case, the possible relationship with 1 Enoch), needs to keep the whole picture in view and not make exclusive claims that thus and such is the hermeneutical key to the text.

As Robert Doran evidently did not know when he wrote his response, the matter (and my fascination with Tobit) became further complicated by a piece written by Dennis MacDonald, who built on Carl Fries's article and did for Tobit and the Odyssey what I had done for Tobit and 1 Enoch. Thus came to be my third article, "Tobit, Genesis, and the Odyssey: A Complex Web of Intertextuality."[3] Here I affirmed much of MacDonald's insightful expansion and refining of Fries's study, but I argued that some of his parallels between Tobit and the Odyssey are better explained by the patriarchal narratives in Genesis—*albeit as they are interpreted in* Jubilees *and the Qumran "Reworked Pentateuch"*! The skein of yarn had become even more tangled that either of us had thought. I reiterated my plea for an imaginative rethinking of the complicated worlds that generated the texts we study.

Where does this leave my initial probe and Doran's skepticism about a genetic connection between Tobit and 1 Enoch? I believe that these two texts are historical artifacts accidentally preserved from a complex world where sapiential and apocalyptic activity were not as distinguished from one another as our genre analysis and other

---

[3] "Tobit, Genesis, and the *Odyssey*: A Complicated Web of Intertextuality," in Dennis R. MacDonald, *Mimesis and Intertextuality in Antiquity and Christianity* (Harrisburg, 2001), pp. 41–55. For MacDonald's article, "Tobit and the Odyssey," see ibid., pp. 11–40.

heuristic tools have led us to believe. The authors of Tobit and the Enochic texts shared something of a common dualistic (our term) cosmology and a common angelology. Moreover, as 1 Baruch and Sirach indicate, sapiential literature of the Greco-Roman period was not immune to eschatology or an interest in revelation, notably as they saw these attested in the biblical prophets.[4] If we acknowledge this jumbled state of affairs and seek to sort out the pieces, the precise relationship between Tobit and 1 Enoch will be less important than that recognition that reality back then was immensely complicated, just as our experience tells us it is right now. We shall see that models of antiquity are just that—models—and are not substitutions for the real thing. In reconstructing history, we see darkly as in a spotty, unpolished mirror.

Doran's response nicely lays out some of those complications and the diversities they reflect, and his observations suggest some others. Tobit rejoices over the destruction of Nineveh, but also envisions the inclusion of some of the gentiles. The same is true of 1 Enoch[5]—though this does not indicate a genetic connection between the texts. Ezra and Tobit, on the one hand, and Esther, on the other hand, evince very different attitudes about marriage and about *kashrut*. On both counts, his observation may provide a partial explanation for the absence of Esther and the presence of Tobit in the Qumran collection. 1 Enoch and Tobit do, indeed, indicate different valuations of the Mosaic Torah, but this is part of a larger puzzle. The author of Jubilees presumes to write in the name of Moses and paraphrases two books of the Pentateuch, but he also incorporates substantial parts of 1 Enoch into his work, and in this context celebrates Enoch as the first to have given a "testimony"—something that Moses did later (in the form of Jubilees).[6] Similarly, the Qumran community prizes the Enochic writings but places the Mosaic Torah at the center of its piety.[7] Although, in my view, some of the Enochic authors were highly critical of the Jerusalem temple, they imagined an eschatological temple located at the place[8] and, as I have noted, one text describes it in words similar to those in Tobit.

---

[4] On Tobit, 1 Baruch, and Sirach, see Nickelsburg, "Wisdom and Apocalypticism," below, pp. 272–273.

[5] Nickelsburg, *1 Enoch 1*, pp. 62–63.

[6] Ibid., pp. 71–76.

[7] For 1 Enoch at Qumran, see ibid., pp. 76–78.

[8] Ibid., pp. 54–55.

Finally, I believe that Doran's observations about Judaism and Hellenism are most important and indicate a major step forward since the landmark monographs by Tcherikover and Hengel.[9] Hellenism was a complex, multifaceted phenomenon. Jewish writers like the authors of Tobit and parts of 1 Enoch participated in the phenomenon, even if not as blatantly as Philo of Alexandria and the authors of the Wisdom of Solomon and 4 Maccabees. In this respect, as in others mentioned above, we must be careful that our categories and pigeonholes do not get in the way of the data.

[9] Victor Tcherikover, *Hellenistic Civilization and the Jews* (Philadelphia, 1961); Hengel, *Judaism and Hellenism*, cited by Doran.

CHAPTER NINE

WISDOM AND APOCALYPTICISM IN EARLY JUDAISM: SOME POINTS FOR DISCUSSION

GEORGE W.E. NICKELSBURG

I. INTRODUCTION

A renewed interest in the description, definition, and categorization of apocalypticism has been a major preoccupation for scholars of early Judaism during the past two and a half decades (Hanson 1985; Collins 1986). Catalyzed by the discovery and analysis of the Qumran Scrolls and spurred on by the pioneering monograph of Klaus Koch (1972), the discussion of apocalypticism has been advanced by such persons as Paul D. Hanson, Michael E. Stone, John J. Collins, and other scholars who have worked on the problem in general or certain apocalypses in particular.

So radical have been the shifts in emphasis and method and in the primary materials discussed, that some of the giants who dominated the discussion in the late nineteenth and early twentieth centuries (R.H. Charles, Hermann Gunkel, and Paul Volz) would find the current discussion of apocalypticism as much alien territory as they often found the apocalypses themselves. Because apocalyptic literature holds such a central place in the study of Israelite religion in the Greco-Roman period, a revolution in the understanding and assessment of this literature was bound to have a ripple effect in the broader discussion of the history of Israelite religion. And so it has, as one can see by reviewing the burgeoning literature on early Judaism.

Ripples, however, do not always follow their predetermined path, either because they meet with counterforces or because they run up against the inertia of stationary objects. For reasons too complex to analyze here, much New Testament scholarship has had a love-hate, attraction-avoidance relationship with the modern study of early Judaism—drawing deeply from it at times and blissfully ignoring or even actively resisting it at other times.

Perhaps the two places where the ripples have most often been diverted or blocked have been in discussions of Torah and in the use of the term "apocalyptic." My interest here is with the latter, specifically, the manner in which this adjective-become-noun is sometimes used with little or no concern for the discussion during the past two decades and no evident knowledge that *much in that discussion remains unresolved and unclarified.*

II. The Present Project

Two related objectives have been set for a new SBL Consultation on Wisdom and Apocalyptic in Early Judaism and Early Christianity. The initiators of the consultation believe that the achievement of these objectives will require the full five-year term of an SBL seminar, and we would like to structure the consultation sessions this year and next year in order to shape such a scenario.

The first objective is some clarification of the nature and interrelationship of the wisdom, prophetic, and eschatological components in Jewish apocalyptic writings. Like the study of Jewish apocalypticism, the discussion of Israelite wisdom literature has made substantial advances over the past decades (Crenshaw 1985; Mack and Murphy). Two developments are especially significant for our present concern. The first is the increasing frequency with which works like Sirach and the Wisdom of Solomon are discussed in connection with the wisdom literature of the Hebrew Bible (von Rad; Crenshaw 1981). The second is a recognition of wisdom elements in apocalyptic literature, as well as a debate about their origin, function, and importance. During the first half of the life of our projected seminar, we propose to look at the apocalyptic literature with a view toward identifying wisdom elements and their relationship to analogous elements in post-biblical Jewish sapiential literature, including, possibly, some of the texts from Qumran.

Our second proposed objective is to shed light on some relevant New Testament texts, such as "Q" and the Epistle of James. Is it appropriate to ascribe wisdom and apocalyptic elements in Q to separate sources and separate communities? What might our study of the Jewish texts tell us about the coexistence of sapiential and eschatological elements in Q and in James?

Two considerations will guide our discussion of the Jewish and Christian material. The first is some serious reflection on the way in which the study of our primary sources has tended to distill, abstract, and often reify terms like "wisdom" and "apocalyptic" without recognizing that the abstraction is the result of a (necessary) process of historical reconstruction. The second is a concerted effort to reconstruct aspects of the social and cultural realities that gave rise to, and are reflected in the relevant primary sources: the institutions, offices, roles, and functions that resulted in the Jewish sapiential and apocalyptic literature and made use of it. These two considerations, in turn, have immediate implications for our understanding of the rise of Christianity, the genetics and functions of its literature, and perhaps our reconstructions of the career of Jesus of Nazareth.

The program for the initial session of the consultation will provide entree into the two segments of the life of the projected seminar. The present paper offers for discussion in the first part of the session some observations about wisdom and apocalypticism in early Judaism. The second half of the session will consider the paper of Richard Horsley, entitled "Wisdom Justified by all her Children: Examining Allegedly Disparate Traditions in Q," a review and evaluation of the discussion of Q as it relates to the topic of the consultation.

The relationships between wisdom and apocalypticism and the implications that these might have on the current discussion of Q have already been taken up in an article by John Collins (1993), which focuses on "generic compatibility." The present project was conceived with no knowledge of the Collins article, yet both his article and mine have reached similar conclusions: Jewish wisdom and apocalypticism cannot be cleanly separated from one another. Our conclusions are also complementary; he focuses on genre and on distinctions within the sapiential literature. I have attempted a more detailed comparison of a broader range of sapiential and apocalyptic texts with less concern for generic matters as such. Collins concludes that a posited dichotomy between the wisdom and apocalypticism must be used with caution in the analysis of Q. Considerations of space, a companion paper on the Q discussion, and the prospect of a multi-year seminar have led me to omit any explicit discussion of relevant NT texts, but in general, I am wary of the wisdom/apocalyptpic dichotomy that has become an important part of the Q discussion. It is my hope that the extended discussion of our topic will bring some clarity to the issues.

The thesis of this paper is that the entities usually defined as sapiential and apocalyptic often cannot be cleanly separated from one

another because both are the products of wisdom circles that are
becoming increasingly diverse in the Greco-Roman period. Thus,
apocalyptic texts contain elements that are at home in wisdom literature, and wisdom texts reflect growing interest in eschatology.
Moreover, claims to revelation, inspiration, or divine enlightenment
can be found in both "sets" of texts. Our subject matter is complex
and the issues are often not clear. The presentation in this paper is
intended only to be suggestive—to present briefly *some* issues for discussion, some pointers toward an agenda.

III. SOME ESTABLISHED FINDINGS OR POINTS OF CONSENSUS

The renewed discussion of apocalypticism that began in the early
1970's has produced some important results; in some cases they have
found wide consensus.

It is useful to distinguish between three terms: the literary genre
"apocalypse"; the "apocalyptic eschatology" found in such documents
and, according to some scholars (e.g., Hanson 1975, 1976), in texts
antecedent to the apocalypses; and "apocalypticism," "the symbolic
universe in which an apocalyptic movement codifies its identity and
interpretation of reality" (Hanson 1976, 29–30).

In order to be semantically meaningful, the terms "apocalyptic"
and "apocalypticism" should designate entities for which revelation
is a significant component. In this respect, it makes a great deal of
sense to begin a study of apocalypticism with an analysis of texts
that are widely agreed to be apocalypses, such as 1 Enoch, Daniel,
the Apocalypse of Abraham, 4 Ezra, 2 and 3 Baruch, and the Book
of Revelation (Koch).

While all of these texts contain, in part or as a whole, revelations
of a hidden past or future and/or of hidden parts of the cosmos
mediated through a revealer figure, they vary widely in their specific
content and emphases (Collins 1979). For example:

> 1 Enoch is a complex text attributed to a pre-Mosaic sage, which con-
> tains mythic narratives about the primordial past, a prophetic call based
> on a heavenly ascent, guided tours of the cosmos interpreted by angels,
> detailed torah about the movement of the heavenly bodies, dream
> visions about the future of human history, and discourses composed
> of ethical admonitions and prophetic exhortations.

> In the Book of Daniel, the narrative section consists of a cycle of leg-
> ends about the wisdom and faithful conduct of Jewish sages in exile.

Revelation comes through dream visions and their interpretation, through inspired sages.

Like Daniel the Apocalypse of Abraham combines legend (Abraham's rejection of idolatry), an ascent to the divine throne, and visions about shape of the cosmos and (mainly) the future of Israel.

The contemporary apocalypses 4 Ezra and 2 Baruch, claim to base their information on auditions and visions about the future of Israel, mediated or interpreted by angels. 4 Ezra in particular eschews the notion that one can know the kind of cosmic secrets revealed in 1 Enoch (Stone 1976), and both 4 Ezra and 2 Baruch understand wisdom in terms of the Mosaic Torah and its post-prophetic interpretation by scribes and sages.

In short, even when we tie the notion of apocalypticism to texts that are formally apocalypses, we find wide diversity in the content of what is revealed and the form through which it is mediated. *We must use the generic terms with caution and the recognition that we do not know exactly what we are talking about.*

It has long been recognized that Jewish apocalyptic texts are rooted, in part, in Israel's prophetic tradition. The throne visions in 1 Enoch 12–16, Daniel 7, and the Apocalypse of Abraham recall Isaiah 6, 2 Kings 22, and Ezekiel 1–2. 1 Enoch roots the sage's authority as a revealer in a prophetic call scene that draws heavily of Ezekiel 1–2 and prepares Enoch to be preacher against the sins of the watchers. Although Daniel 7 is not a call scene, the seer describes the heavenly tribunal taking action against the rebellious kingdoms and kings of the earth. Both within and outside the framework of dream visions about the future, apocalyptic texts from 1 Enoch to 2 Baruch have an eschatological focus and emphasis that has much in common with the biblical prophetic texts.

The discussion of apocalyptic literature has also recognized that these texts draw on the language, genres, and motifs of Israel's wisdom literature. Even if von Rad overemphasized this point (Collins 1986, 355), scholars have continued to discuss the sapiential elements in apocalyptic texts (Smith; Coghenour 1978 and 1982; Argall).

In short, a careful study of Jewish apocalypses from 1 Enoch to the post-70 texts places us in a religious and intellectual world that is strongly reminiscent of the prophetic and sapiential corpuses of the Hebrew Bible. The texts also reflect the influence of ancient near eastern myth and Mesopotamian mantic wisdom (e.g., Collins 1977a), but that is not our concern at present.

IV. SOME POINTS FOR A DISCUSSION OF THE JEWISH LITERATURE AND ITS SETTINGS

Working from the findings of a generation of scholarship and my own investigation especially of 1 Enoch, I suggest that it is worthwhile to discuss the following issues, observations, and theses about the sapiential and apocalyptic literatures, their possible social settings, and the modern discussion of these bodies of literature.

A. *Jewish Literature*

1. *Wisdom Literature: Its Interest in Prophecy and Claims to Inspiration*
Although Israelite wisdom texts like Tobit, Sirach, and Baruch hold the Mosaic Torah in high regard and contain much (proverbial) instruction about (sometimes Torah-related) human conduct, they also have a high regard for the *prophetic* tradition, including its concern about future events, and they place the sage, scribe, or teacher in the role of an inspired spokesman of God and interpreter of Torah and prophets.

a. *The Book of Tobit*   The righteousness of Tobit and his family is tied to the Mosaic Torah, and Israel's exile is due to the people's apostasy from the Torah. Although Tobit is not a sage, as such, he speaks in proverbs, some of which are tied to the concerns of the Torah. His function as a court official is reminiscent of the sage Daniel and his colleagues, and his association with Ahikar recalls the heavily proverbial content of The Story of Akikar. Nonetheless, the Book of Tobit ends with a look toward the future. The Zion hymn in chapter 13 draws on the tradition of Second and Third Isaiah. Tobit predicts the time when the words of the prophets will be fulfilled in detail, and his scenario for the future in chapter 14 is reminiscent of 1 Enoch's periodized Apocalypse of Weeks (Nickelsburg 1988, above, 227–28). Tobit is the recipient of revelation when Raphael discloses his identity as one of the seven holy ones in the divine throne room, and Tobit's predictions presume a certainty about the future that, while tied to prophecy, functions as new revelation.

b. *The Wisdom of ben Sira*   For ben Sira, the Torah is the repository of heavenly wisdom, which the sage, inspired by God, expounds like prophecy (chap. 24). Wisdom instruction—both the exposition of Torah and practical advice—is the primary content of ben Sira's book. Nonetheless, ben Sira's fascination with the prophets is evident in chapters 44–50, which feature Moses, Samuel, Nathan, Elijah, Isaiah, Jeremiah, Ezekiel, and the Twelve. He also evidences a deep concern about the unfulfilled oracles of the prophets (notably Second and Third Isaiah) and the need that these divine spokesmen be found faithful (36:11–16). Moreover, he employs traditional prophetic literary forms (Baumgartner).

c. *The Book of Baruch*   The book of Baruch has important sapiential elements, makes explicit reference to the Mosaic Torah, and speaks in prophetic idiom. The book is attributed to the scribe of Jeremiah. The wisdom poem in chapter 3 is reminiscent of Job 28. In 4:1–9, the Torah is said to be the repository of heavenly Wisdom (cf. Sirach 24), and both in these verses and in 3:29–30, the author takes up the idiom of the wisdom material in Deut 30:11–14. In the early chapters, Baruch speaks and acts like a prophet, employing the language of Jeremiah and Ezekiel, as well as the prophetic voice of Moses in Deuteronomy. Israel's Exile was predicted by "your servant Moses" (Bar 2:28). The Book of Baruch concludes as the author predicts Israel's return from Exile (Deut 30:1–5), employing the idiom of Second and Third Isaiah (Bar 4:9–5:9).

To summarize, in various ways, the authors of Tobit, Sirach, and Baruch focus on the importance of the Mosaic Torah, employ the idiom of the wisdom texts of the Hebrew Bible, and evidence high respect for the predictions of Israel's prophets, either referring to them explicitly or speaking in the language of their writings. While we might debate whether these authors have an eschatological emphasis, they do operate with a teleology that anticipates a time when the prophetic oracles will reach their goal or fulfillment.

2. *Apocalyptic Literature: Its Focus on Revelation and Use of Wisdom Elements*

Although the heavy emphasis on prediction has led scholars to see the apocalypticists as successors to the prophets, at many points these apocalyptic texts speak in the idiom, motifs, and forms of Israelite *wisdom* literature. The variety in these texts, which span four hundred years (300 B.C.E. to 100 C.E.) is especially evident in their attitudes toward the Mosaic Torah, their relationship to the prophets, and the emphasis that they place on the newness or derivative character of the revelation that they present.

a. *1 Enoch*   The collection known as 1 Enoch is especially remarkable for its wisdom components (Coughenour 1978, 1982; Argall).[1]
The content itself is described as "wisdom" (5:6; 37:1; 92:1; 93:10).
The heart of the opening oracle is an appeal to observe the created
world (2:1–5:4). Much of the content of Enoch's journeys is paralleled in wisdom texts like Job (Stone 1978). The two-ways instruction that runs through chapters 91 and 94–105 (e.g., 91:3–4, 18–19;
94:1–4; 99:10; 105:2) speaks the wisdom vocabulary of Proverbs,
Tobit, and Sirach. The relationship of Enoch's wisdom to the Mosaic
Torah is ambiguous. His revelations preceded those of Moses by
millennia. At least in the Animal Vision, the giving of the Torah is
deleted from the account of the Sinai experience (89:28–35). Instruction
focuses on cosmology and, where it deals with ethical issues (chaps.
92–105), it parallels the concerns of the prophets and the wisdom
corpus (Nickelsburg 1977), though not ignoring "the commandments
of the Most High" (99:10). Especially striking is the use of the wisdom myth in 81:1–82:4, where, in contrast to Sirach 24 and Baruch
4:1, it is Enoch's books rather than the Mosaic Torah that are the
earthly repository of heavenly wisdom (Argall, 91–98). Enoch's relationship to the prophets is also ambiguous. His use of prophetic
forms is evident in the opening oracle of salvation and judgment
(chaps. 1–5), which employs the vocabulary of the Balaam oracle
and language reminiscent of Third Isaiah. Enoch's ascent to heaven
is cast in the form of a prophetic call vision (chaps. 12–16). The
Woes, Exhortations, and predictions of the future in chapters 92–105
also recall prophetic usage (Nickelsburg 1977). Nonetheless, the
prophets are never cited, and the long recitation of Israel's history
in the Animal Vision barely alludes to them (89:51–53). As with the
Mosaic Torah, here Enoch's primordial prophecy long precedes the
voice of the prophets.

b. *The Book of Daniel*   The Book of Daniel offers a narrower spectrum of wisdom components when compared to 1 Enoch. Its chief
feature is the mantic wisdom that dominates the stories in chapters
1–6 and runs through the visions in chapters 7–11. Daniel and his
colleagues are skilled interpreters of dreams and visions, greatly

---

[1] To my knowledge the first systematic attempt to compare in detail a sapiential text and a apocalyptic text is the dissertation of my student Randal A. Argall
(1992). At many points my discussion is indebted to his work.

exceeding the capabilities of their Babylonian counterparts. Lacking in Daniel are the many sapiential literary forms found in 1 Enoch, the Enochic books' heavy emphasis on cosmology, and any equation between wisdom and Torah, even if the piety of Daniel and his friends relates to *kashrut* and the avoidance of idolatry. Daniel's relationship to the prophetic corpus has two aspects. The last vision draws on the prophecies of Isaiah (Ginsberg 1953), though it does not cite them. Alongside this use of prophetic material, which parallels 1 Enoch's approach, is the explicit concern with the fulfillment of Jeremiah's prophecy in 9:2, 24.

c. *2 Baruch*   In 2 Baruch, an extensive apocalypse from around the year 100 c.e., wisdom is especially equated with the Torah (51:1–10). Although Baruch is the scribe mentioned in Jeremiah, he is the recipient of dream visions and, like the prophets, of the word of the Lord (1:1; 10:1). Different from Daniel, his interpretation of dream visions derives not from innate wisdom, but from conversation with God or an angel (e.g., chaps. 41–42, 55). Nonetheless, the use of prayer to trigger these interpretive conversations is reminiscent of Daniel 9 and Sir 39:5–8, and some of the wisdom vocabulary in these prayers is noteworthy (38:1–4; 54:1, 13).

d. *4 Ezra*   For Baruch's contemporary, the author of 4 Ezra, wisdom is less tied to Torah than to the understanding of eschatological secrets, and though Ezra is inspired to rewrite the Torah (14:1–26), similar inspiration results in Ezra's dictation of the twenty-four secret books (14:37–48). 1 Enoch's strong interest in cosmological wisdom, however, appears to be the object of polemic in 4 Ezra (Stone 1976). Finally, the literary form of both 2 Baruch and 4 Ezra, with their argumentative dialogues between the sage and God over the issue of theodicy, are reminiscent of the Book of Job.

3. *Different Emphases in Wisdom and Apocalyptic Texts*
Our survey has identified ways in which texts that are usually categorized as sapiential can equate wisdom with Torah and also transmit elements of the prophetic tradition, and how they can even make claims of revelation or inspiration. Conversely, we have noted wisdom components in the apocalyptic texts, with wisdom and Torah being equated especially in 2 Baruch. The prophetic element, especially noteworthy in the many strata of 1 Enoch, is to some extent retained in the ongoing interest in eschatology.

In short, both sapiential and apocalyptic texts display a number
of common elements:

> wisdom forms; an interest in Torah and prophets; prediction of future
> events; ethical admonitions; claims of revelation. Of course, there are
> many variations among the texts in each group. Nonetheless, in the
> paragraphs that follow, I shall suggest some differences in nuance and
> emphasis that may help us to distinguish the one group from the other.
> In making these generalizations, however, I shall also indicate some
> exceptions and qualifications, which reflect the complexity in the his-
> torical development of sapiential and apocalyptic literature.

a. *Dualism*   Some apocalypses are strongly dualistic in their orientation. Enoch, for example, is marked by: a spacial dualism between
earth and heaven, or the inhabited world and the recesses of the
cosmos inaccessible to humanity; a temporal dualism between the
present time and the eschatological future, and, perhaps, the primordial past; an ontological dualism between humans and a vast
world of good and, especially, evil spirits (Nickelsburg 1991). The
Book of Daniel reflects the same general viewpoint.

> *Exception 1*: The Book of Tobit posits a heavenly throne room from
> which emissaries are sent to earth to do battle with a world of evil
> spirits who inflict illness on human beings (Nickelsburg 1988).

> *Exception 2*: Although 4 Ezra and 2 Baruch have a strong eschatolog-
> ical emphasis, neither focuses on a heaven/earth dichotomy or the
> activity of evil spirits.

b. *Eschatology*   Although wisdom texts like Tobit, Sirach, and
Baruch work with prophetic eschatological themes, eschatology is
more dominant in most of the texts that we describe as apocalypses.

> *Qualification 1*: For some apocalypses like 2 Enoch and 3 Baruch, escha-
> tology focuses more on the fate of the individual than on a general
> conclusion to history (Collins 1984, 198–201).

> *Qualification 2*: 1 Enoch is striking for the diversity with which it deals
> with eschatology. Little space is devoted to periodized reviews of his-
> tory. The judgment is rooted in creation, where the places of reward
> and punishment are located (chaps. 17–36). Reward and punishment
> are referred to in woes and exhortations typical of the prophetic tra-
> dition (chaps. 92–105).

c. *New or Derived Revelation*   The claims of revelation in the wisdom literature tend to be tied to traditional texts, namely, the Mosaic

Torah and the prophets. The authors of apocalyptic texts, while they actually draw heavily on the Torah and the prophets, present new revelations, although they attribute them variously to pre-Mosaic authors (Enoch and Abraham), Moses himself, and post-Mosaic figures (Daniel, Ezra and Baruch). The sources of these new revelations are said to be cosmic journeys and dream visions, interpreted by angels

> *Exception*: On occasion, the association with scripture is explicit in apocalyptic texts: Daniel obtains an explicit interpretation of Jeremiah, albeit from an angel. Both the Book of Jubilees and the Testament of Moses are expanded versions of parts of the Pentateuch, which, however, are said to be part of a revelation to the author of the biblical text.

4. *Texts that Complicate the Categories*

a. *The Wisdom of Solomon*   Its attribution to the author of the Book of Proverbs and Qoheleth, its frequent references to wisdom, and its use of the literary form of the proverb situate the Wisdom of Solomon within the tradition of sapiential literature. Other characteristics of the work suggest close analogies with apocalyptic thought (Collins 1977), even if they are expressed in ways that seem closely related to Greek philosophy. The story of the righteous one in chapters 2 and 5 is dominated by eschatology. In this context immortality is an important conception, but the description of the judgment in chapter 5 reflects a Jewish apocalyptic tradition attested also in 1 Enoch 62–63 (Nickelsburg 1972, 70–78). The cosmic dualism that governs the story also suggests Platonic thought, while reflecting Jewish apocalyptic cosmology. Moreover, the form of the story of the persecuted and exalted righteous one recalls the genre attested both in the wisdom tradition of Genesis 39 and the stories included in chapters 3 and 6 of the apocalyptic Book of Daniel. Finally, wisdom for this author involves revelation of divine mysteries and an understanding of the secrets of the heavenly realm, unknown to the ungodly (2:22–3:4).

An intriguing aspect of the Wisdom of Solomon is its parallels to the Book of Enoch (Larcher 1969, 106–12). Enoch is the epitome of the righteous person (4:10–15). In addition to the judgment scene in chapter 5 which is paralleled in 1 Enoch 62–63, the general form of argumentation in chapters 2–5 is reminiscent of 1 Enoch 102:4–104:8 (Nickelsburg 1972, 128–29). It appears, therefore, that the first part of the Wisdom of Solomon is a Hellenizing and philosophizing version of Jewish apocalyptic tradition. The transformation is possible because of the perceived compatibility of the alternate forms of expression.

The interest in prophetic tradition, which we have observed in both sapiential and apocalyptic writings is present also in the Wisdom of Solomon. The story of the persecution and exaltation of the righteous one in chapters 2 and 5 is a traditional, rewritten form of Isaiah 52–53 (Nickelsburg 1972, 70–78), set in part in the context of other material drawn from Third Isaiah. Like other texts in the apocalyptic tradition, the author reshapes rather than quotes the prophetic prototype. Strikingly, the prophetic figure in the Deutero-Isaianic text looks like the sages in Genesis 39 ff. and Daniel 3 and 6.

b. *The Qumran Scrolls*   The Qumran Scrolls are a treasure trove and a mine field for students of apocalyptic literature. Although no apocalypse has been identified as originating at Qumran, the Scrolls contain many motifs characteristic of apocalyptic literature. The Community Rule (1QS) offers an example of the complexity of the situation, attesting both sapiential and apocalyptic conceptions and characteristics.

1QS 3:13–4:26 is a section of two-ways teaching with many analogies in sapiential literature (Nickelsburg 1972, 156–64). A major difference from these wisdom texts, however, is the pronounced dualism that governs the section. Human works are functions of the good and evil spirits. The section concludes with reference to an eschatological confrontation between the two spirits and an eschatological purifying of the earth (4:18–26), both with analogies in apocalyptic literature (Nickelsburg 1972, 158; see, in addition, 1 Enoch 10:11–11:2).

Although the two-ways section lacks the revelatory component necessary for our definition of apocalyptic literature, 1QS 11:3–9 is startling for its saturation with language and conceptions at home in accounts of visionary experiences recorded by the apocalypticists: revelation in the form of enlightening and seeing; the mystery to come; the fount of righteousness; knowledge hidden from humans; the dwelling place of glory; standing in the presence of the holy ones, the sons of heaven.

Thus while 1QS is not generically an apocalypse and should not be defined as apocalyptic in a technical sense, its dualism, eschatology and use of apocalyptic conceptions indicate that the authors of this wisdom and legal text worked within an apocalyptic orbit.

B. *Institutions and Social Settings*

Since texts are products of persons and communities, the discussion of apocalyptic and sapiential material should include an attempt to reconstruct the institutions, social settings, and functions that gave rise to this literature and made use of it. Such a focus may also help us to avoid the elusive abstraction that sometimes attends the history of ideas.

1. *Figures and Functions in the Texts*

A brief survey of some of the texts surveyed above may enable us to identify types of figures who were involved in the generating and use of sapiential and apocalyptic literature and some of their roles or functions.

a. *The Wisdom of ben Sira* Among all our texts, the Wisdom of ben Sira is the only one attributed to a named historical figure; hence, it may be useful to start in his "non-fictional" world with his own self-description. Ben Sira's title, according to 38:24, is "scribe" (*grammateus*), here and elsewhere his work involves not only the ability to write, but also divinely given "wisdom" (*sophia*). The prologue of the book, written by ben Sira's grandson and translator, and three passages in the book describe his activity. According to the prologue (7–13), ben Sira read and studied the Torah, the Prophets, and the other books of the fathers and then wrote his book for the purpose of instruction and wisdom (*paideia* and *sophia*). The third person singular self-description in 39:1–11 also refers to the study of "the Torah of the Most High," "the wisdom of the ancients," which includes proverbs and parables, and "prophecy" (vv. 1–3). The use of "ponder" (*dianoeomai*) with reference to the Torah, "occupy oneself with" (*ascholeō*) of the prophets, and "seek out" (*ekzēteō*, twice) of wisdom indicates a thorough, ongoing scholarly process, one that excludes the possibility of an other occupation (38:24). This daily activity is preceded by prayer, which, the Lord willing, results in the scribe's being filled with "the spirit of understanding" (*pneuma syneseōs*) that enables him to pour forth words of wisdom (*sophia*), rightly direct "counsel" and "knowledge" (*boulē* and *epistēmē*) (cf. Isa 11:2–3, of the king's inspired wisdom for judgment), ponder "secrets" (*apokrypha*), and "make the instruction of his teaching shine forth" (*ekphanei paideian didaskalias autou*). In 24:27, 32–34, ben Sira speaks again of his teaching activity as enlightenment, analogous to inspired prophecy, which extends the life-giving power of Torah's wisdom, preserving it in ben Sira's book. In 51:21–29 the wording suggests that his teaching activity has a specific locus, in his "house of instruction" (*oikos paideias*). In addition, 39:4 describes the scribe as a travelling scholar, who presents his knowledge before rulers and in foreign lands.

Thus, ben Sira the scribe is a *scholar* of the Torah, the Prophets, and the wisdom texts, who is also a *teacher*. The form of his teaching, to judge from his book, is not halakic exposition of the Torah, but proverbial. A text like 3:1–16 suggests a kind of homiletical exposition on the implications of the Torah, and the form of many of his proverbs embodies the notion that obedience and disobedience result in divine blessing or judgment.[2] Taken as a whole, the body of his teaching has a strong ethical and admonitory character, rather than being directed simply to the transmission of knowledge.

b. *1 Enoch*   A discussion of the real-life figures behind 1 Enoch is difficult because of the pseudepigraphic character of the text. But a few observations are possible, first with reference to Enoch. The authors' term is "scribe" (12:3; 92:1) and "scribe of righteousness" or "scribe of truth" (*grammateus tēs dikaiosynēs* [12:4], *grammateus tēs alētheias* [15:1]). Most basically, the scribal designation relates to his alleged writing of the Enochic corpus, whose character as book is emphasized in 81:6–82:3, 100:6, and 104:12–13. In addition, his writing and reading of the watchers' petition in 12:3–13:7, which has an analogy in Ezra 9–10, places him in the role of a religious mediator, if not, strictly speaking, a priest. Like ben Sira, the fictional Enoch presents his books as the embodiment of life-giving heavenly wisdom, intended for "all the generations of eternity" (82:1–4; cf. Sir 24:33). Though he does not call his instruction "prophecy," he repeatedly speaks in the idiom and forms of the biblical prophets (see above, IV.A.1), and though the text does not cite them, it knows them well.

If we move from the fictional world of the primordial sage to the real world of the authors, we find figures who parallel Enoch the scribe. In 98:9 and 99:10 they are "the wise" (*phronimoi*), and their "words" are heard and, to judge from 98:15 (where their opponents are mentioned as writing books), they write their words in books that are read. Thus the fictional Enoch has real life counterparts,

---

[2] Ibid., 225–339.

known as "the wise" and functioning as scribes. They are, in fact, the persons who compose and utter the prophetic woes that run through chapters 94–103. In this respect they parallel Enoch's role as God's spokesman of doom against the wicked. The form of much of the material in chapters 94–105 is typical of sapiential literature (e.g., two-ways sayings), but a passage like 99:2 (Greek) suggests that they are also engaged in halakic disputes about the proper interpretation of the Torah (Nickelsburg 1982, above, 106–13). Much of the content in 1 Enoch relates to the rewards and punishment that will come to those who obey or disobey Enochic torah. In addition, Stone has rightly seen behind the cosmology of the journey accounts in chapters 17–36 the activity of learned scholars (1978), and there are remarkable parallels between 1 Enoch and the Wisdom of ben Sira in this respect (Argall, 99–164). However, it needs to be emphasized that the authors of 1 Enoch 17–19 and 20–36 have put their cosmological wisdom at the disposal of their eschatological message (Nickelsburg 1981, 54–55).

c. *The Book of Daniel*   Different from Sirach and 1 Enoch, the Book of Daniel places little emphasis on the role of the scribe. Daniel is alleged to have written down the visions in chapters 7–12, but even in 12:9 this is not explicit; in all of Daniel's visions the emphasis is on his receipt of, or participation in the visions, the interpretations that he heard, and his undefined transmission of them. The chief quality of Daniel and his friends, apart from their faithfulness to their God (1:17), is their wisdom as inspired interpreters of dream visions, similar to, but vastly superior to their Babylonian counterparts.[3] Different from Enoch, who received and recounts visions, these persons belong to a professional class of interpreters. In addition, though they are not interpreters of the Torah, both the three youths and Daniel are God's spokesmen, preaching, on the basis of revealed information, against the arrogance of Nebuchadnezzar and Belshazzar and announcing God's judgment. The role is prophetic, even if they are not called prophets.

A hint of the real world of Daniel's authors appears in 12:3 in the reference to the *maśkilîm*, who "cause many to be righteous." The teaching role of these wisdom figures may be suggested in the

---

[3] Although Ben Sira is suspicious of dream interpretation (34:1–8), his description of the sage who travels to foreign courts (39:4) is reminiscent of the stories in Daniel 1–6.

claim that they will "shine" (*yazhiru*) like the firmament, perhaps an allusion to the metaphor of teaching as enlightenment (cf. Sir 24:24:27; 39:8; cf. 1 Enoch 5:8 Greek; 1QH 4:5–6, 27). The teaching role is explicit in the statement that they cause many to be righteous. Striking in 12:3 is the author's use of Isa 52:13 and 53:10; the prophetic Servant of that text is identified with the wise teachers of the Maccabean period. In view of the issues at stake in chapters 1–6 (observance of *kashrut* and rejection of idolatry) and in the Maccabean period, these teachers are rightly seen as teachers of the Torah, encouraging other Jews to stand fast in righteous conduct.

d. *The Wisdom of Solomon*   The protagonist in the Wisdom of Solomon 2 and 5 is not only a righteous person, but one who, inspired by the knowledge given by God (2:13) and privy to divine secrets (2:22), speaks against the sins of the godless (2:12), claiming to be God's son or servant (2:13). Combining motifs in Daniel 1–6 and 12:3, he is the righteous and wise spokesman of God, persecuted and exalted, and he is described in the language of Isaiah 52–53. Once again, the prophet-like figure emerges as a wise man. The role of scribe or writer is implied in the book only in Solomon's authorship of the book. The real author, of course, is an expositor of Torah and prophets, who speaks in the idiom of Israelite wisdom and Greek philosophy.

e. *The Qumran Texts*   The Qumran texts provide many hints about their authors and their roles. The sapiential and eschatological instruction in 1QS 3:13–4:26 is for the *maśkil* to use in teaching the community (3:13). The Damascus Document describes a plurality of sages (*ḥkmym*) and persons of perception (*nbwnym*) who are led by one who "searches" (*drš*) the Torah (CD 6:2–11). A continued process of Torah study is reflected in 1QS 8:12–16, and 1QS 5:7–9 makes it clear that the community's definitive interpretation is revealed. The author of 1QH 4:5–5:4 describes himself as an enlightened teacher of the Torah, cast in the image of Second Isaiah's Servant (Nickelsburg 1981, 138–39), who stands in opposition to a cadre of false interpreters and seers (cf. 1 Enoch 98:8–99:10; Nickelsburg 1982, 334–43, above, 106–13). The Teacher of Righteousness (cf. Enoch, the scribe of righteousness) is both an expounder of the Torah and an inspired interpreter of the prophets (CD 1:10–12; 1QpHab 6:1–5). In addition to the study of the Torah and the prophets, the sapiential ambience of Qumranic activity (ben Sira's third area of activity) is evident not just in the term *maśkil*, but in the language and conceptions of texts like 1QS 11 and 1QH 1.

f. *2 Baruch and 4 Ezra*   I note only briefly that the alleged authors of two post-70 apocalypses, Ezra and Baruch, although they speak like prophets at times, are both scribes. Their activity, moreover, involves the receipt and transmission of revelation. Ezra's function is to reconstitute the Torah, while Baruch makes heavy allusion to the wise interpreters of the law who will follow him as community leaders (chap. 77; see Sayler, 116–17). Thus, again, we are led toward scribes as prophetic successors with responsibility for teaching Torah and interest in eschatology.

2. *Synthesizing our Information: Developments in Israelite Wisdom Circles*
Our review of texts has pointed us toward a related set of figures with specific roles or functions. Of course, it is not possible to equate all of these types of figures with one another, but I shall risk framing an hypothesis about the situation in the fourth to the second century B.C.E.

In the Greco-Roman period, the study of the Torah and the collection and study of prophetic oracles became a major occupation among "scribes" and "the wise." Although these persons worked with the vocabulary and conceptions of the proverbial wisdom tradition, they were interpreters of the Mosaic Torah and understood themselves to be the heirs of the prophets.[4] Theirs was a learned profession, dedicated to "searching" (Heb. *drš*) ancient texts for new meanings.[5] As such, they were scholars and teachers. However, standing in the train of the prophets, they also played the role of preachers, though precisely in what settings is not clear. Through their interpretation of Torah *and* prophets, a new thing was coming into being. While some of the prophets surely knew some of the Mosaic traditions and could speak in a sapiential idiom, "the wise" framed their ethical instruction with reference to the *Torah*, in the genres used by *the prophets*, and in *wisdom* idiom. In addition, their sensitivity to the realities of their historical circumstances led them increasingly to employ the language and historical scheme of Deuteronomy 28–32 and the eschatological scenarios of the prophets, notably Second and Third Isaiah, to describe problem and solution.

---

[4] See Hengel 1:134–35.
[5] See Smith, who concludes that apocalypticism is a learned, scribal phenomenon.

There was clearly a close relationship between these interpreters of the tradition and the "apocalypticists," those who claimed that the new teaching they presented was *revelation* apart from the Torah and the prophets. This is attested in the manifold similarities evident in their common use of the literary forms and vocabulary of the wisdom tradition and the titles "the wise" and "scribe," their keen de facto interest in both the Torah and the prophets, and their focus on the future resolution of present troubles.

As we compare the sapiential and apocalyptic literatures, we shall *not* discover that ben Sira and the authors of Enoch and Daniel were really clones of one another. Indeed they had some serious points of disagreement. Nonetheless, they appear to be different species of the same genus, and as is often the case, one argues most heatedly with those most similar to oneself, or those using different methods to draw divergent and sometimes conflicting conclusions from a common starting point.

The activity of interpreting the Torah had its own variations, developing alternatively into halakic refinement and sapiential instruction. The former may well reflect the belief that the circumstances of the nation or one's community reflected the covenantal curses and required careful searching of the Torah to determine precisely how it was to be obeyed (Jub 23:17; CD 1).

In discussing the social settings in which the wise did their exposition and admonition, we need to consider the issue of community and community setting. Here caution is important, because diversity is likely. The detailed evidence that we have about the Qumran community is helpful but can send us in wrong directions. Some of the apocalyptic texts in 1 Enoch do suggest a sectarian setting (Nickelsburg 1982), though of what sort is unclear. Closed groups can be the function of halakhic disputes, but 1 Enoch breaks the mold with its openness to outsiders (indeed, Gentiles, it would appear). Daniel is an apocalypse that suggests an open, non-sectarian setting with anyone in Hellenizing Israel as the potential object of the author's admonition.

The spectrum of allusions in the sapiential and apocalyptic literature suggest many possibilities for consideration as one thinks of concrete settings: school (of what sort); synagogue (with what meaning); temple court; closed conventicles; the open market place. All of this requires hard work with Jewish and non-Jewish texts, as well as epigraphic and archeological evidence, using the tools of philology, literary criticism, and social scientific methods, and keeping an open mind that is not bound to traditional categories and conclusions.

3. *Two Cautions about Compartmentalization*

a. *Confusing Functions with Institutions and Offices*   Although I wish to avoid the notion than everyone was like everyone else, it seems important to emphasize that the differentiation of functions need not indicate a corresponding differentiation in offices and institutions. We need not suppose that first century teachers of the Torah and the prophets were professors of the academic study of religion, who might never take to the pulpit or the soap box. Indeed, texts as different as 1 Enoch, the Wisdom of ben Sira, and certain Qumranic texts referring to the Teacher of Righteousness seem to indicate that sages of very different dispositions engaged in analogous (though not totally identical) sets of functions. It would be worthwhile to set up a table or grid in which one could plot: text, titles or self-designations, functions, and settings.

b. *Confusing Scholarly Terminology and Historical Reality*   The history of scholarship indicates that we have sometimes confused our scholarly abstractions and heuristic categories with flesh and blood realities in the ancient culture that we study. Terms like sapiential, apocalyptic, and eschatological are useful and, indeed, necessary, but they must be seen for what they are: windows into another world, means for trying to understand that to which we do not have first hand access. It is imperative that the means not be construed as the end, or the window, as the landscape.

The history of scholarship also attests the ways in which our categories have become hermetically sealed compartments that give the impression that each refers to, or contains something totally different from the other. Thus "wisdom" or "sapiential" is distinct from "apocalyptic." By focusing intently on one or the other, as the thing itself, we fail to see that in the world from which they have come to us, they were related parts of an organic whole, each with some of the same genes as the other. Having used the terms "wisdom" or "sapiential" and "apocalyptic" in this paper to describe discreet bodies of literature, I have drawn conclusions that suggest that these are flawed categories.

4. *Thinking Holistically about the Past*

My observations, as rough and flawed as they are, invite us to think holistically about the past. In synchronic terms, we can consider the following:

—How did the apocalypticism variously attested in the texts we have surveyed relate to broader currents and counter-currents in the circles of the learned successors of the prophets?
—In what various ways were eschatology and ethics related to each other in the texts of the Greco-Roman period and the activities of those who created and read them?
We also need to think about the crucial diachronic dimension:
—Can we find a continuum from prophet to sage?
—Is it really meaningful to use the term "*apocalyptic* eschatology" to refer both to the prophet Third Isaiah, whose oracle is not an apocalypse, and his successor, the author of 1 Enoch 26–27, who cast material from Isaiah 65–66 into the form of an apocalypse?
—What were the different nuances in the notions of revelation or inspiration held by the prophets and their various successors?

Above all, I wish to emphasize the need to study text in context. Part of the bind that scholarship has gotten itself into is the result of dealing with texts and our abstract descriptions of them apart from the real worlds that created the texts. In fact, texts are historical artifacts. As we try to understand the functions that they fulfilled and the settings in which they were employed, we may discover that the similarities in texts that *we have decided* belong to different categories are not really all that strange after all, because in the wholeness of life in antiquity they were tied together in ways that we have yet to understand.[6] In short, the problem may not be in the texts, but in the categories and methods that we have used to describe and interpret them.

BIBLIOGRAPHY

Argall, Randal A. 1992. 1 Enoch and Sirach: A Comparative Literary and Conceptual Analysis of the Themes of Revelation, Creation and Judgment. Diss. The University of Iowa. Ann Arbor: UMI. Published as SBLEJL 8. Atlanta: Scholars Press, 1995.

[6] In my SBL paper, "Tobit and Enoch: Distant Cousins with a Recognizable Resemblance" (1988, above, 217–39) I struggled with the problem of the similarities between a sapiential and an apocalyptic text. The configuration of these similarities will not go away, and we need to find some appropriate tools and categories to explain the common genes in these family members.

Baumgartner, Walter 1914. "Die literarischen Gattungen in der Weisheit des Jesus Sirach," *ZAW* 34:161–98.

Collins, John J. 1977. "Cosmos and Salvation: Jewish Wisdom and Apocalyptic in the Hellenistic Age," *HR* 17:121–42.

———. 1977a. *The Apocalyptic Vision of Daniel.* HSM 16. Missoula: Scholars.

———. 1979. "Jewish Apocalypses," *Semeia* 14:21–59.

———. 1984. *The Apocalyptic Imagination.* New York: Crossroad.

———. 1986. "Apocalyptic Literature," in Robert A. Kraft and George W.E. Nickelsburg (eds.), *Early Judaism and its Modern Interpreters.* Philadelphia/Atlanta: Fortress/Scholars: 345–70.

———. 1993. "Wisdom, Apocalypticism, and Generic Compatibility," in Leo Perdue et al. (ed.), *In Search of Wisdom.* Philadelphia: Westminster.

Coughenour, R.A. 1978. "The Woe Oracles in Ethiopic Enoch," *JSJ* 9:192–97.

———. 1982. "The Wisdom Stance of Enoch's Redactor," *JSJ* 13:47–55.

Crenshaw, James L. 1981. *Old Testament Wisdom: An Introduction.* Atlanta: John Knox.

———. 1986. "The Wisdom Literature," in Knight and Tucker 1985:369–407.

Koch, Klaus 1972. *The Rediscovery of Apocalyptic.* SBT 2:22. Naperville: Allenson.

Ginsberg, H.L. 1953. "The Oldest Interpretation of the Suffering Servant," *VT* 3:400–404.

Hanson, Paul D. 1975. *The Dawn of Apocalyptic.* Philadelphia: Fortress.

———. 1976. "Apocalypticism," *IDBSupp*: 28–34.

———. 1985. "Apocalyptic Literature," in Knight and Tucker 1985:465–88.

Hengel, Martin 1974. *Judaism and Hellenism.* 2 vols. Philadelphia: Fortress.

Knight, Douglas A. and Gene M. Tucker 1985. *The Hebrew Bible and Its Modern Interpreters.* Philadelphia/Atlanta: Fortress/Scholars.

Larcher, C. 1983. *Études sur le livre de la Sagesse.* Paris: Gabalda.

Mack, Burton L. and Roland E. Murphy 1986. "Wisdom Literature," in Kraft and Nickelsburg: 371–410.

Nickelsburg, George W.E. 1972. *Resurrection, Immortality, and Eternal Life in Intertestamental Judaism.* HTS 26. Cambridge: Harvard University.

———. 1977. "The Apocalyptic Message of 1 Enoch 92–105," *CBQ* 39:309–28.

———. 1981. *Jewish Literature Between the Bible and the Mishnah.* Philadelphia: Fortress.

———. 1982. "The Epistle of Enoch and the Qumran Literature," *JSJ* 33 = *Essays in Honour of Yigael Yadin*: 333–48. Reprinted above, pp. 105–122.

———. 1988. "Tobit and Enoch: Distant Cousins with a Recognizable Resemblance," in David J. Lull (ed.), *SBL 1988 Seminar Papers*: 341–60. Reprinted above, pp. 217–239.

———. 1991. "The Apocalyptic Construction of Reality of 1 Enoch," in John J. Collins and James H. Charlesworth (eds), *Mysteries and Revelations: Apocalyptic Studies since the Uppsala Colloquium.* JSPSupp 9. Sheffield: Sheffield Academic: 51–64. Reprinted above, pp. 29–43.

von Rad, Gerhard 1972. *Wisdom in Israel.* Philadelphia: Westminster.

Sayler, Gwendolyn B. 1982. *Have the Promises Failed? A Literary Analysis of 2 Baruch.* SBLDS 72. Chico: Scholars.

Smith, Jonathan Z. 1975. "Wisdom and Apocalyptic," in Birger A. Pearson (ed.), *Religious Syncretism in Antiquity.* Missoula: Scholars.

Stone, Michael E. 1976. "Lists of Revealed Things in the Apocalyptic Literature," in Frank M. Cross, Werner E. Lemke, and Patrick D. Miller (eds.), *Magnalia Dei: The Mighty Acts of God: Essays on the Bible and Archaeology in Memory of G. Ernest Wright.* Garden City; Doubleday: 414–52.

———. 1978. "The Book of Enoch and Judaism in the Third Century," *CBQ* 50: 479–92.

RESPONSE TO "WISDOM AND APOCALYPTICISM IN EARLY JUDAISM: SOME POINTS FOR DISCUSSION"

Sarah J. Tanzer*

George Nickelsburg's 1994 essay, "Wisdom and Apocalypticism in Early Judaism: Some Points for Discussion," defined the problem and tentatively proposed half of the agenda for a new Society of Biblical Literature Consultation (and later a Group) working on Wisdom and Apocalypticism in Early Judaism and Early Christianity.[1] Although I had an opportunity to respond to Nickelsburg's essay when the paper was originally presented, returning to it eight years later I am struck by: (1) the impressionistic style of the essay and, yet, its clarity of insight into the issues involved in rethinking the interrelationship of wisdom and apocalypticism and the producers of these early Jewish texts; (2) how much our SBL group has been guided by the agenda proposed in this essay; (3) that so many of the stumbling blocks still remain in understanding the dynamic interrelationship of Jewish wisdom and apocalyptic literature, the communities and individuals behind these texts and the ways in which we might learn from the interrelationship of Jewish wisdom and apocalyptic about what we see in some New Testament and early Christian writings.

The core of Nickelsburg's thesis about Jewish texts from the Greco-Roman period is beyond dispute: "that the entities usually defined as sapiential and apocalyptic often cannot be cleanly separated from one another. . . . Thus, apocalyptic texts contain elements that are at home in wisdom literature, and wisdom texts reflect growing interest in eschatology."[2] Some of the details of his thesis will be discussed below.[3] Nickelsburg's "cautions" offered at the end of his essay

---

* McCormick Theological Seminary.

[1] While Nickelsburg's paper considered the issues from the early Jewish side of things, Richard Horsley made suggestions about the other half of the agenda—looking at issues raised by the study of Early Christianity—in his essay, "Wisdom Justified by All Her Children: Examining Allegedly Disparate Traditions in Q," in *SBL Seminar Papers*, 1994 (Atlanta, 1994), pp. 733–751.

[2] George W.E. Nickelsburg, "Wisdom and Apocalypticism in Early Judaism: Some Points for Discussion," in *SBL Seminar Papers*, 1994 (Atlanta, 1994), above, pp. 269–270.

[3] In fact, a more detailed thesis about the scribes and "wisdom circles" that pro-

should not go unnoticed: we have a tendency to confuse scholarly constructs with the realities of the ancient cultural world which we are studying: "Terms like sapiential, apocalyptic, and eschatological are useful and, indeed, necessary, but they must be seen for what they are: windows into another world, means for trying to understand that to which we do not have first hand access. It is imperative that the means not be construed as the end, or the window, as the landscape" (p. 285). So too, he cautions us away from setting impermeable boundaries between the categories of wisdom and apocalyptic and advises us to think more holistically about life in antiquity and the producers of these texts: ". . . our categories have become hermetically sealed compartments that give the impression that each refers to, or contains something totally different from the other. . . . By focusing intently on one or the other, as the thing itself, we fail to see that in the world from which they have come to us, they were related parts of an organic whole, each with some of the same genes as the other" (p. 285).

What follows includes a more detailed look at Nickelsburg's points for a discussion organized around his two larger categories, "Jewish Literature" and "Institutions and Social Settings." While it highlights some of the prescient strengths of his essay as well as offering some of my reservations, its primary purpose is to look at how the conversation has developed in the eight years since, how the work of the Wisdom and Apocalypticism Group relates more broadly to scholarly trends, and to note where we seem no further along and what some of the questions and issues are that remain.

JEWISH LITERATURE

Nickelsburg reminds us that over the last three decades we have learned to distinguish the literary genre of apocalypse[4] from "apocalypticism" or an "apocalyptic worldview,"[5] and perhaps very cautiously

---

duced this literature can be found in Nickelsburg, ibid., pp. 283–284, and is taken up further in this essay.

[4] Revelation, mediated by an otherworldly being to a human recipient, dealing with matters that are in principle beyond ordinary human knowledge and involving supernatural powers, a final judgment and eschatological salvation. This definition is drawn from John J. Collins' work, both his response to Nickelsburg's essay given at the 1994 annual SBL meeting and *Apocalypse. The Morphology of A Genre (Semeia 14;* Missoula, 1979), pp. 21–59.

[5] A constellation of elements drawn from apocalypses (lots of variations, but

to speak of apocalyptic movements (such as the Qumran community),[6] even while admitting that the diversity of what is included in these categories belies the thought that these are any more than necessary scholarly constructs (pp. 270–271).

What needs to be added to Nickelsburg's observations about definitions of apocalypse—apocalyptic worldview—apocalypticism is that there has not been any corresponding discussion around the issues of definitions of wisdom, either as a literary genre or as a worldview, and that, while the general character of the category has been thoughtfully described by many, Wisdom Literature as a literary genre has eluded definition. This too should remind us that genre definitions are scholarly constructs and limited. Complicating the issue of definitions of wisdom is that unlike apocalyptic it has no single large genre (such as an apocalypse), which would make it easily identifiable and from which one could seek a constellation of features that would contribute to defining a worldview. A lot depends on the literary context in which the various broad types and smaller forms of wisdom are found. What has been defined is a literary corpus, including: Proverbs, Qoheleth, Job, Sirach and the Wisdom of Solomon—with Proverbs typically being considered as the norm when discussing wisdom forms, themes and language. James Crenshaw in his intelligent study, *Old Testament Wisdom*, states: "However much these literary productions differ from one another, they retain a mysterious ingredient that links them together in a special way."[7] The difficulty comes in attempting to isolate that 'mysterious ingredient.' All five of these texts are formally, thematically, and linguistically diverse, just as they also differ in their attitudes towards Wisdom— her theological connections, her attainability, and her benefits or lack thereof. In fact, Qoheleth and Job are often seen as both related to and yet a critique of the sort of wisdom found in Proverbs. The diversity of these texts is one problem.

---

typically: interest in otherworldly regions, angels and demons, eschatology, emphasizing judgment of the dead and a promise that the faithful would rise for their rewards). Again, so much of Collins' work has been formative here.

[6] Collins has pointed out the dangers inherent in moving from literary works to social movements in "Genre, Ideology and Social Movements in Jewish Apocalypticism," in J.J. Collins and J.H. Charlesworth, eds., *Mysteries and Revelations: Apocalyptic Studies Since the Uppsala Colloquium* (Sheffield, 1991), pp. 11–32.

[7] J.L. Crenshaw, *Old Testament Wisdom: An Introduction* (Atlanta, 1981), p. 17.

On the other hand this corpus (despite its Hellenistic members) may be too circumscribed to be helpful in describing the evolving and more pervasive character of wisdom in early Judaism as it shows up within different literary genres. This lack of distinctiveness means that wisdom "threatens to become an all-encompassing category. Any form of knowledge that is recognized as good may be dubbed "wisdom," and it is difficult to pin down any one literary form that might provide a criterion for identifying material as sapiential."[8] One strategy which is useful is to look for a constellation of wisdom elements, e.g., smaller forms, themes, and language that are found in the five member wisdom corpus to assess what makes them distinctive (e.g., context in which they are found, etc.) and to evaluate other texts on the basis of clusters of these distinctive features.[9]

Five distinct, broad types of wisdom have been identified: (1) Wisdom sayings; (2) Theological wisdom; (3) Nature wisdom; (4) Mantic wisdom; (5) Higher wisdom through revelation.[10] These typologies of wisdom seem useful, but need more attention than they have so far received and more precision about the scope and features of the literature that fits under each heading. These categories should be looked into closely both with texts which have been widely acknowledged as Wisdom literature and with those texts that challenge the boundaries between apocalyptic and Wisdom (such as many of the

---

[8] John J. Collins, "Response to George Nickelsburg" (paper presented at the annual meeting of the SBL, Chicago, IL, November 1994), p. 2. It is difficult to know where one should draw the line. Different scholars have included different texts under the heading "wisdom." Nickelsburg, for example, has included Tobit and Baruch in this category ("Wisdom and Apocalypticism," pp. 272–273).

[9] Cf., Michael V. Fox, *Proverbs 1–9* (*The Anchor Bible* 18A; New York, 2000), p. 17: "No definition of Wisdom literature will identify precisely which works belong and which do not. But we should not think of Wisdom literature as a field that can be marked out and fenced in. Wisdom literature is a *family* of texts. There are clusters of features that characterize it. The more of them a work has, the more clearly it belongs in the family. In fact, in the case of Wisdom literature, the family resemblances are quite distinctive. . . ." There is a problem, however, with this issue of distinctiveness, because of the universalism of Israelite wisdom. It means that the forms, themes and language tend not to be the exclusive property of Wisdom and so when found by themselves (not in clusters) it would be difficult to argue that they are indicators of a wisdom tradition at work.

[10] John J. Collins, "Wisdom, Apocalypticism and Generic Compatibility," in Leo G. Perdue, et al., eds., *In Search of Wisdom: Essays in Memory of John G. Gammie* (Louisville, 1993), p. 168, expanding on the threefold typology of James Crenshaw ("Method in Determining Wisdom Influence Upon 'Historical' Literature," in *JBL* 88, 1969, p. 132).

Qumran texts). It has often been acknowledged that mantic wisdom is very much a part of apocalyptic writings, whereas wisdom sayings are rare in such a context. It is not too difficult to speculate on the reasons for this. Apocalyptic texts may show a preference for mantic wisdom and higher wisdom through revelation, because of their orientation to the supernatural world, and because of their reliance upon revelation as the source of wisdom. By contrast, wisdom sayings, which draw upon human experience and observation, are less compatible with an apocalyptic worldview.

It has also been noted that some Wisdom literature in which wisdom sayings predominate actively shuns mantic wisdom.[11] Sirach is one such text that actively rejects the sort of apocalyptic revelation (mantic wisdom) found in 1 Enoch, Daniel, and other apocalyptic texts. The issue is less related to categories and more related to the issue of esoteric vs. exoteric wisdom and the worldviews that underlie this tension. Jon Berquist has noted that: "Both wisdom and apocalyptic seek hidden knowledge. For sages, this knowledge hides within the structure of reality and presents itself eagerly to the observant sage. Knowledge provides solutions to the problems of life. Such knowledge makes itself available to everyone, . . . Apocalyptists, on the other hand, find a hidden knowledge that limits itself to those who are righteous. . . . The knowledge is not universally helpful; it tells of the destruction of some and thus comforts only the apocalyptists."[12] Further work needs to be done in thinking through the different typologies of wisdom that are attested in varieties of texts; where different types of wisdom seem compatible and where they clash; and how these relate to the perceived worldview of the text.

Another feature of Wisdom literature that has been noticed and deserves further exploration is that while revelation is not absent as

---

[11] Cf., Sirach 34:1–8. See Collins, ibid., p. 172, Richard A. Horsley, "The Politics of Cultural Production in Second-Temple Judah" (paper presented at the annual meeting of the SBL, Denver, CO, November 2001), pp. 7, 9, 11, and 12, and Lester L. Grabbe, "Papers by D. Harrington and B. Wright: A Reply" (paper presented at the annual meeting of the SBL. New Orleans, Louisiana, November, 1996), p. 2.

[12] Jon L. Berquist, *Judaism in Persia's Shadow: A Social and Historical Approach* (Minneapolis, 1995), pp. 187–188. See also Randal A. Argall, "Reflections on I Enoch and Sirach: A Comparative Literary and Conceptual Analysis of the Themes of Revelation, Creation and Judgment" in *SBL Seminar Papers*, 1995 (SBLSP 34; Atlanta, 1995), pp. 350–351. Argall's essay is really a synopsis of what can be found in much more detail in his book, *1 Enoch and Sirach: A Comparative Literary and Conceptual Analysis of the Themes of Revelation, Creation and Judgment* (Atlanta, 1995).

a source for wisdom, the writers of Wisdom literature draw much more heavily on traditional opinions. They aspire not to originality, but rather they are concerned with "adapting religious traditions for use in their own time."[13] This, of course, is a feature that helps to differentiate wisdom from apocalyptic writings in which revelation plays the determinative role.

Identifying how the specific characteristics of a text are linked to a worldview holds promise for understanding the interrelationship of wisdom and apocalyptic, yet also cautions us away from sliding once more into the dichotomy of labeling a text as either apocalyptic or wisdom. Contributing to the tendency to dichotomize (and to label more texts as apocalyptic rather than wisdom) is our clarity about the constellation of elements that would indicate an apocalyptic world-view (even acknowledging several variations), whereas we are less certain about what it means to say that a text exhibits a wisdom worldview. So, for example, typical of an apocalyptic worldview is the important role that supernatural agents and the heavenly world play in human affairs; the expectation of eschatological judgment and reward or punishment beyond death; and the perception that something is fundamentally wrong with the world.[14] The wisdom worldview has been characterized as beginning "with humans as the fundamental point of orientation. It asks what is good for men and women. And it believes that all essential answers can be learned in experience. . . ."[15] "This worldview involves more than a point of ori-entation. It also involves a set of assumptions about the universe. It affirms a world where there is an organic connection between cause and effect; where human fulfillment, such as it is, is to be found in this life; and where wisdom can be attained from accumulated expe-rience without recourse to special revelations."[16] Two things limit the usefulness of this characterization of wisdom: (1) It works better as a characterization of the Hebrew wisdom texts, but doesn't charac-terize the Wisdom of Solomon or other texts from the Hellenistic and Roman periods.[17] (2) This worldview may not be distinctive to wisdom alone in ancient Israel.

---

[13] Jon L. Berquist, *Judaism in Persia's Shadow*, p. 165. Cf., Collins, "Wisdom, Apocalypticism and Generic Compatibility," pp. 169–170.

[14] Ibid., p. 171.

[15] Crenshaw, *Old Testament Wisdom*, pp. 17–19.

[16] Collins, "Wisdom, Apocalypticism, and Generic Compatibility," p. 169.

[17] Cf., Collins, "Response," pp. 4–5 ("Even when Job and Qoheleth question this worldview or dissent from it, it still frames the discussion.").

These observations about the state of definitional issues especially
in the study of wisdom, but also to some degree in apocalyptic, lead
me back to Nickelsburg's thesis and his cautions about these scholarly categories: (1) that we tend to dichotomize wisdom and apocalyptic when studying a text—insisting that the categories are mutually
exclusive or at least that one label should prevail—that we assume
"generic incompatibility" when the opposite is true; (2) that we believe
too much in our definitions of these categories and forget that they
are merely constructs, "windows" onto an "ancient landscape;" (3)
that we don't tend to give the categories enough flexibility to understand texts which come from different times, locations and contexts.
While I would agree completely with all of these observations, in
the area of Wisdom literature the reverse problem is at least as great:
before we can more fully understand the relationship between wisdom and apocalyptic, and where the boundaries between these categories are most permeable, we need to work text by text on the
definitional issues of wisdom. And as we look at texts in which the
boundaries between wisdom and apocalyptic are blurred (the texts
in which there is generic compatibility), we need to ask about types
of wisdom, context, worldview, tradition and revelation as sources
for wisdom and how the themes which are found in both wisdom
and apocalyptic are shaped by the specific worldview of the text.[18]

I find Nickelsburg's designation "*texts that complicate the categories*"
especially helpful for a few reasons: the texts in which both wisdom
and apocalyptic features are clearly evident most strongly push us
to work out the interrelationship of wisdom and apocalyptic with
some precision—they force the issue of definitions, dichotomous labeling and what it is that we seek to know through the use of these
categories; from the period following the Maccabean revolt as the
ideas in apocalyptic literature became more acceptable in Judaism
(e.g., resurrection, judgment, the impact of the heavenly world on
human lives, etc.) one finds many more texts that combine elements
of wisdom and apocalyptic in ways that challenge our understanding; texts that in form are neither apocalypses nor fit simply within
the types of wisdom literature (e.g., Qumran rule codes, testaments,

---

[18] A good example of this is Argall's "Reflections on 1 Enoch and Sirach," pp.
337–351, in which he examines shared themes, literary and conceptual features of
1 Enoch and Sirach and comes to the conclusion that it is their worldviews which
set these two books apart.

etc.);[19] it is also a designation that fits well with the challenges of early Christian texts (for example Q, James, and the Epistle of Barnabas). The Qumran corpus seems especially rich here, allowing us to look at this designation from many different angles: by noting the features of an apocalyptic worldview in texts that are not apocalypses and that are varied in form; by studying four of the five different types of wisdom (excluding mantic wisdom) that are reflected in these texts; lastly, by comparing the range of ways apocalyptic and wisdom are brought together in these texts. For example, there is 4QInstruction that has many similarities to Sirach in form and content and yet also repeatedly calls upon the sage to gaze upon the "mystery that is to come." On the other hand, there are the Hodayot and the hymnic parts of 1QS that are clearly not wisdom texts and yet are loaded with all sorts of wisdom elements (especially revelatory and theological wisdom) and also exhibit an apocalyptic worldview.

Institutions and Social Settings

In the second part of his essay, Nickelsburg argues that in order to understand the interrelationship of wisdom and apocalypticism we need to try "to reconstruct the institutions, social settings, and functions that gave rise to this literature" in order "to avoid the elusive abstraction that sometimes attends the history of ideas" (pp. 269 and 279). In particular, we need to work at understanding the producers of these texts and their real-life social worlds to the extent that we are able, even though this is not an interest of the texts themselves. He has risked framing an early hypothesis about "Developments in Israelite Wisdom Circles," following a first assessment of figures and functions in early Jewish texts.[20] His observation that as we look at the interrelationship of wisdom and apocalyptic literatures, "we shall *not* discover that ben Sira and the authors of Enoch and Daniel

---

[19] Collins considers the form and content of testaments in "Wisdom, Apocalypticism and Generic Compatibility," pp. 178–179.

[20] The hypothesis can be found on pp. 283–284. This hypothesis, as Nickelsburg acknowledged, is risky; in my view it raises the complexities involved in moving from literary texts and figures to institutions and social settings. Similarly, I don't find the terminology, "wisdom circles," to be helpful—it is too general and too poorly defined.

were really clones of one another.... Nonetheless, they appear to
be different species of the same genus . . ." (p. 284) challenges us to
notice their close proximity in terms of geography, education, functions and class even as we recognize how strikingly different are their
worldviews and the different scribes and scribal allegiances represented by these texts.[21]

The issue of specifying the social locations of the producers of
these texts, the scribes, has been the focus of much scholarship over
the past dozen years and has also been a central focus of the SBL
Wisdom and Apocalypticism group. On the one hand, what has
emerged are more detailed, but broad hypotheses about who these
various scribes were and their background in society. For example,
Jon Berquist provides rather full hypotheses about the social locations of the producers of wisdom literature and apocalyptic literature in the post-exilic period. His observations about the scribes who
produced Wisdom literature include: they were among the most lit-
erate segment of Jerusalem society; although they may well have
been active within the Temple they sought other truths to be found
outside of the Temple system; they were trained in foreign languages
and their education had an international character to it which would
allow them to oversee the bureaucratic affairs involving other nations
and provinces; they worked for the government, the Temple, local
merchants and other employers; they contributed to the social maintenance of society's power institutions; they presented the opinions
of society's chief authorities as immutable; while their social functions included educating the young, they served the powers that be
in a daily way through their scribal activity.[22] Berquist sees the scribes
who produced apocalyptic literature as deriving from the same social
location as the scribes who produced wisdom: "the knowledge experts
of Jerusalem, who operate within the middle management of the
imperial-colonial bureaucracies."[23] But unlike the scribes who produced wisdom, those who produced apocalyptic literature felt themselves to be in a position of relative deprivation by comparison to

---

[21] P. 729. In fact, his call for setting up tables or grids to plot "text, titles or
self-designations, functions, and settings" would be useful for bringing precision to
our descriptions of the scribes who produced these writings.

[22] Berquist, *Judaism in Persia's Shadow*, pp. 161–172. On the issue of a wisdom
school or wisdom schools, see ibid., p. 162, and Fox (*Proverbs 1–9*, pp. 7–8), who
summarizes the scholarship on this subject.

[23] Berquist, p. 187.

their superiors and were frustrated by their lack of power to change the system.[24] Aware that they could not change the systems in which they worked, these groups of scribes undertook different responses: in wisdom literature the scribes teach people how to succeed within society and the current institutions, whereas in apocalyptic literature the scribes "create a rhetorical power that legitimates their own dis-satisfaction by claiming God's displeasure at the system led by their superiors. Destruction of the system seems inevitable . . ."[25] though it will happen through God's intervention and not by human hands. These very full hypotheses provide helpful reconstructions against which to test out the evidence of individual texts, but may mislead people into thinking that we know more about these scribes than we possibly can, and also lump together wisdom scribes as over against apocalyptic scribes by too simplistically attributing to them one sort of stance in relationship to the systems within which they live and work.

On the other hand, another approach has been to try to discern the specific social world of the scribes on a text by text basis, ask-ing a variety of social world questions such as: where are they located socially? For whom would these scribes have worked? With whom would they have associated? What was their relationship to the peo-ple in power? What do they advocate for/against in society? What sort of authority do they seem to have? What was authoritative for them? Does the polemic in the text give hints of possible rivalries between scribal groups?[26] Richard Horsley represents a growing trend in this text by text scholarship in his conclusion that we learn a great deal about the producers of these texts through an examina-tion of their attitudes toward the current imperial regime(s), and their attitudes toward the Temple, the priesthood and the ruling aristoc-racy in Judea.[27] Further, according to Horsley's analysis, their choice

---

[24] Ibid., pp. 184–187.

[25] Ibid.

[26] So, for example, Benjamin G. Wright III, "Putting the Puzzle Together: Some Suggestions Concerning the Social Location of the Wisdom of Ben Sira," in *SBL Seminar papers*, 1996 (Atlanta, 1996), pp. 133–149, concludes (p. 148) after looking at Sirach, 1 Enoch, and Aramaic Levi, that despite many common interests, they held "competing notions of scribal wisdom and priestly legitimacy. Their concerns and claims show that in the late third to early second century B.C.E., besides hav-ing to confront and to deal with outsiders and foreign cultural influences, different Jewish groups who had varying assessments of the Jerusalem priesthood and Temple were actively engaged in an inner-Jewish struggle for power."

[27] Horsley, "The Politics of Cultural Production."

among differing types of wisdom depended precisely on these things
(thus: traditional proverbial wisdom is found in texts which are basically pro-status quo whereas mantic wisdom and higher wisdom
through revelation tend to be the wisdoms of choice for those who
are opposed to the status quo or those who are part of a resistance
movement).[28] While quite helpful for its detailed text-by-text analysis and for its attention to the social indicators in different texts, one
wonders whether this sort of approach will also lead us to new way
of dichotomizing.

Eight years down the road are we any wiser for George Nickelsburg's
essay, "Wisdom and Apocalypticism in Early Judaism"? Certainly
many of the same stumbling blocks remain in trying to understand
the interrelationship of wisdom and apocalypticism in early Judaism,
and although we have been wary of the dichotomizing tendencies
of the past, much in current research has led to different (but still
somewhat dichotomizing) ways of defining the divide between the
various types of wisdom and the differing perspectives of the scribes
who produced it. Yet his essay has proved tremendously generative
in any number of ways. His comment about scholarly reification and
abstraction of wisdom and apocalyptic (p. 269)—has prompted a
putting aside of the terms and working more deductively and de-
scriptively out of the texts. His concern that we try to reconstruct
the social and cultural realities around the production of the texts
(p. 269) has challenged us to search in the details of each individual text for what we might learn about the producers of these texts,
their commitments and relationship to their social world. He has
reminded us that our definitions of the genre apocalypse and related
terminology only take us so far—that there is great diversity and
there really aren't any pure genres out there (pp. 270–271). Especially
helpful in recognizing that the boundaries between wisdom and apoc-

---

[28] This simplified overview does not begin to do justice to Horsley's rich analysis. For more on 1 Enoch, see his, "The Politics of Cultural Production," pp. 8–10;
Patrick A. Tiller, "Israel at the Mercy of Demonic Powers: An Enochic Interpretation
of Post-Exilic Imperialism" (paper presented at the annual meeting of the SBL,
Boston, MA, November 1999) and Argall, "Reflections on 1 Enoch and Sirach,"
pp. 350–351. For more on Sirach, see Horsley, "The Politics of Cultural Production,"
pp. 6–8, and Benjamin G. Wright III, "'Put the Nations in Fear of You:' Ben Sira
and the Problem of Foreign Rule" in *SBL Seminar papers, 1999* (Atlanta, 1999), pp.
77–93. For more on Daniel, see Horsley, "The Politics of Cultural Production,"
pp. 11–12.

alyptic are very permeable and not sharply drawn when looking at Jewish literature in the Greco-Roman period is his designation, "texts that complicate the categories" (p. 723). Although Nickelsburg cautiously included only the Wisdom of Solomon and the Qumran Scrolls under this heading in his essay, I suspect that eight years later he would include many more texts under this designation. Perhaps the best way to bring this response to an end is to remind us of Nickelsburg's challenge to think holistically about these texts, because "the similarities in texts that *we have decided* belong to different categories are not really all that strange after all, because in the wholeness of life in antiquity they were tied together in ways that we have yet to understand" (p. 286).

RESPONSE TO SARAH TANZER

After eight years of study on the topic of "Wisdom and Apocalypticism," Sarah Tanzer's response to my paper and her reflections on these years of study suggest that we still find ourselves on terrain that we have not clearly mapped and that we do not understand very well. We have worked through many texts, tried to place them in their generative contexts, and asked many good questions about texts and contexts. Yet the answers continue to elude us. She notes that while we know quite a bit about apocalypticism, having at hand as a partial control an analysis of the genre of apocalypse, we are still in the dark about the category that is generally called "wisdom."

I will comment briefly on the larger picture, suggesting three overarching commonalities between "wisdom" and apocalypticism, and within them, some points of difference. In doing so, I offer three possible areas of investigation and propose three theses for consideration in this investigation.

(1) The "mysterious ingredient" in "wisdom" to which Crenshaw refers in his study of "Old Testament Wisdom" is the purposeful, "systematic," and sometimes obsessive quest to understand how things are or should be and why. Crenshaw hints at this in the chapter headings of his 1998 edition (italics, mine): "The *Pursuit* of Knowledge," "The *Search* for Divine Presence," "The *Chasing* after meaning," "The *Quest* for Survival, "The Widening *Hunt*." One seeks to understand one's world, how to live aright in it, and how it relates to God's greater designs and purposes. The notion of searching and seeking is important. One does not simply know these things; one must think about them, ask about them, and observe nature and human conduct to (try to) find some answers. If we tie this to the question of social location, we arrive at the one description of the sage that has been preserved from ancient Israel. The verbs speak for themselves.

> On the other hand he who *devotes* himself
>   to the *study* of the law of the Most high
> will *seek out* the wisdom of all the ancients,
>   and will *be concerned* with prophecies;
> he will *preserve* the discourse of notable men
>   and *penetrate* the subtleties of parables;

> he will *seek out* the hidden meanings of proverbs
> and be at home with the obscurities of parables (Sir. 38:1–3 RSV).

As ben Sira notes, this is a full-time profession and not an avocation (38:24). One must have the leisure to think that is not available to those whose trades and occupations demand their attention. The sage or scribe, however, must direct his attention to a consideration of how things are or should be. It would be worth considering to what degree the "wisdom" literature, broadly construed, is permeated with language about seeing, thinking, and considering.[1] The activity that I have in mind is typical of literature like the Wisdom of ben Sira, as the passage above indicates. It also pertains the a work like 1 Enoch, where one is exhorted to "observe" the heavens and the earth and to understand what one sees, and where the seer to taken to see the hidden places of the universe and to peer into the obscure future. However, to confuse the categories further, the process also pertains to the activity of those who study the Torah. Striking here, as in Sir. 39:1, and 3, is the use of the verb *darash* or *baqash*.[2] To study the Torah is to search after a meaning that is not immediately apparent and that may be completely elusive, and this may involve great effort (Jub. 23:17; 1QS 6:6; 8:14–15). Thus, though we may distinguish between "sapiential" texts and halakhic exegesis, as I have, they have in common the search for right knowledge and understanding of God's will.

(2) This pursuit of understanding focuses on the issue of what is right and what is wrong and on the consequences that follow from this. On a mundane, albeit very practical level, it may involve boorish conduct at a banquet that leads to social ostracizing, or foolish companionship with the powerful that puts one in their debt. More seriously, proverbial wisdom lays out, often in poetic parallelism, the consequences of obeying or disregarding the will of God. Halakhic exegesis asks what God's will is. Apocalyptic wisdom takes on the big issues of whether divine justice is, in fact, present in the (history of) the phenomenal world. But as Wisdom of Solomon 1–5 indicates, this issue is not limited to the writings that we call apocalypses.

---

[1] Here I am indebted to a graduate seminar paper on 2 Baruch written some years ago at the University of Iowa by Frances Flannery.
[2] Rodney A. Werline, *Penitential Prayer in Second Temple Judaism: the Development of a Religious Institution* (Atlanta, 1998), pp. 111–113.

Indeed, these big issues of "theodicy" leap across categories and types of apocalyptic and other sapiental thought. Koheleth and Job are concerned with the issue. And like Job, the authors of 2 Baruch and especially 4 Ezra wrestle with the issue, Ezra to the point of obsession.

(3) Finally, there is the issue of how one knows, or where one goes for the knowledge that leads to understanding. One may reflect on the results of practical experience. "There is some one who . . . and this happens to him/her." One may appeal to nature—often with the admonition to "observe." The admonition may occur in an apocalypse (1 Enoch 2:1–5:4; 101:1) and in other non-apocalyptic "sapiential" contexts. Thus, Matt. 7:26–30 and Luke 12:24–31, as they draw on their Q source, appeal to the example of the birds and the flowers. The appeal to observe the heavens and the earth appears also in 2 Macc. 7:28 in a mother's exhortation that her son act rightly by dying for the Torah. Common to all these texts is not only the appeal to "observe" nature, but also the purpose of such observation—to act rightly or to see that others have acted wrongly. For ben Sira, the scribe looks for enlightenment in the tradition, which for him includes the Torah, the prophets, and the writings and traditions of the wise. Here the Enochic authors part company with him. Although, in fact, they draw on Scripture at many points, they do not acknowledge the fact. Instead they claim to have received a special revelation, through dreams, visions, and heavenly journeys. They assert that this is an ancient revelation (to Enoch), but, in fact, it is new revelation. Scripture is not sufficient. The author of chapters 24–26 draws on the imagery of Isaiah 65–66, but he anchors the authority of his information not in the prophetic word about the new Jerusalem, but in a visionary journey in which Enoch himself actually saw these future realities. For the author of the Animal Vision, the history of the world—including the sins of Israel, the enlightenment of the chosen, and the judgment that will set things right—was seen in Enoch's dream vision. This striking difference in epistemology may well be tied to the apocalypticist's world view, as Sarah Tanzer suggests. Because the Enochic authors experience their world as an alienating environment, they appeal to special revelation that will resonate with their audience and thus guarantee the veracity of their claims that the end is at hand and that God's judgment will right the injustices that they now perceive.

Three questions follow from this.

(1) Are the three rubrics proposed in these theses shared by all the texts generally thought to be "sapiential" or "apocalyptic," and/or can the rubrics be refined to fit the evidence better?
(2) If so, do the rubrics help to distinguish this group of texts from the macro-contents of other types of texts?
(3) Do the rubrics provide a tool for dividing the texts in the group into sub-groups?

As modern scholars, we get caught in traps of our own making, when we attempt to lock certain clusters of motifs and emphases into exclusive categories like "wisdom" and "apocalyticism." We shall do better to study the texts broadly and comparatively, in order to see what we find where—especially when we do not expect to find it there—and to observe what patterns emerge from this comparative endeavor.